The Virtuous Therapist
Ethical Practice of
Counseling & Psychotherapy

ELLIOT D. COHEN
Indian River Community College

GALE SPIELER COHEN
Indian River Community College

Brooks/Cole • Wadworth

 I(T)P An International Thomson Publishing Company

Belmont • Albany • Bonn • Boston • Cincinnati • Detroit • Johannesburg • London • Madrid • Melbourne • Mexico City
New York • Pacific Grove • Paris • Singapore • Tokyo • Toronto • Washington

Sponsoring Editor: *Eileen Murphy*
Marketing Team: *Steve Catalano, Christine Davis*
Marketing Representative: *Alston Mabry*
Editorial Assistant: *Julie Martinez*
Production Editor: *Mary Vezilich*

Manuscript Editor: *Patterson Lamb*
Cover & Interior Design: *Laurie Albrecht*
Art Editor: *Jennifer Mackres*
Typesetting: *WestWords, Inc.*
Printing and Binding: *Webcom*

For more information, contact:

WADSWORTH PUBLISHING COMPANY
10 Davis Drive
Belmont, CA 94002
USA

International Thomson Publishing Europe
Berkshire House 168-173
High Holborn
London WC1V 7AA
England

Thomas Nelson Australia
102 Dodds Street
South Melbourne, 3205
Victoria, Australia

Nelson Canada
1120 Birchmount Road
Scarborough, Ontario
Canada M1K 5G4

International Thomson Editores
Seneca 53
Col. Polanco
11560 México, D. F., México

International Thomson Publishing GmbH
Königswinterer Strasse 418
53227 Bonn
Germany

International Thomson Publishing Asia
60 Albert Street #15-01
Albert Complex
Singapore 189969

International Thomson Publishing Japan
Hirakawacho Kyowa Building, 3F
2-2-1 Hirakawacho
Chiyoda-ku, Tokyo 102
Japan

Printed in Canada

10 9 8 7 6 5 4 3 2 1

Library of Congress Cataloging-in-Publication Data

Cohen, Elliot D.
     The virtuous therapist : ethical practice of counseling and
psychotherapy / Elliot D. Cohen, Gale Spieler Cohen.
          p.   cm.
     Includes index.
     ISBN 0-534-34408-9 (pbk.)
     1. Counselors—Professional ethics.   2. Psychotherapists—
Professional ethics.   3. Counseling—Moral and ethical aspects.
4. Counseling—Moral and ethical aspects—Case studies.
5. Psychotherapy—Moral and ethical aspects.   6. Psychotherapy—
Moral and ethical aspects—Case studies.   I. Cohen, Gale Spieler,
1952–   . II. Title.
BF637.C6C46   1998   98-37866
174'.915—dc21   CIP

To
our children,
Tracey and William,
our parents,
Elaine and Jack Spieler,
Ruth Cohen and
the memory of Walter Cohen

CONTENTS

PART ONE
ETHICS AND VIRTUOUS PRACTICE   1

CHAPTER ONE
ETHICS AND VIRTUE   3

Laws, Codes of Ethics, and Ethical Decisions   3
Types of Ethics   5
   Descriptive and Philosophical Ethics   5
   Ethical Theory   6
   Rule Ethics   7
   Rule Ethics and the Concept of a Right   13
   Care Ethics   14
   Virtue Ethics   19
Applied Professional Ethics: A Proposed Eclectic Approach   24
Summary   25
Review Questions   26
Discussion Questions   27
Cases for Analysis   28

CHAPTER TWO
FOUNDATIONS OF COUNSELING VIRTUES   31

The Purpose of Counseling Practice   32
The Value of Counseling Virtues   33
Professional and Moral Virtues   34
Welfare, Interests, and Needs   34
Moral Problems, Dilemmas, and Responsibility: A Framework
   for Ethical Decision Making in Counseling   35
   Identifying and Defining Moral Problems   35
   Identifying Morally Relevant Facts   38
   Conducting a Philosophical Analysis of the Defined Problem in Light
     of All Morally Relevant Facts   39

Reaching a Decision That Is Reasonable in Light of the Philosophical Analysis 42
Implementing the Decision in Action 44
Client Welfare, Autonomy, and Trust 47
Summary 48
Review Questions 50
Discussion Questions 50
Cases for Analysis 51

CHAPTER THREE
AUTONOMY-FACILITATING VIRTUES 55
Facilitating Client Autonomy: The Person-Centered Approach 55
Congruence 57
Unconditional Positive Regard 58
Empathy 61
The Autonomy-Facilitating Attitudes as Moral Virtues 64
The Autonomy-Facilitating Virtues and Client Trust 65
Summary 65
Review Questions 66
Discussion Questions 66
Cases for Analysis 67

CHAPTER FOUR
TRUST-ESTABLISHING VIRTUES 71
The Therapist-Client Trust 71
Principles of Trustworthiness 73
Honesty 74
Principle of Honesty 74
Honesty and Deception 75
Candor 76
Principle of Candor 76
Candor and Informed Consent 78
Discretion 82
Principle of Discretion 82
Discretion and Confidentiality 83
Professional Competence 88
Principle of Beneficence 88
Competence, Benevolence, and Beneficence 89
Nonmaleficence 92
Principle of Nonmaleficence 92
Nonmaleficence, Nonmalevolence, and Due Care 93

Diligence   94
  Principle of Diligence   94
  Diligence and Promotion of Client Welfare   95
Loyalty   98
  Principle of Loyalty   98
  Loyalty and Conflicts of Interest   99
Fairness   102
  Principle of Fairness   102
  Fairness, Equality of Treatment, and Managed Care   102
Principles, Standards, and Substantive Moral Problems   104
Summary   105
Review Questions   106
Discussion Questions   107
Cases for Analysis   108

PART TWO
MORAL PROBLEMS AND ISSUES   **113**

CHAPTER FIVE
MULTICULTURALISM AND COUNSELING ETHICS   **115**
Multicultural Counseling   115
Case Studies   117
  Case 1: Sexual Orientation as Minority Culture   117
  Case 2: Counseling the Devoutly Religious Client   123
  Case 3: Assimilation, Enculturation, and the Minority Client   128
Guidelines for Multicultural Counseling   133
Summary   134
Review Questions   134
Discussion Questions   135

CHAPTER SIX
AVOIDING ETHICAL IMPROPRIETY: PROBLEMS OF
  DUAL-ROLE RELATIONSHIPS   **137**
Dual-Role Relationships Involving Conflicts of Interest   138
Case Studies   141
  *Case 1: Sexual Dual-Role Relationships: A Case of Mutual Sexual
    Attachment   141*
  *Case 2: Counseling Students: A Case of a Nonelective Dual-Role
    Relationship   149*
Ethical Standards for Addressing Dual-Role Relationships   156
Summary   160
Review Questions   160
Discussion Questions   161

CHAPTER SEVEN

SUSPECTED CHILD ABUSE: A THERAPIST'S RESPONSIBILITIES 165

Child Abuse: Some General Facts 165
Sexual Abuse 165
Physical Abuse 167
Case Studies 167
Case 1: A Therapist's Responsibility to Report 167
Case 2: Child Abuse and a Custody Battle: A Therapist's Responsibility to Promote Clients' Autonomy 173
Ethical Standards for Managing Suspected Child Abuse 179
Summary 181
Review Questions 182
Discussion Questions 182

CHAPTER EIGHT

DOMESTIC VIOLENCE AND ABUSE: ETHICAL AND THERAPEUTIC CONSIDERATIONS 185

Facts About Domestic Abuse and Violence 185
Case Studies 187
Case 1: Domestic Abuse, Client Autonomy, and Confidentiality 187
Case 2: Safeguarding the At-Risk Client: Therapist Moral Objectivity and Nonmaleficence 192
Case 3: Male Victimization: Gender Scripting and Domestic Violence 198
Guidelines for Counseling Victims of Domestic Violence 202
Summary 204
Review Questions 204
Discussion Questions 205

CHAPTER NINE

CONFIDENTIALITY, THIRD-PARTY HARM, AND CLIENTS WHO HAVE HIV 207

Some General Facts about HIV 207
The Virtuous Therapist and the HIV-Seropositive Client 208
Case Studies 208
Case 1: Harm to an Identifiable Third Party 208
Case 2: Harm to Unidentifiable Third Parties 211
Case 3: Harm to a Third-Party Client 214
Standards for Disclosure of Confidential Information 217
Summary 221
Review Questions 222
Discussion Questions 222

CHAPTER TEN

PATERNALISTIC INTERVENTION, INVOLUNTARY
COMMITMENT, AND CLIENT AUTONOMY

225

Paternalism in Counseling and Psychotherapy   225
Autonomy   226
Mental Competence   227
Justified Paternalism   228
Involuntary Commitment   229
Case Studies   231
   Case 1: A Pregnant Client with a Bipolar Disorder   231
   Case 2: Involuntary Commitment of a Child   236
   Case 3: A Question of Rational Suicide   240
Ethical Standards of Paternalism   249
Summary   253
Review Questions   255
Discussion Questions   255

REFERENCES   259

Appendix A   ACA *Code of Ethics* and *Standards of Practice*   269
Appendix B   *Ethical Principles of Psychologists* and *Code of Conduct*   293
Appendix C   NASW Code of Ethics   315
Appendix D   Ethical Standards of Human Service Professionals   333
Appendix E   AAMFT Code of Ethics   337

The growing trend toward professionalization in mental health—psychology, counseling, social work, and other fields—has brought increased awareness of and concern with ethical problems in therapy. This interest has been evidenced by the frequent inclusion of ethics courses in the curricula of graduate training and 2-year programs, and state licensure requirements. Many professional associations have recently revised their professional codes of ethics to address new as well as persistent moral challenges. An increasing number of statutes and court decisions have also emerged that affect mental health practice.

Notwithstanding the existence of codes of ethics and law, mental health professionals are often left in quandaries about questions of ethics. Codes of ethics provide important guidelines but are often not sufficient to resolve problems. Statutes and legal precedents can be useful, but they do not always provide unequivocal answers, and a legal resolution to an ethical problem may not necessarily be a moral one.

Unfortunately, most literature in counseling ethics tends to be superficial, avoiding philosophical analysis, citing law and codes of ethics without an organized framework for interpreting and applying these standards. This literature typically cites legal and mental health sources in an effort to display different moral and legal perspectives. Philosophical arguments and analyses are not developed, and many of the important questions raised are left for students to ponder on their own amid a labyrinth of conflicting legal and moral perspectives. For instance, the distinction between confidentiality and privileged communication is discussed; legally permissible exceptions to confidentiality are noted; and the general statements contained in ethics codes are quoted. However, no attempt is made to wed these distinctions to a systematic, philosophical approach to ethical decision making. Even when ethical principles and standards other than law and ethics codes are introduced, these standards are presented as a barebones list of criteria. No systematic development and application of the criteria are provided.

The Virtuous Therapist is intended to provide a systematic, philosophical approach to mental health ethics. In Part 1 (Ethics and Virtuous Practice), a comprehensive, philosophical model of ethical decision making is developed as a basis for addressing a number of hard ethical problems that are raised in Part 2 (Moral Problems and Issues).

Chapter 1 (Ethics and Virtue) explores fundamental concepts and theories of ethics and introduces a "virtues" approach to ethics in relation to two other key theories—namely, rule-based and care-based approaches. In Chapter 2 (Foundations of Counseling Virtues), the distinctions introduced in Chapter 1 are employed to define key concepts undergirding a theory of counseling virtue. In Chapters 3 and 4 (Autonomy-Facilitating Virtues and Trust-Establishing Virtues, respectively), a substantive theory of counseling virtues is built on the foundations set in the previous chapters. The emerging theory is then used as a basis for analyzing ethical issues raised in Part 2. All chapters contain review and discussion questions. Review questions check the reader's familiarity with and understanding of important chapter information. Reviewing these questions is helpful before working through the discussion questions, which presuppose this knowledge base. Discussion questions invite students' own critical thinking about key ethical issues raised in the chapter. Each chapter in Part 1 also includes Cases for Analysis, which challenge students to apply chapter contents to instructive case scenarios raising moral problems.

Although we have attempted to show the legitimate role of rules including law and ethics codes, and ethical principles in ethical decision making, we have also emphasized the development of character or virtue in counseling as fundamental. In contrast to rule-based approaches, our virtues perspective emphasizes the therapists' development of character traits that include emotional, attitudinal, and motivational dimensions and are important if not essential to working through moral problems in therapy successfully. For example, it is not possible to be empathetic toward clients merely by following legal or moral rules; yet an empathetic therapist possesses a virtue that may indeed be a necessary condition for the moral resolution of a counseling problem.

This emphasis on emotions can also be found in recent feminist notions of ethics in terms of the human capacity for caring. It is our thesis that a therapist must care about the welfare of others, especially clients, although not to the exclusion of nonclients. Such care ethics emphasize the role of case-based reasoning in ethical decision making. Instead of applying abstract rules to settle moral problems, these approaches start with prior cases as bases for dealing with subsequent cases. Much as a past legal decision can establish a precedent for making later decisions, particular situations can provide "moral precedents" for helping to resolve similar moral problems.

We have adopted a case-based approach and incorporated it into the fabric of this text. Each chapter in Part 2 presents two or more carefully developed case studies intended to provide useful precedents for resolving related cases. Based on actual situations—names and other identifying details have been disguised—these cases represent a wide variety of persistent, moral dilemmas in therapy and are intended to provide practical, concrete focal points for confronting such exigencies.

Each case analysis relies on the philosophical framework developed in Part 1. Philosophical analyses conclude with standards that provide guidance for the moral problems presented in the cases by directing practitioners' attention to key ethical considerations. They provide no formula, but these standards are more specific than the general ethical principles addressed in Part 1 and supplement current codes of ethics such as those addressed in Chapter 4—namely, the American Psychological Association's *Ethical Standards*, the National Association of Social Workers' *Code of Ethics*, the American Counseling Association's *Code of Ethics*, and the National Organization for Human Service Education's *Ethical Standards of Human Service Professionals*. (The full text of these codes is also reprinted in the appendixes.)

The issues addressed in Part 2 are timely, ethically engaging, and of practical importance to practitioners in their day-to-day work. For example, the expanding AIDS epidemic has prompted pressing questions about the ethics of counseling sexually active clients who are HIV-seropositive. Many of the issues addressed here have not often been philosophically examined elsewhere. For example, whereas legal definitions of child abuse abound, there is little philosophical literature on psychotherapists' ethical responsibilities in cases of suspected child abuse.

The ethical approach developed here is intended to work within many different psychotherapeutic modalities. Its ethical model is consistent with and applicable to cognitive-behavioral approaches as well as to existential and humanistic approaches. Similarly, it applies to a wide range of mental health professionals, including psychologists, counselors, marriage and family therapists, psychiatric nurses, social workers, and human service workers. Accordingly, the terms *psychotherapist* and *therapist*, used interchangeably throughout this book, are meant to encompass a wide latitude of professionals. The term *counseling* is also used generically to encompass the range of activities pursued by these professionals.

The Virtuous Therapist is co-authored by a philosopher with training and clinical experience in counseling and by a counselor with a background in philosophy. By combining these professional credentials, we have attempted to avoid philosophical short-sightedness while remaining in tune with the practical realities of psychotherapy.

The book is intended as a primary text for professional ethics courses in graduate programs such as counseling, psychology, social work, and psychiatric nursing. It may also be used with traditional primers on ethical and legal issues, including professional association casebooks, and as a primary text in human services ethics courses such as those offered in human services associate degree programs at 2-year colleges. Finally, it may supplement undergraduate courses in medical ethics, professional ethics, and applied ethics. We hope the ultimate value of this book will be in its ability to guide therapists and prospective therapists in morally responsible practice.

We wish to thank the following reviewers for their suggestions and comments: Peggy Kaczmarek, New Mexico State University–Las Cruces; Ken Merrell, The University of Iowa; Paul Sharkey, Emeritus, University of Southern Mississippi; and Robert E. Wubbolding, Xavier University.

Elliot D. Cohen
Gale Spieler Cohen

PART ONE

Ethics and Virtuous Practice

CHAPTER 1
Ethics and Virtue
CHAPTER 2
Foundations of Counseling Virtues
CHAPTER 3
Autonomy-Facilitating Virtues
CHAPTER 4
Trust-Establishing Virtues

CHAPTER ONE

Ethics and Virtue

LAWS, CODES OF ETHICS, AND ETHICAL
   DECISIONS
TYPES OF ETHICS
   Descriptive and Philosophical Ethics
   Ethical Theory
   Rule Ethics
   Rule Ethics And The Concept of a Right

Care Ethics
Virtue Ethics
APPLIED PROFESSIONAL ETHICS: A
   PROPOSED ECLECTIC APPROACH
SUMMARY
REVIEW QUESTIONS
DISCUSSION QUESTIONS
CASES FOR ANALYSIS

When therapists provide therapy, they typically bring training in counseling theory to the fore of their practices. Knowledge of several different theoretical approaches (for example, humanistic and existential as well as cognitive and behavioral approaches) may often help them in confronting the myriad of counseling settings, client populations, and presenting problems they encounter. Similarly, grounding in different kinds of *ethical theory* can provide them with useful guidance in confronting the diverse ethical problems arising in counseling and psychotherapy. Having a theoretical framework for making ethical decisions that is informed by major ethical traditions may be as important to ethical practice as counseling theory is to the provision of competent therapy. Indeed, a thesis of this book is that, in the real world of counseling practice, separating the provision of competent therapy from the exercise of sound ethical judgment may be difficult or impossible!

With an eye toward providing such an enlightened theoretical framework, this chapter explores general ethical concepts and theories. Starting by distinguishing between law and morality, it defines the nature and scope of ethics as a distinct study. It then addresses major types of ethical theory: (1) rule or principle ethics, (2) care ethics, and (3) virtue ethics.

This chapter presents case vignettes illustrating the relevance of each of these types of theories to counseling practice. It discusses advantages and limitations of each theory and proposes a "virtues" approach that incorporates advantages of both rule and care ethics. The emerging *eclectic* approach in turn supports the idea of a "virtuous therapist" (as suggested by the title of this book) that is developed and applied in subsequent chapters.

Laws, Codes of Ethics, and Ethical Decisions

Part of being a morally virtuous professional involves the awareness of the legal and ethical standards that govern the profession. A therapist who cares about ethical propriety in professional matters will be privy to the content of relevant laws, both case law and statute. He or she will also be familiar with the professional codes of ethics. It is, however, a grandiose mistake to suppose that familiarity with these standards and even singlemindedness in one's effort to comply with them, makes one moral.

First, there is a difference between law and morality. We may hope that law and morality intersect (that what is legal is moral, and what is moral is legal) but this is not always true. The history of racial and religious persecution including slavery affords good examples of legally sanctioned immoralities. Not so long ago women, with the sanction of law, were denied the right to vote and could legally be beaten for disobeying their husbands, according to "the rule of thumb," which permitted such beating when done with a stick no thicker than a thumb. The holocaust affords a chilling reminder of how blind conformity to law alone can have tragic results. The morally virtuous therapist is on notice and does not accept something as right and good simply because it has been given the status of law.

Second, legal rules state minimum requirements below which conduct may be deemed unacceptable. Such minimum standards fail to define what it means to do an excellent job as opposed to merely an acceptable one. Indeed, there is a higher calling of propriety beyond compliance with what is legally required. This higher calling engages our skills, challenges us to aspire to the higher reaches of our professional capacities, summons us to go that extra mile. Indeed, even a therapist with marginal skills who charges unusually high rates and does no pro bono work could still manage to practice within the law.

Third, obedience to law and codes may be motivated merely by self-interest—for instance, a desire not to be fined, imprisoned, or have one's certification or license revoked. Although these can be respectable desires, they are not sufficent to make one a virtuous therapist. As we see in Chapter 2, virtuous therapists are motivated by a desire to promote client welfare. As we see in Chapters 3 and 4, virtuous therapists must act with requisite feelings and emotions such as empathy and unconditional positive regard for their clients, and they must take client welfare as an intrinsic value, not merely a way of making money.

Fourth, even therapists who obey relevant laws and ethics codes out of regard for their clients might still not be virtuous. To see this, try to imagine a computer that had been programmed with all relevant legal rules and ethics codes of a given profession, say counseling. Would it do a good job in making ethical decisions? Putting aside philosophical questions as to whether machines, which do not have free will, can make choices in the first place, there are practical reasons for doubting it.

What, for example, would the computer say if it were asked whether it was all right for a therapist to begin a sexual relationship with someone she had counseled four years earlier? For example, according to Florida statute, "for purposes of determining sexual misconduct, the counseling relationship is held to continue into perpetuity." But according to the American Counseling Association (ACA) Code of Ethics, "Counselors do not engage in sexual intimacies with former clients within a minimum of two years after terminating the counseling relationship" (A7b). Torn in two contradictory directions, the computer would probably shut down! Similarly, the ACA Code states, "The primary responsibility of counselors is to respect the dignity and to promote the welfare of clients" (A.1a). We can agree with this rule, but what will the computer tell us in such cases when the welfare of the client is inconsistent with the welfare of a third person?

Perhaps the computer software can be expanded to include rules for deciding conflicts among primary rules such as the ones just mentioned. ("When such and such a rule conflicts with such and such further rule, choose the first rule.") Even if possible, such an elaborate system would include rules that did not, strictly speaking, belong to either the legal system or codes of ethics. In other words, it would require knowledge not afforded by an ability to cite legal rules and codes of ethics.

Further, such a system would need to cover an infinite set of possible contexts and situations in which ethical problems might arise. If this system were to do a good job at making ethical decisions, it would inevitably have to develop the power to exercise moral discretion, to draw conclusions about cases that did not appear to fall clearly under any particular rule. For example, what should a family therapist do when to seek the welfare of one family member will cause harm to the welfare of another family member? In such a case, a therapist may need to exercise discretion enlightened by prior clinical experience, not merely by mechanically applying a set of preestablished rules. It is therefore easy to see how a therapist who knew all relevant legal rules and codes of ethics would not, by this knowledge alone, do a good job at making ethical decisions.

On the other hand, the approach to ethical decision making that we take in this book does not suppose that an ethical decision can simply be deduced from a set of rules. As we will see, such decisions also rely fundamentally on experience, perception, and emotion. It is a purpose of this book to help stimulate such additional moral fuel.

Types of Ethics

DESCRIPTIVE AND PHILOSOPHICAL ETHICS

This book deals with a certain type of ethics—namely, counseling ethics. Generally, ethics may be defined as the study of morality. There are, however, two distinct but related ways in which one could study morality: (1) descriptively and (2) philosophically. First, one could simply describe the moral outlooks of others, reflected in a particular culture. For example, in speaking of traditional Latin values, Olivia M. Espin (1995) states that Latin women

> receive constant cultural messages that they *should* be submissive and subservient to males in order to be seen as "good women." To suffer and be a martyr is also a characteristic of "good women." . . . To enjoy sexual pleasure, even in marriage, may indicate *lack of virtue*. (p. 425, emphasis added)

In this passage, the author is using the moral term *good women* (as well as the words *should* and *lack of virtue*) to report or describe what she takes to be the moral outlook of a Hispanic cultural tradition, not to advance her own moral perspective or even one held by all Hispanics today. Note the author's use of quotation marks surrounding the term *good women* to make clear that she has intended to quote—report or describe—a moral outlook, not to prescribe one. This is an example of *descriptive ethics.*

On the other hand, ethics can also signify the *philosophical* study of morality. In this sense, we would not merely use moral terms to describe the moral outlooks of others; we would also use them to advance our own moral outlooks as developed through a careful process of reasoning and reflection on key concepts and issues. For example, it is in this sense that we might argue that respect for client self-determination morally obligates counselors to work within the culturally defined belief systems of clients.

Although descriptive and philosophical ethics are distinct, they are also related. That is, the philosophical study of ethics may presuppose the descriptive study of ethics insofar as knowledge of alternative cultural perspectives might be relevant to the formulation of morally justified responses to culturally diverse client populations.

For example, consider the case of Suki, a 30-year-old Japanese female:

> Suki met Kimo, a Japanese-American, while he was on business assignment in Japan. The two married and settled in the United States. At Kimo's request, the two sought couples counseling with Jon Westfield. Mr. Westfield, who had been in practice for only a few months, had no previous experience counseling Oriental couples. Moreover, he was unfamiliar with Oriental culture. At the initial session, Mr. Westfield noted that Suki did not make eye contact with him, sat quietly, deferred to her husband, and appeared to be uncomfortable with personal questions—for example, questions about her sex life. At first, Mr. Westfield interpreted Suki's behavior to be "highly resistant." He also perceived her unwillingness to speak for herself to be indicative of a dependency problem. However, realizing his own unfamiliarity with Japanese culture, he decided to research the subject before the next session. Consequently, he learned that the lack of eye contact, which he had perceived as a sign of resistance, was actually proper Oriental etiquette, and that the personal questions he had asked were probably culturally received by Suki as being in poor taste. Moreover, he now realized that his evaluation of Suki's deference to her husband as dysfunctional behavior was culturally biased. The next time Mr. Westfield saw the couple, he was more aware of his own Western biases and more open to, and tolerant of, Oriental cultural perspectives.

As the case of Suki demonstrates, philosophically defensible moral outlooks are not likely to bear much fruit if applied in a cultural vacuum. Thus, respect for Suki's self-determination required that Mr. Westfield understand the cultural bases of Suki's behavior. Without this understanding, Mr. Westfield was bound to impose his own cultural values on Suki and, thereby, to diminish her freedom.

Keeping in mind the relationship between descriptive and philosophical ethics, we have placed the primary focus of this book on developing and applying a *philosophically* defensible counseling ethic. There are two distinct but related branches of philosophical ethics: (1) ethical theory and (2) applied ethics.

ETHICAL THEORY

Ethical theory is that branch of philosophical ethics that attempts to formulate general criteria or standards for distinguishing the morally good from the morally bad. This is the branch that attempts to provide general directions for avoiding evil and for living the morally good life. Two major types of ethical theory have dominated Western philosophy: (1) *rule (or principle) ethics* and (2) *virtue ethics*. The first—rule ethics—proposes and philosophically defends certain rules or principles of moral conduct. The second—virtue ethics— defines and defends certain traits of character, the possession of which is said to make one a morally good person. Rule ethics have typically focused on morally good action; virtue ethics have typically focused on morally good character. A third, more recent, variety of ethical theory is *care ethics;* as developed by feminist thinkers, it takes relationships of caring to be central to the mission of ethics. The theory proposed in this book is a form of virtue ethics, which also incorporates aspects of rule and care ethics.

RULE ETHICS

One variety of rule ethics is *utilitarianism* (or the ethics of utility). Formulated in the 19th century, this theory has become a major current in contemporary ethical theory. According to this theory, actions or types of action are morally justified (right) or morally unjustified (wrong) according to the amount of good and evil they can be expected to bring into the world by their performance. When the conduct in question, taken from all available alternative courses of action, can be expected to produce more good than evil, it is morally justified; otherwise, it is wrong. Thus, the principle of utility emerges as the sole standard of moral action.

In its classical form, as articulated by the English philosophers Jeremy Bentham and John Stuart Mill, utilitarianian ethics was hedonistic (from the Greek root *hedone,* meaning pleasure) in its theory of the good. That is, "good" signified "pleasure"; its contrary, "evil," signified "pain." So understood, the moral rightness of actions could be calculated by determining their overall tendency to produce pleasure and prevent pain.

For the classical utilitarians, moreover, the pleasures and pains of all those affected by the action in question were to be taken into account and weighted equally in the "hedonic calculus." Thus, as a principle of social utility, the theory went beyond the narrow self-serving concern for the agent's—the actor's— own pleasures and pains or those of significant others, and sought to consider equally the welfare—or the pains and pleasures—of others.

Two types of utilitarianism have been distinguished: (1) *act* utilitarianism and (2) *rule* utilitarianism. The former—act utilitarianism—requires that a separate calculus be undertaken for each individual action that is contemplated; the latter—rule utilitarianism—applies the principle of utility toward the justification of rules and, thus only indirectly, to acts.

Consider, the case of John, a client experiencing suicidal ideation:

> John had unsuccessfully attempted suicide 2 months prior to entering therapy with Dr. Weinick. The suicidal attempt was precipitated by his having been fired from his job after his wife had divorced him. John had taken both these events as proof of his own worthlessness and the futility of going on with his life. He had been in therapy

for just 3 weeks when he requested to see his counseling records. State laws normally entitle clients to view their records, but Dr. Weinick was convinced that revealing the clinical diagnoses contained in these records—which included borderline personality disorder—would be viewed by John as further confirmation of his own worthlessnesss and could, at this early stage in therapy, not only jeopardize prospects for successful therapy but could very likely precipitate a second suicide attempt. What was Dr. Weinick to do?

If Dr. Weinick were to apply the act utilitarian principle, he would approach this question by considering whether in this instance the disutility (pain, frustration, and potential loss of life) resulting from allowing John to see his records would be an overriding reason not to permit such access. On the one hand, Dr. Weinick would need to consider John's prior history and clinical assessment and decide what the probabilities of another suicide attempt would be if he were permitted to view the records as written. On the other, Dr. Weinick would have to consider the probable outcomes of all other possible alternatives—from an outright refusal to reveal the records to selective editing of the records before opening them. This calculus would also need to weigh the effects of each option on all those concerned, including the therapist himself. For example, Dr. Weinick would need to consider whether there were legal risks involved in altering these records and whether the harm prevented to John was worth the risks to Dr. Weinick.

From a *rule* utilitarian perspective, the challenge would be to formulate a professional rule governing client access to records that could be justified by virtue of its tendency to maximize overall utility, at least in the long run, when it was generally obeyed. Given such a rule, Dr. Weinick could find out what to do without first having to perform a complex "utility calculus."

Of course, it is possible that two such rules, in a given situation, might conflict. For example, in the present situation, a general rule prescribing respect for client self-determination would seem to require disclosing the records to the client at his request. On the other hand, such a rule would appear to conflict with one proscribing doing harm to clients. Given that each of these rules is utility maximizing, which rule should take precedence?

One classical response to this question proposed by J. S. Mill (who appears to have been a rule utilitarian) is to appeal directly to the "first principle" of utility in case of conflict between two "secondary rules." According to Mill, "If utility is the ultimate source of moral obligations, utility may be invoked to decide between them when their demands are incompatible. . . . We must remember that only in these cases of conflict between secondary principles is it requisite that first principles should be appealed to" (Mill, 1971, p. 30). Thus, where the obligation to respect clients' autonomy in viewing their own records conflicts with the obligation not to harm clients, the psychotherapist may appeal directly to the principle of utility to resolve the conflict. However, in situations in which no such conflict exists, says Mill, such a utility calculus is not necessary and appeal to a secondary rule—such as a rule granting clients autonomy in viewing their own records—will suffice.

In the formulation of utility-maximizing rules, exceptions to the rules may be made a part of the rules themselves. For example, a rule permitting client access to records may be more likely to maximize overall utility if it includes a qualification excepting cases when such access would (or probably would) cause serious psychological or physical harm to clients. However, for all exceptions to be conceived of and built into a rule in advance is highly unlikely; therefore, such an approach may still require some utility calculation for a therapist to determine whether an exception to the rule actually applies in the first place. For example, Dr. Weinick would still need to assess the risk of harm to John in permitting him to view his counseling records.

Nevertheless, the recognition of exceptions to rules, including legal ones, is important from a rule-utilitarian perspective. Consider the case of Jeannie, a 15-year-old female who was 2 months pregnant:

> When Jeannie first began therapy, she told her therapist, Dr. Jamieson, that she was pregnant because she had had sexual intercourse with her boyfriend. As therapy progressed, however, she revealed to Dr. Jamieson that she had lied about how she had gotten pregnant, that she had never even had a boyfriend, and that the pregnancy was really the result of having been sexually molested by her father, who had repeatedly abused her since she was a little girl. Moreover, Jeannie said that her father had threatened her about revealing this fact to anybody and had forbidden her, on religious grounds, to get an abortion despite her pleas for one. In the state in which Jeannie resided, however, parental consent was required before a minor could have an abortion. Thus, Jeannie was being forced, against her protests, into having the child.

Although a legal rule requiring parental consent for minors to receive abortions may arguably be held to maximize utility in the majority of cases, such a rule may overlook important exceptions in which much disutility—pain and suffering—is generated. This would appear to be true in Jeannie's case. Thus, from the rule-utilitarian perspective, a better rule—that is, a rule that more closely attained the goal of maximal utility—would be one that avoided the disutility of requiring parental consent in cases where the parent from whom consent is required was also the prospective father of the unborn child. Formulating and implementing the rule practically, however, present difficulties for the rule utilitarian: Proving that the minor's father is also the prospective father of the unborn child and also that the father sexually molested his daughter must itself proceed in a manner that maximizes overall human happiness. As the rule in question is part of a larger system of rules, the system itself must be examined for its conduciveness to human happiness. Hence, avoiding the disutility of such exceptional cases may demand changes in other parts of the system—for example, changing standards for proving sexual abuse. What might have seemed to be a simple utility adjustment can thus end up being a rather complex attempt to balance a number of rules within a system of rules.

One criticism of *act* utilitarianism has been its purported ability to justify unjust acts as long as they maximized overall utility. For example, suppose conducting a psychological experiment on certain clients would probably provide valuable insights that would, in the long run, benefit many clients suffering from serious psychopathology. However, imagine that the experiment designed required that these clients not be informed that they were being used as experimental subjects; and imagine also that there were substantial risks that a certain drug administered under false pretenses to these subjects would cause irreversible brain damage resulting in mild intelligence deficits. Nevertheless, given that the experiment would likely benefit many mentally ill clients, the theory of act utilitarianism could still justify conducting the experiment. However (so the criticism goes), such action would be unjust, for it would be a violation of the right of these clients not to be made subjects of the experiment without their freely given, informed consent.

Rule utilitarians have responded to the above criticism by maintaining that such unjust acts could never be justified by a system of utility-maximizing rules, as such a system would never contain any rule that legitimized conducting psychological experiments on clients without their freely given, informed consent. Indeed, were such a rule to exist, many individuals in need of psychotherapy would not seek it for fear of becoming the unwitting "guinea pigs " of experiments.

A further criticism of utilitarianism—which would appear to apply to both act and rule forms—has been its insistence that the consequences of actions alone are ultimately a sufficient standard of moral action. Critics argue that an adequate assessment of the morality of action must also consider the *motive* from which the action proceeds. For example, a person who helps the police rescue a kidnapped child for purposes of collecting a reward—and who, without promise of such reward, probably would have let the abductors kill the child—produces good results by his deed. Nonetheless, it is questionable that an act so ill-motivated could be called morally good. The consequences of such an action could reasonably be called good, but the ascription of the term *moral* or *morally good* to such an ill-disposed act is not as clear-cut.

Some utilitarians, for instance Mill, have responded to this criticism by maintaining that the principle of utility is a standard for assessing the morality of action, not one for assessing the morality of motives or character (Mill, 1971, p. 25, n. 3). However, this response merely assumes the possibility of morally assessing actions independently of their motives; and it is precisely this assumption that some wish to deny.

Immanuel Kant, the famous 18th-century German philosopher, proposed a rule-based ethics that emphasized motive exclusive of consequences (Kant, 1964). Whereas utilitarians try to assess the morality of action exclusively in terms of consequences, Kantians go to the opposite extreme of trying to assess the morality of action exclusively in terms of motive. Thus, for Kant, neither the intention to bring about results nor the actual results of action are relevant to assessing moral worth. Rather, moral action proceeds from a "good will" as manifested in action performed for the sake of duty.

According to Kant, an act is performed for the sake of duty when motivated by respect for an unconditional command of reason known as "the categorical imperative." In one form, this principle of duty prescribes acting only in ways that any rational being could consistently accept as universally binding: "Act as if the maxim of your action were to become through your will a universal law of nature" (Kant, 1964, p. 89). For example, suppose that a psychotherapist, moved by the desire for money, extended the duration of a client's therapy beyond its usefulness. For Kant, to expose the impropriety of such conduct, the therapist in question need only ask whether her "maxim" or motive of action—in order to make money I will provide services whether needed or not—could be accepted as a universal law of nature by any rational being. Because no rational being would herself consent to being so treated were she a client—as a client would need to trust her therapist in order for therapy to be useful—no rational being could consistently accept such a practice as universally binding.

Consider the case of Dr. Schneider, a 57-year-old male psychologist with a thriving practice:

> Dr. Schneider has recently gone through a divorce after 32 years of marriage. Experiencing depression over the ending of his marriage, he has had difficulty keeping his attention focused on what his clients tell him in session. Although his case notes in the past have been quite accurate and complete, he has begun to fill them out in a cursory fashion, adding further to his lack of recall of case details. On the one hand, Dr. Schneider regrets the present state of his ineptness in treating clients. On the other, the mere thought of referring his present clients only seems to add to his feelings of dispair and forlornness. He wonders whether he can get through the present crisis without sacrificing any of his practice, yet he still has the conscience to ask himself if attempting to do so would even be right.

As stated, from Kant's perspective, the moral propriety of actions must be assessed in terms of motive alone. However, if Dr. Schneider were to give up all or some of his clients out of concern for their welfare, he would still not—contrary to the utilitarians—be acting morally. Nor would he be acting morally if he were to give up any of his case load because of a guilty conscience. For Kant, such acts might be expedient and even in accordance with what Dr. Schneider's duty requires, assuming it is his duty to give up clients; however, these actions would lack *moral* worth because, they would not be done for the sake of duty. To accomplish the latter, Dr. Schneider would need to transcend mere expedience and emotionality and act out of respect for what reason—in the form of the categorical imperative—would prescribe. In looking rationally and dispassionately at his own problem, Dr. Schneider would see that he could not make a universal law out of his maxim: In order to work through my own psychological difficulties, I will provide psychological services inferior to what my clients could obtain elsewhere. Instead, this maxim would be inconsistent with the way any rational being, including Dr. Schneider himself, would want to be treated. Accordingly, to be moral, Dr. Schneider would have to surrender his present maxim, no matter how emotionally trying for him this might be. This, in turn, might require him to refer present clients for more competent services as well as not take on new clients until he had satisfactorily worked through his present crisis.

In ceasing to perceive his clients as mere psychological crutches, Dr. Schneider would have begun to treat his clients with the respect that they as persons deserve. That is, for Kant, only motives that can be rationally made into universal laws respect the inherent dignity of persons. Kant accordingly accepts a further formulation of his categorical imperative: "Act in such a way that you always treat humanity, whether in your own person or in the person of any other, never simply as a means, but always at the same time as an end" (Kant, 1964, p. 96). As in the case of Dr. Schneider, to present inferior or unnecessary services on the pretense of providing competent therapy would be to treat clients as objects used or manipulated ("mere means") instead of as rational, self-determining agents ("ends in themselves").

One difficulty of Kantian ethics is its failure to recognize the importance of *context* in ethical decision making. For example, Kant has argued that suicide for self-interested reasons such as to end one's own suffering is *always* wrong, as a universal law of destroying life in order to improve it would be self-contradictory (Kant, 1964, p. 89). Nevertheless, against Kant, a cogent argument can be made that in some extreme situations of unmitigated pain and suffering, the disutility of continued existence makes suicide both a reasonable and a moral option. Thus, Kant's attempt to settle ethical questions—such as whether suicide is ever justified—by abstract calculations without careful consideration of concrete situations appears to oversimplify the realities of ethical decision making.

Consider, for example, the case of Larry, a person with acquired immune deficiency syndrom (AIDS):

> Larry has been seeing his therapist, Dr. Adler, for 8 years. During this time, Dr. Adler has seen Larry's health progressively decline. He has witnessed him waste away from a robust man to one of virtual skin and bone. He has seen the ravages of Kaposi's sarcoma and the rise of other opportunistic infections; currently, early signs of cognitive/motor deterioration associated with human immunodeficiency virus (HIV) encephalopathy are appearing. It is evident to Dr. Adler that Larry has made his peace with himself and his loved ones and is prepared to die. Larry explains to Dr. Adler his well-organized plan to end his own life before the ravages to his brain foreclose this opportunity. Dr. Adler considers Larry's desire to be a reasonable one under his special circumstances and he sees no point in trying to stop him. Rather, Dr. Adler is deeply sympathetic toward this client whom he has come to know and respect.

Not only are the legal implications unclear concerning Dr. Adler's complacent attitude toward Larry's intentions to end his own life (see Chapter 10); the moral question is also not cut and dried. Yet, Kant's view leaves little left to argument. For Kant, Dr. Adler is effectively condoning and permitting an unreasonable and immoral act. There is no allowance for the context in which Larry and his therapist find themselves, and no accounting for the dignity that accrues from taking control of one's own death.

Nor is there any flexibility for Dr. Adler's compassion for his client as a basis for noninterference with Larry's suicide; Kant's theory does not recognize feelings and emotions as morally legitimate motives of action. Some philosophers—for example, Hume—have made sentiments such as sympathy the foundation of morality; for Kant, an action performed out of such a motive, "however right and however amiable it may be, has still no genuine moral worth" (Kant, 1964, p. 66). By emphasizing reason to the exclusion of emotion, Kant has made moral action an affair of cool and dispassionate calculation. However, moral actions occur within the context of interpersonal relations and such relations are often emotionally charged. Although intense emotions can destroy moral objectivity—as when one flies into a rage—emotional detachment can produce insensitivity toward, and lack of regard for, the welfare, interests, and needs of others. Thus some degree of emotional engagement, within reason, would appear relevant to moral action.

According to a third formulation of Kant's categorical imperative, we should "act always on the maxim of such a will in us as can at the same time look upon itself as making universal law" (Kant, 1964, p. 100). In other words, our actions should be rationally autonomous, grounded in universal laws that we rationally and freely choose. Consider, for example, the case of Kathy, a 40-year-old housewife and mother:

> Kathy is in therapy with Dr. Lipkin for depression. As she explains, "It is as though I am going through the motions of living without feeling like anything really matters. I don't know what's wrong with me. I have a husband who takes good care of me and three lovely children, but I'm still not happy." Kathy had earlier hoped to attend college to become a high school Spanish teacher, but she got married after graduating from high school, became pregnant, and did not attend college. When Dr. Lipkin asked her if she had considered going back to school for teaching, she declared, "It is more important for the man to have a career than the woman anyway. The woman should be at home with the kids." When Dr. Lipkin asked her why it was more important for the man to have a career, however, and why women and men could not share in parental duties, she became agitated. Eventually, she admitted to not being sure why men's careers should be considered more important than women's except that this is what her mother had repeatedly told her when she was a young girl.

From Kant's perspective, in Kathy's uncritical acceptance of male and female gender roles, she had not autonomously and rationally conformed her will to "universal law." Rather, she was moved by forces of emotion and socialization. For Kant, such determination is bondage, not freedom. On the other hand, by beginning to see an inconsistency—a double standard—in the differential social treatment of women and men, Kathy had begun to transcend these forces, to fashion her will according to universal law rationally determined, and, accordingly, to assert her freedom.

Indeed, for Kant, only through such conformity of the will to reason can one attain freedom and realize one's nature as an end in itself. For him, we are otherwise no different from physical objects that are acted on and completely determined by external forces. However, although some rational engagement may be requisite to our freedom, we need not suppose that emotional engagement or the acceptance of cultural norms cannot themselves be rational and free. Although Kant issues an important reminder to avoid being carried away by blind emotion or blind adherence to social rules, this does not mean that a will that is at least partly moved by such extrinsic factors must always be unfree. Kant's emphasis on pure reason as the ground of human freedom may thus be unrealistic.

RULE ETHICS AND THE CONCEPT OF A RIGHT

In the context of discussing moral problems, one freqently argues for or against a particular ethical stance by appealing to rights. For example, one might argue against abortion on the grounds that the unborn child has a right to life. Talk about rights can be understood only within the context of *rule* ethics. In general, a *right is an interest that is protected by a rule.* To say that a person has a right to something of interest implies that there is a rule that prohibits others from interfering with that interest. Thus, one has a right to life because there is a rule that forbids others from taking away one's life. When the rule in question is a legal rule, the right in question can be considered a *legal right;* the right is a *moral right* when the rule in question is a moral one. For example, a client may have a legal right to refuse to disclose confidential information in a court of law in a state that recognizes such privilege by statute. This is the so-called legal right of privileged communication to be addressed in Chapter 4. In a state where no such statute exists, no such legal right exists. On the other hand, one could argue that a person has a moral right to such privileged communication even if there is no corresponding legal right. This is possible because courts morally should respect clients' private communications with their therapists.

Insofar as a theory of ethics accommodates rules, talk about rights makes sense from that theoretical perspective. For example, according to *rule* utilitarianism, one has or should have a right to something of interest when general conformity to a rule forbidding interference with that interest can be calculated to maximize overall happiness. Thus we have a right to life, from this perspective, because general respect for life maximizes overall happiness. On the other hand, Kantian ethics would countenance a right to life because such a rule or maxim can be turned into a universal law of nature and it is just what is required to treat others as "ends in themselves."

Because *act* utilitarianism does not accommodate rules, it cannot talk about rights. In this theory, we are supposed to use the utility standard to justify concrete actions, not abstract rules or maxims. For example, in this theory, a particular promise should be kept if keeping it, on the whole, is best, not because promise keeping *as a rule* is justified. A further type of ethics that also does not accommodate rules, and accordingly does not talk about rights, is *care ethics,* to which we now turn.

CARE ETHICS

Whereas Kantian ethics proposes a master rule—the categorical imperative—for the abstract calculation of morality, care ethics links morality to the concrete situation. As advanced by the Harvard psychologist Carol Gilligan, care ethics perceives morality in terms of concrete interpersonal relationships that can be understood only by people who have compassion and empathy for the predicaments of other people. It is about the preservation of such relationships and the prevention of human suffering. In care ethics, the primary motive is "the wish not to hurt others and the hope that in morality lies a way of solving conflicts so that no one will get hurt" (Gilligan, 1994a, p. 728). Caring does not mean that nobody ever actually gets hurt, however, because in the real world our capacity to help others may be limited by time and circumstances. "Although inclusion is the goal of moral consciousness, exclusion may be a necessity of life" (Gilligan, 1982, p. 148).

Although care ethics resembles act utilitarianism in its concentration on context (as against abstract rules and talk about rights) and on the consequences of action, it denies that morality is a matter of rational calculation or adding up of pleasures and pains. Rather, moral action involves a sense of what is right in a given situation, a kind of perception as opposed to the product of applying an algorithm. Thus, an ethics of care would not justify wholesale sacrifice of the welfare, interest, or needs of any individual because doing so could be calculated to maximize overall utility.

Moreover, unlike the act-utilitarian calculation, the act of caring is infused with emotion. In clarifying the notion of caring, Lawrence M. Hinman states:

> Caring has an irremediably emotive component to it. To care about someone is not just to act in particular ways; it is also, and necessarily, to *feel* in particular ways. There would be something odd if a parent tried to add up impersonally all the hedons and dolors for a particular choice that will affect the family. Part of caring is to feel something for the other person. (Hinman, 1994, p. 336)

Consider, for example, a case of Dr. Engle, a psychologist in private practice:

> Mrs. Johnston, a single mother of a 13-year-old female, Cindy, called Dr. Engle and explained that Cindy had threatened to kill herself after she received news that a close friend had attempted suicide. Mrs. Johnston said that she worked three jobs and that Cindy was often left on her own after school and evenings. She also stated that Cindy was now very distraught over the possibility of being involuntarily placed in an inpatient facility for evaluation, but that no other therapist had agreed to see her on an outpatient basis. Mrs. Johnston was crying and indicated that although she had no insurance and could not afford Dr. Engle's usual fee of $125, she did not know what to do if Dr. Engle refused to help her. Dr. Engle recalled her own sense of futility and quiet desperation when, as a young adolescent, a close friend of hers committed suicide. As a mother and an experienced professional, she also understood what Mrs. Johnston was going through: the pain of watching her baby suffer, the anxiety of not knowing how to make the suffering go away, the feeling of helplessness and loss of control over something so precious. Dr. Engle could not see Cindy that day without imposing on other clients, but she was willing to see her before regular hours at 7:00 A.M. the following morning at a substantially reduced fee. She advised Mrs. Johnston not to go to work that evening and to keep a close watch on her daughter.

In this case, Dr. Engle did not simply weigh the pluses and minuses of seeing Cindy on an outpatient basis. Had she done so, she might well have advised Mrs. Johnston to check Cindy involuntarily into a free psychiatric facility. Dr. Engle's response to Mrs. Johnston's desperate plea was itself infused with emotion. She was emotionally in tune with both mother and daughter and with her own feelings. She really cared, and such caring could not be extracted from such emotionality and relegated to a purely rational process of abstract calculations. She was not simply performing a utility calculus in which the welfare of one person was balanced over that of another. Nor did she consult pure reason in the form of the categorical imperative to find out what her duty was. Rather, her motive was to address the needs of everyone concerned—Cindy, Mrs. Johnson, her other clients—without sacrificing anyone's needs.

Although such caring involves an irremediably emotive component, this should not be taken to mean that it does not also include a rational component. Thus, according to Maxine Morphis and Christopher Riesbeck, the ethics of care may be viewed as a function of "case-based reasoning" as opposed to "rule-based reasoning." For example,

> a rule-based model of planning a dinner party might use rules to calculate when to have the party, who to invite, what level of formality to impose, what food to serve, and so on. A case-based approach, on the other hand, would use previous dinner parties as a model, and make modifications based on those experiences. Thus, unfortunate combinations of guests would be avoided, the kind of food that has been popular before would be an obvious option, realistic starting and ending times would be assumed, and so on. (Morphis & Riesbeck, 1990, p. 16)

Similarly, in responding to Mrs. Johnston's plea for help, Dr. Engle did not simply apply ethical principles or other prepackaged rules—for example, "If a prospective client can't afford your services, then make a referral" or "If you can't see a potentially suicidal client immediately, then advise placement in an inpatient facility for evaluation." Instead, in coming to a conclusion about how to respond to Mrs. Johnston's plea for help, she began with her own past experiences—as a child in a similar situation, as a mother, as a professional in dealing with similar crises. Whereas these past experiences were infused with emotion, they also provided rational bases for proceeding in the present case. Indeed, these experiences provided reliable information precisely because they were emotional. Much as understanding colors requires seeing in color, understanding the present case—which was emotional—called for emotional understanding, not just cold, dispassionate perception.

Carol Gilligan provides a further illustration of the case-based nature of care ethics in contrast to a rule-based perspective. In discussing the short story, "A Jury of Her Peers" by Susan Glaspell, in which the character of Minnie Foster is suspected of killing her husband, Gilligan relates the following:

> A neighbor woman and the sheriff's wife accompany the sheriff and the prosecutor to the house of the accused woman. The men representing the law, seek evidence that will convince a jury to convict the suspect. The women, collecting things to bring Minnie Foster in jail enter in this way into the lives lived in the house. Taking in rather than taking apart, they begin to assemble observations and impressions, connecting them to past experience and observations until suddenly they compose a familiar pattern. . . . Discovering a strangled canary buried under pieces of quilting, the women make a series of connections that lead them to understand what happened. The logic that says you don't kill a man because he has killed a bird, the judgment that finds these acts wildly incommensurate, is counterposed to the logic that sees both events as part of a larger pattern—a pattern of detachment and abandonment that led finally to the strangling. . . . Mrs Peters, the sheriff's wife, recalls that when she was a girl and a boy killed her cat, "If they hadn't held me back I would have—" and realizes that there had been no one to restrain Minnie Foster. . . . Seeing detachment as the crime with murder as its ultimate extension, implicating themselves and also seeing the connection between their own and Minnie Foster's actions, the women solve the crime. (Gilligan, 1994b, p. 270)

According to Morphis and Riesbeck, a case-based understanding of care ethics helps to explain its contextual as well as its intuitive nature (Morphis & Riesbeck, 1990, p. 20). Case-based reasoning must pay close attention to the details of the individual contexts in which interpersonal relationships occur in order to make comparative judgments of present contexts with past ones; therefore, such reasoning is indisoluably contextual in nature rather than abstract. To compare Minnie Foster's life to her own, Mrs. Peters first had to absorb intimate details of the way Minnie Foster lived; she was then able to put together (intuit) what really happened. This ability to see deeply into the situation required that Mrs. Peters exercise her powers of empathetic understanding, to sense what Minnie Foster sensed. It also required what feminist thinkers have recently characterized as *connected knowing*, a way of knowing based on a commitment to understand the views of others rather than to look for flaws in them (Goldberger, Tarule, Clinchy, & Belenky, 1996). These concepts are examined in Chapter 3. As will become apparent, the ability of therapists to relate personally to intimate aspects of clients' lives—including clients' feelings and emotions—is fundamental to a viable counseling ethic.

The comparative or analogical structure of case-based reasoning may be contrasted to rule-based reasoning insofar as the latter begins with rules and deductively applies them to specific contexts to reach conclusions. For example, from the rule that "You don't kill a man because he has killed a bird," it follows that Minnie Foster must have had other motives for killing her husband. As Gilligan suggests, such abstract and detached logic would have failed to reach a true conclusion (Gilligan, 1994b, p. 270). On the other hand, in case-based reasoning, prior cases, such as Mrs. Peters's own experience of what it felt like to have her cat's life destroyed by another human being, stand as precedents for adducing conclusions about present cases; thus such reasoning begins with cases rather than with rules.

Nevertheless, in care ethics, rules may still serve heuristically as guidelines. The Kantian rule of treating persons as ends in themselves and not as mere means may help to call attention to a moral problem inherent in treating people in a certain way—for example, if a therapist lied to a client or, as in the previous example, if Dr. Engle had treated Mrs. Johnson or Cindy in a way she herself would not want to be treated. From the perspective of care-based ethics, moral rules provide only a moral minimum to moral action. The rest must be provided by attention to the nuances and relevant details of individual contexts such as facts about the lives of concrete people affected by contemplated actions and appeals to one's own prior experiences, observations, and emotions. In general, moral action must be informed by sensitivity to relevant factors that may be too complex or by their nature not readily captured and formulated by a pre-arranged set of rules. Such a set of rules may thus be "only as good as its role in the correct articulation of the concrete" (Nussbaum, 1990, p. 95). As Gilligan (1982) suggests,

> moral judgment must be informed by "growing insight and sympathy," tempered by the knowledge gained through experience that "general rules" will not lead people "to justice by a ready-made patent method, without the trouble of exerting

patience, discrimination, impartiality, without any care to assure whether they have the insight that comes from . . . a life vivid and intense enough to have created a wide, fellow feeling with all that is human." (p. 148)

And, as Morphis and Riesbeck (1990, p. 23) suggest, caring itself is

not definable by a set of conditions, but rather will be repeatedly tested and will evolve with individuals and with families as well as with culture and with technology. Caring is an art, not a science.

As first proposed by Carol Gilligan, care ethics was intended to call attention to differences between the ways males and females approach morality, as well as the distinct developmental stages women go through in reaching moral maturation. Thus, while morally mature men have been characterized as tending to settle ethical problems by impartially applying universal rules—for instance, Kantian ones—protective of human rights (Gilligan, 1994b, p. 264), morally mature women have been characterized in terms of the informal, concrete "injunction to care, a responsibility to discern and alleviate the 'real and recognizable trouble' of this world" (Gilligan, 1994a, p. 731). Moreover, this injunction to care does not exclude self-regard. Indeed, for Gilligan, what distinguishes morally mature women from many who lack such maturity is appreciation that responsibility to care includes caring about oneself as well as about others (Gilligan, 1994a, p. 731).

Nevertheless, as Gilligan herself maintains, "development for both sexes . . . would seem to entail an integration of rights and responsibilities through the discovery of the complementarity of these disparate views" (Gilligan, 1994a, p. 731). Thus, an ethics of care need not be viewed as the exclusive domain of women. Indeed, "men can have both masculine and feminine dimensions to their moral voices just as women can have both" (Hinman, 1994, p. 334).

As stated, care ethics perceives morality in terms of the preservation of concrete interpersonal relationships. However, whereas some relationships may be worthy of maintaining, others such as abusive marriages may not be. One might argue that care ethics, with its focus on preservation of relationships, may promote the preservation of even those relationships that are better off terminated (Beabuot and Wennemann, 1994, p. 42).

For example, a marriage counselor who perceives his primary professional goal to be the preservation of the marital relationship may tend to see counseling that ends in divorce as a professional failure. Such singlemindedness may be incompatible with the well-being of the client involved in an abusive or otherwise untenable relationship. Given the proclivity of abuse victims to remain in abusive relationships, any cue from the therapist that divorce should be avoided if at all possible may lead the client, to her detriment, to continue in the relationship.

Although there is a potential problem in applying care ethics to psychotherapy, remember that care ethics also stresses the responsibility to prevent pain and suffering. As abusive relationships promote pain and suffering, preserving them would appear to be inconsistent with the ethics of care.

A further difficulty with care ethics still remains, however. Care ethics emphasizes acts of caring, but it does not provide any account of the *agents* themselves who act with care. As caring persons are the ones most likely to perform caring acts, some account of what it is to be such a person would seem to be in order. This account would not replace a care ethics; it would instead provide a more complete framework for its development. Such a framework can be provided by a virtue ethics, to which we now turn.

VIRTUE ETHICS

In contrast to the other types of ethical theories surveyed here, virtue ethics looks at moral action within the context of moral agency. As defined by Aristotle, the ancient Greek philosopher, moral virtues are states of character concerned with rational control and direction of emotions. Moreover, such states of character are, according to Aristotle, habits acquired from repeatedly performing virtuous actions. A person who has acquired a habit of confronting life situations without being deterred by undue or irrational fears possesses the virtue of courage; and a person who has acquired a habit of rationally indulging—neither overdoing nor underdoing—bodily desires such as for food or sex possesses the virtue of temperance.

As moral virtue is thus a function of both reason and emotion, it avoids the Kantian pitfall of defining ethical motivation purely in terms of reason while also acknowledging, along with care ethics, the important role of emotion in ethics. Yet, unlike care ethics, it provides a philosophical framework for defining the relationship between moral action and moral agency.

Like act utilitarianism, virtue ethics stresses the context-dependent nature of moral action. For example, what is courageous in one situation may amount to foolhardiness in another. A mark of a virtuous person is the ability to know when a certain line of conduct is morally in order and when it is not.

However, virtue ethics does not assume that moral determinations are simply the result of a rational calculus (Aristotle, 1941, Bk. 2, Ch. 9, 1109b20). Rather, such decisions are concerned with "particulars, which become familiar from experience" (Bk. 6, Ch. 8, 1142a14–15), and like "anything else that is perceived by the senses . . . the decision rests with perception" (B2, Ch. 9, 1109b20). In this regard, virtue ethics is similar to the case-based understanding of care ethics as presented by Morphis and Riesbeck.

This knowledge from experience is practical in that it is used for deliberation about how to achieve ends sought effectively. Hence, in contrast to Kant, morally virtuous acts are motivated by concern for the consequences of actions. For example, morally virtuous therapists would need not only to care about helping clients work through their difficulties but would also need to know how to do so competently.

On the other hand, a morally virtuous person is more than simply a clever person who, armed with a fund of knowledge from experience and acute observation powers, knows how to attain the desired target. The morally viruous person also aims at morally good ends; and this is undertaken not for any ulterior motive such as fame or money, but for the sake of the ends themselves. A morally virtuous psychotherapist would seek to be honest with her clients not merely because this behavior is itself a way toward the goal of maximizing profit (supposing that "morality pays" by attracting clients) but because honesty itself is to be valued.

Consider the case of Joel Cosgrove, M.D., a psychiatrist in practice for 20 years:

> Joel Cosgrove, M.D., has appeared on nationally televised talk shows to promote a new book in his field. Dr. Cosgrove has, by his own admission, enjoyed the media attention, but he has always been critical of those who have proffered ideas purely for the sake of pursuing fame and fortune. Recently, he was asked to host a nationally syndicated talk show in which viewers would be encouraged to call in about their personal problems. Although he found the offer tempting at first, his conclusion was that such a show would constitute "morally irresponsible practice by trivializing the nature of the therapeutic process, and undermining client welfare." Accordingly, Dr. Cosgrove turned down this very lucrative offer to concentrate on research and private practice.

The desire for money and fame did to some extent motivate as well as tempt him, but Dr. Cosgrove was, in the end, unwilling to transgress his moral principles for the sake of these external goods. Acting instead according to perceived standards of morality and professionalism, he attained rational control over his material desires. This did not mean that Dr. Cosgrove was untrue to his values by making money from his book or by accepting publicity; as Aristotle recognized, virtue does not require that a person completely abstain from indulging such human desires. On the other hand, had Dr. Cosgrove accepted the TV offer, he would have indulged these appetites by embarking on a career—and cultivating a habit—of dealing dishonestly with his clients.

As a morally virtuous person, however, Dr. Cosgrove had internalized general principles regarding morally good ends such as that of dealing honestly with others. To say that he had internalized these principles means that he thought they should be respected, that it would be unjust or wrong in itself to violate them. Accordingly, he was willing to give up substantial material gain for their sake.

Note that although virtue ethics is informed by ethical principles, these principles are general in character. For example, "Be honest" does not tell you exactly how to be honest or what is to count as honesty in a given context. As in care ethics (as understood on the case-based model of Morphis and Riesbeck), rules or principles, including Kantian and utilitarian ones, may serve to point one in the right direction. Much is left to assessing the situation, which is a process informed by prior experience and enlightened perception, not the mere product of applying a moral algorithm. Dr. Cosgrove was able to draw the line between the pursuit of material gain consistent with professionalism and the principles of honesty and the practices that fell short of this professionalism and honesty because his perception was enlightened by 20 years of private practice.

Aristotle's virtue ethics is based on a certain view of human nature. According to Aristotle, although human beings are animals, they are distinct from all other animals by virtue of their ability to reason. For Aristotle, it is rational living that provides the standard of human virtue. For example, much as the merit of a life raft lies in how well it fulfills its end or purpose of keeping one afloat, the merit—virtue, excellence—of a human being lies in how well this being fulfills his or her natural purpose or end (of living rationally). Because moral virtues always involve the exertion of rational control over passions, a virtuous life represents one befitting a human being as a rational animal. Thus the moral virtues are essential components of a life of prosperity, happiness, or flourishing for human beings.

Aristotle's theory of moral virtues has been dubbed an internal theory because it considers moral virtues to be part of the very definition of what it means for human beings to be happy or prosperous (MacIntyre, 1982). This is why Aristotle regards virtuous action as good in itself, the primary reward being in *acting* virtuously, not in any external reward, such as money or fame, derived from it.

Aristotle's theory rests on the assumption that there is, indeed, some ultimate human end or purpose, a determinable human nature, according to which all human prosperity is to be defined. This assumption has, however, not enjoyed universal acceptance by philosophers. For example, according to the French existentialist, Jean-Paul Sartre (1985), human beings define their own unique purposes and meanings through their life decisions; there is no preestablished human nature as there is, say, a lifeboat nature or a chair nature. Rather, human beings possess the freedom to make of themselves what they will.

Consider, the case of Diane, a 55-year-old widow and mother of two adult children:

> Diane was in counseling with Dr. Rodner to work through the recent loss of her husband of 37 years. At the start of therapy, Diane, who had been a housewife since 18, expressed serious doubts about the meaningfulness of life because she no longer had a husband and her children had since moved away and were preoccupied with their own lives. She stated, "I had a purpose; I was a wife and mother, and now I'm a nothing." However, after six months of therapy, Diane came to see that she had the power to create new goals and purposes for herself. Diane, who had always wanted to get a college education, enrolled in a degree program at a local community college. Although she believed it was difficult to stand up to the anxiety, self-doubt, and uncertainty she confronted in making such sweeping changes in her life, she had, by her own admission, found new meaning and vitality in living.

As long as Diane looked on herself as a kind of human machine that served certain useful functions—as a mother and a wife—she felt safe. But this security was purchased at the expense of failing to see that she had many other possibilities open to her, depending on what she herself decided. She was not, after all, like a lifeboat or a chair that functioned only according to a preexisting design. She instead came to see that her life was whatever *she* made of it. Realization of such personal autonomy brought with it renewed hope for the future. On the other hand, her previous outlook—that human purposes precede and negate such freedom—thwarted her prospects for happiness. From the existentialist perspective, it was her capacity to exert such control over the course of her own existence that made the idea of a fixed, preordained, human nature unrealistic and self-stultifying. As we see later (Chapter 3), this value of personal autonomy—the freedom to make independent choices, the exertion of control over one's own life—is itself a major goal of therapy.

In contrast to Aristotle, Alasdair MacIntyre (1982) has maintained that there is not necessarily one ultimate end or purpose defined by one universal set of human virtues. Rather, there is a plurality of *practices*—coherent, complex, socially established, cooperative human activities—each with its own specific purpose and respective set of virtues. For MacIntye, such practices include the activities of art, science, game playing, the professions, the family, the community, and other social relationships. For example, in MacIntyre's view, clarity of delivery—the habit of presenting information in a clear form—would presumably be a virtue of the practice of teaching, as intelligibility is an essential aspect of the learning process.

According to MacIntyre, there are always certain goods *internal* to a practice that can be realized only through engaging in the particular practice. Thus, goods internal to medical practice would include cultivation of a certain bedside manner, diagnostic skills, and mechanical skills—such as those of surgery. On the other hand, fame, honor, and money accruing from work done in one's profession (medicine, mental health, etc.) would be goods *external* to the specific practice as these can be realized in many other ways. Insofar as MacIntyre holds that internal—as opposed to external—goods can provide sufficient rewards for participation in practices (the activities involved in practices themselves constituting the end of participation), his theory, like Aristotle's, is an internal theory.

However, unlike Aristotle, MacIntyre offers no independent standard for distinguishing between practices that ennoble human beings and those that do not. It is thus possible to imagine evil practices that satisfy MacIntyre's characterization. For example, some "hired guns" (persons employed to kill others) might take great pride in the skills they have cultivated through their line of work. Indeed, relative to the end of this work, the cunning needed to outsmart authorities is a virtue; and such internal goods as fine marksmanship and the skillful use of special surveillance techniques, not to mention the thrill literally of getting away with murder, may amply provide the internal rewards. It is also possible to imagine such a "professional" who is quite willing to do pro bono work, thus being no more in it for the money—the external rewards—than are certain other professionals such as doctors and lawyers.

There is, however, an important difference between practices like law and medicine and the practice pursued by the hired assassin: The practice of law or medicine can be plausibly justified by appeal to the general happiness principle; the practice of killing people for money cannot. Whereas the assassin aims to destroy human life regardless of the social consequences including human suffering, law and medicine, as social institutions, exist to prevent human pain and suffering through the preservation of life and liberty. This distinction suggests a further external way of justifying practices and their virtues.

According to this utilitarian approach, the specific virtues within a given practice and ultimately the practice itself are morally justified when the cultivation of these virtues within the practice can be expected to maximize overall happiness in the hedonic sense of maximizing pleasure and minimizing pain and suffering. On this view, virtue is seen as possessing its moral worth in relation to its social utility. Such a view has been entertained by J. S. Mill (1971).

Regarding virtue, Mill holds that "there was no original desire for it or motive to it save its conduciveness to pleasure, and especially to protection from pain. But through the association thus formed it may be felt a good in itself, and desired as such with as great intensity as any other good" (Mill, 1971, p. 39). According to Mill, social utility thus emerges as the principle for deciding what specific traits of character are virtuous—namely, those that promote overall happiness. However, whereas virtue is ultimately justified on grounds of utility, the internal perspective of Aristotle and MacIntyre is still preserved as a psychological fact. That is, in Mill's view, those who have cultivated virtuous habits will still want to act virtuously for virtue's sake—not just as a means of maximizing utility.

Consider the case of Dr. Firestone, a medical researcher:

> Dr. Firestone had evidence pointing to the anticarcinogenic properties of a certain psychotropic drug. However, he also had reason to believe that the drug could have certain untoward, albeit temporary, psychiatric side effects including the production of paranoid ideation when taken in quantities consistent with its potential therapeutic value. Although he was aware of the prospective benefits of further research with human subjects, Dr. Firestone realized the importance of getting informed consent, which, for him, included informing subjects of possible psychiatric effects of the drug regimen. On the one hand, he knew that failure to provide informed consent could later result in lawsuits and loss of funding for the research; and he was aware that not informing subjects of material risks of experimentation could, in the long run, discourage would-be subjects from participating. Given the prospective benefits of the research, failure to provide informed consent would, therefore, be a bad idea. Still, Dr. Firestone did not consider informed consent to be a mere expedient to promoting his research goals. To the contrary, he thought it only fair that subjects be provided with all relevant information about harmful side effects of the drug. In his view, providing such information would be necessary, even if failure to do so would not jeopardize his research goals, and even if disclosure would severely limit the number of subjects willing to participate.

For Dr. Firestone, honesty was the best policy from an internal, not just an external, perspective. He considered it to be right in itself to be honest with experimental subjects, not merely because there was utility in doing so. His motive for disclosing the relevant information was therefore at least in part the desire to act virtuously, for virtue's own sake.

In Mill's view, this motive of virtuous action is distinct from the justification of virtuous practice. Whereas virtuous actions are motivated, at least in part, by the desire to act virtuously, the practice of virtue—the cultivation of virtuous habits as part of a practice—is to be justified by the principle of utility. For example, the general practice of being honest with subjects in human experimentation might be justified on utilitarian grounds, but such grounds need not define the primary motivation of individual researchers, as was true in Dr. Firestone's case. Rather, the principle of utility applies as a basis for determining whether given practices qualify as virtuous; it applies as a *criterion of virtues selection*, not necessarily as the motivation behind individual virtuous actions.

Applied Professional Ethics: A Proposed, Eclectic Approach

In this book, the principle of utility, as it relates to welfare of clients and others affected by counseling practice, is employed as a criterion of virtues selection for construction of a virtue-based counseling ethics. The emerging theory will have the advantage of recognizing the internal nature of virtuous motivation as emphasized by Aristotle and MacIntyre. However, unlike Aristotle's view, it will not assume any general theory of human nature; unlike MacIntyre's view, it will provide a moral criterion for assessing virtuous practices.

Among the further advantages to be gained from a virtues approach to counseling ethics of the sort to be developed here is the recognition of the relevance of therapists' character in dealing with moral problems arising in professional practice. For purposes of constructing such a theory, this personality aspect will include consideration of the motives for which moral actions are undertaken—for instance, the desire to act honestly or courageously. The emerging theory will also acknowledge the role of emotion as a legitimate component of a morally good motive—for instance, the role of such emotional states as empathy and compassion in promoting among therapists greater understanding of and sensitivity toward the plights of clients and other relevant persons. The theory will accordingly recognize that moral action is no mere affair of rules but is instead infused with emotion, human relatedness, and sensitivity to the nuances of individual context.

Part II of this book presents and analyzes concrete cases concerning problems of multicultural counseling, religion, dual-role relationships, child abuse, domestic violence, HIV, suicide intervention, and involuntary commitment. These case studies will set precedents for therapists' future reference as the therapists confront similar cases in their own counseling practices.

The approach taken herein also acknowledges the significant role of ethical theories, principles, rules, and standards in helping to guide moral problem solving. In Part I, a system of general principles, including trust-establishing principles, is developed and related to many rules contained in professional codes of ethics, notably those of the American Counseling Association, the American Psychological Association, and the National Association of Social Workers. In Part II, these principles and rules, together with broader ethical theories, are employed in case analyses. More specialized sets of rules called standards are also derived from the case analyses. These standards specifically address concrete moral exigencies of the sorts mentioned above and thus provide therapists with problem-specific guidelines to moral decision making that go beyond those found in the professional codes.

The perspective presented here further recognizes that to accomplish virtuous ends and to be caring, therapists must also consider the consequences of their actions. However, such concern for consequences is tempered by the realization that morality is no mere matter of detached, quantitative analysis. In general, the emerging theory weaves together important aspects of Kantian, utilitarian, and care ethics within the framework of a virtue ethics while attempting to avoid some of the pitfalls of these theories.

Part I of this book develops the theory. Part II applies the developed theory to persisting moral problems arising in contexts of counseling and psychotherapy. This book is thus an example of the branch of philosophical ethics known as *applied ethics* (Martin, 1989, p. 13). Theories are said to be applied when they serve the practical mission of helping to solve or clarify specific moral problems or issues. These issues may range from issues of general interest—for instance, whether gun control is morally justified, whether abortions are morally permissible—to those of concern to specific professions, such as the ethics of lawyers, engineers, doctors, or nurses. Insofar as applied ethics is concerned with moral issues of practical importance for professionals, it is called *professional ethics* (Bayles, 1989, pp. 3–4). Because it is concerned with moral problems of counseling and psychotherapy, this book is an example of professional ethics.

Summary

As evident from the discussions and case illustrations in this chapter, an enlightened ethical decision is a product of several factors and is often characterized by tensions between competing interests and considerations. On the one hand, ethical decision making is not simply a mechanical process of deducing a conclusion from a set of cut-and-dried rules. An ethical problem is not like a math problem in which a formula is applied in reaching a solution. On the other hand, it is not a merely subjective process in which there are no validating standards. There are important principles—such as those proposed by Kant, Bentham, and Mill—useful codes of ethics, standards, statutes, and case law, but these rules are not hard and fast. They must be applied and enlightened by perception and experience, by the ability to draw inferences from perceived similarities and differences between the presenting case and past ones, and by sensitivity grounded in our ability to feel as well as to reason.

On the one hand, ethics is an affair of reason and rules; on the other, it depends on emotion and experience of particulars. Ethical decision making requires that we act to achieve good results, but it also requires that we act with character and good motive. It involves dedication to principle even in the face of serious risks. Yet it involves knowing when we have gone too far in pressing one principle at the expense of another; it involves knowing when we have attained "the golden mean" between excess and deficiency. It involves balancing competing interests such as truth and honesty against risk of harm to self or others. It involves drawing a line between self-interest and mere selfish disregard for one's professional responsibilities.

Such are the tensions that tug at ethical choice, and they are fully captured only when we see the different ethical theories in their relation to (and often disequilibrium with) one another. Kantian ethics gives us part of this overview, utilitarianism gives us another part, and care ethics adds yet another fundamental component. Kantian ethics features motive, bidding us to act on motives we would be prepared to have others act on. It enjoins us to treat others as autonomous persons and not as mere objects to be used and manipulated. In contrast, utilitarianism stresses good consequences. Rule utilitarianism justifies rule-governed activities or practices in terms of their tendency to promote pleasure over pain. It can provide us with a standard for deciding what counseling practices should be regarded as virtuous. Act utilitarianism applies the utility standard directly to individual acts. It stresses acting to promote the greatest happiness in the face of competing alternative actions. On the other hand, care ethics drives home the primacy of preserving concrete interpersonal relationships and reminds us that acting to promote human happiness is not likely to be achieved through dispassionate, emotionally detached utilitarian calculation.

With its emphasis on character, a virtue ethics that avoids appeals to inflexible theories about human nature and gender roles envelops these other theories. It encloses them within a framework of practical habits comprising character traits to act, think, and feel in ways that incorporate and balance Kantian, utilitarian, and care-based considerations. Within this framework, reason, emotion, perception, motive, consequences of action, principles, and the concrete situation can all count and have a voice. The individual ethical decision maker is left with the challenge of conducting the chorus, with knowing when and where each voice is to be sounded.

The choral analogy above suggests that ethics may be more like art and less like science in at least some respects. But as in art there are forms and structures that can help to guide the creative process, so can there be in counseling. In seeking the terms of ethical practice of counseling and psychotherapy, we can expect at least as much help from a careful study of applied ethics.

REVIEW QUESTIONS

1. What is ethics? Explain the difference between descriptive and philosophical ethics. What relevance does each have to counseling practice?

2. What is ethical theory? Explain the difference between rule and virtue ethics.

3. What is utilitarianism? Explain the difference between act and rule utilitarianism.

4. What are the three formulations of Immanuel Kant's categorical imperative? In what ways is Kantian ethics similar to utilitarianism? In what ways is it different?

5. What is care ethics and how does it differ from act utilitarianism? In what sense, according to Morphis and Riesbeck, is care ethics a function of both reason and emotion?

6. What is virtue ethics? What is the difference between virtue ethics and care ethics? In what ways are these two approaches related?

7. What role do rules serve in virtue ethics? In what respects is concern for consequences an aspect of virtue ethics?

8. What does Aristotle mean by a moral virtue? What, according to Aristotle, is the difference between being a virtuous person and merely a clever one?

9. What is the difference between an internal theory of virtue and an external one?

10. What is applied ethics? What is professional ethics?

DISCUSSION QUESTIONS

1. Do you think that the moral rightness or wrongness of an action can always be determined by looking solely at the consequences of the action? What problems, if any, might there be in trying to base the morality of action solely on the consequences of action?

2. Can Kantian ethics be useful to therapists in making ethical decisions? Provide examples to illustrate your response. What problems, if any, might there be in trying to base the morality of action solely on Kantian principles?

3. In comparison to rule-based ethical theories such as Kantian ethics and utilitarianism, what advantages might there be in approaching ethical decision making in counseling practice from the perspective of care ethics? What disadvantages, if any, might there be in taking this approach? What problems, if any, might there be in trying to base the morality of action solely on care ethics to the exclusion of Kantian and utilitarian ethics?

4. In comparison to both care and rule ethics, what advantages, if any, might there be in approaching ethical decision making in counseling practice from the perspective of virtue ethics? What disadvantages, if any, might there be?

5. Compare and contrast the theories of virtue of Aristotle, MacIntyre, and Mill. What problems, if any, are inherent in each of these theories, especially as they are applied to counseling practice? What, if anything, do you like about each of these theories? Defend your responses.

6. Can a truly virtuous therapist be motivated, at least in part, by something other than the desire to act virtuously—for example, the desire to make money?

7. The following ethical dilemma (so-called "Heinz's dilemma") was originally devised by Lawrence Kohlberg (1987, p. 88) to measure moral development in adolescents:

> In Europe, a woman was near death from a very bad disease, a special kind of cancer. There was one drug that the doctor thought might save her. It was a form of radium that a druggist in the same town had recently discovered. The drug was expensive to make, but the druggist was charging 10 times what the drug cost him to make. He paid $200 for the radium and charged $2,000 for a small dose of the drug. The sick woman's husband, Heinz, went to everyone he knew to borrow the money, but he could get together only about $1,000, which was half of what it cost. He told the druggist that his wife was dying and asked him to sell it cheaper or let him pay later. But the druggist said, "No; I discovered the drug and I'm going to

make money from it." Heinz got desperate and broke into the man's store to steal the drug for his wife.

The question posed by Kohlberg was this: "Should Heinz steal the drug?" Kohlberg claimed that morally mature individuals would autonomously rank the dying woman's right to life over the druggist's property right in the medicine and would accordingly agree with Heinz's decision to steal the drug. Carol Gilligan (1982), however, arguing from a care ethics perspective, claimed that morally mature individuals might try to find other ways instead of stealing that would satisfy everyone's interests.

How, in your estimation, would utilitarians—both act and rule variants—resolve the dilemma? How would adherents of Kantian ethics resolve it? Discuss applications of all three formulations of Kant's categorical imperative.

8. Looking at the situation from a care ethics perspective, what sorts of problems might occur with each of the rule-based approaches mentioned in question 15 in dealing with Heinz's dilemma?

9. Does trying to solve Heinz's dilemma resemble a math problem in which values can and should be clearly defined, quantified, or balanced? Should emotion play a role in the decision? Would a virtuous person have stolen the drug? Briefly develop and defend your own approach to this dilemma.

10. Generalizing from your answer to question 9, how would you characterize your own approach to ethics? Rule based? Utilitarian? Kantian? Care based? Virtue based? Eclectic? Explain.

11. What, in your estimation, can one reasonably expect to gain from studying applied or professional ethics in the areas of counseling and psychotherapy?

Cases for Analysis

Applying the theories and concepts of ethics developed in this chapter, discuss each of the following cases:

CASE 1

Sarah is a 40-year-old widow. Her husband, Sam, was a police officer. The day prior to the couple's 17th aniversary, 2 years ago, Sam was shot and killed in the line of duty while attempting to apprehend a robbery suspect. After her husband died, Sarah had a mental breakdown and was hospitalized for 6 months. She has since been seeing psychologist Roger Sculio as an outpatient. In the past 6 months, Sarah has made significant progress in working through her husband's death. Before his death, Sarah worked as a photographer for a magazine. She has not worked since Sam was killed, but she has been contemplating accepting her former boss's invitation to return to work for him. She has also been thinking about agreeing to have dinner with an old high school boyfriend of hers who has recently called and asked her out.

Two weeks ago Sarah visited her gynocologist, Dr. Brady, with complaints of uterine pain and abnormal vaginal bleeding. On investigation, Dr. Brady found that Sarah had highly progressed, uterine cancer that had metasticized. At the request of Sarah's brother, Warren, Brady did not inform Sarah of the test results. Instead, he told her that she had a benign tumor. However, Warren informed Dr. Sculio of his sister's medical condition. He told Sculio that, while he considered this information pertinent to Sarah's therapy, he did not want his sister to know. He argued that Sarah had been through too much already and she deserved to live out the little time she had left without suffering the trauma of knowing.

Dr. Sculio had always believed in the importance of honesty and candor in his practice as well as in his private life. If he did not disclose this information to Sarah, he would fail to be honest and candid with his client. On the other hand, if he did disclose, the knowledge could jeopardize Sarah's prospects for happiness before confronting the onslaught of her disease. What was Sculio to do?

Case 2

In the past 6 years, Holbrook Senior High School had witnessed the death of three homosexual students who took their own lives. Believing that these deaths might have been prevented if the students had had Holbrook counselors with whom they could relate, Ralph Anderson, a counselor at Holbrook, proposed that the school employ at least one homosexual counselor who would be available for homosexual students.

Several faculty members and parents of students voiced objections to Anderson's proposal, arguing that such a provision would encourage homosexuality among Holbrook students. One other Holbrook counselor argued that there is no reason why homosexual students cannot speak to heterosexual counselors and that sexual orientation was entirely irrelevant. One teacher argued that what homosexual clients need is therapy, not support for a homosexual lifestyle. What should the administration at Holbrook do?

Case 3

Jane Feeney, a 28-year old, practicing Jehovah's Witness, was 5 months pregnant when she was rushed to Crestmount Hospital after having been in an automobile accident. Although the fetus was still alive, Jane had lost a large amount of blood from the injuries she had sustained and she needed a blood transfusion if she and her fetus were to survive. Jane clearly indicated that she could not accept the blood because to do so would be a sacrilege. Her husband, also a practicing Jehovah's Witness, concurred with his wife's decision.

An emergency meeting of the hospital ethics committee was convened to make a recommendation on the matter. Mary Didereau, a hospital social worker who had visited Jane, argued that Jane's decision was competent and that she therefore had a right to refuse treatment, even if it meant the loss of the fetus. Larry Damiano, an examining physician, argued that such a decision to destroy two lives was irrational and that the transfusion should be given immediately. Paul Flynn, a hospital administrator, suggested that the hospital needed a judge's determination to avoid a potential lawsuit. Dr. Damiano, however, emphasized that waiting for court action was risky because the decision had to be made *right now*. Diane Flemming, the head nurse, argued that the fetus's right to life was overriding. What should the committee recommend?

Case 4

Brixton High School currently has a program on safe sex. In addition to providing instruction and counseling services, the school also provides free condoms to any student who requests them. However, the school has come under fire from the community for encouraging sex instead of abstinence. Prominent religious and community leaders have repeatedly charged that the only safe sex is no sex at all. Some parents have written to the local newspapers protesting the school policy, and the local TV station has provided coverage of the controversy. As a result of the bad press, the school principal is now considering abandoning the program. What should be done about this situation?

CHAPTER TWO

Foundations of Counseling Virtues

INTRODUCTION
THE PURPOSE OF COUNSELING PRACTICE
THE VALUE OF COUNSELING VIRTUES
PROFESSIONAL AND MORAL VIRTUES
WELFARE, INTERESTS, AND NEEDS
MORAL PROBLEMS, DILEMMAS, AND
    RESPONSIBILITY: A FRAMEWORK FOR
    ETHICAL DECISION MAKING IN
    COUNSELING
Identifying and Defining Moral Problems
Identifying Morally Relevant Facts

Conducting a Philosophical Analysis of the
    Defined Problem in Light of All Morally
    Relevant Facts
Reaching a Decision That Is Reasonable in
    Light of the Philosophical Analysis
Implementing the Decision in Action
CLIENT WELFARE, AUTONOMY, AND TRUST
SUMMARY
REVIEW QUESTIONS
DISCUSSION QUESTIONS
CASES FOR ANALYSIS

As common human experience will confirm, ethical decisions are often complicated choices involving many factors. In the midst of involvement with such decisions, we may have difficulty keeping these factors straight. Concepts and issues may seem vague, and our ability to distinguish the relevant from the irrelevant may wane. The presenting moral problem may itself not be clear and we may have only a vague notion of how to proceed.

Recognizing the inherent ambiguity of ethical decision making, this chapter is intended to bring some order to the confusion that may surround our ethical decisions. It begins by examining the broad purpose of counseling practice itself and defines the primary counseling goal in terms of human welfare. (The emerging definition also serves to identify key counseling virtues in Chapters 3 and 4.)

The concept of human welfare is clarified, related to, and distinguished from *interests* and *needs*. The welfare, interests, and needs of clients and others is offered, in turn, as a basis for identifying *moral problems* and *morally relevant facts*. According to these terms and distinctions, a five-stage process for making ethical decisions is presented. Discussion of each stage includes illustrative vignettes and definitions of pertinent concepts. At the heart of this decision-making process is the *conducting of a philosophical analysis*. The nature of this analysis is explained and illustrated; key ethical principles and standards for avoiding illogical thinking in the process are provided. The nature and grounds of *morally responsible action* are treated in the final stage ("Implementing the Decision in Action").

This chapter concludes by introducing two counseling objectives that play a central role in promoting client welfare: (1) *facilitation of clients' autonomy* and

(2) *establishment of a bond of trust between therapists and their clients.* These two counseling objectives are discussed in Chapters 3 and 4, respectively.

The Purpose of Counseling Practice

As discussed in Chapter 1, virtues are defined within the contexts of specific social activities or practices and in relation to the particular purposes of those practices. Thus, the main point of baseball is to score the most runs, and the virtues of baseball are those skills that best promote this primary purpose—for instance, being skillful at batting or pitching. However, although the goal of the game is to score the most runs, a player may also value his baseball skills for their own sake—for example, seeing a good hit or a finely orchestrated catch as being instances of "internal goods" carrying their own intrinsic merit. From one perspective, the player is trying to score the most runs for his team through the exercise of his skillful activities. From this external perspective, baseball virtues are to be valued for the sake of scoring the most runs. Yet, from the other, internal, perspective, they are to be valued and sought after for their own sake; so even a player on the losing team can still take pride in a skillful play.

Counseling may also be conceptualized as a practice with its own set of internal virtues that are definable in relation to a primary end or purpose. Such a conceptualization, however, requires that this primary purpose be specified. If a satisfactory account of such a purpose can be given, then a standard of virtue selection for counseling ethics will have been established; and accordingly, the virtues requisite to being a virtuous psychotherapist may also be specified.

What, then, is the primary purpose of counseling? One quite obvious response to this question is that counseling aims to achieve clients' mental health. The concept of mental health is, however, a value-laden concept, the flip side of which is mental illness. Given these various values and the philosophical controversy surrounding these concepts, this line is not pursued here (see, for example, Szasz,1960; Lazarus,1969).

Consider the usual reasons why people seek therapy. These include the alleviation of anxiety, depression, stress, guilt, inability to cope, dysfunctional relations, drug and alcoholic addictions, and co-dependency. The reasons for entering therapy are many; still, all the reasons just stated share a common feature, for they all involve seeking relief from pain and frustration or finding a more pleasurable mode of living and relating. This response is reminiscent of the way the classical utilitarians define the good (see Chapter 1). That is, the primary purpose of counseling may be stated in hedonic terms—namely, *to promote clients' pleasure and the alleviation of pain.* In this book, the term *welfare* is used to refer to such hedonic states of pleasure or alleviation of pain.

The primacy of therapists' responsibility to clients is apparent in this formulation of the purpose of counseling practice. Still, it would be naive to suppose that the "client" in counseling practice can be adequately defined and understood apart from the broader social and professional context in which clients seek therapy (Corey, 1996). Because the client does not typically live in isolation from other members of society and social institutions (for example, family, friends, co-workers, human service agencies of origin and referral, and insurance providers), therapists also have moral and professional responsibilities to these third parties who may be significantly affected by the conduct of therapist or client.

When counseling practice is viewed in this larger social context, therapists also emerge as promoters of human welfare—that is, as promoters of clients' welfare as well as the welfare of other human beings, and social institutions that serve human beings, who may not necessarily be clients. Therapists ordinarily promote general human welfare by tending primarily to client welfare, but this may not always be possible. Situations may arise in which therapists must also consider the welfare of relevant nonclients. Such cases arise when clients' actions threaten the welfare of third parties—for example, when HIV seropositive clients are sexually active with uninformed sexual partners (see Chapter 10). When a third person is in such a state of vulnerability—liable to harm from a client unless the therapist intervenes—the therapist has a moral responsibility to help that third person (Cohen, 1995).

However, the responsibility of the therapist to act on behalf of an endangered third party may be limited by that person's own degree of responsibility for his or her actions. For example, a virtuous therapist need not be expected to compromise client welfare to safeguard third parties from harm arising largely from their own recklessness (Cohen, 1994).

Virtuous therapists thus seek to promote client welfare while avoiding harm to others and safeguarding the vulnerable and dependent. The chief end of counseling practice is client welfare thus qualified, and the standard for selection of counseling virtues will therefore be conduciveness to this end. Insofar as counselors collectively promote the welfare of their clients without harming nonclients in the process, they also serve the broader utilitarian mission of promoting "the general welfare of society" (NASW, 1997, 6.07).

The Value of Counseling Virtues

The virtuous therapist will perceive his or her own virtuous conduct as crucial to attainment of client welfare. From this external perspective, all counseling virtues are to be valued for their benefit to clients. From the internal perspective, counseling virtues are to be valued for their own sake. Thus, a virtuous therapist will value competent and diligent therapy even if, in a particular instance, therapy fails to contribute to client welfare, perhaps because the client refuses to cooperate in the counseling process. The virtuous therapist will regret not having helped the client to feel better, but she will still recognize the intrinsic value of having conducted herself in accordance with virtue, not unlike the baseball player on the losing team who recognizes the intrinsic merit of having played an excellent game.

Professional and Moral Virtues

Counseling virtues may be at the same time professional and moral. As these virtues are conditions of viable therapy, they are professional. As they are instruments of human welfare, they are moral. The fusion of moral and professional virtues helps to show why these virtues are not optional in the practice of psychotherapy. As far as therapy is concerned, the question "Why be moral?" can be answered thus: because this is what it means to provide professional counseling services. A therapist who is dishonest in rendering services acts unprofessionally.

The term *professional* as used above needs clarification. Professional conduct is conduct that befits a professional; unprofessional conduct is behavior that does not befit a professional. Being a professional means being a member of a select group of individuals who are specially trained and skilled in the performance of an important public service. These services are ones that promote the serious welfare, interests, and needs of humans (or other animals) including legal, health, and educational services. Because counselors and psychotherapists provide such a service in helping their clients to attain greater satisfaction and less pain and frustration in their lives, counselors and psychotherapists are among the ranks of professionals. If they perform this service well, they act professionally. When they act professionally, they act morally.

Welfare, Interests, and Needs

The concept of client *welfare* must be distinguished from the idea of client interests. Psychotherapists necessarily serve the welfare of clients, but they do not necessarily serve their interests. A depressed client may irrationally desire to commit suicide, in such a case, client welfare would best be served by paternalistic intervention, perhaps in the form of involuntary hospitalization. (The subjects of paternalism and involuntary hospitalization are treated in Chapter 10.)

Therapists do not generally serve clients' *unethical* interests. Thus, a therapist may, and ordinarily should, refuse to honor a client's request if it is perceived to be unjust. Without moral impunity, a therapist may refuse to help a client commit a crime. Determining the moral weight of the interest in question will, of course, require moral analysis in terms of broader theories or principles of ethics. The Kantian categorical imperative would not, for example, approve clients' use of therapists as mere means to accomplish illicit ends.

This should not be construed to mean that virtuous therapists freely interfere with clients' self-determination. On the contrary, virtuous therapists are disposed to maintain a general climate of respect for what clients want. Nevertheless, client interests that therapists serve must be consonant with long-term client welfare as well as with those personality attributes or virtues of a therapist that tend to promote that welfare.

The question of whether psychotherapists serve client needs is philosophically more complex. First, controversy surrounds the distinction between physical needs on the one hand and mental needs on the other. Some theorists (Ellis

& Harper, 1975) deny the existence of mental needs; others (Fromm, 1955) affirm their existence. Thus, the question of whether virtuous psychotherapists serve mental needs of clients is not answerable without first taking a theoretical stand on the existence of such needs.

Still, it is a matter of fact that certain commonplace, human interests exist. For example, most people want to love and be loved, have sexual relations, belong to a group, achieve desired goals, exert control over their lives, and expand their knowledge base. Whether these are universal human needs is not addressed here. Insofar as such interests promote client welfare, however, psychotherapists may be deemed to serve them.

The existence of certain physical needs is also a fact. Although psychotherapists are concerned primarily with clients' mental welfare, the psyche cannot easily be separated from the soma, and what is necessary for the survival of the body is also necessary for the survival of the mind. Client welfare can be compromised by bodily conditions—as when medication is indicated to help control severe depression or schizophrenia—so virtuous psychotherapists do not disregard clients' physical integrity and bodily needs.

The primary purpose of counseling in terms of clients' welfare must be qualified by avoiding and preventing harm to others. Hence, concern for the welfare, interests, and needs of nonclients may also fall within the purview of virtuous therapists. This does not require the virtuous therapist to *advance* the welfare, interests, and needs of nonclients. Rather, his or her concern is to safeguard others from harm in the process of helping the client.

Moral Problems, Dilemmas, and Responsibility: A Framework for Ethical Decision Making in Counseling

Ethical decision making can be conceptualized in five stages, based on consideration of the welfare, interests, and needs of clients and relevant others. The stages are somewhat interdependent, and no hard and fast separation between them is realistic; however, they do provide a broad, systematic framework for making ethical decisions. These stages progress from identifying and defining the problem to implementing the decision.

IDENTIFYING AND DEFINING MORAL PROBLEMS

In general, having a problem means having an unresolved question for which the answer is not immediately apparent. Two types of problems can be distinguished according to the type of question raised: intellectual problems and practical ones. Intellectual problems ask "What should I think or believe?"; practical problems ask "What should I do?" A mathematician's question about whether a theorem can be proven is an intellectual problem, a physician's question about what therapy to try on a patient with a newly discovered strain of HIV is a practical problem. Although answers to practical problems can assume answers to intellectual problems (the use of a drug may hinge on an understanding of its chemical properties), the focus of a practical problem is always on action, not merely on belief.

Moral problems are a form of practical problem regarding the treatment of people or animals by people. The central question raised by a moral problem can be expressed in terms of welfare, interests, and needs, as previously defined. This question is what to do when there is risk to the welfare, interests, or needs of persons, either individually or collectively.

Therapists ordinarily have moral problems when the welfare, interests, or needs of clients or related others may be compromised depending on what therapists do. The seriousness of the moral problem is directly proportional to the degree of harm at stake. Thus, when the survival of a client or third party is at risk, the moral problem may be very serious indeed. The degree of harm also needs to be assessed in terms of the probability that the harm will occur. That is, other things being equal, the greater the probability of the harm's occurring, the more serious is the moral problem.

In this context, failure to help the client through therapy does not necessarily constitute client harm; however, leaving the client worse off than he or she was prior to therapy does constitute client harm. Because the latter is a possible consequence of the therapy, psychotherapists face a moral problem in the provision of therapy.

To resolve a moral problem, one must first identify and define what that problem is. In effectively identifying and defining a moral problem, the therapist must perceive how welfare, interests, or needs are at risk. In the case of a client whose spouse beats her in the presence of their 2-year-old child, the presenting moral problem may be defined in terms of what to do when there is risk to the physical as well as emotional welfare of both client and child. An adequate definition of the problem will include specification of persons at risk along with a description of the risks at hand. This description should state the welfare, interests, or needs that are at risk. The definition should take the form of what to do given such and such risks to such and such individuals. It should be generally stated, leaving details for subsequent stages.

Defining moral problems therefore requires moral sensitivity—that is, insight and awareness of human welfare, interests, and needs as these are affected in actual life contexts. Such insight, rather than being an inborn trait, appears to increase with exposure to moral contexts and practice in moral reasoning (Kitchener, 1986). Such insight is also conditioned by therapists' ability to empathize with clients as well as related others (see Chapter 3).

Consider the case of Dom Fulton, Ph.D., psychologist:

> For 6 months, Maria Mangrove saw Dr. Fulton once or twice a week for depression and suicidal ideation. In the course of therapy, Maria came to believe that she had fallen in love with Dr. Fulton and, in session, began to declare her love for him openly. Although Dr. Fulton believed Maria's feelings to be a result of transference, he found her very attractive and had strong sexual feelings toward her. In one session, Dr. Fulton admitted to Maria that he harbored such strong sexual feelings toward her. However, he still sincerely believed that he could help her. Refusing her overtures to begin a personal, sexual relationship, he continued to meet with her as client. As the sessions continued, Maria became increasingly more and more

despondent over Dr. Fulton's lack of personal attention until one day she failed to keep her appointment. She had committed suicide.

Dr. Fulton's failure to perceive adequately the nature and scope of his moral problem contributed to the deterioration of his client's mental condition. His lack of moral sensitivity toward the welfare, interests, and needs of his client preempted him from acting in a professionally appropriate manner. Dr. Fulton's general moral problem was one of discerning what to do given the potential risk to Maria's emotional and physical well-being caused by the interplay between his own strong sexual feelings and Maria's depressed, vulnerable, dependent state. Had he correctly discerned and appreciated this complex potential for harm, he would have found a viable solution to his problem—for instance, referring his client to another competent mental health practitioner. His failure to assess the problem with a clear head may have meant the difference between life and death for his client.

In defining a moral problem, therapists must also be morally objective; they must avoid building into the definition their personal biases, prejudices, values, or preconceived solutions. For example, "How to convince my pregnant client to carry to term instead of getting an abortion" would assume the therapist's personal aversion to abortion. Such a definition would not be consistent with furthering the client's welfare as it would undermine her personal autonomy to decide for herself. A more objective definition would consider what to do in the case of a pregnant client given specified risks to maternal welfare, interests, and needs, and specified risks to the fetus. Resolution of this broadly defined moral problem can then give rise to a more specific problem. The therapist may conclude that the answer rests with client self-determination and, accordingly, he may move to another moral problem: "How to facilitate the clients' own rational decision according to her own personal values and circumstances."

Moral objectivity also requires that therapists avoid the use of strong, emotive language instead of more descriptive, neutral language; for example, the labeling of a client as "schizo" instead of as a person who has schizophrenia, or as "Mongoloid" instead of a person with Down's syndrome. Such sweeping and pejorative personality ascriptions or similar emotive expressions are dehumanizing and thus are likely to impede humane and considerate treatment of the labeled person.

A moral dilemma may be defined as a moral problem in which no matter what is done, there is risk to someone's welfare, interests, or needs as defined. Resolution of a moral dilemma is not likely to be without regrets even though it may be an appropriate response to the problem at hand. There is thus a distinction between feeling good about what one has done and having done what was right in the given situation. In responding to a moral dilemma, a therapist may do the right thing and still feel bad about what she has done.

Consider the case of Nurse McBride, a 24-year-old, female registered nurse, who had been employed at her current job in a psychiatric hospital for just under 6 months:

> On duty late one evening, Nurse McBride saw Kurt Baller, M.D., injecting himself
> with heroin. Dr. Baller, a psychiatrist, had an excellent reputation among the staff

and was, in Nurse McBride's estimation, a talented physician. When Nurse McBride confronted Dr. Baller, he denied what was clearly evident—that he had a drug addiction problem. The doctor told Nurse McBride either to mind her own business or "kiss her job goodbye." The nurse was accordingly confronted with a moral dilemma. If she disregarded the doctor's threat and informed her superior, the allegations could be dismissed and her own job possibly jeopardized. On the other hand, if Dr. Baller continued to practice without getting the help he needed, client welfare could be jeopardized. In the end, Nurse McBride informed her superior. Dr. Baller was required to enter a drug rehabilitation program and, unfortunately, never returned to the practice of medicine. Nurse McBride felt sad about the plight of this talented physician, but she nonetheless believed that what she had done was right and good.

Had this newly employed nurse considered only her own job security, she might indeed have decided to say nothing. This, action however, would have failed to address the extent of her moral problem, which required due regard for the welfare, interests, and needs of her clients.

IDENTIFYING MORALLY RELEVANT FACTS

Morally relevant facts are those pertaining to the welfare, interests, and needs of people who may be affected by the decision. These facts include clients' psychological and medical profiles such as test results, clinical evaluations, history, intentions, and other emotional/cognitive/behavioral states. The fact that a client has a history of violent behavior and has disclosed to his therapist a detailed plan to harm or kill a specific person is morally relevant to the welfare of this person. In the case of a depressed client (such as the case of Maria discussed above), whether the client has a previous history of attempted suicide would be morally relevant to client welfare. To call these facts morally relevant signifies that resolution or clarification of the moral problems in question requires attention to these facts. Thus, the moral problem of third-party endangerment cannot be satisfactorily resolved without consideration of the client's violent history and expressed plan.

Other morally relevant facts may also include socioeconomic conditions such as financial, familial, and religious ones. The fact that the parents of a female adolescent client refuse on religious grounds to allow the client to dress and wear makeup like her peers must be considered in addressing the moral problem raised by the client's interest in peer acceptance.

Consider the case of Jennifer, a 14-year-old female adolescent, and her mother Lilly, who have come to Jane Riley, Licensed Mental Health Counselor (LMHC), for family counseling.

> Jennifer complains of her mother's strict rules. The teenager is not being allowed to dress the way her peers dress, to wear makeup, and to do many of the things that they do. Lilly complains that Jennifer is disobedient and "out of control." Toward the end of the first session, Lilly reveals to Ms. Riley that she is a Jehovah's Witness.

The presenting moral problem in this case is what to do when the welfare of an adolescent girl and her interest in peer acceptance are in apparent conflict with her mother's religious interests. Thus, the tenets of Jehovah's Witnesses concerning activities that are "of this world" emerge as relevant factors in the search for a satisfactory resolution to the conflict between mother and daughter. As we will see (Chapter 5), cultural and religious factors can often be dismissed only at the expense of alienating clients and compromising their welfare, interests, and needs.

CONDUCTING A PHILOSOPHICAL ANALYSIS OF THE DEFINED PROBLEM IN LIGHT OF ALL MORALLY RELEVANT FACTS

Philosophical analysis of moral problems includes the reflective activity of clarifying key terms and concepts. A therapist attempting to help a homosexual client adopt a more "normal" lifestyle must first get clarification from his client as to what the client means by "normal."

Although justified moral judgments must be based on facts, facts by themselves are not a sufficient decision-making basis. Such decisions must be influenced by more general standards that can help to guide inferences from *is* to *ought*. For example, should I (a therapist who finds himself in serious need of more money) raise the counseling fee of a regular client who most likely cannot afford an increase? In this instance, applying Kant's categorical imperative may help me to clarify my moral commitment to the client's welfare. Could I make a universal law out of my maxim so that I would be willing to be similarly treated were I in this client's shoes? A negative answer to this question may lead me to seek alternative routes to improve my financial situation.

In cases of a moral dilemma in which the welfare, interests, or needs of two or more people are in conflict, the importance of having ethical principles as guides is apparent. A basic principle undergirding the practice of a virtuous therapist (given the primary counseling objective of improving client welfare without harming others) is that of *moral considerateness:* A virtuous therapist cares for the welfare, interests, and needs of everybody concerned so that everybody's harms are mitigated to the extent possible in the situation.

In the case of Lilly and Jennifer mentioned above, Jane Riley, as a virtuous therapist, will try to recognize both client's interests as far as possible. Thus, she will work within the bounds of Lilly's religious tenets to find mutually agreed-on activities such as permitting Jennifer to go bowling with her friends instead of limiting her options to seeing a G-rated movie.

Consider the case of Tom, a 16-year-old male who had been referred to Dr. Seltzer by his school counselor for aggressive behavior in school (fighting with other students, swearing at his teachers, and so on).

> In the course of therapy, Tom revealed to Dr. Seltzer that he had been regularly using drugs, including amphetamines and marijuana. He explained that his mother, Bridget, who works two jobs, is often not home and is unaware of his drug habit, and that his father, who is divorced from his mother, sees him only occasionally on weekends. Tom confided in Dr. Seltzer that he "hates" both his parents and that he often feels like doing something "bad" just to get back at them for being such "assholes." He made clear, however, that he does not want his parents to know anything about his feelings or his drug problem.

The general moral dilemma here is what to do when keeping client trust presents an imminent risk to client welfare—the danger that Tom might overdose on drugs, for instance. In cases like this when client welfare appears to require disclosure of confidential client information, a virtuous therapist would attempt to go as far as possible in both opposing directions with as little sacrifice to anyone as is reasonably possible under the circumstances. This may mean, for example, that Dr. Seltzer would take care not to release any more information than is absolutely necessary, and to make disclosure only to Tom's primary caretaker, his mother. Thus Dr. Seltzer might inform Bridget that her son is taking certain dangerous drugs. He would probably do so, however, only after first informing Tom of his intention to disclose this information; and he would carefully convey this information without disclosing other facts told to him in trust if they are not directly relevant to the immediate danger. In no case would there be wholesale departure from the conflicting concerns. The intent would be to reconcile as much as can be reconciled, with the understanding that a "perfect" solution—one with no sacrifices whatsoever—is not an option. Without such concerted efforts in both opposing directions, the probability of causing unnecessary pain or injury would increase.

According to the principle of considerateness, an unreasonable sacrifice or harm is one that is unnecessary or excessive. A harm is unnecessary or excessive when a therapist can accomplish his goal without incurring it. In the above case, it would be unreasonable to disclose certain confidential information to Tom's mother if the disclosure would not help to prevent Tom from overdosing on drugs. Telling Tom's mother that Tom said he hates her would be unnecessary for the purpose of reducing the immediate risks of a drug overdose. It would also be excessive because it is more than is needed for this purpose.

The principles given below represent versions of some broad ethical principles addressed in this book. These principles can be useful as guidelines in conducting a philosophical analysis of a defined problem.

Some Basic Ethical Principles

- Act Utilitarianism: Act in ways that maximize overall happiness (that is, choose from the possible alternatives those actions that create the greatest balance of pleasure over pain).
- Rule Utilitarianism: Act according to rules or policies that tend to maximize overall happiness.
- Universal Law (First Formulation of Categorical Imperative): Act according to reasons that you could, as a reasonable person, accept as universal law (that is, as binding on everyone without exception).
- Respect for Persons (Second Formulation of Categorical Imperative): Act so that you treat persons, including yourself, as ends in themselves (that is, as rational, self-determining agents) and not as mere means (that is, not as objects to be manipulated).
- Autonomy (Third Formulation of Categorical Imperative): Act autonomously (according to your own free and informed perspective) and not out of blind conformity to social pressures, the wills of others, fear, or similar unreflective motives.

- Vulnerability: Take reasonable measures to protect vulnerable individuals—those who are unable to help themselves and who might suffer significant harm without your assistance.
- Considerateness: Be attentive to the welfare, interests, and needs of everybody concerned, mitigating harm to the extent reasonably possible.

In addition to these, further principles can be derived that may assist counselors in conducting philosophical analyses of moral problems. Such principles include those intended to promote trust between therapist and client (Principles of Trustworthiness) such as honesty, candor, diligence, and loyalty. These principles in their relation to more specific rules from major codes of professional ethics are addressed in Chapter 4.

Philosophical analysis here also requires that therapists carefully inspect their own reasoning for illogical thinking (not merely psychological impediments such as defense mechanisms and countertransference). The following are some questions that therapists can ask themselves in attempting to get rid of irrational thinking that might block satisfactory analysis of moral problems.

Checking for Illogical Thinking

- Am I *stereotyping* others?
  Example: Thinking that my black clients are all alike
- Am I *hastily generalizing* from unrepresentative samples?
  Example: Beginning to think that all males are sexual predators on the basis of my intensive work with male sex offenders
- Am I *catastrophizing* about what might happen?
  Example: Exaggerating what might happen to me if I don't get more clients
- Am I wearing *cultural blinders?*
  Example: Discounting my clients' religious beliefs in favor of my own
- Am I *demanding perfection* of myself or others?
  Example: Demanding that my clients always or almost always get better
- Am I *jumping on a bandwagon?*
  Example: Providing an inaccurate *DSM-IV* (*Diagnostic and Statistical Manual of Mental Disorders;* American Psyciatric Association, 1994) diagnosis to collect from an insurance company because other therapists I know are doing it
- Am I *damning or degrading other persons or myself?*
  Example: Using degrading terms such as *no good* or *worthless* to characterize an uncooperative client
- Am I *exaggerating my inability to tolerate situations or persons?*
  Example: Telling myself that I couldn't stand it if I made a mistake in treating a client

Logical mistakes such as those illustrated above may be easier to observe in others—for example, in clients—but they may also infect therapists' own thinking, impairing the therapist-client relationship and thereby adversely affecting client welfare. Virtuous therapists will therefore have cultivated critical reflective habits regarding their own thinking, thus realizing that, like their clients, they too are not beyond the perils of faulty thinking (Cohen, 1994).

As virtuous therapists seek to promote client welfare, they will also be cognizant of the philosophical distinction between *shoulds of expedience* and *moral shoulds*. They will perceive the difference between saying that "I should really refer this resistant client if I want to make it easier for myself" and "I should really try to work with this client if I think I can help him." The first should is one of mere expedience; the second is a moral should—that is, one concerned principally with the client's welfare.

REACHING A DECISION THAT IS REASONABLE IN LIGHT OF THE PHILOSOPHICAL ANALYSIS

The state of not having reached any decision because of procrastination or vacillation can itself become a decision—that is, a decision by indecision—which can itself have regrettable consequences. In making decisions by indecision, a therapist surrenders his opportunity to use rational judgment to control outcomes. Since there are typically more ways for things to go wrong than for them to go right, when decisions are made by indecision, the chances are substantially diminished that things will go right. In the context of therapy, this mode of deciding can have significance for the welfare of clients and other relevant third parties. For example, procrastination about whether to notify the authorities about a dangerous client can allow another's injury or death. When this is the consequence, the therapist has, in effect, made the decision, albeit by indecision. Although a virtuous therapist will not act without giving the matter at hand due consideration within the constraints of allowable time, such a therapist will not commit the converse mistake of allowing the passage of time to settle the matter randomly.

Consider, the case of Jack, a 30-year-old client with schizophrenia, and his therapist, Dr. Eldridge.

> Jack told Dr. Eldridge that a voice was persistently commanding him to "slash the throat" of Leisa, his former girlfriend. Jack, also said that he knew this would be a "horrible thing" and that he was "trying his best to resist." Dr. Eldridge asked Jack if he would agree to inpatient treatment, but Jack angrily protested the idea. Because Dr. Eldridge believed that she was finally beginning to make significant progress with Jack, she questioned the merit of involuntarily committing him at this point. Further, she was not certain that Jack presented any serious threat to Leisa's welfare. What was Dr. Eldridge to do?

Virtuous therapists will not withhold a decision until they are absolutely sure what the correct decision is. Rather, they will be prepared to tolerate some measure of ambiguity in making moral decisions, realizing that there may be more than one right answer to a moral problem and that there is no litmus test of moral correctness, no algorithm for calculating the morally right thing to do (Aristotle, 1941, Bk. 1, Ch. 3). Indeed, a therapist who required absolute certainty before reaching a decision would make the decision by indecision. In Dr. Eldridge's case, procrastination about whether to involuntarily commit Jack would be tantamount to deciding not to detain a potentially dangerous client.

Because Dr. Eldridge is competent, she realizes that being schizophrenic does not itself make Jack homicidal, but she knows that schizophrenics who do commit such crimes typically do so as a result of their schizophrenia. In addition, Jack has been clear about his struggle with a homicidal impulse. Thus, although Dr. Eldridge cannot be sure that Jack will act on this impulse, it is reasonable for her to believe he will. She has good or adequate reason for this belief.

Part of ethical decision making is making such a normative assessment of the purported facts. The basis of the conclusion is probability, not certainty. Relative to one set of facts, a conclusion may be justified; relative to another, it may not. In considering all reasonably available and morally relevant facts, a therapist does what is humanly possible. Hindsight is, of course, better than foresight. Whereas the virtuous therapist will learn from her mistakes, she will understand these distinctions and will not blame herself for what she could not reasonably have foreseen.

If Dr. Eldridge is a virtuous therapist, she will also be aware of her legal obligation to notify endangered third parties and to detain dangerous clients in cases where there is clear and imminent danger to third parties. She will also be aware that therapists are not legally expected to "render a perfect performance" but "need only exercise `that reasonable degree of skill, knowledge, and care ordinarily possessed and exercised by members of [that professional specialty] under similar circumstances'" (*Tarasoff v. Regents*, 1976, p. 25). Legal as well as moral standards therefore require reasonable or justified determinations rather than absolute certainty.

Virtuous therapists will understand and generally comply with laws, codes of ethics, agency policies, and other professional regulations. They will, however, distinguish between legal and moral acceptability, for what is moral and what is legal are not always identical. For example, as we shall see (Chapter 4), the decision to disclose confidential patient information to the authorities may in certain exceptional circumstances be morally defensible; nonetheless, it may be in violation of a state statute.

Accordingly, virtuous therapists will not apply laws, codes of ethics, agency policies, and other professional regulations unreflectively or mechanically as if the solutions to moral problems could be made simply by looking them up in the rule books. Nor will they apply such rules without understanding their rationales or without being prepared to exercise discretion when the rules do not clearly apply or when they conflict with the welfare of clients or other relevant third parties. Accordingly, they will be morally autonomous—that is, disposed toward making their own moral decisions. They will "come to their own decisions about moral issues on the basis of their own moral principles [and consideration of the morally relevant facts]; and then in turn to act upon their considered judgments" (Cohen, 1988, p. 84). Psychotherapists who blindly follow rules or orders without wrestling with moral problems or who pass the burden of making ethical decisions onto others are not morally autonomous. These therapists cannot be virtuous because they are mere cogs, not truly moral agents.

IMPLEMENTING THE DECISION IN ACTION

As suggested above, part of being morally autonomous is acting by one's own ethical lights. However, in standing on principle, therapists may encounter opposition and risk personal loss including time, money, popularity, and employment; also, they may incur legal penalties. Hence, counseling virtue requires moral courage whereby a therapist is "disposed toward doing what he thinks is morally right even when he believes that his doing so means, or is likely to mean, his suffering some substantial hardship" (Cohen, 1988, p. 83). Morally courageous therapists will avoid unnecessary personal sacrifices, but they will also be prepared to challenge agency policies that they reasonably believe are contrary to client welfare, even at risk of losing their jobs.

In standing on their ethical principles, virtuous therapists will also be morally responsible. A primary factor that creates moral responsibilities for one person rather than another is "a difference of power, which usually consists of superior knowledge and ability to affect outcomes" (Ladd, 1982, p. 67). Thus, moral responsibility is

> oriented toward consequences while, at the same time, it relates these consequences interpersonally to particular people who are able to effect and to those who are affected by these consequences as they relate to their needs, their problems, and their welfare. (Ladd, 1982, p. 66)

Furthermore, moral responsibilities are situation dependent, which means that they require

> thought and reflection about the situation in which the person finds himself and serious attention to the variety of possible courses of action open to him. All this in turn means that the person in question must make a determined effort to find out all the relevant facts concerning the situation and the possible outcomes of the choices open to him. Mindlessness is inconsistent with moral responsibility. (Ladd, 1982, p. 67)

Because of their training, access to personal client information, and position of authority, therapists can have substantial knowledge and power in relating to their clients. Hence, in the present context, being morally responsible means that a therapist is disposed toward applying this knowledge and power toward promoting clients' welfare, interests, and needs. Clients are often in vulnerable (psychological) states, and unscrupulous therapists may use their knowledge and power to manipulate and take advantage of them—as when a therapist lies to a client about the seriousness of his or her condition in order to prolong therapy. Still, other therapists may simply lack the conviction to use their facilities toward promoting client welfare—as in cases of client abandonment. On the other hand, morally responsible therapists are steadfast in their conviction to help the client; they genuinely care and therefore, to the best of their ability, within reason, use the facilities with which they are furnished toward affecting this end. As applied to acts, in contrast to agents, saying that a therapist has a moral or professional responsibility to perform a specific act means that performing it best utilizes such special knowledge and power toward fulfilling the primary counseling mission.

Therapists may also be morally responsible for nonclients who are relevantly situated. Because of their privileged access to the personal thoughts of clients, therapists are privy to information that may affect the welfare of third parties. Such knowledge and power underscores a therapist's moral responsibility to clients, and it may also be the basis of moral responsibility to nonclients. In the case of Dr. Eldridge, the therapist's privileged access to Jack's thoughts placed her in a position of knowledge and power with respect to Leisa. In this case, Dr. Eldridge was morally responsible for both individuals.

Moral responsibility cannot be deemed "all or nothing"; nor can one moral responsibility properly be said to override another as can specific duties or obligations. Thus, Dr. Eldridge's responsibility for Jack did not negate her responsibility for Leisa, nor was the reverse true. Being morally responsible meant doing her absolute best, under the circumstances, to promote the welfare of each person. The principle of considerateness thus applies to and regulates morally responsible conduct. Whereas Dr. Eldridge was presumably justified in taking action to prevent harm to Leisa, consideration for Jack also meant taking care to support and protect him. The precise details of the resolution would show that a cost was involved, but wholesale disregard for the welfare of either would not be compatible with moral responsibility.

A therapist has moral responsibilities because therapists are people, and people have moral responsibilities. In general, moral responsibilities exist because people are social creatures who depend on each other for help. Whether and to what extent people can be expected to be their brothers' and sisters' keepers in general depend on four factors: (1) the extent to which a person is dependent on another for help; (2) the seriousness of the welfare, interest, or need at stake; (3) the extent to which one has the knowledge and power to help the dependent person; and (4) the amount of personal sacrifice the provision of help will require. In some cases these factors may weigh against claiming moral responsibility, as when helping a person will require great personal sacrifice—for example, risking one's life—in order to prevent a lesser harm to another, such as loss of money. At the other extreme are cases in which people are dependent on others for their very survival, they have no available means of saving themselves, and relatively little effort from others is required to effect a favorable outcome.

Consider the case of Kitty Genovese, who was murdered in 1964 in Queens, New York:

> At 3:20 A.M. Kitty Genovese returned home from her job as a manager at a bar. As she walked the hundred feet to her home, she noted a man in a parking lot nearby. Concerned, she turned in the direction of a police call box, but before she reached it, the man attacked her with a knife. She screamed, "Oh, my God, he stabbed me! Please help me! Please help me!"
>
> The screams awoke thirty-eight people living in a seven-story apartment house overlooking the scene. One man yelled, "Let that girl alone." No one else did anything. The attacker was scared away by the lights that went on, the windows that opened, and the excited talk that ensued. He walked toward his car but a few minutes

later returned to find Kitty Genovese staggering toward her apartment. He then stabbed her again, and she again screamed loudly, "I'm dying!" And again no one did anything. The man went to his car and drove away, only to return yet a third time. Kitty Genovese was still alive. This time he killed her. (Martin, 1989, p. 116)

Whether any of the 38 onlookers had a moral responsibility to attempt to fight off the assailant, there is no question that each had a moral responsibility to do the bare minimum of calling the police. This was within the power of all 38 witnesses, yet not one of them did so. Every one of these people failed to meet his or her minimum moral responsibility, even if only one person needed to make the call.

As the case of Kitty Genovese demonstrates, moral responsibility is not the same as legal responsibility. None of the witnesses was held legally responsible even though each was clearly morally responsible. In general, the primary purpose for holding people legally responsible for a misdeed is to punish or make them pay for it. Assignments of legal responsibility are typically made in retrospect to mete out a penalty, provide a remedy, or redress a grievance. In some cases, the person who is held legally responsible may not even be the one who perpetrated a wrongdoing as when a non-negligent employer is held accountable for the wrongful act of an employee (so-called vicarious liability). In civil litigation, the basis for assigning legal responsibility is often not who deserves to pay but rather who has the most money! On the other hand, the primary purpose for holding people morally responsible is not to punish or collect money but rather to effect positive future outcomes, to satisfactorily resolve presenting moral problems in the future (Ladd, 1982).

The concept of moral responsibility must also be distinguished from job-related responsibilities. For example, it may be the responsibility of a member of a crime syndicate to lie, cheat, steal, and kill under certain conditions. Although these tasks may go with the job, they are not moral responsibilities. Consider, for example, the case of Larry, an activities director at Stone Top Home for Children:

> When Larry signed a contract to work at Stone Top, he understood that part of his job would be to do community outreach work for the facility. This included going to schools, civic organization meetings, and other community and statewide functions to help raise money and support for the home. After 6 months on the job, Larry had witnessed several instances in which children were physically and mentally abused by staff. In one instance, Larry actually witnessed a 10-year-old boy being sexually molested. Larry considered going to the police but was afraid that the chief administrator, whom Larry considered to be dangerous, would take revenge on him. Moreover, he doubted his ability to prove any allegations he might make.
>
> Although he received a high measure of respect within the community and was paid well for his work, Larry questioned the propriety of mustering up support for the school. On consideration, Larry decided to quit. Unable to get a similar job, he took a job for lesser pay working as a clerk.

In accordance with Larry's contract at Stone Top, he had a job-related responsibility to do community outreach work for his employer. However, given the abusive school environment, he had a moral responsibility not to do such work.

Larry's decision to quit his job, notwithstanding foreseeable personal sacrifices, was also within the purview of his moral responsibilities. It is also arguable that, by virtue of his knowledge and position, he had a moral responsibility to go to the authorities or to find some other way to "blow the whistle"—for example, by contacting the press. Yet it is likely that no matter how Larry chose to resolve his moral problem, he would not be held legally responsible.

Sometimes it is easy to confuse doing one's job with meeting one's moral responsibilities, but it is important to realize that the two are not necessarily the same. As the case of Larry suggests, doing one's job does not ensure that one acts in a morally responsible manner. Where welfare, interests, or needs of clients conflict with the fulfillment of job-related responsibilities, a dedicated and responsible employee may not equal a morally responsible professional.

Client Welfare, Autonomy, and Trust

Promotion of client welfare is the primary end of counseling, but therapists are not likely to realize this part without realizing two further counseling objectives: facilitation of clients' autonomy and establishment of a bond of trust between therapists and their clients. These related ends are themselves instrumental in achieving client welfare and are used here to set general parameters for identifying and classifying individual counseling virtues.

Helping clients achieve autonomy or self-determination is a defining feature of the counseling process; this element may, at least in part, be defined as "a process by which clients learn how to make decisions and formulate new ways of behaving, feeling, and thinking" (Gladden, 1996, p. 8). Thus, instead of telling clients what to do, think, or feel, therapists serve as facilitators of change, providing clients with the support and understanding for making their own decisions according to their own considered judgments, interests, and chosen goals. "It is the facilitation of self ownership by the client and the strategies by which this can be achieved; the placing of the locus of decision-making and the responsibility for the effects of these decisions" (Rogers, 1977, p. 14). Therapists thereby help to "unleash the client's capacity for making independent and individual decisions within the context of rationality, which involves the ability to reason logically, clearly, and intelligibly; to distinguish means from ends; to use empirical evidence for supporting factual beliefs; to be impartial when judging beliefs; and to hold values conducive to freedom and enlightenment" (Van Hoose & Kottler, 1985, p. 7). In so doing, therapists help clients to free themselves from self-stultifying, irrational dependence on others—including the counselor—and consequently, to increase the likelihood of experiencing greater pleasure and less frustration in the course of living.

Similarly, establishing a bond of trust between client and therapist may be seen as a central aspect of counseling. Given the propensity of many clients to resist disclosure of personal facts, especially to someone they do not know, establishing such trust may be essential for free and open communication between therapist and client. Without this free and open exchange, there is little chance that clients will work through their problems in therapy. Where such disclosure occurs, however, these chances significantly increase.

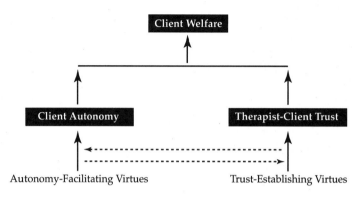

FIGURE 1.   *Flowchart depicting relations between counseling values and virtues*

Accordingly, both counseling objectives—facilitation of clients' autonomy and establishment of a therapist-client trust—themselves emerge as vital means to the promotion of clients' welfare. In short, if counseling is to serve its primary function, these two objectives must be realized.

This is not to deny the intrinsic goodness of such values as autonomy and trust. Nor is it to suggest that no other counseling values are equally as important. Nevertheless, these two values provide standards for identifying and classifying a comprehensive set of counseling virtues.

Because these two values are conducive to client welfare, counseling habits that promote one or both of them will tend to promote client welfare also. Like guiding lights, they will serve to direct the quest for counseling habits that properly characterize the virtuous psychotherapist.

Accordingly, two broad classifications of virtues are distinguished in this book: those that promote client autonomy and those that promote client trust. The former are called *autonomy-facilitating* and the latter, *trust-establishing*. Whereas each class of virtue is distinct, they are also related. Virtues that establish trust will facilitate client autonomy by encouraging clients to work through their problems in therapy (especially when the problems for which therapy is sought are themselves rooted in the loss of autonomy); conversely, virtues that facilitate client autonomy will also promote therapist-client trust by stimulating mutual understanding and respect. In Chapter 3, we consider autonomy-facilitating virtues; and in Chapter 4, we consider trust-establishing virtues.

Summary

Ethical decision making in counseling and psychotherapy is a dynamic process in which therapists confront moral problems. A moral problem is a practical problem about what to do when there is risk to the welfare, interests, or needs of people, individually or collectively.

Effective responses to these risks call for moral sensitivity—insight and awareness of human welfare, interests, and needs as these are affected in actual life contexts. Therapists need to cultivate and rely on such insight in identifying, defining, and addressing their moral problems. Such sensitivity is at the heart of what it means to be a caring professional. It makes the difference between a cold, detached awareness of facts and a deeper, more in touch, connected appreciation of the human dimensions of moral problems.

There is no formula for resolving moral problems, but procedural guidelines can provide a broad systematic framework for making ethical decisions. According to the five-stage procedure presented here, one should (1) clearly and nonprejudicially define the moral problem at hand; (2) take a careful inventory of the facts pertinent to the risks at stake; (3) conduct a philosophical analysis, applying ethical guidelines in the form of general theories, principles, and rules including those of pertinent ethics and legal codes, drawing important logical distinctions and avoiding logical pitfalls or fallacies in evaluating these facts; (4) reach and be prepared to live with a reasonable decision even if it is somewhat ambiguous and lacks certainty; and (5) implement the decision in action.

To reach a decision means avoiding making that decision by indecision. Implementing a decision can require moral courage, which implies consistent and undaunted commitment to helping the client or to preventing harm to an endangered third party even in the face of reasonable personal sacrifice.

Implementing a decision also involves moral responsibility. Because of their training, access to personal client information, and perceived position of authority, therapists can have considerable knowledge and power in relating to their clients and other affected individuals. With such knowledge and power comes moral responsibility. Acting as a morally responsible professional means harnessing this knowledge and power to promote or safeguard the welfare, interests, and needs of dependent, vulnerable clients or others. This involves having consideration, countenancing as little sacrifice to human welfare as reasonably possible.

Therapists typically also have legal and job-related responsibilities, but these may not always coincide with their moral responsibilities. Moral responsibility can sometimes militate against performing actions that are within the bounds of law or one's job. Therapists who unreflectively assume that they are acting morally because they are acting in conformity to law or job expectations may fail to act as autonomous, morally responsible professionals.

The primary purpose of counseling is to promote the welfare, interests, and needs of clients and other affected individuals. This counseling objective cannot, however, be attained in isolation of concern for promoting client autonomy and trust. Counseling effectively achieves client welfare by facilitating client autonomy. Self-reliant, independent clients are happier and less frustrated. Therapeutic progress is also unlikely without free and open communication between client and therapist. Without a bond of trust between client and therapist, such communication is unlikely to occur.

As professionals, therapists provide an important public service, one that promotes the serious welfare, interests, and needs of others. Therapists who as a matter of course fulfill this primary counseling objective possess professional virtue. To this extent they also possess moral virtue. Moral and professional virtue coalesce as both concern the promotion of human welfare.

REVIEW QUESTIONS

1. What is the primary purpose of counseling?

2. What professional responsibility can psychotherapists have to nonclient third parties? How does this responsibility differ from psychotherapists' responsibility to their clients?

3. What is a moral virtue? What is a professional virtue? How are these related?

4. Explain the difference between client welfare and client interests. How are they related?

5. What is a moral problem?

6. What is meant by being morally objective in defining a moral problem?

7. What is a moral dilemma?

8. Do appropriate responses to moral problems necessarily "feel good"? Explain.

9. When is a fact morally relevant?

10. Can facts alone provide a sufficient basis for making a moral decision? Explain.

11. What does the principle of moral considerateness state? Why might this principle be said to be basic to psychotherapy?

12. What is moral courage?

13. In the context of therapy, what does moral responsibility mean?

14. What is client autonomy and how is it related to the counseling process?

15. Given the primary purpose of counseling, what is the significance of the value of trust between therapist and client?

DISCUSSION QUESTIONS

1. Comparing the primary purpose of counseling to that of other professions such as law and medicine, discuss some similarities and differences between counseling and psychotherapy and these other professions.

2. In your estimation, can a therapist who fails to help a client resolve the problem for which therapy was sought still have provided virtuous therapy? Defend your response.

3. Are all moral virtues professional virtues? Are all professional virtues moral virtues? In your estimation, can a therapist be professionally virtuous yet lack moral virtue? Defend your response.

4. In your estimation, are there such things as psychological human needs? Explain, illustrate, and defend your response.

5. Discuss the nature and importance of moral objectivity in defining moral problems as a requisite to resolving them. Illustrate your point using at least

one example of a moral problem that you have confronted in your personal life or work-related experience.

6. Do therapists ever have a professional responsibility to serve client interests that are against the therapists' own moral principles? Do they ever have a professional responsibility not to serve such interests? Provide examples to illustrate your responses.

7. Discuss some of the main characteristics of philosophical analysis. What, in your estimation, is the value of conducting a philosophical analysis of presenting moral problems in psychotherapy?

8. Why is decision by indecision not a good approach to moral problem solving in psychotherapy or elsewhere? Discuss some ways in which therapists might avoid this pitfall.

9. Is moral courage a counseling virtue? Provide an example that illustrates your response.

10. Briefly describe a moral problem that you have encountered in your personal experience and describe several facts of your case that you think would be morally relevant to the problem at hand.

11. Provide at least three examples of morally irresponsible therapeutic tactics and explain why each is morally irresponsible.

12. Can a course of action be legal and not moral? Can a course of action be moral and not legal? Provide examples to illustrate your responses.

Cases for Analysis

Using the standards of decision making provided in this chapter, provide a critique of the therapists' approaches in the following cases. Considering the five stages of decision making, explain how you think the cases should have been handled by the respective therapists.

CASE 1

Jack and Freda Lober have been married for one year. In the first 5 months of their marriage, the two enjoyed an active sex life. Although they had an occasional quarrel, they generally got along, had an open and honest relationship, and enjoyed each other's company. However, their relationship suddenly began to deteriorate. The couple began to argue more frequently and Jack began to feel as though Freda was "shutting him out." Moreover, despite repeated sexual overtures by Jack, Freda was either "too tired" or "just not in the mood." After 6 months of a sexless and ungratifying relationship, Jack insisted that the couple seek marriage counseling.

Jack thumbed through the Yellow Pages in search of a therapist. Locating Mary Salmon, Licensed Professional Counselor (LPC), he set up an appointment. On the first session, Salmon informed the two that she would sometimes be meeting with each individually and sometimes together as a couple. She informed them that any secrets that were disclosed in private sessions—except for a few noted exceptions involving harm to self or others—would be kept "in the strictest confidence."

In sessions when Jack was present, Freda appeared guarded and spoke very little. When challenged by Jack that she had "become frigid," Freda denied the allegation but refused to comment further. One month into therapy, in a private session, Freda informed Salmon that she was a lesbian, that she was trying to go straight because that was "what was expected of her." She explained that about 6 months earlier, she had met a woman with whom she had begun a sexual relationship. She explained that her guilt was what kept her from "keeping up the sexual facade" with Jack.

In response, Salmon told Freda that she "deserved to feel guilty for what she had done to Jack." She told Freda that once she made a commitment to Jack, she should have stuck with it instead of getting involved with a lesbian relationship. Salmon told Freda that she would work with her to put the marriage to Jack "back together." She advised Freda to break off the relationship with the other woman and not to say anything about the affair to Jack because "no man could ever understand why his wife would cheat on him with another woman." This would, she stated, "destroy his male ego." Freda agreed to try to do what she had advised but that she would need her "help."

CASE 2

On August 20, 1969, Prosenjit Poddar, who was a voluntary outpatient receiving therapy at Cowell Memorial Hospital at the University of California at Berkeley, told his therapist, Dr. Lawrence Moore, that he intended to kill a certain unnamed girl, readily identifiable as Tatiana Tarasoff, when she returned home from a summer in Brazil. Moore, in agreement with Dr. Gold who had initially examined Poddar, and Dr. Yandell, assistant to the director of the Department of Psychiatry, decided to commit Poddar for observation in a mental hospital. Moore orally notified campus police officers Atkinson and Teel of his intention to commit Poddar. Moore then sent a letter to Police Chief William Beall requesting the police department's assistance in securing Poddar's confinement.

Officers Atkinson, Brownrigg, and Halleran took Poddar into custody. Convinced, however, that Poddar was rational, they released him on his promise to stay away from Tatiana. Dr. Harvey Powelson, director of the Department of Psychiatry at Cowell, then asked the campus police to return Moore's letter and he ordered the destruction of all copies of the letter and notes Moore had taken as Poddar's therapist. Powelson "ordered no action to place Prosenjit Poddar in 72-hour treatment and evaluation facility." Shortly after Tatiana returned home from Brazil,

Poddar went to her residence and stabbed her to death (Majority Opinion in *Tarasoff v. Regents of the University of California,* California Supreme Court, July 1, 1976. *131 California Reporter* 14. Dr. Moore also maintains that he wrote a "SECOND letter of commitment—again to no avail—and contacted the police several more times urging them to save Ms. Tarasoff" but the police refused to act. Moore, L. E. [1997, August 18] Psychologist warned of murder plot [Response to Dear Abby letter]. *Port St. Lucie News,* p. C4.)

CASE 3

Bridget Handsley was married for 2 years to George Handsley. She had been married once before at age 17 to Greg Brooks, who abused her both physically and sexually for a decade of their marriage. The marriage, however, came to an end when Greg died of a sudden heart attack at the age of 41. About 6 months after Greg died, Bridget began to date George, whom she soon married.

George, like Bridget's first husband, continued the history of abuse. Bridget was not permitted to socialize with many of her former friends whom he regarded as "cheap tramps." When she did go out, he monitored and determined where she could go, with whom, and when she was to return. If she returned home late, he interrogated her and sometimes accused her of "having an affair" for which she received a beating. She was not permitted to work and was expected to keep the house "spic and span." He chose her clothes and refused to allow her to wear makeup because it made her "look like a whore." He censored the type of music she could listen to and occasionally read her mail. George often drank, and he became physically aggressive when drunk. Not infrequently, he would beat her if she said something that "ticked him off." She would then be forced to lie at his feet and "beg" his forgiveness. After a beating, he would be "nice" to her for a while and bring her "gifts." These periods were short-lived, however, and the relationship would soon become abusive.

After an exceptionally severe beating, in which she was taken to the emergency room with a broken arm and some fractured ribs (she told the physician that she had fallen down a flight of stairs), Bridget decided to do something about her situation. When George was at work, she made an appointment with Kathleen Farmington, LCSW. Farmington listened attentively to Bridget's words that echoed a life of abuse. Farmington relayed to Bridget her own experience with an abusive relationship and she told Bridget how she finally "got up enough nerve" to get out of the relationship by leaving. She told Bridget that she should do the same. That afternoon, after this first meeting with Farmington, Bridget decided to "get up enough nerve" to leave. She packed some of her belongings, got into her car and began to drive down the highway, destination unknown. After a few hours of travel, Bridget became disenchanted with the idea of leaving. She was lonely and did not know where to go. She questioned whether it was really a good idea to leave. After all, he provided for her and he was basically "a good man." So Bridget turned around and returned home to an angry George who was standing in the driveway, fists clenched. Grabbing her by the collar, he dragged her into the house and began to punch her repeatedly. When he finally stopped, Bridget lay motionless on the floor. She was dead.

When Farmington heard about Bridget's death, she thought to herself. "Stupid woman. Why did she go back to him?"

CHAPTER THREE

Autonomy-Facilitating Virtues

FACILITATING CLIENT AUTONOMY: THE
   PERSON-CENTERED APPROACH
CONGRUENCE
UNCONDITIONAL POSITIVE REGARD
EMPATHY
THE AUTONOMY-FACILITATING ATTITUDES AS
   MORAL VIRTUES

THE AUTONOMY-FACILITATING VIRTUES AND
   CLIENT TRUST
SUMMARY
REVIEW QUESTIONS
DISCUSSION QUESTIONS
CASES FOR ANALYSIS

As discussed in Chapter 2, clients' welfare, interests, and needs are not likely to be served unless attention is paid to client autonomy. This chapter offers a set of mutually supportive counseling virtues that serves this central objective. The list is derived from Carl Rogers's person-centered approach to counseling. Three counselor attitudes embraced by this theory—congruence, unconditional positive regard, and empathy—are shown to be key moral virtues in a counseling ethic. Each is defined, illustrated, and related to other key ethical and philosophical concepts.

Inherent in this approach is the therapist's nonjudgmental acceptance of the client as a human being—someone to be valued and cared for regardless of his or her beliefs or behaviors. For many clients, this experience of feeling intrinsically worthy is a uniquely rare and empowering experience.

Facilitating Client Autonomy: The Person-Centered Approach

In addressing the nature and role of autonomy-facilitating virtues in the field of psychotherapy, we should examine the *person-centered* approach. Formulated by Carl Rogers, this approach operates from a humanistic and phenomenological perspective with the primary purpose of self-actualization of clients as independent, autonomous persons. Phenomenological approaches hold that true understanding of others is accomplished only when the therapist is able to enter the subjective world of the client. As Rogers said, "None of us knows for sure what constitutes objective reality and we live our whole lives in the reality as perceived" (Rogers, cited in Evans, 1975, p. 10). Although Rogers was primarily interested in constructing a theory of personality and psychotherapy, elements of his counseling approach can also be used to construct a theory of autonomy-facilitating counseling virtues.

According to Rogers, "Therapy is not a matter of doing something to the individual, or inducing him to do something about himself. It is instead a matter of freeing him for normal growth and development, of removing obstacles so that he can again move forward" (1977, p. 6). In this view, those in need of therapy have been in some manner deprived of certain requisite conditions of normal psychological growth and have consequently had their naturally forward-moving growth potential thwarted. The job of therapy is to introduce, or reintroduce, those conditions into the client's life and thereby "to free the client to become an independent, self-directing person"(p. 7).

Rogers holds that "the individual has within himself vast resources for self-understanding, for altering his self-concept, his attitudes, and his self-directed behavior—and that these resources can be tapped if only a definable climate of facilitative psychological attitudes can be provided" (Rogers, 1977, p. 7). From the Rogerian standpoint, this "definable climate of facilitative psychological attitudes" can be completely expressed in three counseling attitudes: (1) congruence, (2) unconditional positive regard, and (3) empathetic understanding. According to Rogers, these conditions are both *necessary and sufficient* conditions for client growth and development. Moreover, they apply to constructive change within all personal relations, not just therapist-client ones—for instance, parent and child, leader and group, teacher and student (Rogers, 1977).

In this book, we do not suppose that humans have a fixed human nature toward independence and self-direction. We agree that such values are desirable as a basis of human happiness, but the assumption that becoming autonomous is part of normal growth and development fails to recognize that the goal of autonomy is itself a human choice, one for which clients are responsible. The autonomous client is thus one who realizes that nonautonomous existence, like autonomous existence is a possibility, but who freely chooses autonomy because he or she prefers it, not out of conformity to some preestablished human "nature" or "essence" (Sartre, 1985).

Furthermore, we need not assume Rogers's claim that the three stated counseling attitudes of congruence, unconditional positive regard, and empathy constitute a *sufficient* vehicle of positive client change. Still, these attitudes may be considered *necessary* therapeutic conditions of such change. For example, according to Gerald Corey, these "therapeutic core conditions are necessary for therapy to occur, yet I do not see them as being sufficient conditions for change. I see them as the necessary foundation on which therapists must then build the skills of therapeutic intervention" (Corey, 1991, p. 219). This weaker stance appears in some form in other counseling theories, including cognitive-behavior theories (Whalen, DiGiuseppi, & Dryden, 1992, Ch. 2).

In this book, our position is that Rogers's three attitudinal conditions, if not necessary therapeutic conditions of positive client change, tend to increase the probability that clients will become more self-directive and independent, at least when these attitudes are combined with other appropriate skills, techniques, and modalities. It is in this sense that Rogers's counseling attitudes are assumed to facilitate client autonomy. Following is a discussion of each of the three Rogerian attitudes viewed as counseling virtues.

Congruence

According to Rogers (1977, p. 9), the more congruent the therapist is—that is, the more genuine she is, permitting herself to be "herself in the relationship, putting up no professional front or personal facade"—the more likely the client is to realize a similar freedom. Such openness or transparency about oneself means that the congruent therapist will be disposed against hiding her true beliefs, feelings, and attitudes from the client. She is thus prepared to "own" her own thoughts and feelings, to take responsibility for them. Consequently, she provides an impetus for clients to take similar responsibility for theirs.

The congruent psychotherapist would also appear to take responsibility for her actions in the sense of "consciousness of being the incontestable author of an event or of an object" (Sartre, 1985, p. 52). Such authorship requires that the therapist realize her free will in deciding on one course of action rather than another. For example, a therapist who decides to work with a suicidal client on an outpatient basis instead of having him committed to an inpatient facility must accept the consequences of this decision as her own, even if these consequences are negative, as when the client commits suicide. This acceptance of responsibility would require that the therapist not make excuses for or rationalize what has happened—for instance, telling herself that the client would have eventually committed suicide anyway. Instead, it would require that the therapist authentically, without excuse, pretense, or self-deception, confront the anxieties and frustrations of choosing in an uncertain universe (Sartre, 1985, p. 59).

The therapist who denies his role in shaping therapeutic outcomes, denies his autonomy. For example, the therapist who blames his failure to help clients on agency policies rather than on his own decision to comply with these policies tries to purchase relief from frustration and anxiety about past and future failure at the expense of reducing himself to a mere cog. The congruent therapist does not try to hide his responsibility behind an excuse. As clients' problems stem from their reticence to accept responsibility, the congruent therapist serves as a positive model for them to emulate.

This does not mean, however, that therapists must be congruent in an absolute sense. "Congruence exists on a continuum rather than on an all-or-nothing basis" (Corey, 1991, p. 213). Therapists do not have to disclose everything about themselves to clients, for not all self-disclosures are even relevant to clients' situations. Similarly, some information may be confidential and therefore should not be disclosed. In this case, it may be enough to say that the information in question is confidential. There are, therefore, some rational limits to the extent of therapists' self-disclosure.

Given that therapists' congruence, as described above, facilitates clients' autonomy, it will be included within an autonomy-driven counseling ethic. The virtuous therapist must then be congruent. Moreover, this virtue would appear to go beyond a client-restricted sort of genuineness. The virtuous therapist, in this model, would need to have acquired a disposition toward genuineness with others if he is to be genuine with clients. Otherwise, such client-restricted genuineness would be itself a sort of professional posture that is not congruent with the therapist's private self. The congruent therapist must therefore be disposed to present himself as the person he is, both inside and outside therapy.

The importance of congruence for human happiness is illustrated by the case of Bill Franklin, a former client of Dr. Alexander Mercer, Licensed Marriage Counselor.

> Bill had been married for 2 years when he and his wife, Blanche, came to Dr. Mercer, at Blanche's insistence, for marriage counseling. The presenting problem, as Blanche described it, was a lack of communication.
>
> Bill had been raised in a very strict, religious environment and was expected by his parents to become a clergyman. He honored this parental mandate by earning a divinity degree and becoming a minister. After serving in his capacity as minister for several years, he subsequently resigned his position, and became a corporate manager. Bill had been married once before. His first marriage came to an end after 10 years when his wife "threw him out." Soon after, he married Blanche.
>
> Six months into therapy, Bill revealed to Blanche that he was a homosexual who had had frequent homosexual encounters during the 2-year course of their marriage. This revelation came after Blanche confronted him about homosexual literature Bill had left on the bathroom vanity. Although Blanche continued therapy with Dr. Mercer to work through her unfinished business, Bill never returned to therapy.
>
> Separated from Blanche, Bill took an apartment. He decorated his apartment walls with pictures of naked women and invited some of his "straight" friends (from whom he had tried to conceal his homosexuality) into his living quarters. After a few months, Bill began to date another heterosexual woman, whom he subsequently married.

Bill's refusal to accept himself as a gay man led him to pursue a heterosexual facade and a self-defeating game plan in which he would ultimately and repeatedly set himself up for rejection. Bill's inner torment and desire to reaffirm his own unworthiness appeared to stem from and feed on his lack of self-acceptance. Like a cog in a machine whose functions were predictably determined by the mechanism, Bill was not a free, autonomous agent but instead a product of forces that perpetually denied his dignity and personal being. Only by mustering the courage to relinquish this role, bringing his inner being into alignment with his outer being, and making himself congruent, could he establish himself as autonomous.

Unconditional Positive Regard

On the Rogerian model, a second condition of constructive client change toward greater independence and autonomy is satisfied when therapists are disposed toward having "unconditional positive regard" for their clients as individuals. This is an attitude of deep, genuine caring for the client, that does not depend on what the client thinks, feels, or does. "It is not an attitude of `I'll accept you when . . .'; rather it is one of `I'll accept you as you are'" (Corey, 1991, p. 213). It is an attitude that "resembles the love that a parent sometimes feels toward an infant" (Rogers, 1977, p. 10). This does not mean that therapists must always share their clients' perspectives or that therapists must always approve of what their clients say or do. It does mean that therapists will continue to care deeply for their clients regardless of what their clients think, feel, or do; and it means that therapists will communicate this feeling to their clients. Thereby, clients encounter a therapeutic environment in which they are free to be whatever they are without jeopardizing their therapists' regard for them as people.

Not only are clients free to be whatever they are; they are also free to be whatever they *can* be. The therapeutic environment is thus one in which clients can freely and safely explore their potential for positive growth and development (Nuttin, 1962, p. 120). It is the client, however, who must decide how and what to change; and therapists who show unconditional positive regard do not answer these queries for their clients. Indeed, it is in precisely this process of freely deciding how and what to change that clients experience positive growth and development, for it is in this process that clients begin to actualize their potential for autonomous and independent existence.

Unconditional positive regard for a client does not imply that the therapist agrees with a client's behavior or attitudes. In being congruent, therapists express what Rogers terms "persistent" feelings relevant to what is transpiring in the session (Rogers, 1982). Such expression of feelings further serves as a model of genuineness and openness characteristic of the Rogerian modality. The virtuous therapist shares his feelings in a nonjudgmental and noncoercive manner. He does not label clients; such a practice thwarts autonomy, treats clients as means, and is not consonant with the quality of unconditional positive regard. Therapists who have unconditional positive regard for their clients will be disposed against condemning them—for instance, "Because you have harmed another, you are a bad person." The type of evaluation that is an assessment of client behavior is consistent with a caring attitude toward clients; the sort that degrades clients as persons is not.

The noncondemnatory, caring disposition of therapists with unconditional positive regard also gives dignity and pays tribute to clients as "ends in themselves" or seats of intrinsic value. Because the value of clients is not made conditional on what the client does or says, such value is intrinsic, attaching unconditionally to the client as a person. Thus, the dependent client who has come to see himself as a conditional value (as an object of sorts) experiences through therapy an environment that helps him develop self-respect and, consequently, increased self-reliance and independence.

Respect for the intrinsic dignity of clients requires that therapists avoid resorting to threats, coercion, blackmail, emotional manipulation, or other ways to exert power and control. A virtuous therapist will avoid giving the client the impression that for the therapist to continue providing therapy or emotional support is in some way contingent on the client's thinking or doing what the therapist wants or expects. Creating this impression (either deliberately or inadvertently, explicitly or implicitly) exploits the client's dependency and hampers development of the person's autonomy and independence.

Therapists' intrinsic respect for clients must, in consistency, also extend to nonclients. Having respect for the intrinsic dignity of clients without a similar respect for other persons would appear psychologically difficult or impossible, as such a schism would require the therapist to be one sort of person with clients and another sort with others. Even if such contrary habits could be cultivated, they would destroy congruence because the therapist's posture toward clients would only be a professional one that would not be consistent with the therapist's private self.

Virtuous therapists, in their dealings with nonclients and clients, will avoid personal attacks—for example, name calling—and other verbally manipulative or abusive expressions. Rather, in stating their claims and voicing their grievances, they will stick to the facts, respectfully and rationally arguing for conclusions on their own merit.

In general, therapists' posture of unconditional positive regard implies acceptance of Kant's "respect for persons" formulation of the categorical imperative: "Act in such a way that you always treat humanity, whether in your own person or in the person of any others, never simply as an end, but always at the same time as an end" (Kant, 1964, p. 96; see Chapter 1). Thus, the therapist who has the virtue of unconditional positive regard will be disposed to treat clients as well as nonclients as "ends in themselves" and not simply as "means."

Unconditional positive regard is illustrated in the case of Joe, a 17-year-old boy who had been placed in a juvenile detention center for car theft and who had met weekly with George Baslo, Licensed Clinical Social Worker (LCSW), the center's resident therapist, during Joe's 2-year period of incarceration.

> For the first year of therapy, Joe overtly displayed resistance to the therapeutic process. He routinely referred to Mr. Baslo using profanity and threatened to kill him on numerous occasions. Despite such frequently occurring outbursts and temper tantrums, Baslo continued to show respect for Joe as a person. Joe's conduct was typically met with retaliatory name-calling and derogation by a number of the staff—responding, for example, by calling him a "worthless scum"—but Baslo refused to accept or dignify Joe's low opinion of himself. Nor did he denounce Joe's right to feel and express his anger. Joe, who had been abandoned by his father when he was 5 and was raised by an abusive, alcoholic mother did not have an easy childhood and Baslo could understand Joe's burning anger, even though he did not agree with the many things Joe said and did. As time passed, Baslo's refusal to give up on Joe began to pay off. Joe's outbursts gradually diminished and Joe began to express and explore possibilities for the future. As Joe appeared to have a talent for working with computers, he began to entertain the idea of becoming a computer programmer as a career goal. By the time Joe was released, his self-esteem had greatly increased and he no longer engaged in his previous "games" of inviting others' disrespect.

Mr. Baslo's consistent attitude of unconditional positive regard for Joe provided a solid role model for Joe to emulate. If Mr. Baslo could care for Joe, then maybe Joe could care for himself. Perhaps for the first time in his life, Joe had been provided with an atmosphere where he was safe to be himself and to explore who he might want to be. In this environment, Joe was able to relinquish a vicious, self-defeating game of self-denigration, which he had unhappily played with the support of society for 17 years.

Empathy

According to Rogers, the third facilitative condition of constructive client change is satisfied when therapists are disposed toward experiencing empathetic understanding of clients' subjective worlds. Such a therapist "senses accurately the feelings and personal meanings that are being experienced by the client and communicates this understanding to the client." In so doing, the empathetic therapist "assists the client in gaining a clearer understanding of, and hence a greater control over, her own world and her own behavior" (Rogers, 1977, p. 11).

Because empathetic therapists are able to attain a compassionate understanding and perception of the subjective life of clients, these therapists are also morally sensitive—that is, they possess a deep appreciation for clients' welfare, interests, and needs. An empathetic therapist would sense the loneliness, isolation, fear, and vulnerability of a seriously depressed client who had AIDS (acquired immune deficiency syndrome). The therapist would appreciate the nature and magnitude of the ethical and social problems, such as discriminatory and exclusionary social practices, confronted by this client and other persons in similar circumstances. A therapist can demonstrate empathy in a variety of ways. One way is to use minimal responses, appropriate verbal and nonverbal replies that let the therapist affirm "being with" the client. Therapists can show this, for example, by saying "uh huh" and "I see" as well as by nodding the head.

Empathy can also be demonstrated by the therapeutic use of Rogerian *reflection*. In reflection, the therapist states back to the client the essence of what the client is feeling. Reflection requires the therapist to use new language in this restatement and not merely "parrot back" the exact words of the client. Accurate reflection lets the client see that the counselor truly understands what he or she is feeling, and it may further serve to put a situation into sharper focus for the client. Consider the following example:

Client: I just don't know where to start. There are so many things that I need to do.

Therapist: You're feeling overwhelmed thinking about everything that you want to accomplish.

Whereas empathy involves a sense of personal identification with the client's subjective world, therapists must be careful not to overidentify with the client's feelings; that is, they must not lose a sense of their own identity and sep-arateness. Otherwise, therapists may be unable to help clients clarify and under-stand their own subjectivity. An example is when a therapist allows his own negative feelings toward his wife to interfere with the client's working through his own similar feelings. According to Rogers, clients' self-understanding helps them gain greater control over their own world and behavior, and therapists who overidentify with clients' subjective worlds, thereby failing to help clients arrive at this self-understanding, are apt to thwart client autonomy. Therefore, an autonomy-driven counseling ethic would justify the cultivation of a type of empathy that does not absorb therapist identity but instead enables the thera-pist to "sense the client's private world as if it were [the therapist's] own, but without ever losing the 'as if' quality" (Rogers, 1961, p. 284).

Empathetic understanding is based on an epistemology of *connectedness* as opposed to *separateness*. As characterized by Blythe McVicker Clinchy (1996), the *separate* knower looks at someone's idea with doubt and incredulity, trying to find exceptions to the stated idea, shooting holes in it, looking for fallacies, checking for validity. Alternatively, *connected* knowing engages an "empathetic receptive eye." Instead of looking for flaws, the connected person looks for what is right in an idea rather than for what is wrong even if the idea is not at first appealing. He or she tries diligently—not simply believing what comes easy—to see it from the other person's perspective; to become an ally or advo-cate, not an adversary, of what is being examined. This approach to knowing aligns one with the other rather than driving a wedge between them.

Nevertheless, as Clinchy acknowledges, there is still a difference between *understanding* a point of view and *agreeing* with it. By trying to believe a point of view, one can come to understand it. Such attempts at believing make up a *"procedure* that guides . . . interaction with other minds; it is not the *result* of the interaction" (Clinchy, 1996, p. 208).

Further, as Rogers recognizes, although therapist and client are connected, they must still remain separate and distinct centers of experience (Clinchy, 1996). Within this context of separate but connected experiencing and believ-ing, there can be more than reflection. There can also be collaborative discovery, sharing of new ideas, revision and expansion of previous ideas, and abandon-ment of old ones. As Michael J. Mahoney (1996) suggests,

> My experience has been that the most helpful therapists are those who can resonate deeply with their clients' experiences, and, importantly, who can dance the dialectic between their own and the other's experiencing. Differences then become impor-tant not because they create or maintain a separating distance but because they afford opportunities for both participants to learn about and explore new ways of being themselves. (p. 138)

Such resonating back and forth may be a necessary condition of the "as if" quality of empathetic regard. Moreover, were the therapist to surrender her dis-tinctness, the therapist would be nonautonomous and as such not a model capable of facilitating autonomy by example.

Empathetic understanding goes beyond a mere sensing of others' feelings. It is more than having an affect similar to that of the client. It also includes inference, judgment, belief, and other aspects of thinking and reasoning. In empathy, thought and feeling, reasoning and emotion, heart and mind are all represented. To empathize with what another is feeling, one must also understand the other's circumstances (Clinchy, 1996, p. 224–225). For example, as Kohn suggests,

> The issue is not just how weepy I become upon learning that your spouse has died; it is also whether I am merely recalling and reacting to a comparable loss in my own life or whether I am resonating to your unique set of circumstances—the suddenness of the death, the particular features of this person you loved that are especially vivid for you, your rocky marital history and the resultant prickles of guilt you are now feeling, the way your initial numbness is finally giving way to real pain, the respects in which your unconscious fears of being abandoned are about to be freshly revived by this event, the relationship that you and I have had up to now, and so on. (Kohn, quoted in Clinchy, 1996 p. 225)

Empathetic understanding thus involves informed feeling. To empathize, therapists must surrender the commonplace assumption that thinking and feeling are contrary actions, rivals at war with one another (Clinchy, 1996). To empathize, a therapist must be privy to personal knowledge of the client's life. An empathetic therapist must carefully listen and attend to what the client is saying; otherwise, the therapist will not have attained sufficient understanding of the client's circumstances. But information without affect is not empathy any more than is affect without information. Empathy includes both; however, in the *experience* of empathy, there is no simple division into affect plus understanding. These elements interact and combine; affect fuels understanding and understanding fuels affect.

Some critics have questioned the merits as well as the possibility of attaining such genuine subjective sharing within the professional context. Thus, J. Haley has claimed that

> we must accept the fact that the therapeutic situation is not an honest human experience; it is a paid relationship. The therapist is receiving money to be human with a patient, which is rather inhuman. Second, it can be argued that no therapist of any school can share with a patient all of his observations and understanding. Third, it is doubtful that a patient can actually achieve autonomy when exposed to the understanding therapeutic approach. Finally, and most important, it is unlikely that an honest sharing of understanding within a paid relationship solves the problem the patient is paying his money to recover from. (cited in Van Hoose & Kottler, 1985, p. 121)

The inference from the premise that a relationship is a paid one to the conclusion that it is not an honest, human experience is unsound and defies the experiences of many professionals. When the fee charged is fair (see Chapter 4) and the client has agreed to the terms of payment, then the fact of compensation for services rendered is consistent with the possibility of an honest relationship and it need not disrupt the quality of the therapeutic encounter. Second, it is an oversimplification that an honest relationship requires the therapist to share with a patient all observations and understanding. As already discussed, congruent disclosure exists on a continuum and is not all-or-nothing. Third, an understanding therapeutic approach may not always be sufficient to increase client autonomy or to solve the problem for which the client seeks therapy, but it is an important if not necessary condition of therapeutic progress.

The concept of empathetic understanding as well as unconditional positive regard is illustrated in the case of Clive, a 26-year-old male who sought therapy with Dr. Stuart for the presenting problem of "marital difficulties":

> Clive's wife had left him for reasons which he first described as "minor"—"losing my temper and screaming at her." However, as therapy progressed, Clive slowly and tentatively began to reveal a history of having physically abused both his spouse and his dog. Though not approving of such actions, Dr. Stuart was able to listen actively as Clive shared with her not only his abusive behaviors but also a recounting of his own childhood abuse at the hands of his father. By reflecting back to the client the client's own feelings, Dr. Stuart was able not only to clarify these feelings for Clive, but also to demonstrate that she was trying to understand the feelings he was experiencing. This understanding served to strengthen the bonds of trust between therapist and client and to facilitate further client self-disclosure. Feeling cared for and accepted, Clive began to explore the implications of his actions and the deleterious effects they had on others. As he was now more comfortable with self-disclosure, Clive began to express a wide gamut of feelings including sorrow, fear, unresolved childhood anger, and remorse.

Dr. Stuart's success in empathizing with Clive was partly a result of her ability to maintain unconditional positive regard for her client, despite his commission of acts that were counter to her own moral values. Had Stuart permitted her moral disapproval for Clive's actions to influence her acceptance of him as a person, she probably would not have been able to "connect" with her client. As a result, Clive would probably not have been motivated to make further disclosure. Without such disclosure, Dr. Stuart's ability to empathize would, in turn, have been limited by her lack of cogent background information.

The Autonomy-Facilitating Attitudes as Moral Virtues

The three attitudinal conditions considered in this chapter—congruence, unconditional positive regard, and empathy—may be considered *moral virtues* in the Aristotelian sense and not merely counseling styles or techniques. First, they are states of character as constituted by specific habits or dispositions that can be improved or diminished in relation to time, experience, and practice. Second, they involve both rational and emotional components. Whereas empathy demands that the therapist identify emotionally with clients, therapists must also be guided by a sense of objectivity; and whereas congruent therapists must be open about their emotions, they also need to exercise rational judgment about the appropriateness of emotional expressions. Also, whereas unconditional positive regard requires that therapists care deeply for their clients, such care does not require the therapist to surrender his own judgment of right and wrong, or to accept as true everything the client says or does. In short, these three conditions are habits involving rational direction of emotion within the therapeutic context, and as such, may, in the Aristotelian sense, be appropriately considered moral virtues, albeit counseling ones.

The Autonomy-Facilitating Virtues and Client Trust

In general, congruence, unconditional positive regard, and empathy, as counseling virtues, promote client trust. When therapists are genuine, caring, and understanding, clients are more likely to express and explore their private thoughts and feelings in the therapeutic context without fear of reprisal. As this free expression and exploration facilitates ownership of their own thoughts, feelings, views, decisions, and actions, clients become more independent and self-directing.

For therapist and client to build a bond of trust is a central condition in promoting client autonomy in the therapeutic context. This trust is also the basis of further counseling virtues beyond the three described in this chapter. In the next chapter, we consider these additional virtues.

Summary

This chapter has explored the nature and scope of autonomy-facilitating virtues and the ways they bear on the counseling process. Congruence, unconditional positive regard, and empathy were presented as moral virtues rather than merely as counseling techniques. Reflection and minimal responses, avenues through which therapists demonstrate empathetic understanding of the client's world, were also explained. Examination of the concepts of separate and connected knowledge further helped to clarify the epistemological underpinnings of empathetic understanding.

To codify the virtues described here would be difficult, if not impossible. These qualities are essential aspects of the affective, care-based side of virtuous practice and decision making. Ethical choices require perception to be infused with emotional appreciation of concrete reality. Empathetic understanding supplies this perception and increases the therapist's moral sensitivity to the welfare, interests, and needs of clients. Unconditional positive regard for clients undergirds Kantian respect for clients as ends in themselves and ensures that the definition, analysis, and resolution of moral problems will proceed without recourse to personal attack or other self-defeating responses to client realities. Congruence implies forthrightness and authenticity, and supports moral courage to adhere to one's moral convictions even in the face of adversity. These three counseling attitudes collectively stand in intimate relation to other key counseling values as facilitators of client autonomy and pillars of therapist-client trust. They condition virtuous practice and make it possible.

REVIEW QUESTIONS

1. What is Rogers's view of human nature?

2. What is meant by being *congruent*? Must a congruent therapist tell the client everything that is on his mind? Explain.

3. What is meant by *unconditional positive regard?* Must a therapist who has unconditional positive regard for her clients always agree with what these clients think or do? Explain.

4. What is the relationship between unconditional positive regard and other counseling values such as trust and autonomy? What is the relationship between the categorical imperative and unconditional positive regard?

5. What is empathy? What relation does it have to other counseling values such as trust and autonomy?

6. How can understanding the client's circumstances increase a therapist's ability to empathize with a client?

7. What is *connected* knowing and how is it different from *separate* knowing?

8. What is reflection, and how does reflection differ from parroting back what someone has said? Why might reflection be considered an important element of a counseling ethic?

DISCUSSION QUESTIONS

1. Discuss some aspects of the congruent therapist. What relationships exist between congruence and other counseling values such as trust and autonomy?

2. Can a virtuous therapist have congruence with regard to his clients and lack this characteristic with regard to others? Explain.

3. Consider the problems Bill Franklin had coping with his homosexuality. Do you think therapists are ever justified in helping their homosexual clients to try to *become* heterosexual in order to fit into a heterosexual culture? In your estimation, could a homosexual client ever be helped to live *congruently* as a heterosexual?

4. What steps can a therapist take to increase the possibility that she will treat clients with unconditional positive regard?

5. In your estimation, could Baslo have had the same measure of success with Joe had he taken a more "no nonsense" approach toward him? Did Baslo have a moral responsibility to continue counseling Joe despite his displays of hostility toward Baslo, including threats on his life? What would you have done if you were Baslo?

6. In the case of Clive, discuss how the outcome of the case might have differed had the therapist scolded him for the abuse of his wife.

7. Respond to the following: behaviors that clients engage in are sometimes unethical and hurtful to others. The virtuous therapist therefore has a moral responsibility to express actively to the client his disapproval of such actions.

8. In Chapter 1, *care-based ethics* was discussed. In what respects does the Rogerian approach to therapy resemble this ethic?

9. Compare and contrast the concepts of empathy and sympathy.

10. With respect to empathy, is it necessary to have experienced the same life events as one's client to understand the client? Explain.

11. Discuss whether and how so-called connected and separate ways of knowing might each have a place in a virtuous counseling approach.

12. Do you agree with Haley that because the therapeutic relationship is a paid one, it can never be "an honest human experience"? Does the fact that it is a paid relationship destroy or at least lower the prospects that the relationship will produce genuine trust and empathetic understanding? If not, why not? If so, why? If so, what reasonable steps could a therapist take to address this problem?

13. Are congruence, unconditional positive regard, and empathy types of *moral virtue*? Explain.

14. In your estimation, are congruence, unconditional positive regard, and empathy *sufficient* conditions of positive client change? That is, do you think that clients will ordinarily improve when therapists display all three of these traits toward their clients? Explain.

15. Are congruence, unconditional positive regard, and empathy *necessary* conditions of (positive) client change? That is, will clients typically *fail* to improve when therapists *lack* any one or all of these traits? Explain.

Cases for Analysis

Using the concepts introduced in this chapter, discuss the adequacy of the approaches taken by the therapists in each of the following cases:

Case 1

Jack Brenner, a 35 year-old, married client of Dr. Max Riethman, suffered from anxiety related to his job as a psychiatric nurse. Jack, who was also pursuing a degree in mental health counseling, felt overwhelmed by the pressures of his job, school, a newborn infant, and a wife who was frustrated by Jack's lack of time for her. Dr. Riethman, who used a form of cognitive-behavior therapy, made virtually no disclosures about his personal life to

Jack. For example, he never mentioned whether he was married or had children. Dr. Riethman believed that disclosure of such personal facts was generally unnecessary, and he was especially cautious not to make such personal disclosures in the present case. This was because Dr. Riethman's wife, Donna, was, unknown to Jack, one of Jack's classmates, and Dr. Riethman believed that if Jack knew Donna Riethman was his wife, this knowledge might be uncomfortable for Jack. Thus, when Jack asked Dr. Riethman if he was married, Dr. Riethman retorted, "I would prefer to stick to your marital issues."

As therapy progressed, Jack made significant progress and reported that "he no longer had any issues to work through." Therapy was accordingly phased down. On the last session, Jack began to cry, stating that he would miss meeting with Dr. Riethman. He also stated, "I know nothing about you; you're like a blank screen; still, I will really miss you." Dr. Riethman responded, "I will miss you too, Jack." The two stood up, stared into each other's eyes, and smiled. Jack turned toward the door, and exited.

CASE 2

Rita Lancaster, Ph. D., is a psychologist. According to Dr. Lancaster, clients will not learn how to take control over their lives unless the therapist points them in the right direction. According to Lancaster, "Manipulation, sometimes subtle, sometimes not so subtle, is inevitable. Even therapists' choice of questions is largely controlled by the direction in which therapists want therapy to go. In such cases, clients are led to the right conclusions."

In support of her stance, Dr. Lancaster often cites the case of Shelly, a 21-year-old client of Lancaster's who came to counseling because she was having trouble getting dates. Dr. Lancaster told Shelly that she needed to be more assertive and not "such a wallflower." Accordingly, she gave Shelly a behavioral assignment to ask a boy whom she liked out on a date. When Shelly indicated that she was not ready to do this, Lancaster told her that she could not then help Shelly. She stated, "If you're not willing to cooperate, then there's no point to continuing with therapy." As a result, Shelly asked the boy out. He accepted the invitation, and Shelly recently announced her engagement to this same boy.

CASE 3

Cynthia Hatley works as a counselor in a domestic violence shelter. She had herself been an abuse victim and has devoted herself to trying to help other victims. Ms. Hatley is also active in state outreach programs and gives lectures on problems of domestic abuse and violence throughout the nation.

Presently divorced, she was married twice and was physically and emotionally abused by both her former husbands. In addition, as a young child she had been the victim of both physical and sexual abuse by her stepfather.

Ms. Hatley has prided herself on being in touch with her clients' feelings because she was "there" herself. She stated the following:

Every time I hear clients tell me about how they were brutalized, those old feelings of fear and humiliation swell up inside me again, and I can feel the pain these women are experiencing. Sometimes we just sit and cry together. It helps them to know that I am just like them, and that I am there for them, and they usually have little trouble opening up to me. I also encourage them to express their anger and outrage. I know that these women are blaming themselves for what some monsters did to them.

CHAPTER FOUR

Trust-Establishing Virtues

THE THERAPIST-CLIENT TRUST
PRINCIPLES OF TRUSTWORTHINESS
HONESTY
    Principle of Honesty
    Honesty and Deception
CANDOR
    Principle of Candor
    Candor and Informed Consent
DISCRETION
    Principle of Discretion
    Discretion and Confidentiality
PROFESSIONAL COMPETENCE
    Principle of Beneficence
    Competence, Benevolence, and Beneficence
NONMALEFICENCE
    Principle of Nonmaleficence
    Nonmaleficence, Nonmalevolence,
        and Due Care

DILIGENCE
    Principle of Diligence
    Diligence and the Promotion of Client Welfare
LOYALTY
    Principle of Loyalty
    Loyalty and Conflicts of Interest
FAIRNESS
    Principle of Fairness
    Fairness, Equality of Treatment, and Managed
        Care
PRINCIPLES, STANDARDS, AND SUBSTANTIVE
    MORAL PROBLEMS
SUMMARY
REVIEW QUESTIONS
DISCUSSION QUESTIONS
CASES FOR ANALYSIS

The primary counseling purpose of promoting client welfare is served by two mutually supportive counseling objectives: (1) facilitation of clients' autonomy and (2) establishment of therapist-client trust. The first of these objectives was addressed in Chapter 3. In this chapter, the second of these objectives is addressed through articulation of counseling virtues that are vital to the creation and maintenance of a bond of trust between therapist and client. In particular, the virtues of honesty, candor, discretion, competence, diligence, loyalty, and fairness are presented as character traits that collectively mark therapists as trustworthy.

In this chapter, general principles of trustworthness that undergird the conduct of trustworthy therapists are formulated. Pertinent professional codes of ethics and legal standards are related to these principles, and their implications for virtuous practice are explored.

The Therapist-Client Trust

The bond of trust between therapist and client is a central value in counseling ethics. Where such a bond exists, the probability is good that the client will confide in his therapist and therefore work out his problems. Take away this bond of trust, and clients will be reluctant to disclose their deepest secrets; thus, client welfare will likely not be served by therapy. Therapeutic habits that build trust between therapist and client can be called counseling virtues as such habits serve the primary counseling mission of promoting client welfare.

One account of professional virtues as defined in relation to the professional-client trust is set forth by Michael Bayles (1989). Although he intended his so-called fiduciary model to apply to professional ethics in general, what he says, with some qualifications, can be applied to counseling ethics.

Bayles believes the fiduciary model is justified because "the weaker party [the client] depends upon the stronger [the professional] in ways in which the other does not and so must trust the stronger party" (Bayles, 1989, p. 78). In the case of counseling, clients may be especially vulnerable to the unethical therapist. Frequently, clients come to counselors because they have dependency issues to work through. Unethical counselors can use their position of power to exploit this client dependency for self-serving purposes. However, a counseling ethic that uses trustworthiness as its central criterion for selection of virtues will include those virtues likely to act against exploitation of client weakness.

According to Bayles, seven virtues can be justified on the standard of trustworthiness: honesty, candor, discretion, competence, diligence, loyalty, and fairness. A professional—in particular, a counselor—who does not exemplify each of these virtues would, in the Baylsian analysis, not be worthy of clients' trust.

Before discussing these virtues, note the distinction between saying that a therapist is *trustworthy* and saying that the therapist is *trusted*. In this context *trustworthy* means "can generally be counted on to keep clients' trusts." A therapist who is trusted by her clients may not be trustworthy; conversely, a therapist who is trustworthy may not be trusted by her clients. For example, in the former case, a client may be deceived by an unscrupulous therapist into trusting him; and in the latter, a client may not have been in therapy long enough to have established a bond of trust with her therapist.

There is no guarantee that a trustworthy therapist will in time be trusted by her client. A skeptical client may continue to offer resistance to the therapeutic process due to her lack of confidence in therapists in general, thereby making progress unlikely. Yet, in comparison to untrustworthy therapists, trustworthy ones stand a greater chance of coming to be trusted by their clients. For example, therapists who routinely lie to their clients or who do not usually follow through on their promises are likely, at least eventually, to be distrusted by their clients. On the other hand, trustworthy therapists avoid such deeds and are thereby more likely to earn their clients' trust. Moreover, deceitful or manipulative therapists could not be congruent. As the absence of congruence thwarts trust, untrustworthy therapists are not apt to gain clients' trust. Given the primary end of counseling as the promotion of client welfare, virtuous therapists will be those who possess virtues that make them trustworthy.

Manipulation and deception, while sometimes viewed by the therapist as being in the best interest of the client, ultimately damage the client-therapist relationship irreparably by violating and betraying the client's trust. As many clients have experienced lifetimes of such betrayals, the therapeutic relationship may provide the first haven for unconditional positive regard and trust. Such trust may have been hard won. In violating the sanctity of this trust, a therapist not only risks sabotaging the therapeutic relationship but also risks inflicting serious harm to the client who finally believes that someone can be trusted only to be deceived again. The physician's dictum, "first do no harm," can aptly be applied to the virtuous psychotherapist. Client welfare can be seriously damaged by deceptions.

In manipulating a client, a therapist is treating that client as a means, not as an end. If this were universalized, therapists could routinely use manipulation, deception, and coercion to induce clients to do whatever the therapist thought was in the best interest of the client. Such a practice serves to thwart client autonomy and thus to undermine the primary counseling mission.

Principles of Trustworthiness

The virtuous therapist must have cultivated trustworthy habits of honesty, candor, competence/benevolence, diligence, loyalty, discretion, and fairness. The client would otherwise not be inclined toward self-disclosure, and the primary counseling mission of promoting client welfare would be impaired.

These trust-establishing virtues can be partly defined in terms of certain general principles of ethical conduct. This chapter provides a formulation of each principle as well as supporting ethics code citations from the National Association of Social Workers (NASW), *Code of Ethics* (1997); American Psychological Association (APA), *Ethical Principles of Psychologists* (1992); American Counseling Association (ACA), *Code of Ethics* (1995); and the National Organization for Human Service Education (NOHSE), *Ethical Standards of Human Service Workers* (1994). These citations represent important implications of the principles. Although each citation refers to a specific profession—social work, psychology, counseling, human services—each is understood here to transcend these designations and to apply universally to all mental health care professions. (Unabridged versions of these codes of ethics are contained in the appendices of this book.)

Although the virtuous therapist respects all principles of trustworthiness, *these principles are not unconditional and their application to actual cases may require the therapist to weigh and balance competing ethical interests.* For example, the principle of discretion may permit disclosure of confidential client information to prevent harm to a third party. As we have already seen (Chapter 2), the virtuous therapist is morally considerate and tries to harmonize conflicting standards as far as the situation allows. Thus, rather than make a wholesale betrayal of confidence, the virtuous therapist will disclose the least information necessary to prevent the impending harm (ACA, 1995, B.1.f).

Also, a habit of conformity to the principles is an essential aspect of counseling virtue, but conforming alone does not make therapists virtuous. The virtuous therapist must also harbor appropriate motives such as intrinsic regard for the welfare of clients and others. As we have seen, the virtuous therapist must be empathetic and congruent, and must have unconditional positive regard for clients and others. These autonomy-facilitating virtues cannot easily be cast, even partly, in terms of action-guiding rules; they are largely emotive in character, and emotions cannot effectively be prescribed by a set of rules.

Principles of trustworthiness will not provide an algorithm for ethical decision making as they are too general. Yet, as will become evident from an inspection of respective code citations, these principles are specific enough to circumscribe the range of morally permissible counseling practice. Within the broader context of virtue ethics, which includes the further elements of habit, motive, and feeling, the principles of trustworthiness gain import and help to define what it means to be a virtuous therapist.

Honesty

PRINCIPLE OF HONESTY
Avoid deception in relating to clients and other relevant third parties.

• Human services professionals act with integrity, honesty, genuineness and objectivity (NOHSE, 1994, 28).
• Psychologists do not make public statements that are false, deceptive, misleading, or fraudulent, either because of what they state, convey, or suggest or because of what they omit, concerning their research, practice, or other work activities or those of persons or organizations with which they are affiliated. . . . psychologists do not make false or deceptive statements concerning (1) their training, experience, or competence; (2) their academic degrees; (3) their credentials; (4) their institutional or association affiliations; (5) their services; (6) the scientific or clinical basis for, or results or degree of success of their services; (7) their fees; or (8) their publications or research findings (APA, 1992, 3.03.a).
• Counselors are accurate, honest, and unbiased in reporting their professional activities and judgments to appropriate third parties including courts, health insurance companies, those who are the recipients of evaluation reports, and others (ACA, 1995, C.5.c).
• Psychologists terminate a professional relationship when it becomes reasonably clear that the patient or client no longer needs the service, is not benefiting, or is being harmed by continued service (APA, 1992, 4.09.b).
• Counselors claim or imply only professional credentials possessed and are responsible for correcting any known misrepresentations of their credentials by others (ACA, 1995, C.4.a).
• Counselors do not attribute more to their credentials than the credentials represent, and do not imply that other counselors are not qualified because they do not possess certain credentials (ACA, 1995, C.4.d).
• If psychologists learn of misuse or misrepresentation of their work, they take reasonable steps to correct or minimize the misuses or misrepresentation (APA, 1992, 1.16.b).
• Counselors plan, conduct, and report research accurately and in a manner that minimizes the possibility that results will be misleading. They pro-

vide thorough discussions of the limitations of their data and alternative hypotheses. Counselors do not engage in fraudulent research, distort data, misrepresent data, or deliberately bias their results (ACA, 1995, G.3.b).

• Psychologists never deceive research participants about significant aspects that would affect their willingness to participate, such as physical risks, discomfort, or unpleasant emotional experiences (APA, 1992, 6.15.b).

• In forensic testimony and reports, psychologists testify truthfully, honestly and candidly and, consistent with applicable legal procedures, describe fairly the bases for their testimony and conclusions (APA, 1992, 7.04.a).

HONESTY AND DECEPTION

The connection between honesty and trustworthiness is undeniable as "by definition, a dishonest professional is not worthy of a client's trust" (Bayles, 1989, p. 80). In the context of providing psychotherapy, a therapist can be called honest insofar as she is disposed against deceiving or tricking clients or other relevant third parties.

Whereas *truthfulness* is sometimes used as a synonym for the generic virtue of honesty, being truthful can also refer to the more specific habit of speaking the truth. In the latter sense, being truthful is only one type of honesty, a person could be truthful yet still not be honest in other ways. For example, "a person could steal or cheat but admit it truthfully when questioned"(Bayles, 1989, p. 81). Moreover, notwithstanding such a person's truthfulness, we would be hard put to call her an honest person.

A therapist can be called dishonest if she is disposed toward intentionally engaging in deceit or trickery. Examples of dishonesty may include therapists' deliberate acts of misinforming (lying); misleading (presenting information in vague or misleading ways as in misleading advertising or misrepresenting credentials); telling half truths (omitting relevant facts); leaving false impressions (failing to correct client misunderstandings); stealing (taking time or money from clients under false pretenses, defrauding insurance companies); and being disingenuous, inauthentic, or insincere (thinking or feeling one way, and saying or doing another). On the other hand, trustworthy therapists are congruent and act with integrity, honesty, genuineness, and objectivity (NOHSE, 1994, 28).

In the context of psychotherapy, dishonesty may be motivated by self-interest, as when a therapist extends the duration of therapy beyond what she believes to be beneficial to the client to continue to receive payment (APA, 1992, 4.09.b). Because such conduct involves stealing from the client, it is incompatible with the primary end of counseling (client welfare); and virtuous therapists will be disposed against engaging in it.

On the other hand, dishonesty may also be motivated by the desire to help clients, as when a therapist gives a client paradoxical directions to deter the client from self-destructive behavior. Some claim that the end of client welfare justifies engaging in such deceit and that "it is unlikely that an honest sharing of understanding within a paid relationship solves the problem the patient is paying his money to recover from" (Haley, 1976, p. 208).

The issue of the "therapeutic" use of deceit has previously been addressed. In addition to the problems with such practices mentioned earlier, giving paradoxical directions to a suicidal client may prove disastrous. "These procedures [paradoxical procedures] are not advisable in crisis situations, suicide, homicide, violence, abuse, or excessive drinking. Paradox in these situations is likely to be counterproductive and irresponsible" (Corey, Corey, & Callanan, 1988, p. 111).

Any warranted use of manipulation could be justified only in the most extreme circumstances, such as cases involving actively psychotic clients. In justifying "dishonesty" in this type of situation, note that to be honest requires only that a therapist be in the habit of acting honestly; it does not require that she always do so. A therapist habitually disposed toward telling lies may be called a "liar," but it could not sensibly be argued that anyone who has ever told a lie is a liar. To accept this inference would mean that all or most individuals are liars (Cohen, 1994).

An application of Kant's categorical imperative points to the same conclusion. A universal law that therapists always tried to deceive or trick clients into getting better would be self-defeating, as nobody would then be tricked or deceived; and the practice of therapy would accordingly be destroyed. Short of such a universal law, widespread use of deceit by therapists would probably serve to impede substantially the primary counseling purpose—promotion of client welfare—by weakening the bond of trust between therapist and client.

In addressing honesty, Bayles (1989, p. 80) notes that the sense of honesty he is considering amounts to "an obligation to the client" and "does not directly require honesty towards others." He notes that "professionals can be honest with their clients and in acting in their behalf be dishonest with others." Nevertheless, Bayles does suggest that professionals who act dishonestly toward others are more likely to do the same to their clients. Moreover, he maintains that, as part of the fiduciary relationship, "a professional is not completely directed by the client but offers independent advice and service. To the extent professionals are free moral agents, they are responsible for effects on third parties and subject to obligations to them" (Bayles, 1989, p. 112).

Some have argued that professional virtue is consistent with disregard for the welfare of nonclients. For example, Charles Curtis (1951) claimed that good lawyers must learn to treat everybody but their clients as "barbarians and enemies." We have, already seen (Chapter 2), however, that persons who are not clients can also have legitimate moral claims on therapists as the primary purpose of counseling also includes regard for third-party welfare.

Candor

PRINCIPLE OF CANDOR
Keep clients informed about matters related to the counseling process consistent with what clients would reasonably want to know.

• When counseling is initiated, and throughout the counseling process as necessary, counselors inform clients of the purposes, goals, techniques, procedures, limitations, potential risks and benefits of services to be performed, and other pertinent information. Counselors take steps to ensure that clients understand the implications of diagnosis, the intended use of tests and reports, fees, and billing arrangements (ACA, 1995, A.3.a).

• In obtaining informed consent for research, counselors use language that is understandable to research participants and that . . . identifies any procedures that are experimental or relatively untried (ACA, 1995, G.2.a).

• Social workers should discuss with clients and other interested parties the nature of confidentiality and limitations of clients' right to confidentiality. Social workers should review with clients circumstances where confidential information may be requested and where disclosure of confidential information may be legally required. This discussion should occur as soon as possible in the social worker–client relationship and as needed throughout the course of the relationship (NASW, 1997, 1.07.e).

• When counselors work as subcontractors for counseling services for a third party, they have a duty to inform clients of the limitations of confidentiality that the organization may place on counselors in providing counseling services to clients. The limits of such confidentiality ordinarily are discussed as part of the intake session (ACA, 1995, D.4).

• Psychologists obtain appropriate informed consent to therapy or related procedures, using language that is reasonably understandable to participants. . . . informed consent generally implies that the person (1) has the capacity to consent, (2) has been informed of significant information concerning the procedure, (3) has freely without undue influence expressed consent, and (4) consent has been appropriately documented (APA, 1992, 4.02.a).

• Psychologists make reasonable efforts to answer patients' questions and to avoid apparent misunderstandings about therapy. Whenever possible, psychologists provide oral and/or written information using language that is reasonably understandable to the patient or client (APA, 1992, 4.01.d).

• When persons are legally incapable of giving informed consent, psychologists obtain informed permission from a legally authorized person, if such substitute consent is permitted by law (APA, 1992, 4.02b).

• Psychologists (1) inform those persons who are legally incapable of giving informed consent about the proposed intervention in a manner commensurate with the persons' psychological capacities, (2) seek their assent to those interventions, and (3) consider such persons' preferences and best interests (APA, 1992, 4.02c).

• Social workers should provide clients with reasonable access to records concerning the clients. Social workers who are concerned that clients' access to their records could cause serious misunderstanding or harm to the client should provide assistance in interpreting the records and consultation with the client regarding the records. Social workers should limit clients' access to their records, or portions of their records, only in exceptional circumstances when there is compelling evidence that such access would cause serious harm to the client. Both clients' requests and the rationale

for withholding some or all of the records should be documented in clients' files (NASW, 1997, 1.08.a)
• Counselors obtain permission from clients prior to electronically recording or observing sessions (ACA, 1995, B.4.c).

CANDOR AND INFORMED CONSENT

According to Bayles (1989, p. 81), the virtue of candor requires full disclosure and not merely truthfulness that may be consistent with the withholding of relevant information. What constitutes full disclosure will, however, be a function of what a rational client would reasonably want to know (*Canterbury v. Spence*, 1972).

In this context, full disclosure means disclosure of all information the client would need to know to be able to give informed consent to therapy. This would generally include any information having potential bearing on the welfare, interests, or needs of the client. As stated by Corey, Corey, and Callanan (1988, p. 169), "issues of violating the rights of clients are raised when practitioners fail to provide clients with adequate information that may affect their welfare." This information may vary according to the idiosyncrasies of individual clients, but there are certain common human interests that clients concerned about their own welfare would want or expect their therapists to address in the initial meetings.

First, a client would reasonably want to know about *the modality of therapy* to be used because this information has bearing on how the client will be treated and what she can expect in the provision of therapy. This would include the risks as well as the benefits of the therapy. For example, the client receiving Gestalt therapy should be advised of the strong experiential, emotional, and confrontational nature of the approach (ACA, 1995, A.3.a).

Clients would also reasonably want to know whether the employed modality or variations of it represent a conventional approach or is of an experimental nature (ACA, 1995, G.2.a). It is reasonable for clients who care about their own welfare not to be willing subjects to experimental trials, so therapists who engage in such experimentation without clients' informed consent would undermine the clients' autonomy by treating them as manipulated objects. Obviously, such manipulative acts would render therapists unworthy of their clients' trust.

Second, clients would reasonably want to know whether the *information disclosed in therapy sessions will be shared with others*. Because this type of information is personal, the client should be told the nature and extent of confidentiality (NASW, 1997, 1.07.e). This would include informing the client about general exceptions to confidentiality including general conditions under which disclosure might be legally required (see section on Discretion and Confidentiality, this chapter). It would include keeping the client apprised of the possibility that her case will be discussed among colleagues—regardless of whether the client's identity will be disclosed (Corey, Corey, & Callanan, 1988, p. 172)—or whether sessions will be observed or electronically recorded (ACA, 1995, B.3.c). It would also include informing the client about what information is to be sent to third-party payers such as insurance companies or managed care providers (ACA,

1995, D4). Clients would reasonably want to know what diagnostic classification is being sent into the insurance company as a condition of reimbursement by the company. For example, some clients may not want the classification "borderline personality disorder" to go on record.

It is understandable that therapists should wish to receive reimbursement from third-party payers for services provided, but they must remember that client information disclosed for these purposes belongs to the client. Therapists should first apprise the client of what information will be submitted to the third-party payer and receive the client's consent prior to submitting the information. It is also the therapist's responsibility to learn what information the third-party payer requires and tell the client as close to the start of therapy as possible (ACA, 1995, D.4). With this information, the client will have maximum autonomy to decide whether he wishes to pursue therapy in accordance with the requirements of a specific third-party payer or to pursue an alternative course.

Third, clients would reasonably want to know *how much the therapy will cost and when payment is due* (ACA, 1995, A.3.a). They would also want to know the length of time this commitment of time and money is likely to last. If there are limits to the number of sessions permitted, clients should also be told this (Corey et al., 1988, p. 172).

Fourth, clients would reasonably want to know their *therapists' credentials* and whether the therapists are qualified to address the specific problem for which the client seeks therapy (ACA, 1995, A.3.a). A therapist who fails to tell a client seeking treatment for bulimia about her lack of previous experience and background in the treatment of eating disorders places the client at risk of harm. This lack of candor exploits clients' trust by failing to correct false impressions clients are likely to have—in particular, that the therapist is qualified to address the problem.

In such a case, candor would require therapists' disclosure of lack of qualification. Still, therapists can expand their experiential base only by taking on new and different types of cases and all therapists must get their start somewhere. If a therapist believes that with consultation with colleagues and research, she has a reasonable chance of helping the client or at least of not placing the client in jeopardy, then candor would require that the therapist disclose this to the client, thereby leaving the choice to the client (Bayles, 1989, p. 71). In this way, the values of trust and autonomy are preserved.

Fifth, clients would reasonably want to know what *alternative treatments*, if any, are available. A therapist who proposes to treat a client's panic attack according to a cognitive-behavior modality should inform the client of other possible approaches, even if the alternatives are outside the purview of the therapist—for example, as in the case of drug therapy when the therapist is not licensed to prescribe drugs (Bayles, 1989, p. 85).

Sixth, clients would reasonably want to know whether *sessions will be electronically recorded or observed* (ACA, 1995, B.3.c). To record them without the client's prior express consent is to treat the client as an object that is manipulated. The therapist should understand that information disclosed by the client in the course of therapy is the client's possession with which she has entrusted the therapist. To duplicate this information electronically without the client's express, advance permission is to deprive the client of her autonomous control over her own property.

Seventh, clients would reasonably want to know *what information about the client has been placed on file* (NASW, 1997, 1.08.a). The therapist should tell the client of his right to such information. "It seems logical that counselors who are not willing to explain and to be open and honest with their clients, to the extent of allowing clients to see their own files, cannot expect to create an atmosphere and relationship of trust and safety" (Mappes, Robb, & Engels, 1985, p. 251).

There are some situations in which a virtuous counselor would arguably be justified in at least temporarily withholding client information despite the client's interest in knowing it. For example, if a client with a history of attempted suicide is experiencing suicidal ideation at a given time, the counselor might reasonably decide, out of consideration for the client's welfare, to withhold certain personal information requested by the client—for instance, the results of a psychological evaluation that the counselor believes would adversely affect the client's psychological state.

It is questionable, however, whether exceptions to candor like the one above are essential to preserving clients' trust in their counselors, as counselors who did not make such exceptions but instead maintained an unconditional policy of candor might arguably merit greater client trust.

Nevertheless, a policy of unconditional candor would inevitably run into conflicts with client welfare as in the case just noted. The disclosure of the results of a psychological evaluation to a suicidal client, who is likely to be further disturbed by those test results, might serve the client's *interest*—in knowing what the diagnosis is—without also serving the client's *welfare*. The virtuous therapist would be disposed toward respecting client interests, but he or she would realize that if knowing can harm the client, it would defeat the primary counseling mission of promoting client welfare.

This therapist may well regret having to surrender respect for the client's interests and she will not make withholding information a common practice. However, when the client's life hangs in the balance, the therapist will not stand on ceremony. On the other hand, out of consideration for the client's interest, the therapist will inform the client of his tests results as soon as the information can be safely disclosed without serious impunity to the client (Bayles, 1989, p. 83).

Clients not provided with these seven types of information cannot be said to have given informed consent to therapy. Because the therapeutic process itself aims at promoting clients' powers of self-directiveness and independence, the provision of therapy requires clients' informed consent as a condition of this central therapeutic goal. Obtaining clients' informed consent gives clients a voice in decisions concerning their own lives and thus supports and respects clients as autonomous agents.

Two other related conditions are absolutely essential for a client's consent to therapy to be valid legally as well as morally. In addition to being informed, such consent must also be *free of coercion*, and *competent*.

Mere provision of information to a client does not respect the client as a rational, autonomous agent. For a client's consent to therapy to serve this vital function, it must be *free and uncoerced* (APA, 1992, 4.02.a). Otherwise, it is manipulative and at odds with clients' autonomy. Threatening, intimidating, or frightening clients into submission does not constitute gaining their valid consent to therapy.

Informed, autonomous consent must also be competent consent. In this context, competence means that "the client is able to understand the nature of the procedure or course of treatment, the possible risks and benefits, and any other information relevant to treatment, such as confidentiality, fees, timing, counseling approach, and credentials of the counselor" (Anderson, 1996, p. 13). A cognitively impaired client who is unable to comprehend what is being explained to him does not give such consent. The client's impairment should not, however, remove the requirement for obtaining informed consent before treating an incompetent client. When the client has a legal guardian, the informed consent may be obtained from that guardian (APA, 1992, 4.02.b), assuming that the guardian represents the client's welfare and, as such, would reasonably want to know how the client is to be treated.

Because minors are also clients, the doctrine of informed consent applies to children to the extent of their capacity to comprehend (APA, 1992, 4.02.c). Treating children as objects who have no say in what happens to them can, no less than with adults, prevent the development of therapist-client trust and can destroy their sense of self-worth. While parents and legal guardians often have serious interest in the welfare of the minor client, the virtuous therapist does whatever is reasonably possible to protect client welfare, and does not, self-defeatingly, sacrifice minor clients' welfare in order to satisfy concerns of guardians.

If informed consent is to promote trust, autonomy, and ultimately the welfare of clients, it must be an ongoing process by which clients are kept adequately informed throughout the duration of therapy (ACA, 1995, A.3.a). Thus, information imparted to the client may require updating as therapy progresses. For example, the therapist should inform the client if she decides to try a different modality or to consult with another therapist.

Finally, the values of trust, autonomy, and welfare of client require that disclosure of information be made clearly so that clients understand it (APA, 1992, 4.02.a; 4.02.d). The therapist should not assume that the client understands technical distinctions; nor should she present the information in oversimplified ways, thereby creating misunderstandings. The manner of presentation will vary to some extent with the ability of the client to comprehend, but assuming that the client cannot understand or simply does not want to know tends to subvert the client's active participation in therapy. Therapists behaving this way treat the client as a passive object and thereby undermine the promotion of client autonomy.

The therapist may give the client information about fees and the nature of confidentiality in written form, but doing so cannot be assumed as gaining the client's informed consent. There may be no real consent if the client does not fully comprehend what she has read. Nor can the consent be considered freely given if a form is simply presented for signature without allowing clients the opportunity to consider and explore its contents carefully, both with and without the therapist. In the context of exploration, the therapist may ask the client to verbalize her understanding of specific items and correct any misunderstandings. Unless the therapist has reasonable belief that the client adequately understands the document, the consent cannot be considered valid.

Discretion

PRINCIPLE OF DISCRETION

Safeguard clients' confidences and avoid disclosure of confidential information without clients' fully informed and freely given consent.

• When counseling clients who are minors, or individuals who are unable to give voluntary, informed consent, parents or guardians may be included in the counseling process as appropriate. Counselors act in the best interests of clients and take measures to safeguard confidentiality (ACA, 1995, B.3).

• Counselors make every effort to ensure that privacy and confidentiality of clients are maintained by subordinates, including employees, supervisees, clerical assistants, and volunteers (ACA, 1995, B.1.h).

• Counselors are responsible for securing the safety and confidentiality of any counseling records they create, maintain, transfer, or destroy whether the records are written, taped, computerized, or stored in any other medium (ACA, 1995, B.4.b).

• It is the responsibility of the human service worker to protect the integrity, safety, and security of client records. With the exception of the supervisory relationship, all client information that is shared with other professionals must have the client's prior written consent (NOHSE, 1994, 1.6).

• The general requirement that counselors keep information confidential does not apply when disclosure is required to prevent clear and imminent danger to the client or others or when legal requirements demand that confidential information be revealed. Counselors consult with other professionals when in doubt as to the validity of an exception (ACA, 1995, B.1.c).

• A counselor who receives information confirming that a client has a disease commonly known to be both communicable and fatal is justified in disclosing information to an identifiable third party, who by his or her relationship with the client is at a high risk of contracting the disease. Prior to making a disclosure the counselor should ascertain that the client has not already informed the third party about his or her disease and that the client is not intending to inform the third party in the immediate future (ACA, 1995, B.1.d).

• When court ordered to release confidential information without a client's permission, counselors request to the court that the disclosure not be required due to potential harm to the client or counseling relationship (ACA, 1995, B.1.e).

- When circumstances require the disclosure of confidential information, only essential information is revealed. To the extent possible, clients are informed before confidential information is disclosed (ACA, 1995, B.1.f).
- Social workers should not disclose identifying information when discussing clients with consultants unless the client has consented to disclosure of confidential information or there is a compelling need for such disclosure (NASW, 1997, 1.07.q).
- Use of data derived from counseling relationships for purposes of training, research, or publication is confined to content that is disguised to ensure the anonymity of the individuals involved (ACA, 1995, B.5.a).
- Social workers should not discuss confidential information in any setting unless privacy can be ensured. Social workers should not discuss confidential information in public or semipublic areas such as hallways, waiting rooms, elevators, and restaurants (NASW, 1997, 1.07.i).
- In group work, counselors clearly define confidentiality and the parameters for the specific group being entered, explain its importance, and discuss the difficulties related to confidentiality involved in group work. The fact that confidentiality cannot be guaranteed is clearly communicated to group members (ACA, 1995, B.2.a).
- In family counseling, information about one family member cannot be disclosed to another member without permission. Counselors protect the privacy rights of each family member (ACA, 1995, B.2.b).

DISCRETION AND CONFIDENTIALITY

The discreet professional respects the privacy of the client by not disclosing information about the client. Bayles (1989, p. 96) uses the term *discretion* to include information that is a matter of public record as well as information that is, strictly speaking, confidential—learned from the client in the course of therapy. On this broad use, the discreet therapist would be disposed not to speak openly to others about what has transpired in a court proceeding in which one of his clients was a litigant, even though such information was a matter of public record. In this book, we use the term *discretion* in a manner compatible with this broad sense although our focus is on discretion exercised with respect to information that is learned from clients in the course of therapy.

From the perspective of promoting clients' welfare, interests, and needs, therapists' discreet handling of such confidential information is of primary importance. In many cases, clients come to therapy with personal problems they are reluctant to share with anybody, including the therapist. Without reasonable assurance that their therapists will respect their confidentiality, these clients would probably not tell their therapists the whole truth; or they would not seek therapy in the first place. On the other hand, when clients can trust their therapists to respect confidentiality, the probability is substantially improved that they will become more self-disclosing and therapy can progress meaningfully.

In the context of therapy, clients' control of information about themselves is an expression of personal autonomy or self-determination. As therapy aims to promote client autonomy, a therapist's breach of confidentiality is counterproductive and self-defeating. In Kantian terms, the client so treated is reduced to "a mere means" or object that is manipulated. No rational person, including the therapist herself, would ordinarily consent to being treated this way, so therapist's behavior portends a model of inconsistency and double standards, not one of trustworthiness.

Violating clients' autonomy presupposes a nonconsenting client. When the client freely gives his informed consent to the disclosure, it is not a breach or betrayal of trust but rather the client's autonomous expression. Discreet therapists will thus be disposed against disclosing clients' confidences when such disclosure is without clients' consent (ACA, 1995, B.1.f).

This does not mean that a discreet therapist will never disclose confidential client information without client consent. As we have seen, the avoidance of harm to third parties as well as to clients falls within the purview of the primary purpose of counseling. When a client is intent on killing or otherwise seriously injuring himself or someone else, a therapist's disclosure of confidential information to the extent necessary to stop the assault may be warranted (ACA, 1995, B.1.c). In addition, as we shall see (Chapter 10), such disclosure may be warranted when a sexually active client who has tested positive for the human immunodeficiency virus (HIV) jeopardizes the welfare of an unsuspecting, identifiable sexual partner (ACA, 1995, B.1.d).

These occasions for disclosing confidential information assume, however, that the other person is vulnerable to the harm in question and is thus unable to escape it on his own without help from the therapist. There is a vulnerability principle undergirding justified disclosures: In the provision of counseling services, the therapist has a moral responsibility to protect from harm all those who are vulnerable or dependent on the therapist's actions or decisions. On the other hand, third parties who take calculated risks or behave in reckless ways are not considered vulnerable in these cases as they can foresee or comprehend the risk of harm without help from the therapist. If disclosure of confidential information without client consent impedes *client* welfare, the responsibility of third parties to protect themselves, when they are reasonably situated to do so, cannot be dismissed (Cohen, 1995, pp. 240–242).

A candid therapist will not consult with other professionals without informing the client of this possibility when therapy is initiated. Even with client authorization, disclosure need only include information that is essential for receiving an informed opinion from the consultant (NASW, 1997, 1.07.q; ACA, 1995, B.1.f). The name of the client or other identifying facts may well be irrelevant and should not be disclosed.

It is not unusual for therapists associated with agencies to disclose information about clients at staff meetings. In this context, a discreet therapist will again avoid disclosure of any information that is not germane to the purposes at hand. A client's case may still be constructively discussed without mention of her name or other identifying information.

Office staff and paraprofessionals who work with therapists may have legitimate reasons for being granted access to confidential client information; the discreet therapist will strive to safeguard client confidences by helping to educate these personnel about the confidentiality of client information (ACA, 1995, B.1.h).

Discreet therapists will not share their client's cases with acquaintances, friends, family, or others who have no professional expertise or need to know. Nor will they discuss their cases in public places—for example, in the lunchroom where information can be overheard (NASW, 1997, 1.07.i). Such acts show disregard for clients' welfare and for clients' trust in their therapists.

Discreet therapists will not use their clients' confidences as a source of comic relief from the stresses of their professional life. They will not joke about their clients or ridicule them to others. Such behavior is inconsistent with empathetic regard for clients' problems; as the client can be presumed to be nonconsenting, it is also a breach of confidentiality. From a Kantian perspective, it is to treat the client as a "mere means," as an object of ridicule; no rational being, including the therapist, would consent to this treatment. Professional life may be rife with stress, but the discreet therapist will find other ways to deal with it.

Discreet therapists will also not misuse data obtained from counseling relationships for purposes of training, research, or publication (ACA, 1995, B.5.a). Data gathered through work with clients can be instrumental toward advancing the counseling knowledge base, but such advances should not involve violating the privacy of clients. In disseminating their findings, therapists should avoid disclosure of personal client information by carefully disguising any details that might reveal clients' identities. A client's name, place of employment, and residence may easily be changed without defeating didactic purposes. From a Kantian perspective, disclosure of identifying details for purposes of advancing counseling could not consistently be turned into a universal law as no one would then submit himself or herself to counseling. The practice would destroy the very trust that made advances in counseling possible in the first place.

The confidential treatment of client information learned in the course of therapy also has legal as well as moral standing. Hence, indiscreet therapists may also confront civil as well as criminal liability for mishandling confidential client information.

In some states this information is legally protected as privileged communication by statute, meaning that, as a rule, it may not be disclosed in a court of law without the client's consent. According to Florida statute, for example, "a patient has a privilege to refuse to disclose, and to prevent any other person from disclosing, confidential communications or records made for the purpose of diagnosis or treatment of his mental or emotional condition" (Florida Rules of Evidence, Title VII, 90.503[2]).

Note, however, that such privilege is not absolute and may not be legally recognized under certain conditions. For example, according to Florida statute, there is no privilege for "communications relevant to an issue of the mental or emotional condition of the patient in any proceeding in which he relies upon the condition as an element of his claim or defense" (Florida Rules of Evidence, Title VII, 90.503[4]).

In general, in states where privileged communication is recognized, privilege may still not apply under conditions such as the following (Anderson, 1996; Knapp & Vandecreek, 1985; Shah, 1969):

- The state orders a mental examination of the client.
- The client initiates a malpractice suit against the therapist or brings the therapist before a state agency such as a licensing board.
- Parents make their mental health an issue in situations such as a custody suit.
- Child abuse is suspected.
- The client has already disclosed the information to or in the presence of a third party such as a friend or associate.
- The client voluntarily testifies or authorizes disclosure.
- The therapist has to disclose confidential information for purposes of self-protection.

Recently, support for recognizing privileged communication in the federal courts has been provided in the case of *Jaffee v. Redmond* (1996). In this case concerning a policewoman who was in counseling after fatally shooting a suspect, the therapist, a licensed clinical social worker, refused to disclose confidential client information to a trial court. On hearing, the United States Supreme Court ruled in favor of recognizing privilege between psychotherapist and client. According to the majority opinion as delivered by Justice Stevens, there are private as well as public interests served by recognition of privileged communication between a psychotherapist and her client that override any evidentiary benefits accruing through required court disclosure. Because successful psychiatric treatment assumes an environment in which clients feel free to speak openly, protection of confidential communications as privileged serves important private interests. On the other hand, the psychotherapist privilege also serves the public interest by promoting the mental health of citizens, which is a "public good of transcendent importance." The Court's ruling was explicitly extended to psychologists, psychiatrists, and social workers; whether it also extends to other therapists such as licensed mental health counselors still remains to be seen. However, according to Remley et al. (1997, p. 216), there is a "substantial possibility" that licensed counselors who practice in states that have statutes recognizing counselor-client privilege and that consider counselors to be psychotherapists will be afforded privilege in federal as well as state courts.

In states where privileged communication is not explicitly provided for by statute, courts may nevertheless grant privilege when the public interest in protecting privacy is deemed to outweigh the court's legitimate interest in obtaining the information. According to Anderson (1996), four standards have been applied by courts in determining whether privilege should be extended:

1. The communications must originate in confidence that they will not be disclosed.
2. The element of confidentiality must be essential to the full and satisfactory maintenance of the relationship between the parties.
3. The relation must be one which, in the opinion of the community, ought to be sedulously fostered.
4. The injury that would inure to the relation by the disclosure of the communications must be greater than the benefit thereby gained for the correct disposal of litigation.

In states where privilege is explicitly granted by statute, a therapist would not be in contempt of court by refusing to comply with a subpoena issued to obtain confidential client information. Even in jurisdictions where privilege does not exist, a therapist has the legal option of filing a motion to protect the information as confidential, a motion that may or may not be honored by the court. The discreet therapist will therefore need to be aware of this option as well as the legal status of privilege in the jurisdiction in which she is practicing. Knowing this status and being concerned about protecting client welfare, a therapist will not unnecessarily or prematurely divulge the requested information (ACA, 1995, B.1.e). Nor will the discreet therapist normally disclose any more information than has been requested, adhering instead to the policy of keeping disclosure to a bare minimum (ACA, 1995, B.1.f).

Whether or not privileged communication is explicitly recognized, state statutes routinely permit disclosure of confidential information in order to prevent death or serious bodily injury to the client or another person. Similarly, case law has also recognized such limits to confidentiality. According to the landmark decision in *Tarasoff*, "the privacy ends where the public peril begins." When probable harm to a third party exists, the therapist is held to have a legal duty to warn the relevant person or to detain the dangerous client (*Tarasoff v. Regents of the University of California*, 1976). Further, a legal duty to prevent harm to others may still exist according to an "unidentifiable but foreseeable standard" where the client poses "a danger to the public in general rather than to any particular individual" (Pietrofesa et al., 1990, p. 132).

Similar limits to confidentiality have also been recognized in codes of professional ethics (for example, ACA, 1995, B.1.c). However, while codes, statutes, and case law help to clarify the nature and limits of confidentiality, these sources generally set minimum standards of discretion. A therapist operating below these has violated a legal or professional duty. Even so, the codes may fail to address significant areas in which questions about discretion are raised (Mabe & Rollins, 1986). On the other hand, the discreet therapist is guided by standards of excellence that go beyond what is codified or legally required. Thus, for example, a therapist may not be guilty of a legal violation when he discloses facts about his clients that are a matter of public record anyway; or when he jokes about his clients at a staffing; or when, even with the consent of the client, he discloses more than he really needs to disclose. Nevertheless, a discreet therapist would be disposed against doing such things.

In the context of group therapy, the moral responsibility to respect confidentiality extends beyond the therapist to each group participant. Each group member shares intimate, personal information with the others, and each is dependent on the others for maintaining privacy. From a Kantian view, a universal law in which group members did not maintain confidentiality outside the group would be impossible as no one would then share secrets in the group. Moreover, no reasonable group members would want their own secrets disclosed outside the group and so could not consistently justify similar treatment of others. ("Because you won't want others repeating what you say, then don't do it to others.") From a utilitarian view, outside disclosure can chill inside disclosure. ("We're all in it together. The group will work best when *all* cooperate.")

It is, in turn, the group leader's moral responsibility to explain these rationales for maintaining confidentiality. However, maintenance of confidentiality depends on mutual cooperation, so the candid group leader will also make clear that confidentiality cannot be guaranteed (ACA, 1995, B.2.a).

In the context of family therapy, therapists have a moral responsibility to respect the privacy of each family member and thus should not disclose information to one family member about another family member without the other's permission (ACA, 1995, B.2.b). Although marriage and family therapy cannot function without consideration of family dynamics, the inherent dignity of each family member as client must also be preserved in the process. Respect for the privacy of each is a necessary condition of such respect.

Secretivism in family and couple relationships tends to impede therapeutic progress, so some marriage and family therapists subscribe to a policy of nonsecrecy according to which each client is informed at the start of therapy that no secrets will be kept from other family members, or that any information obtained in the course of therapy may be disclosed to other family members at the discretion of the therapist (Huber, 1994). However, while marriage and family therapists have unique confidentiality concerns, such therapists still have a professional responsibility to "respect and guard confidences of each individual client" (American Association for Marriage and Family Therapy, 1991). Although a policy of nonsecretivism made known to all family members at the start of therapy may be consistent with the principle of candor, such a policy can also undermine the primary counseling mission by chilling prospects of significant disclosure.

Insofar as such a policy gives therapists power to determine whether and to what extent personal information about one family member will be disclosed to another family member, such a policy subverts client autonomy. Family members, including partners, are clients in their own right, ends in themselves, and as such deserve to be treated as autonomous, self-determining persons no less than any other clients.

Professional Competence

PRINCIPLE OF BENEFICENCE
Provide counseling services qualitatively consistent with the types of training, ability, and skills that promote clients' positive psychological growth, relief from frustration and unhappiness, and the diverse, related ends for which therapy may be sought.

• Counselors accept employment only for positions for which they are qualified by education, training, supervised experience, state and national professional credentials, and appropriate professional experience. Counselors hire for professional counseling positions only individuals who are qualified and competent (ACA, 1995, C.2.c).

• Counselors practice in specialty areas new to them only after appropriate education, training, and supervised experience. While developing skills in new specialty areas, counselors take steps to ensure the competence of their work and to protect others from possible harm (ACA, 1995, C.2.b).

• Where differences of age, gender, race, ethnicity, national origin, religion, sexual orientation, disability, language, or socioeconomic status significantly affect psychologists' work concerning particular individuals or groups, psychologists obtain the training, experience, consultation, or supervision necessary to ensure the competence of their services, or they make appropriate referrals (APA, 1992, 1.08).

• Counselors will actively attempt to understand the diverse cultural backgrounds of the clients with whom they work. This includes but is not limited to learning how the counselor's own cultural/ethnic/racial identity impacts her/his values and beliefs about the counseling process (ACA, 1995, A.2.b).

• Counselors recognize the limits of their competence and perform only those testing assessment services for which they have been trained (ACA, 1995, E.2.a).

• Human service workers should know the limit and scope of their professional knowledge and seek consultation, supervision, and/or referrals when appropriate (NOHSE, 1994, 5.1).

• Counselors take reasonable steps to consult with other counselors or related professionals when they have questions regarding their ethical obligations or professional practice (ACA, 1995, C.2.e).

• When generally recognized standards do not exist with respect to an emerging area of practice, social workers should exercise careful judgment and take responsible steps (including appropriate education, research, training, consultation, and supervision) to ensure the competence of their work and to protect clients from harm (NASW, 1997, 1.04.c).

• Social workers should strive to become and remain proficient in professional practice and the performance of professional functions. Social workers should critically examine, and keep current with, emerging knowledge relevant to social work. Social workers should routinely review professional literature and participate in continuing education relevant to social work practice and social work ethics (NASW, 1997, 4.01.b).

COMPETENCE, BENEVOLENCE, AND BENEFICENCE

Obviously, an incompetent therapist is not trustworthy, as a therapist who lacks skill cannot be counted on to promote client welfare. An incompetent therapist is one without the skill, ability, or qualifications needed to address the client's problem effectively. Incompetence also includes "failure to recognize one's fallibility and limitations as a professional and as a person" (Van Hoose & Kottler, 1985, p. 109).

Although Bayles maintains that, strictly speaking, competence is not a moral virtue (1989, p. 84), it can be taken to be both a professional and a moral virtue when it is understood to imply not merely the possession of certain skills, abilities, and qualifications but also the habitual practice of them. As discussed in Chapter 2, counseling virtues are moral virtues insofar as they are instruments of human welfare; and they are professional virtues insofar as they are conditions of viable therapy. Because competence, at least in a sense implying habitual practice, fits both these descriptions, it may therefore be regarded as both a professional and a moral virtue. Moreover, like other moral virtues such as honesty, it can also be valued for its own sake as when a professional takes pride in the rendering of competent services even when such services fail to help the client.

Therapeutic competence is linked to the moral virtue of benevolence. Benevolence may be defined as a habit or disposition "to do good for others when reasonably situated, and to do no harm," this concern for the welfare of others being "for its own sake." Moreover, benevolent therapists are disposed toward "feeling certain ways under certain conditions" such as feeling sorrow at another's misfortune or pleasure in helping a client (Cohen, 1988, p. 84). In the context of therapy, benevolence would seem to imply affective virtues such as empathy and unconditional positive regard (see Chapter 3).

To benefit another, one must first have the requisite knowledge and understanding. Thus benevolence requires competence. A benevolent therapist must know what type of therapy is likely to fit the specific needs of individual clients. Thus, one client, a very young child, may be a good candidate for play therapy whereas an adult client may be a more appropriate candidate for cognitive-behavior therapy. Because benevolent therapists want to benefit their clients and not harm them, they will tend to gather and examine the facts at hand carefully, choosing among alternative treatment plans on the basis of these facts.

Benevolent therapists will be disposed toward applying knowledge and skills toward benefiting clients; such therapists will also be disposed toward having intrinsic regard for the welfare of other human beings, whether or not they are clients. Such regard is intrinsic insofar as it is motivated by the desire to help or avoid harming others rather than by ulterior motives such as the desire for money or fame. Benevolent therapists will normally be motivated by this intrinsic regard to try, within reason, to prevent foreseeable, substantial harm to third parties as well as to clients and will feel remorse when such harm does occur.

Benevolence should be distinguished from the related notion of *beneficence*. Whereas benevolence refers to a virtue involving a disposition of intrinsic regard for the welfare of others, beneficence generally refers to a moral principle according to which one should act to benefit others (Frankena, 1973, p. 64). The term *benefit* refers to increase of positive good or welfare as well as removal or reduction of negative welfare. Thus virtuous therapists subscribe to this moral principle insofar as they work toward helping their clients attain to greater pleasure and less pain and suffering in living.

Because beneficent acts in the context of therapy are most likely to occur when therapists possess relevant knowledge and training in counseling (techniques, interventions, theories, etc.), therapists should, as a general rule, accept employment only in areas in which they are qualified (ACA, 1995, C.2.c). It is one thing to have read and studied a subject matter in graduate school and quite another to have actually practiced such knowledge. It is one thing to have read about dissociative identity disorder (DID) and another to have success-fully counseled someone with this disorder. Accordingly, the requisite sense of being qualified might arguably be taken to include practical experience as well as theoretical grounding.

On the other hand, therapists increase their boundaries of expertise through actual practice. Whereas candor to the client requires disclosure of lack of prac-tical or theoretical grounding, it may not always be inappropriate for a thera-pist to take a case in an area in which she lacks practical experience provided the therapist has taken adequate precautions such as seeking competent super-vision (ACA, 1995, C.2.b).

Similarly, as a profession grows, there will be times when there may not yet be settled standards governing practice in the new area. If standards are to emerge, therapists and related professionals must help define them through their practice, research, and sharing of insights and experiences. In the past decade and a half, as a result of the onslaught of HIV, challenges for counselors have emerged requiring new understandings. According to Odets (1995), "dealing with terminal illness and bereavement are common problems that, in AIDS-afflicted communities, demand modified—and sometimes radically new—conceptualizations if clinical interventions are to be appropriate and helpful for gay and bisexual men living in the epidemic" (p. 3).

As a further example, research and development in genetic science has given rise to genetic counseling, and as this area continues to develop—for example, as our understanding of psychogenetics broadens and as new genetic technolo-gies emerge—further challenges for therapists will arise. In such uncharted ter-ritory where settled standards do not yet exist, therapists must be guided by moral sensitivity for the welfare, interests, and needs of their clients, proceed-ing cautiously, making their contributions through practice enlightened by appropriate education, research, training, consultation, and supervision (NASW, 1997, 1.04.c).

In addition to competence in applying therapeutic techniques and interven-tions, beneficence in the context of therapy may also require knowledge and understanding of human differences such as those related to culture, ethnicity, gender, age, religion, sexual orientation, and socioeconomic status (APA, 1992, 1.08). It is a grandiose error to classify distinct individuals according to broad stereotypes; however, a therapist could also act imprudently by failing to com-prehend culturally significant human differences. For instance, knowledge of Oriental attitudes about male and female gender roles might help a therapist better understand why her Chinese client defers to her husband when she is addressed (see, for example, the case of Suki in Chapter 1 under Descriptive Ethics). This, in turn, might help the therapist avoid misreading such deference. The principle of beneficence accordingly supports multicultural training for therapists.

Competent therapists will also realize that competence includes awareness of available client resources. Competence is relative to available resources. For example, competent health care in the 18th century is not likely to be competent in the 21st century because of health care advances. Competence requires updating of knowledge and skills. Competent therapists will therefore keep current on the literature in their profession and will periodically update their knowledge and skills by attending pertinent continuing education programs (NASW, 1997, 4.01.b).

Nonmaleficence

PRINCIPLE OF NONMALEFICENCE
In provision of counseling services, safeguard the welfare of others, including nonclients, through noninfliction and prevention of pain and suffering.

• The social worker should under no circumstances engage in sexual activities or sexual contact with current clients, whether such contact is consensual or forced (NASW, 1997, 1.09.a).
• Social workers should not engage in sexual activities or sexual contact with former clients because of the potential for harm to the client. If social workers engage in conduct contrary to this prohibition or claim that an exception to this prohibition is warranted because of extraordinary circumstances, it is social workers—not their clients—who assume the full burden of demonstrating that the former client has not been exploited, coerced, or manipulated, intentionally or unintentionally (NASW, 1997, 1.09.c).
• Social workers should not provide clinical services to individuals with whom they have had a prior sexual relationship. Providing clinical services to a former sexual partner has the potential to be harmful to the individual and is likely to make it difficult for the social worker and individual to maintain appropriate professional boundaries (NASW, 1997, 1.09.d).
• Counselors do not engage in sexual harassment. Sexual harassment is defined as sexual solicitation, physical advances, or verbal or nonverbal conduct that is sexual in nature, that occurs in connection with professional activities or roles, and that either (1) is unwelcome, is offensive, or creates a hostile workplace environment, and counselors know or are told this; or (2) is sufficiently severe or intense to be perceived as harassment to a reasonable person in the context. Sexual harassment can consist of a single intense or severe act or multiple persistent or pervasive acts (ACA, 1995, C.5.b).
• If it is suspected that danger or harm may occur to the client or to others, it is the responsibility of the human service worker to act in such a manner to prevent such from occurring. This may involve seeking consultation, supervision, and/or breaking the confidentiality of the relationship (NOHSE, 1994 , 1.4).
• Counselors refrain from offering or accepting professional services when their physical, mental, or emotional problems are likely to harm a client or others. They are alert to the signs of impairment, seek assistance for prob-

lems, and, if necessary, limit, suspend, or terminate their professional responsibilities (ACA, 1995, C.2.g).
• In a group setting, counselors take reasonable precautions to protect clients from physical or psychological trauma (ACA, 1995, A.9.b).

NONMALEFICENCE, NONMALEVOLENCE, AND DUE CARE

Nonmaleficence generally refers to a moral principle according to which one should avoid harm to others, whereas *nonmalevolence* refers to a moral virtue that also includes the lack of malicious intent or motive (Beauchamp & Childress, 1979, p. 98). We include, under the somewhat ambiguous term *nonmaleficence*, both the prevention and noninfliction of harm. Whereas the principle of beneficence supports means of advancing client welfare, the principle of nonmaleficence supports means of avoiding—preventing or not inflicting—harm to others, including nonclients. Note, however, that failure to comply with the principle of beneficence can result in violation of the principle of nonmaleficence. This is true because therapists who fail to recognize the limits of their competence jeopardize client welfare. In this regard, the principle of nonmaleficence also requires respect for the principle of beneficence.

More generally, nonmaleficence requires due care not to place the lives of others at risk of harm. In regard to client welfare, due care extends to respect for professional and legal standards of knowledge, skills, and diligence that have been established for the protection of clients (Beauchamp & Childress, 1979, p. 100). Such standards of due care include state practice laws requiring a minimum level of training (education, degrees, and experience) to practice in a given professional area (mental health, social work, psychology, etc.). They also include professional and legal standards defining the scope of permissible professional relationships.

State laws as well as professional codes of ethics (for example, NASW, 1997, 1.09.a; 1.09.d, respectively) typically forbid sexual activities with current clients or therapy with former sexual partners. Some states proscribe sexual relations with former clients "into perpetuity" (for example, Florida, DPR, Rule Chapter 21CC-10.003); some codes of ethics require a minimum 2-year waiting period after cessation of professional services (ACA, 1995, A.7.b; APA, 1992, 4.07.a). The rationale for such proscriptions against sexual relationships with former clients is to prevent exploitation. As noted earlier (Chapter 2), therapists have intimate knowledge, power, and influence with respect to those for whom they are providing, and have provided, professional services. Consequently, they have a moral responsibility to use their knowledge and power in a manner consonant with the welfare of both client and former client alike. Therapists contemplating sexual relations with former clients should keep in view the potential for serious exploitation if the knowledge and power they acquired through the professional relationship is transferred to a personal, emotionally charged, sexual relationship.

The blending of sexual and professional roles is sometimes referred to as sexual dual-role relationships. As such relationships can have serious potential to harm clients, therapists engaging in them breach nonmaleficence. However, as these relationships pose conflicts of interest for therapists, which in turn threaten client welfare, they also constitute breaches of loyalty. They are therefore considered in this chapter under the principle of loyalty, and they are also examined in greater detail in Chapter 6 on dual-role relationships.

Nonmaleficence also extends to therapists' treatment of clients, employees, or others with whom they work. For example, therapists have a recognized professional as well as legal responsibility to abstain from engaging in verbal and nonverbal conduct that would likely be perceived as sexual harassment by a reasonable person to whom such conduct is directed (ACA, 1995, C.5.b; *Ellison v. Brady*, 924 F.2d. 872 [1991]). Nonmaleficence also extends this responsibility beyond the work environment to the personal lives of therapists. Therapists who engage in unwelcome or offensive sexual conduct outside as well as inside the professional context make a mockery of the counseling mission to regard the welfare of others; and they damage the profession itself by contributing to a chilling stereotype of therapists as sexually unstable and hence not truly worthy of clients' trust.

Diligence

PRINCIPLE OF DILIGENCE
Provide reliable, careful counseling services.

• Counselors do not abandon or neglect clients in counseling. Counselors assist in making appropriate arrangements for the continuation of treatment, when necessary, during interruptions such as vacations, and following termination (ACA, 1995, A.11.a).
• Psychologists discuss with clients or patients as early as is feasible in the therapeutic relationship appropriate issues, such as the nature and anticipated course of therapy, fees, and confidentiality (APA, 1992, 4.01.a.).
• Counselors maintain records necessary for rendering professional services to their clients and as required by laws, regulations, or agency or institution procedures (ACA, 1995, B.4.a).
• Counselors are responsible for securing the safety and confidentiality of any counseling records they create, maintain, transfer, or destroy whether the records are written, taped, computerized, or stored in any other medium (ACA, 1995, B.4.b).
• Psychologists provide proper training and supervision to their employees or supervisees and take reasonable steps to see that such persons perform services responsibly, competently, and ethically (APA, 1992, 1.22.b).
• Counselors take special care to provide proper diagnosis of mental disorders. Assessment techniques (including personal interview) used to determine client care (e.g., locus of treatment, type of treatment, or recommended follow-up) are carefully selected and appropriately used (ACA, 1995, E.5.a).

• Social workers should work to improve employing agencies' policies and procedures, and the efficiency and effectiveness of their services (NASW, 1997, 3.09.b).

• Social workers should be diligent stewards of the resources of their employing organizations, wisely conserving funds where appropriate and never misappropriating funds for unintended purposes (NASW, 1997, 3.09.g).

• Human services professionals promote cooperation among related disciplines (e.g., psychology, counseling, social work, nursing, family and consumer sciences, medicine, education) to foster professional growth and interests with the various fields (NOHSE, 1994, 29).

• Counselors alert their employers to conditions that may be potentially disruptive or damaging to the counselor's professional responsibilities or that may limit their effectiveness (ACA, 1995, D.1.c).

DILIGENCE AND THE PROMOTION OF CLIENT WELFARE

Benevolent therapists are also diligent. As morally responsible agents, they are disposed toward genuinely caring about their clients' welfare to the extent that counseling activities are carefully geared toward accomplishing this end. The term *diligent* applies only to therapists who actually make such an effort. A therapist who, out of forgetfulness or negligence, compromises a client's welfare does not act diligently, even though he may not have intended the harmful result. Thus, having good intentions and being diligent are not the same.

According to Bayles (1989, p. 86), professionals may be competent and still fail to be diligent. For example, a poor diagnosis can result from carelessness as well as incompetence. Thus, professional competence in the sense of possessing the knowledge and ability to help clients does not guarantee professional diligence as it does not assure the efficient application of such knowledge toward helping the client.

As a habit, diligent therapists will make and keep client records (ACA, 1995, B.4.a). In making and keeping records, a diligent therapist shall be guided primarily by concern for clients' welfare. "Self-protection should not be the primary motivation for keeping routine counseling records" (Remley, 1990, p. 164). However, most states require therapists to keep counseling records and failure to do so has sometimes resulted in license suspension. Failure to keep adequate records may also be grounds for malpractice because it violates a standard of due care (Anderson, 1996).

Counseling records should include information that may be of use in helping clients—for example, notes describing what transpired in the session as well as therapists' own observations, hypotheses, and evaluations. Having made such notes for therapeutic purposes, diligent therapists will review them in a timely manner. They will examine these notes prior to and in preparation for the next session, thereby permitting more efficient use of session time. This behavior also conveys to clients, through therapists' ability to recall details of previous sessions, an attitude of care and consideration that promotes client trust.

Diligent therapists will maintain accurate financial records; these records may be instrumental in helping the client secure deserved reimbursement from insurance companies for services rendered. They may, at the discretion of the therapist or counseling facility, be kept separate from counseling records (Anderson, 1996).

As stated by the ACA (1995, B.4.b), "Counselors are responsible for securing the safety and confidentiality" of counseling records. The advent of new computer technology has created new challenges for the protection of records. Computers connected to networks make records stored on one computer accessible through other computers connected to the same network. Security systems, use of passwords, and institutional policies defining information access and protection may help to safeguard records, but no system can ever be completely secure. "Humans are usually the most susceptible point in any security scheme. A worker who is malicious, careless, or unaware of an organization's information policy can compromise the best security" (Comer, 1995, p. 473). Leaving a password where it can be accessed by others can defeat the point of having security in the first place. It is therefore necessary that therapists take reasonable steps to see that they as well as their employees and any personnel they supervise act "responsibly, competently, and ethically" in the protection of client records (APA, 1992, 1.22.b). At the least, this requires that clear policies regarding access and protection of client records be established and that those who are granted access to such information be made aware of these policies.

James P. Sampson, Jr. (1996) has outlined four recommendations that may be built into an institutional policy regarding computer storage of client records:

1. Confidential information should not be maintained on a computer system that can be generally accessed through a computer network.
2. Identification information for computer accounts containing client data needs to be considered confidential and treated as such.
3. Account names and corresponding passwords for confidential data should be kept obscure to decrease the likelihood of unauthorized access.
4. Passwords for accounts containing client data should be changed regularly to limit exposure if security is compromised.

Limiting access to confidential client records through computer networks can reduce risk of unauthorized access, but expecting large organizations such as major insurance and managed care providers to process mass quantities of client information efficiently without the aid of extensive computer networks is probably unrealistic. With today's technological realities, these companies must maintain well-defined and carefully administered policies for accessing and protecting the confidential client information entrusted to them. Individual therapists also have a moral responsibility to avoid entrusting confidential client information to companies that are lax in protecting the privacy of such information.

Therapists may receive speedier reimbursements from insurance and managed care companies when client information is electronically transferred to company computers via the Internet, as opposed to mailing the information in a sealed envelope. However, with electronic transfer, therapists increase the risk that confidential information will be accessed by unauthorized listeners while transfers across networks are in progress. The discreet and diligent therapist will not risk unauthorized intrusions into client privacy for the sake of self-serving purposes, such as more timely reimbursement for services rendered.

The diligent therapist will maintain accessibility to clients through such means as answering services, beepers, and answering machines. Moreover, the therapist will check messages and return calls in a timely manner. Otherwise, the therapist will be unreliable and thus unworthy of clients' trust.

The diligent therapist will avoid canceling and rescheduling appointments, especially for personal reasons. Occasional appointment cancellations and changes for personal reasons can be justified because therapists too have private lives, but the diligent therapist will do everything she can reasonably do to stay on schedule and maintain continuity of therapy for the client's sake (ACA, 1995, A.11.a).

The diligent therapist will not shorten one client's time in order to see another client. This may require taking on fewer clients and hence making less money, but the diligent therapist will hold the welfare of individual clients as the primary and overriding consideration. Similarly, the diligent therapist will not make clients wait an excessive length of time for an appointment. If a therapist cannot accommodate a client in due time, she will make a suitable referral.

The primary purpose of diagnosing mental disorders is to promote client welfare. A diligent therapist will therefore take care in formulating diagnoses, realizing that they can be useful in guiding subsequent courses of treatment (ACA, 1995, E.5.a). Notwithstanding the therapist's reasonable desire to collect from an insurance company, a diligent therapist will not make a diagnosis on intake without sufficient evidence to warrant the diagnosis. Otherwise, the therapist acts negligently and violates the primary mission of safeguarding client welfare.

In their work as employees of agencies, diligent therapists will define efficiency of agency practices in terms of their conduciveness to client welfare, and they will work toward improving such efficiency as far as is feasible (ACA, 1995, D.1.c.). Diligent therapists will be mindful of wasteful or frivolous use of scarce agency money and resources and will work through appropriate agency channels and, if necessary, by taking other appropriate political action, to increase agency efficiency as defined (NASW, 1997, 3,09.b; 3.09.g). For example, in government-funded agencies in which case workers are inadequately trained or are being assigned more cases than they can reasonably accommodate, therapists—including but not limited to employees of the affected agencies—have a moral responsibility to work through appropriate political channels to see that more funds are allocated for human services. Activities might include lobbying at state legislative sessions, writing letters to congressional representatives, and supporting cooperative efforts by state and national professional associations to effect government change.

Diligent therapists also realize that the human services system cannot function at its best to serve clients' welfare, interests, and needs when there is lack of cooperation between various groups of human services workers. Thus, "turf battles" between psychologists, mental health counselors, and social workers can lead to professional resentment and alienation. In the end, the clients suffer when legal barriers supported by one group over another circumscribe the range of valid therapeutic options accessible to clients. Diligent therapists will therefore strive to promote professional growth and interests among related disciplines rather than self-defeating competition (NOHSE, 1994, 29).

Loyalty

PRINCIPLE OF LOYALTY

Maintain independence of judgment when acting in matters related to clients' treatment.

• Social workers should be alert to and avoid conflicts of interest that interfere with the exercise of professional discretion and impartial judgment. Social workers should inform clients when a real or potential conflict of interest arises and take reasonable steps to resolve the issue in a manner that makes the clients' interests primary and protects clients' interests to the greatest extent possible. Occasionally, protecting clients' interests may require termination of the professional relationship with proper referral of the client (NASW, 1997, 1.06.a).

• Psychologists recognize that personal problems and conflicts may interfere with professional effectiveness. Accordingly, they refrain from undertaking an activity when they know or should know that their personal problems are likely to lead to harm to patient, client, colleague, student, research participant, or other person to whom they may owe a professional or scientific obligation (APA, 1992, 1.13.a).

• When psychologists become aware of personal problems that may interfere with their performing work-related duties adequately, they take appropriate measures, such as obtaining professional consultation or assistance, and determine whether they should limit, suspend, or terminate their work-related duties (APA, 1992, 1.13.c).

• Counselors are aware of their own values, attitudes, beliefs, and behaviors and how these apply in a diverse society, and avoid imposing their values on clients (ACA, 1995, A.4.b).

• Social workers should not take unfair advantage of any professional relationship or exploit others to further their personal, political, or business interests (NASW, 1997, 1.06.b).

• Counselors are aware of their influential positions with respect to clients, and they avoid exploiting the trust and dependency of clients. Counselors make every effort to avoid dual relationships with clients that could impair professional judgment or increase the risk of harm to clients. (Examples of such relationships include, but are not limited to, familial, social, financial, business, or close personal relationships with clients.) When a dual relationship cannot be avoided, counselors take appropriate professional pre-

cautions such as informed consent, consultation, supervision, and documentation to ensure that judgment is not impaired and no exploitation occurs (ACA, 1995, A.6.a).
• Social workers should not terminate services to pursue a social, financial, or sexual relationship with a client (NASW, 1997, 1.16.d).
• In choosing consultants, counselors avoid placing the consultant in a conflict of interest situation that would preclude the consultant being a proper party to the counselor's effort to help the client. Should counselors be engaged in a work setting that compromises this consultation standard, they consult with other professionals whenever possible to consider justifiable alternatives (ACA, 1995, D.2.a).
• If students or supervisees request counseling, supervisors or counselor educators provide them with acceptable referrals. Supervisors or counselor educators do not serve as counselors to students or supervisees over whom they hold administrative, teaching, or evaluative roles unless this is a brief role associated with a training experience (ACA, 1995, F.3.c).
• Counselors do not use their places of employment or institutional affiliation to recruit or gain clients, supervisees, or consultees for their private practices (ACA, 1995, C.3.d).
• When counselors agree to provide counseling services to two or more persons who have a relationship (such as husband and wife, or parents and children), counselors clarify at the outset which person or persons are clients and the nature of the relationships they will have with each involved person. If it becomes apparent that counselors may be called upon to perform potentially conflicting roles, they clarify, adjust, or withdraw from roles appropriately (ACA, 1995, A.8).
• Counselors ordinarily refrain from accepting goods or services from clients in return for counseling services because such arrangements create inherent potential for conflicts, exploitation, and distortion of the professional relationship (ACA, 1995, A.10.c).

LOYALTY AND CONFLICTS OF INTEREST

Loyal therapists respect and work to advance the welfare, interests, and needs of their clients. According to Bayles (1989, p. 90), such loyalty requires the professional to exercise "independence of judgment." Therapists may lose independence of judgment when they have conflicts of interest. Such conflicts occur when the therapist has a further interest that tends to interfere with and subvert the therapist's primary professional interest in advancing the client's welfare, interests, and needs.

One way a therapist can lose independence of judgment is to allow personal dislike for the client or disapproval of some action by the client to affect adversely the quality of therapy. For example, a counselor may find it hard to continue counseling a child molester because of her own negative feelings toward the offender.

Another way a therapist can lose independence of judgment is for the counselor to become personally or emotionally involved with the client to the extent that she becomes incapable of making objective discernments (APA, 1992, 1.13.a). One example is the counselor who develops dual relationships with a client—for instance, becomes the client's business or sexual partner while still the client's therapist (ACA, 1995, A.6.a) or terminates the therapeutic relationship to be able to pursue such a relationship (NASW, 1997, 1.16.d). Another example is the counselor who engages in countertransference with the client, thereby using therapy to work through her own problems (APA, 1992, 1.13.c).

The loyal therapist will confront without rationalization or denial the potentially detrimental effects of personal biases on client welfare. Such a therapist will avoid entering into dual-role relationships in which there is serious potential for client harm (ACA, 1995, A.6.a) and will avoid exploiting existing relationships for personal gain (NASW, 1997, 1.06.b). If the therapist believes, after careful consideration, that she is unable to continue counseling a client without jeopardizing his welfare and that progress is more likely to be achieved by referring the client, the therapist will inform the client of her conflict and accordingly make a suitable referral (APA, 1992, 1.13.c). Paradoxically, in cases where therapists are unable to maintain independence of judgment, being loyal to the client may itself require making such a referral (NASW, 1997, 1.06.a).

The therapist's assessment of clients' need for therapy may also be colored by the desire to continue to receive fees for services rendered. The loyal therapist will strive for objectivity in assessing client need, and when it is in the client's best interest to terminate or phase out therapy, she will do so, with the client's informed consent. She will not treat the client as a mere means, taking unfair advantage of or exploiting him for monetary gain (NASW, 1997, 1.06.b).

Similar problems may arise when the third-party payer is a parent or legal guardian of a minor child (or incompetent adult). In the desire to keep the parent satisfied—at least partly to receive fees for services rendered—a therapist may lose sight of the minor client's welfare. While having empathy for parental perspectives and striving to accomplish their legitimate counseling objectives, the loyal therapist will also realize that such perspectives and objectives can be clouded by personal involvement and thus may not always represent the client's best interest. The loyal therapist's response to parental or guardian pressures will thus be tempered by this awareness (ACA, 1995, A.8; NASW, 1997, 1.06.a).

The therapist's independence of judgment in regard to third-party payers may also suffer when her understanding of what is best for the client conflicts with what is required by her employer or supervisor (NASW, 1997, 1.06.a). The therapist receives her paycheck from the employer, so there are self-interested reasons—in particular, keeping her job—for the therapist to do what the employer requires. At times, client welfare may militate against this. In such cases, the loyal therapist will not rationalize or deny the potential for client harm in order to reconcile the conflict. Nor will she unnecessarily sacrifice her job, which would benefit neither the client nor herself. Nevertheless, loyal therapists will need to cultivate the virtue of moral courage. Standing steadfastly on principle, the loyal therapist will be prepared to suffer unavoidable personal loss (of time, money, approval, job, etc.) rather than to do material harm to clients.

When third-party payers are insurance companies, therapists' diagnoses may be affected by consideration of the insurance company's unwillingness to pay for certain classifications. In such cases, loyal therapists will avoid presenting false, inaccurate, or misleading diagnoses for self-serving purposes. Lying or deceiving insurance companies is also illegal and constitutes insurance fraud. The price may be loss of license, civil suit by the defrauded insurance company, and/or criminal prosecution. Engaging in fraudulent activity for self-serving reasons is unprofessional. A virtuous therapist would not risk destroying his practice, discrediting his profession, and making a dishonest person of himself for monetary gain (see ACA, 1995, C.5.c under Honesty).

Therapists' independence of judgment may also be impaired if they fail to draw a distinction between their personal values and those of their clients. Loyal therapists, however, will respect clients' freedom to own their values even if these are not shared by the therapists. Loyal therapists will also be sensitive to cultural differences and will be willing to work within the value systems of clients rather than imposing their own personal or culturally biased perspectives (ACA, 1995, A.4.b). As personal and cultural values are central aspects of a person's self-definition, therapists without such tolerance will fail to respect their clients for the persons they are and will accordingly lack unconditional positive regard for them, and this is of primary importance for promoting clients' autonomy.

Therapists' independence of judgment may be adversely affected when they accept goods or services from clients as payment for counseling services (ACA, 1995, A.10.c). These arrangements blur the boundaries between personal and professional relationships by making therapists' personal satisfaction with the goods or services a logically relevant condition of therapy. The logical presumption of such bartering arrangements is that the client's payment in goods or services satisfies the terms of the agreement and that the therapy rendered is just compensation for the goods or services. Such conditions of reciprocity are implicit in the relationship and raise the potential for conflict between both client and therapist. Even when therapists are unaffected by the quality of clients' goods or services rendered, clients may think they are. Clients may still feel pressure to do better in order to hold onto their therapists' approval. Dependence rather than independence may thereby be fostered; and clients may perceive their therapists' regard as conditional, losing trust in the professional relationship. When clients seek to pay for counseling through bartering arrangements, loyalty may require the therapist to make an appropriate referral.

Clients may sometimes offer therapists gifts over and above fees paid for services. These may be offered in appreciation for the services or as gestures of goodwill. If the gifts are merely symbolic gestures and do not have significant monetary value, therapists' acceptance of them need not blur lines between professional and personal relationships. A therapist who accepts a box of chocolates from a client during the holiday season as a token of the client's appreciation need not create a situation of dependency. In such a case, there is no expectation of client or therapist that the gift meet any mutually agreed-on standard of remuneration. Refusal of the gift may have the effect of alienating the client who may take the refusal as a sign of rejection.

The situation is different when the gift has significant monetary value—for example, a personal computer or television set. In these cases, the gift may blur boundaries if the client expects gratitude and indebtedness from the therapist. The therapist may have an uncomfortable feeling that she "owes" the client something or that the client might think she does. The client may have reciprocal expectations or may worry about whether the therapist is sufficiently satisfied with the gift. The gift may carry implications that disrupt mutual rapport and independence of judgment in the professional relationship and intrude into the therapist's personal life. A loyal therapist will accordingly avoid accepting gifts of significant monetary value although she may be inclined to accept gifts that are no more than symbolic gestures or tokens of appreciation.

Fairness

PRINCIPLE OF FAIRNESS
Provide services of equal quality and magnitude consistent with the maximum promotion of the welfare of each client.

• The social worker should not practice, condone, facilitate, or collaborate with any form of discrimination on the basis of race, ethnicity, national origin, color, age, religion, sex, sexual orientation, marital status, political belief, or mental or physical disability (NASW, 1997, 4.02).
• Human service workers advocate for the rights of all members of society, particularly those who are members of minorities and groups at which discriminatory practices have historically been directed (NOHSE, 1994, 16).
• In establishing fees for professional counseling services, counselors consider the financial status of clients and locality. In the event that the established fee structure is inappropriate for a client, assistance is provided in attempting to find comparable services of acceptable cost (ACA, 1995, A.10.b).
• Counselors contribute to society by devoting a portion of their professional activity to services for which there is little or no financial return (pro bono) (ACA, 1995, A.10.d).
• Counselors provide for equal access to computer applications in counseling services (ACA, 1995, A.12.c).

Fairness, Equality of Treatment, and Managed Care

Fairness here refers to equality of treatment (Bayles, 1989, p. 95). Given the primary purpose of therapy, a fair therapist will be disposed toward providing services of equal quality and magnitude consistent with the maximum promotion of the welfare of each client.

Such a therapist will therefore be disposed against imposing on one client in order to benefit another. For example, she will avoid curtailing one client's session time to accommodate another. If two clients are paying for hourly sessions, they will each ordinarily receive their full hour.

This does not mean that exceptions will never be made. Such exceptions, however, will typically be open to all clients and will not usually be made without a relevant difference—that is, one related to client welfare. Thus an emergency with one client may cut short or preempt the session of another client. For example, if a suicidal client requires immediate attention, another client may have to be rescheduled. Nevertheless, the fair therapist will avoid regular practices that increase the probability of having to make such exceptions. For example, he will avoid overbooking.

Given their lack of cogency to the provision of therapy, such attributes as race, religion, gender, sexual orientation, and physical attractiveness are irrelevant grounds for adjusting quality or availability of therapy (NASW, 1997, 4.02). Therapists as distinct individuals may have their own religious and sexual preferences and they may find some clients more physically attractive than others; however, the fair therapist will be disposed against basing provision of therapy on these personal preferences.

Nevertheless, if any attribute blocks the therapist's ability to provide competent, diligent therapy, the fair therapist would be inclined to refer the client to another therapist rather than provide inferior service. For example, a gay therapist who has not fully worked out problems related to his own homosexuality may find it difficult to counsel other gay clients without countertransferring. In such cases, the fair therapist would not place clients' welfare at risk, at least not without the client's informed consent.

The inability of a client to pay is not in itself a relevant basis for turning a client away, because a person's economic status is unrelated to his or her ability to benefit from therapy. However, it is not irrational to desire to be paid for one's work, and therapists, like other professionals, are entitled to compensation. Moreover, without clients who pay for services rendered, therapists would not be able to maintain their practices and would not be able to serve anyone.

Still, a person who needs therapy is treated unfairly if she is deprived of therapy or is given inferior service simply because she is poor. The fair therapist will do what she reasonably can to address the plight of poor and indigent clients. This would include providing suitable referrals for these clients, helping them to obtain timely appointments from referrals (for instance, by placing telephone calls on their behalf), providing pro bono services to poor and indigent clients as a part of case loads, and using flexible fee schedules such as sliding scales commensurate with clients' ability to pay (ACA, 1995, A.10.d).

Charging clients based on their income does not treat *relevantly* like cases unequally and hence it is not unfair (ACA, 1995, A.10.6). Because clients who are unable to pay the higher fee would otherwise not receive therapy, there is a relevant therapeutic basis for treating their cases differently in the fees they pay for services.

Presently, managed care has begun to exercise a significant role in determining the nature and scope of both mental and physical health care. In particular, this system of health care administration regulates the fees charged for services rendered, the determination of whether services are needed, the types of diagnostic procedures that may be used, and the number of allowable client visits. These arrangements aim at a more equal, affordable distribution of health care services, but they have also created moral challenges for therapists.

The fair therapist must take care to treat managed care clients, clients with other types of third-party payment, and self-paying clients all as equals. Although a therapist may be required to accept reduced payment to become a network provider, the reduced fee should not affect the quality of services offered. Because approval of services, duration of therapy, and continuation of therapy in managed care programs are contingent on approval from the company, the therapist might, in some cases, find himself at odds with such decisions. When this occurs, it is particularly important for the therapist to attempt to remedy any inequities a client may suffer as a result.

If the network approves treatment for a shorter duration than the therapist believes is necessary, the therapist must explore other options to help the client receive services that will work toward her maximum welfare. This may include appealing the decision if the agency has an appeal system in place, doing pro bono work, accepting a sliding scale fee, or referring the client to another, more affordable but competent professional. Requesting a peer review with a practitioner who treats the disorder in question or speaking to a supervisor may also be options for the therapist when practitioners and managed care case managers are in disaccord regarding the course of a client's treatment (APA Online Practice of Psychiatry, 1997).

To anticipate some of the problems that may arise in connection with managed care, the fair therapist should inquire about such options as appeals procedures (Davis, 1995) and criteria used in determining approval of additional services once therapy has been initiated *before* joining a network. As the quality of counseling services may be affected by the qualifications of case managers to make professional discernments regarding therapy, a fair therapist will also need to consider this factor in deciding to enlist with a managed care provider (Golden, 1996).

Vigorous advocacy by the therapist for the client's right to have essential and continuous therapeutic services is fundamental to the principle of fairness. It is through such advocacy that services of equal quality and magnitude consistent with the maximum promotion of the welfare of each client can most readily be achieved.

In summary, the fair therapist is disposed toward being consistent in the provision of therapy. Differences in treatment are generally based on relevant distinctions between clients—that is, differences pertaining to client welfare. Otherwise the therapist would not be worthy of clients' trust.

PRINCIPLES, STANDARDS, AND SUBSTANTIVE MORAL PROBLEMS

In the chapters that follow, we give careful consideration to how the virtuous therapist would approach major substantive, practical problems arising in the therapeutic context. In particular, the principles of trustworthiness, together with their respective virtues, are actively employed in analyzing moral problems in counseling and psychotherapy. These moral problems pertain to culture, religion, dual-role relationships, child and spousal abuse, AIDS, suicide, and abortion. Our approach in each of the respective chapters will include the following as main components:

1. Presentation of particular cases in which hard moral problems are raised
2. Ethical analyses of the given cases in terms of how a virtuous therapist would conceive and respond to these moral problems, understood in terms of the virtues, principles, and concepts presented here and in the preceding chapters
3. In light of the given analyses, presentation of more specific standards of conduct derived from applying the principles and virtues to these moral problems. For example, in Chapter 8, standards of reporting suspected child abuse will be derived from application of principles and virtues to concrete cases involving allegations of child abuse.

Using the ethical framework developed here, we shall, in subsequent chapters, examine a wide variety of substantive ethical problems that are likely to resemble many that practitioners confront in their actual practices. In doing so, we hope to provide practical moral guidance in addressing these problems. Although we will employ general principles as well as more specific standards to light the way, these rules should be understood against the background of an ethics of care that reasons not only from rules to cases but also by comparing and drawing analogies between cases (see Chapter 1). Thus, the cases we present may be compared to other, similar cases. It is in this manner that we hope practitioners, in taking on the challenges of ethical clinical practice, will find our case analyses to set useful precedents.

Summary

In this chapter, principles of trustworthiness were formulated and articulated based on criteria from the codes of professional ethics of psychologists, counselors, social workers, and human service workers. The rules selected and abridged from these ethics codes transcend individual professional boundaries and apply universally to *all* mental health care professionals.

Principles of trustworthiness should provide useful guidelines for therapists who aspire to be honest, candid, discreet, benevolent, diligent, loyal, and fair. They cannot, however, substitute for therapists' own careful reflection. Therapists must exercise their own judgment in determining the priority of principles in cases of conflict. Further, codes of ethics are often cast in general terms requiring interpretation. For example, the APA *Ethical Standards* (1992, 1.22.b) enjoins that "psychologists provide *proper* training and supervision to their employees or supervisees; and take *reasonable steps* to see that such persons perform services *responsibly, competently,* and *ethically*" (emphasis added). The specific meaning of the italicized terms may depend substantially on the judgment of the individual therapist who must apply the given rule in a given practical context.

Virtuous therapists subscribe to principles of trustworthiness; they apply them in daily practice along with sound ethical judgment enlightened by the broader ethical theories that undergird these principles. For example, they understand that respect for informed consent is based on the categorical imperative to treat clients as "ends in themselves and not as mere means." They further understand that acceptance of such broader imperatives provides the foundation of a system of conduct conducive to client trust and ultimately to promotion of client welfare.

Trustworthy therapists are not mere robots who resolve moral problems by logically deducing conclusions from general principles. As morally responsible agents, they truly care about people. They are morally sensitive, empathetic, and congruent; they have unconditional positive regard for their clients. These qualities inform trustworthy therapists' perception and judgment, giving greater credibility to their voices and yielding higher probability that they will earn clients' trust.

REVIEW QUESTIONS

1. What is the fiduciary model of professional ethics and in what respects is this model relevant to psychotherapy?

2. What does being trustworthy mean? What is the difference between being trustworthy and being trusted? What is the connection between being trustworthy and being trusted? What is the connection between client trust and client welfare?

3. What is professional honesty and how does it relate to truthfulness?

4. Under what conditions would a client's consent to therapy be considered invalid?

5. Is informed consent an event or a process? Explain.

6. What is professional candor? How can a therapist determine whether given information should be disclosed to a client?

7. What is professional competence? Can a therapist be benevolent and not professionally competent? Explain.

8. What is professional diligence and how can one determine whether a therapist acts diligently? What relationship, if any, is there between professional competence and diligence?

9. What does professional loyalty require? What does it mean for a therapist to have a conflict of interest?

10. What is professional discretion and how does it differ from confidentiality?

11. What is privileged communication? Under what circumstances may privileged communication not apply?

12. State four recommended measures for safeguarding confidentiality of client records stored on a computer.

13. What does fairness mean in the context of providing therapy? Is it always unfair to treat different clients differently?

14. What is managed care and what does it regulate?

DISCUSSION QUESTIONS

1. Can a therapist be virtuous without being trustworthy? Can a therapist be trusted by her clients without being virtuous? In your estimation, can a therapist be trustworthy but lack any of the autonomy-facilitating virtues of empathetic understanding, congruence, and unconditional positive regard?

2. What might motivate a therapist to be dishonest? In your estimation, is a therapist ever justified in being dishonest with her clients? If not, why not? If so, under what circumstances? What would Kant have to say about professional dishonesty?

3. In your estimation, do therapists have a professional responsibility to be honest with nonclients? Defend your response.

4. Discuss briefly at least four types of information that should be disclosed to clients as part of informed consent to therapy. Explain why therapists have a professional responsibility to disclose each of these types of information. In your estimation, are there any circumstances under which it would be acceptable or even morally incumbent on a therapist not to disclose any of the said types of information to a client? Explain.

5. In your estimation, should professional competence be regarded as a moral as well as a professional virtue? Defend your response.

6. Does professional competence as a therapist require such attitudinal skills or abilities as empathetic understanding, unconditional positive regard, and congruence? Defend your response.

7. Discuss the concept of due care in counseling and psychotherapy. Give at least two examples of cases in which therapists failed to take due care.

8. Discuss at least three ways in which loyalty might be sacrificed in the context of providing therapy to clients. What are some precautions therapists might take to preserve professional loyalty? In your estimation, what relation does professional loyalty bear to moral courage?

9. Is it possible for a therapist to disclose information indiscreetly without violating client confidentiality? Explain.

10. Why is the bond of confidentiality between therapist and client generally regarded as an important if not essential factor in the counseling process? What other professions recognize a similar bond of confidentiality? In your estimation, does confidentiality serve a function in these other professions similar to the one it serves in counseling? Explain.

11. Discuss at least two situations in which virtuous therapists might be morally justified in disclosing confidential client information.

12. In your estimation, can situations arise in the provision of therapy in which it is unlawful to disclose confidential client information but nonetheless unethical *not* to make such disclosure? Explain.

13. Insofar as case records for clients can be court ordered and used against clients in courts of law, should therapists ever take any precautions regarding what they say in these records?

14. Discuss at least two measures, not explicitly addressed in this chapter, that you believe diligent therapists would take in their professional practices.

15. In your estimation, are sliding fee scales that are commensurate with the client's ability to pay a good idea? Are they fair? Explain.

16. In your estimation, are managed care arrangements generally fair to clients? To the provider of services? How might virtuous therapists effect changes to ensure that such decisions by the managed care provider are consistent with competent and informed psychotherapeutic practice?

Cases for Analysis

Using the concepts introduced in this chapter, provide ethical analyses of each of the following cases.

CASE 1

Dr. Susan Fredericks was providing marriage counseling to two couples—Bob and Alice, and John and Betty—who were close friends. As was her usual policy, Dr. Fredericks informed each party at the inception of therapy that what was said in session would be held in confidence (prevention of harm to client or others noted as exceptions). However, because the couples confided in each other, each knew personal facts about the other. Moreover in therapy, each client often discussed the others. As a result, Dr. Fredericks had a difficult time keeping track of what each client disclosed on his or her own and what information was disclosed by a member of the other couple. For example, Bob and Alice were aware that John was recently in an automobile accident in which he demolished the family's new car. In therapy, Bob and Alice spent considerable time talking to Dr. Fredericks about how John was "down" about what had happened. Unfortunately, during therapy with John, Dr. Fredericks "slipped" and alluded to John's automobile accident. John was taken back and asked "How did you know about that?" Dr. Fredericks hesitated for a moment and then responded. "You told me. Don't you recall?" John, somewhat bewildered, said "I don't remember mentioning that. Maybe I just forgot."

CASE 2

Michelle Walton, Licensed Mental Health Counselor, was a provider for a small managed care company. In this capacity, she received about three referrals a month. One of these clients was Carla, a 40-year-old, divorced woman. During her initial sessions, Carla related that she had been having difficulty adjusting since her breakup with Jim, her boyfriend of 4 years. After careful consideration of Carla's case, Walton diagnosed her as having an adjustment disorder. The managed care company approved Carla for 20 sessions of therapy. Carla appeared to be progressing, starting to rebuild her confidence and to socialize. During the 16th session, Walton and Carla began to prepare for termination; Carla appeared prepared to do this. On the 17th session, Carla revealed that she had been sexually molested as a child by a male relative and that the abuse had continued until she was 18 years old. Carla related that she had only recently begun to realize that this "secret" might have interfered with the intimate relationships that she had subsequently developed with men. She stated that she had always suffered from nightmares and hypervigilance, but that she had not connected this with the abuse until recently. She asked that Walton attempt to obtain permission to increase the number of allowable sessions.

Walton called to get permission for more sessions citing the additional diagnosis of posttraumatic stress disorder (PTSD). The case manager appeared to be confused as to why Walton had been unable to provide this diagnosis at the onset of therapy. She questioned her about the progress that Carla had made toward her original goals, and when Walton confirmed that most of these goals had been met, the manager stated that she could not authorize any additional sessions. Carla indicated that she could not afford to pay for additional sessions and that she had, in the past, received counseling at the local mental health center and had been dissatisfied with the quality of service. This center was the only facility in the area to offer sliding scale fees. Walton was aware that Carla needed additional therapy; however, she was heavily in debt and believed that she could not provide this client with pro bono services. She therefore terminated therapy on the originally agreed-on date and recommended several books on sexual abuse and PTSD for Carla to read.

CASE 3

Dr. Tremblay and Dr. Montaigne were both psychologists on staff at the local psychiatric hospital. While the two did not socialize outside their work environment and work-related social functions, they frequently consulted with one another, attended staff meetings together, and had some close friends in common. Dr. Tremblay had a son Rod, age 17, who was a senior in high school. Recently, Rod had begun to hang out with what Dr. Tremblay described as a "wild" crowd. Although Rod had always been a good student and very respectful of adults, he had begun to get into trouble in school, his grades had begun to suffer, and he had started to use profanity when addressing his parents. Convinced that Rod needed therapy, he asked Dr. Montaigne to take his case.

Dr. Montaigne agreed to see Rod. Because Dr. Tremblay realized his own inability to remain objective in clinically diagnosing and treating his own son, he told Dr. Montaigne to treat him as he would any parent of a client. However, whereas Dr. Montaigne ordinarily discussed the nature and course of therapy, the limits of confidentiality, and other pertinent details with both parents and minor children, this time he made full disclosure to Rod but not to Dr. Tremblay whom he assumed was already sufficiently informed. Dr. Montaigne did indicate to Dr. Tremblay that, as a professional courtesy, there would be no charge for services rendered.

After one month of therapy, Rod told Dr. Montaigne that his father wanted him to go to the university next year to study psychology, but that he wanted instead to study music. He told Dr. Montaigne that on one occasion when he told his father about his desire to be a musician, his father struck him hard in the leg with one of his golf clubs leaving a large bruise. Rod revealed to Dr. Montaigne that he had begun to experiment with LSD and to smoke marijuana as a way of dealing with the pressure from his father. He also was very emphatic that he did not want his father to know that he was taking drugs. Because Dr. Montaigne believed that Rod was beginning to open up in therapy, he did not want to destroy his trust. On the other hand, he was concerned about his client's mental as well as physical welfare. What was Dr. Montaigne to do?

CASE 4

Alf Grable received his master's degree in social work. Prior to pursuing his degree he had spent 6 years working for the criminal justice system as a parole officer. After graduating from a local university he took a job doing mental health counseling in a private practice owned by his wife, Gladys, who was a licensed mental health counselor. Gladys, who had earned a reputation as a sexual abuse counselor, had a clientele that consisted largely of sexual abuse victims. Although Alf had not had experience working with this population, he believed that his 6 years of experience as a parole officer had brought him into contact with the dynamics of sexual abuse. Moreover, he and his wife had often collaborated on problems related to sexual abuse and the justice system. Thus, when he entered the practice, he promoted himself as a sexual abuse counselor. After about 6 months, he had established himself as one of the community's foremost specialists in sexual abuse, and he was often called on to present lectures and to participate in outreach programs on sexual abuse education.

CASE 5

At 5:00 P.M., Dr. George, psychiatrist, left the psychiatric facility where he was on staff, taking with him some records on cassettes that he intended to review after dinner. However, on his way home, he had a blowout in his rear tire. Unfortunately, Dr. George's spare tire was also flat, so he locked his records in the glove compartment, walked to the nearest call box, and called a wrecker to take his car to the nearest garage. The wrecker came and his car was towed to the nearest garage. When he arrived, the garage attendant told Dr. George that he would be able to have him back on the road in about an hour. Dr. George said he would get a bite to eat and would return in one hour and he handed the trunk key, which also fit the glove compartment, to the attendant. While Dr. George was at a restaurant, the garage attendant opened the glove compartment, looking for the hub cap key. Finding the key along with the cassettes, he thought he would listen to some music while repairing the tire. So he played the tapes in the car tape player only to hear confidential information about a woman who was having a sexual dysfunction. The garage attendant recognized the client on the cassette as the wife of one of his friends. When Dr. George returned, the attendant began to joke about what he had just learned.

PART TWO

Moral Problems and Issues

CHAPTER 5
Multiculturalism and Counseling Ethics
CHAPTER 6
Avoiding Ethical Impropriety: Problems of Dual-Role Relationships
CHAPTER 7
Suspected Child Abuse: A Therapist's Responsibilities
CHAPTER 8
Domestic Violence and Abuse: Ethical and Therapeutic Considerations
CHAPTER 9
Confidentiality, Third Party Harm, and Clients Who Have HIV
CHAPTER 10
Paternalistic Intervention, Involuntary Commitment, and Client Autonomy

CHAPTER FIVE

Multiculturalism and Counseling Ethics

MULTICULTURAL COUNSELING
CASE STUDIES
    Case 1: Sexual Orientation as Minority Culture
    Case 2: Counseling the Devoutly Religious
        Client
    Case 3: Assimilation, Enculturation, and the
        Minority Client

GUIDELINES FOR MULTICULTURAL
    COUNSELING
SUMMARY
REVIEW QUESTIONS
DISCUSSION QUESTIONS

As counselors and human service workers provide services in a diverse and pluralistic society, they must be aware of and familiar with customs, orientations, traditions, ethnicities, and religions of disparate groups of people. Such knowledge and familiarity should, of necessity, extend to those in our population who, historically, may have been underserved or malserved from a lack of understanding, insufficient attention, or social disenfranchisement. This chapter explores and elucidates ways the virtuous therapist, functioning in a diverse society, can beneficently foster postive client growth irrespective of cultural variables and without falling prey to an ethnocentric and often "mainstream American" bias.

The chapter includes case studies, in-depth analyses, and ethical guidelines intended to provide direction for the mental health professional. The case studies highlight some of the complexities and dilemmas that may confuse and confound practitioners and for which there are no clear answers in either ethical codes or state statutes.

Multicultural Counseling

Increasingly, in the fields of counseling and human services there has been a keener and more in-depth focus on the issues associated with multiculturalism or cultural plurality. To explore thoroughly the goals and behaviors of the virtuous therapist in a culturally diverse society, we first need to define the terms *culture* and *multicultural*. Culture may be defined as "shared constraints that limit the behavior repertoire available to members of a certain socio-cultural group in a way different from individuals belonging to some other group" (Poortinga, 1990 p. 6). These behavioral constraints may be broadly defined to include *demographic variables* including age, sex, and place of residence; *status variables* including social, educational, and economic ones; *affiliations*, formal and informal; and *ethnocentric variables* including nationality, ethnicity, language, and religion. In this broad sense, *multicultural* can have importance and practical significance for virtually all counseling relationships (Pedersen, 1991).

In its traditional sense, *culture* has principally been associated with ethnicity and race. With the acknowledgement today that many communities or populations do not define themselves solely by such criteria, some attention has turned to the counseling of more disparate populations. In this chapter, we consider multiculturalism to include groups defined by commonality of age, sexual orientation, education, or gender.

Historically, in the United States, counseling has proceeded from a mainstream America perspective. Many counselors have tended to base their expectations of client wellness and their counseling styles principally on white, Anglo-Saxon, male standards. These styles are more supportive of the notion of *rugged individualism* (Das, 1995) as opposed to *collectivism;* instrumental traits, such as assertiveness, in contrast to expressive ones, such as emotional expressiveness. By such standards, a person of Asian background who decides to take a certain course of action to prevent "shame to the family" may be regarded as lacking independence or needing to individuate himself from his family of origin. This, of course, ignores the cultural values of that person for whom collectivism or the practice of individuals functioning as a group, is a given.

Devaluation of traits that depart from a mainstream perspective has been pervasive. Traditional Freudian psychoanalysis views females as less capable of sublimation than males. Western culture has traditionally attached more prestige to the "male" traits of assertiveness and confrontativeness than to the "female" traits of emotional expressiveness and nurturing. Even the more recent cognitive-behavioral approaches, in their purest forms, place more importance on the skill and expertise of the counselor than on the quality of the therapeutic relationship. One notable exception to this sometimes polarized perspective is the person-centered approach. With its focus on the subjective world of the client and its emphasis on feelings, genuineness, empathy, and unconditional positive regard, this theory has allowed a legitimatization of those expressive qualities so long disvalued but now more vocalized in contemporary feminist theories of knowledge (see, for example, the discussion on "connected knowledge" in Chapter 3). Because of the inherent goal here of grasping and relating to the client's inner world, many tenets of this approach lend themselves to effective use with clients of varying backgrounds and perspectives.

Virtuous therapists approach counseling in a multicultural world *beneficently.* By providing services that support positive growth and the alleviation of frustration and unhappiness, they attempt to understand and have knowledge of varying worldviews consistent with differences in ethnicity, social or religious affiliation, gender, or sexual orientation (American Psychological Association [APA], 1992, 1.08).

Virtuous therapists do not make acceptance of clients' cultural perspectives a condition of respect. Rather, they have *un*conditional positive regard for their clients. Consistent with the principle of fairness, virtuous therapists remain morally unbiased so that the free expression of such diverse views, though possibly not in accord with those of the therapist, allows for client self-determination and autonomy.

The concept of promoting client autonomy is sometimes seen as contrary to and in conflict with a multicultural framework. Critics argue that autonomy is an American value, inconsistent with the collectivism of many cultures. However, the quest for autonomy described here does not violate other cultural values. In promoting an atmosphere that encourages client self-exploration and self-directedness, the virtuous therapist allows the client, independently and without coercion, to decide what dictates, principles, customs, and/or traditions he or she wants to embrace.

The following cases illustrate, from a multicultural perspective, some challenging ethical problems, dilemmas, and issues confronting therapists in an ever-expanding multicultural world. This chapter explores some of the complexities that may confound therapists and presents a framework, including ethical guidelines, on which to base ethical and moral decisions.

Case Studies

CASE 1: SEXUAL ORIENTATION AS MINORITY CULTURE

Jeff is a 32-year-old homosexual, male high school teacher who has been involved in a 2-year live-in relationship with Sam, 40, a mechanical engineer. Jeff has recently begun to experience anxiety as a result of his family's constant attempts to introduce him to women for the purpose of marriage and their perceived preoccupation with his "bachelorhood." Jeff has known that he was gay since age 15 but has never disclosed this to his family members. He actively dated girls in high school and attempted to keep up the pretense that he was heterosexual. At the age of 20, while he was away at college, Jeff had his first homosexual experience. Since that time, Jeff has engaged only in gay sexual relationships. On graduation from college, Jeff found a teaching job in a different state from where his family lives. His primary reason for relocating was to avoid "coming out" to his family and community. The city Jeff chose as his home was also more "gay friendly" than Jeff's hometown, a small, closely knit, traditional midwestern enclave.

Jeff remained here, living quite happily for 8 years. At that time, his father, Jeff, Sr., became critically ill with emphysema. Jeff's mother, Deidre, felt overwhelmed by the constant care and attention that his father needed. Jeff's sister, Sheryl, who is 2 years older than Jeff, had three young children and was unable to participate in the daily caregiving of their father. With mixed feelings of obligation and regret, Jeff relocated 5 miles away from his parents, secured a teaching job, and later, entered into a relationship with Sam.

Both Jeff, Sr., and Deidre hold "traditional" values. Deidre has never worked outside the home and has encouraged Sheryl to follow her example.

Both parents express intolerance toward homosexuality when the topic comes up on media presentations. Although Sheryl has three children, two of them boys, Jeff, Sr., has begun to worry that the family name will not be carried on. His concern about not having grandchildren with his last name, as well as his failing health have contributed to the family's seemingly relentless attempts to find a "suitable wife" for Jeff. Sheryl often arranges for Jeff to be present at her home at the same time as her eligible female friends. Deidre has also enlisted the help of her friends in seeking out marriageable females.

Jeff has become increasingly torn; his loyalty to Sam and his dislike of the secretiveness of his life are pitted against his concern with his family's probable rejection of him if he discloses his sexual orientation. He is further overwhelmed by the nagging fear that disclosure of his homosexuality would contribute to a further decline in his father's health, possibly hastening his death. He told his family that he and Sam were roommates, living together to save money and make ends meet. Jeff's apartment has two bedrooms and when family members visit, the couple keeps up the facade that they each have a separate room.

Jeff recently has been unable to concentrate at work and the school has started to receive complaints from students who view Jeff as disorganized and erratic. His principal has begun to question Jeff's effectiveness in the classroom and has suggested that he seek counseling. Jeff has told the principal only that his father is ill.

Jeff had ambivalent feelings about therapy. He was eager to rid himself of the overwhelming anxiety he was experiencing and wanted to repair his now faltering relationship with Sam, who was beginning to pressure him to disclose their relationship to his family; but he was hesitant about disclosing to "just anybody." Additionally, because his counseling would be paid for through his school's employee assistance program (EAP), Jeff feared that the contents of his sessions would be made known to his principal. He feared that disclosure of his homosexuality would result in his losing his teaching position and being ostracized by both family and community.

Jeff decided to schedule an appointment with Glenda Gatsby, LPC, a married, heterosexual therapist. Gatsby, in concert with providing clients with informed consent, advised Jeff that information involving his sessions might be requested by the EAP. Jeff affirmed his understanding of this and signed appropriate consent forms. Satisfied with the initial session, Jeff decided to continue therapy. Initially, the issue of sexual orientation was not mentioned; however, during the second session, Jeff decided to share this information with Gatsby. Though not herself homosexual, Gatsby has counseled many gay clients and feels comfortable working with this population. Jeff asked that Gatsby not disclose information regarding his sexual orientation to the EAP for fear that it might jeopardize his job. Gatsby, after careful consideration, agreed to honor Jeff's request.

Jeff had, at this point, come under increasing pressure from Sam to "be honest" with his parents about their relationship. Sam threatened to leave the relationship if Jeff did not comply. Jeff, Sr.'s health was progressively declining, and his "dying wish" was to have grandchildren to carry on the family name. Jeff became increasingly more depressed and confused and requested that Gatsby "talk" to Sam.

Gatsby agreed to invite Sam to participate in conjoint sessions but told Jeff that she would not attempt to influence Sam's thinking in any particular direction. Sam subsequently agreed to participate in the sessions.

In the course of therapy, Sam and Jeff discussed the implications of both divulging their relationship to Jeff's family and of keeping it a secret until Jeff, Sr., passed away. The two considered the impact that such a disclosure could have on the father's health and on their relationship if the revelation appeared to hasten his death. At the end of 10 weeks of therapy, the couple decided to wait until after Jeff's father died to make any pronouncements about their relationship. Jeff assured Sam that after a 4-month mourning period he would inform his family of their relationship.

Gatsby arranged for Sam and Jeff to make a follow-up appointment 3 months from the date of their termination. One week before the scheduled appointment she called to confirm the appointment and received a recording saying that the number had been disconnected. Sam and Jeff did not show for the appointment.

As expressed in sessions, Jeff felt torn between competing loyalties. Regardless of what he did, it appears, he was bound to hurt someone—either his family (particularly his father), his partner, or himself. Gatsby must acknowledge that Jeff is, indeed, in the position of struggling with a moral dilemma. As discussed in Chapter 2, this can be explained as a moral problem wherein no matter what is done, someone's welfare will likely suffer. In accordance with the principle of considerateness, Gatsby should seek to work with Jeff to attempt to minimize the suffering that he, as well as significant others, may experience as a result of his actions. In seeking an acceptable resolution to the moral problem, Gatsby should also be familiar with the various ethical perspectives that shape moral decision making.

In exploring Jeff's position from a Kantian perspective, Gatsby would need to ask herself whether Jeff's deceiving his family could be turned into a universal law. Let us imagine that everyone deceived his family. Would this be something that a rational person could support? Would such a practice treat people as ends rather than means? If these two questions are answered in the negative, a Kantian would see lying as morally wrong. In line with Kant's categorical imperative, as discussed in Chapter 1, Jeff would be bound by duty to tell the truth. Gatsby should recognize, however, that blatant honesty as a categorical imperative could, in this case, cause great harm and potentially fracture several significant relationships. As discussed in Chapter 1, Kantian ethics ignores the importance of context and may oversimplify the realities of ethical decision making.

Gatsby should further be aware that a utilitarian framework would provide different ethical guidelines to follow. As seen in Chapter 1, this perspective decides the moral rightness of actions by determining their overall tendency to produce pleasure and prevent pain. If one were to explore Jeff's situation from an *act* utilitarian framework, deceit could be justified if it maximized pleasure and minimized pain.

In addition, Gatsby should note the importance of context in deciding what an appropriate moral action is. Virtue is acquired through the habitual performance of virtuous actions. Virtues are, in and of themselves, valuable. From this perspective, Gatsby should give careful attention to Jeff's decision not to be honest with his family because honesty is a virtue. However, the context in which Jeff's truthfulness or lack of it will be played out is also important. The seriousness of the consequences of Jeff's openness with his relatives must be fully explored.

As a caring therapist, Gatsby must be committed to helping Jeff examine the situation in such a way as to help preserve interpersonal relationships and to prevent suffering. As indicated in Chapter 1, care ethics is situational in that context and consequences are deemed to be essential ingredients of an ethical decision. Gatsby should help Jeff to explore ways he may choose to preserve all his relationships with an eye toward preventing anyone from suffering.

Of course, the actual decisions about how to act and what to say to family and partner are Jeff's. Gatsby should be aware that client autonomy is fostered when clients are encouraged to make independent and uncoerced decisions about their lives. However, she should also know that a therapist can serve as a model of honesty, integrity, and competence. If Gatsby is to be such a model, she must be comfortable with the moral direction of therapy. This is not to say that Gatsby should direct Jeff to a particular course of action, but rather, that she should help to clarify moral and ethical dilemmas. Virtuous therapists embody empathy, unconditional positive regard, and congruence. These attributes can serve this end by encouraging sincere dialogue about welfare, interests, and needs (one's own as well as those of others). A requisite for practicing psychotherapy virtuously is that therapists be real and without pretense.

As a caring and genuine therapist, Gatsby will show unconditional positive regard for Jeff regardless of his thoughts, feelings, or actions. This posture may allow Jeff free expression without fear of judgment or risk of alienation. Such a posture may, in fact, be unfamiliar to Jeff as a homosexual man living in a predominantly heterosexual society. Because Jeff has felt compelled in the past to conceal his sexual orientation from family, co-workers, and others for fear of ostracism and rejection, this attitude may be rather unexpected. As part of a minority population living in a majority culture, many homosexual persons sometimes find themselves the victims of discrimination and negative stereotyping. They often find it difficult to be open and honest about their lifestyle without taking serious risks, either personally or professionally.

Jeff may expect Gatsby to be judgmental about his lifestyle or his secrecy. He may "test the waters" first with less personal information before making any significant disclosures. Jeff will probably be watching not only Gatsby's verbal responses, but also her nonverbal responses such as body language and tone of voice. A genuine therapist will authentically care about Jeff irrespective of differing lifestyles or values. If Gatsby is genuine, Jeff will likely begin to feel freer to disclose and to explore those feelings and issues that are important to him.

In listening to Jeff, Gatsby should try to sense the fear, alienation, confusion, and vulnerability that her client may be experiencing. She should try to understand how living in a culture that can sometimes be homophobic can foster such feelings and lead people to feel forced to be less than honest about their lives. She is aware that being openly gay often leads to social isolation, discrimination, and, in somes instances, violence (Shannon & Woods, 1995). Though she may never have had the exact experiences as Jeff, she can still empathize with these emotions because they are universal, human emotions.

Jeff asked his therapist to talk to Sam. Gatsby will need to clarify exactly what Jeff means by this. Does Jeff want Gatsby to be an advocate for his position of not revealing his sexual orientation to his family or is Jeff asking Gatsby to facilitate conjoint sessions? If the answer is the former, Gatsby cannot comply. As a loyal therapist, Gatsby must maintain independence of judgment in acting in matters related to her client's treatment. Thus, she must "be alert to and avoid conflicts that interfere with the exercise of professional discretion and impartial judgment" (National Association of Social Workers [NASW], 1997, 1.06.a). The virtuous therapist must not act coercively but should respect the autonomy of the individual. This applies regardless of whether Gatsby supports Jeff's position of secrecy. Virtuous therapists avoid imposing their beliefs on clients (American Counseling Association [ACA], 1995, A.4.b).

If Jeff's intention is to bring Sam into therapy, then Gatsby should explore Jeff's purposes for so doing. Although same-sex marriages are not, at present, legal in any states, Gatsby is aware that Jeff's relationship with Sam is a serious and committed one. The lack of legal sanctioning of homosexual marriages often places partners under considerable stress and hardship. Frequently, they feel disenfranchised or ignored when their significant other is involved in treatment, whether that treatment is of a physical or a psychological nature. The principle of beneficence requires that Gatsby render services that promote her client's positive psychological growth. Inclusion of family members in the therapy process often helps to achieve this end. "Counselors . . . strive to enlist family understanding and involvement as a positive resource, when appropriate" (ACA, 1995, A.1.d). Because Sam represents family to Jeff, and as many of Jeff's struggles are connected to their relationship, such inclusion may well be warranted.

During the course of conjoint therapy, Jeff will probably struggle with the dilemma of choosing between disclosing his sexual orientation to his family and remaining silent on the issue. In choosing disclosure, he will confront his father's condemnation of homosexuality together with his fervent last wishes for a grandchild to carry on the family name. In choosing to remain silent, Jeff must endure his family's relentless activity of introducing hiim to eligible women along with the risks of keeping his relationship with Sam a secret (including the prospects of Sam's walking out). Gatsby must help Jeff navigate between these seemingly incompatible choices. Sam and Jeff may be asked to weigh the impact they would experience from maintaining their relationship in secrecy until the death of Jeff's father. Does honesty, in and of itself, have such value that it should be considered an absolute outside of any context? What positives would be gained by revealing Jeff's homosexuality to his father when the father was dying? What would be the impact on Jeff and Sam's relationship if Jeff, Sr., experienced a major decline after hearing such news? Could Jeff and Sam compromise and wait until Jeff Sr.'s death to reveal their relationship to the rest of Jeff's family?

Jeff has requested that Gatsby not reveal to the EAP (employee assistance program) information relating to his sexual orientation. Gatsby here must consider her obligations to both her client and to the EAP network of which she is a part. She has agreed to supply the EAP with any relevant information they request so that they will have sufficient data for making decisions regarding the coverage of services rendered. Such an agreement involves the principle of honesty, which requires Gatsby to avoid deception in relating not only to clients but to third parties as well. Now, however, she must balance that obligation with her commitment to her client's welfare. That is, she must also consider the principles of candor, discretion, considerateness, and nonmaleficence.

Regarding principles of candor and discretion, Gatsby, at the onset of therapy, should advise Jeff of the limits of confidentiality (NASW, 1997, 1.07.e; APA, 1992, 4.01.a), including the role that the EAP plays in this process. Gatsby did inform Jeff that information related to his sessions would be requested, and she asked how he felt about that. Jeff indicated by signing a consent form that he had no objection to this process.

Discretion requires safeguarding client confidences and avoiding disclosure of confidential information without clients' informed and freely given consent. "When circumstances require the disclosure of confidential information, only essential information is revealed. To the extent possible, clients are informed before confidential information is revealed" (ACA, 1995, Code, B.5.a). Gatsby must decide whether Jeff's sexual orientation is essential for the purposes of service coverage and if such a disclosure would violate Jeff's rights and autonomy. Is it imperative that the EAP be aware of Jeff's sexual orientation to sanction services for the treatment of anxiety and conflicted feelings related to his tenuous family relationships and a terminally ill father? Gatsby decided that such information was not vital to her sharing of information.

As a morally considerate therapist, Gatsby should understand also that she should not engage in any unnecessary sacrifice or harm if her goals can be accomplished without it. She should ask herself if she can loyally fulfill her responsibilities to both her client and the EAP without divulging Jeff's sexual orientation. If the answer is yes, Gatsby has neither reason nor right to make such disclosures.

The principle of nonmaleficence ensures that, through the provision of counseling services, the welfare of both clients and nonclients is safeguarded by the therapist. Nonmaleficent therapists prevent pain and suffering to clients and related others. Gatsby must ask herself whether the disclosure of Jeff's sexual orientation might cause him pain and suffering. She knows that Jeff has concerns about the security of his job if the information were to become known. The worry and concern that the revelation could cause for Jeff may appear to Gatsby to constitute pain and suffering. In addition, despite public proclamations of nondiscrimination, many institutions are quite homophobic. Gatsby may have seen various instances in which a teacher's homosexual orientation became the fodder of parental outrage and protest. Because Jeff's sex life did not constitute a threat to others, disclosure of his sexual orientation would appear not to serve any beneficial purpose.

The conclusion of this case leaves Gatsby unable to address the effectiveness of her client's compromise. Although Gatsby's termination of the case appears to have been justified, she did not have the opportunity to assess the long-term results of therapy. As a virtuous practitioner, she will need to balance this sense of the unfinished with the satisfaction of having acted competently within the therapeutic context. More often than not, a therapist may be unable to know just how well, and to what extent, therapy has succeeded in the long run. In the present instance, Gatsby should be prepared to tolerate such ambiguity.

CASE 2: COUNSELING THE DEVOUTLY RELIGIOUS CLIENT

Trish was a 14-year-old female who had been sexually abused by her step-father since she was 8. Trish had left hints over the years in the hope that her mother would become aware of the abuse, but to no avail. Her mother, Shelby, seemed oblivious to what was occurring. Trish, however, always believed that her mother was really aware of the abuse. The allegations surfaced when Trish revealed her abuse to a friend who subsequently told her mother. The friend's mother then reported the allegations to authorities. When Trish's mother was informed of these allegations, she became very agitated and refused to believe that her spouse could commit acts of this type. Her perceived lack of protectiveness coupled with the suspicion that she had been aware of the abuse for years led authorities to remove Trish temporarily from the home. Trish was placed with friends; however, this placement lasted for only a month. During this time, Trish's stepfather confessed to the molestation and her mother agreed to cooperate in a treatment program.

Both Trish and Shelby were assigned to Lisa Dendrow, a therapist with expertise in family sexual abuse. During their initial interviews, Dendrow apprised both mother and daughter of the dynamics of therapy and the guidelines of confidentiality. Shelby and Trish expressed understanding of what was presented to them in both oral and written form. As Trish was a minor, it was necessary for Shelby to sign consent forms for her; however, Dendrow made certain that Trish understood and felt comfortable with the ground rules and that she also sign the appropriate consent forms. This was done not only to ensure that Trish was truly a part of the process but also to empower Trish as an abuse survivor from whom most vestiges of power probably had been stripped during the process of victimization.

Dendrow learned that Shelby was a 40-year-old Jehovah's Witness who had what she herself described as a wild past. That past included four previous marriages and a history of drug abuse. Since becoming a Witness, Shelby had dedicated herself to the faith and was determined not to divorce again. Shelby maintained that despite what had occurred, she wanted to maintain her marriage. She stressed that her religion placed great emphasis on love and forgiveness and stated that the religious hierarchy to which she was committed dictated that she respect and honor her husband. Shelby believed that she should retain her allegiance to her spouse, and that it was possible to do this and still keep her child safe from further abuse. She entered therapy apprehensively as her efforts were not wholly supported by many of her friends and family members, some of whom believed that such matters should be worked out under the counsel of the congregation's elders. Dendrow had, in the past, counseled several Jehovah's Witness families, read extensively about the religion, and spoken with several Jehovah's Witnesses about religious doctrine and custom. She was aware that Jehovah's Witnesses may sanction divorce scripturally when sexual relations occur outside marriage (Watch Tower Bible and Tract Society of Pennsylvania, 1997).

Shelby's husband, Ty, was sentenced to one year of house arrest and ordered to counseling. Shelby took Ty's confession as evidence of his commitment to change, but she was experiencing difficulty feeling close to him. Because Ty was not allowed to live with Trish until his therapy was complete and until Trish's therapist approved it, Ty took an apartment of his own. He complained bitterly about this, but Shelby remained convinced that it was in the best interest of the family as a whole. Shelby, however, was having problems feeling any sexual attraction toward Ty. On the occasions when she first visited him, he was eager for sexual relations but she refused. This was one of the issues that was explored in group sessions.

Shelby's sessions also revealed much about her relationships with Ty and Trish. She commented that she had always perceived herself as an outsider with them and felt excluded from their jokes and comradery. She often spent weekends away from the family, working overtime. After about 8 months of therapy, Shelby revealed that she had been sexually abused at age 12 by her father. She had never confronted him about this nor told anyone, and she had believed that the abuse was better left in the past. As therapy progressed, Shelby began to divulge more and more about her struggle to deal with the feelings of guilt and betrayal, which were a legacy of that abuse.

Trish struggled with her own issues in sessions. She suffered from feelings of depression, low self-esteem, betrayal, anger, and ambivalence toward her stepfather. Trish's relationship with Shelby was tenuous at best; Trish believed that her mother had been aware of the abuse all along and had chosen to ignore it. Her emotional bond with her mother had never been close, and she struggled now with feeling cut off emotionally from her stepfather, who had provided the only support system she believed she had. Trish vacillated between grieving over the loss of her stepfather and hating him for the years of escalating sexual abuse that eventually culminated in intercourse.

As part of the program, Trish took part in a group comprised of other adolescents who had also been sexually abused by family members. Here she explored the issues mentioned above as well as others that she believed were impacting her life. One of Trish's most frequent complaints was that she "could not live" with her mother's strictness. She constantly expressed discomfort with her mother's religious adherence and stated that she was not allowed to be "like other kids." Trish was not allowed to see PG-13 or R movies like her friends and was neither allowed to socialize with nor visit the homes of friends who were not Jehovah's Witnesses. However, she was allowed to play miniature golf, skate, see PG movies, and visit certain Jehovah's Witness friends. These restrictions were linked to Shelby's religious beliefs and her desire to keep Trish from "worldly" influences. Trish further resented having to attend religious meetings several times a week. In addition, Shelby further restricted Trish from visiting with and sleeping over at the homes of many of her friends who were Witnesses. This was because Shelby did not believe that the parents of these friends provided adequate supervision. Although Lisa Dendrow was herself not a Jehovah's Witness, she was aware of many of the beliefs and practices of the group.

As a competent and diligent therapist, Dendrow should educate herself about a variety of religious and ethnic groups residing in her community. In so doing, she would be adhering to the ACA *Code of Ethics* (1995), which establishes that "counselors will actively attempt to understand the diverse cultural backgrounds of the clients with whom they work" (A.2.b.; see also APA 1992, 1.08). Dendrow should be acutely aware that Shelby's worldview is shaped by her religious convictions. Thus, Dendrow should be committed to working as much as possible within the confines of her client's value system.

Although Dendrow, herself a parent of a teenage daughter, may not embrace many aspects of Shelby's parenting style, she must be a loyal therapist. This means that she should strive to maintain objectivity and respect for Shelby's beliefs. In accordance with the ACA *Code of Ethics* (1995, A.4.b), she should "avoid imposing (her) values on clients." (See also APA, 1992, 1.13.a.) In this regard, Dendrow must act to safeguard Shelby's religious beliefs and her autonomy. Dendrow should be genuinely committed to this end. She should care unconditionally about her client, continuing to demonstrate such care irrespective of the client's worldview. In this way, the therapist will demonstrate that she is indeed trustworthy and will not attempt to manipulate or mold the client in compliance with her own values.

With respect to Trish, Dendrow is faced with several challenges. As a discreet therapist, she should respect the dignity of each of her clients, guarding the privacy of each through nondisclosure of information. When working with minor clients, such as Trish, there are several considerations of which Dendrow must be especially aware. Although both Trish and Shelby were apprised of their rights and of the entailments of therapy, due to her status as a minor, Trish's "informed consent" may be less freely given than is Shelby's. Dendrow must be aware of this and of her obligation to Trish concerning the preservation of privacy (ACA, 1995, A.3.c). She must exercise care not to reveal confidential aspects of the therapeutic relationship to Shelby. However, she must balance Trish's privacy against the therapeutic need of a competent parent to be made aware of circumstances that may threaten the minor's continued well-being.

In concert with working within the value system of her clients, Dendrow should also be careful not to promote divisiveness between Trish and Shelby based on their religious differences. In respecting the parent's right to teach her child religious adherence, Dendrow should not attempt to promote an atmosphere wherein the thrust of therapy is toward challenging the parent's religious directives. Such actions not only serve to undermine the family's religious orientation, but they are also counterproductive to the eventual establishment of a stronger parent-child bond. This does not mean that Dendrow cannot allow Trish to express her anger and disagreement on the subject; to do so would not be in concert with the autonomy-facilitating virtue of empathy. As an empathetic therapist, Dendrow must be committed to enhancing her client's autonomy by encouraging the client's free expression of feelings and communicating back to the client the essence of those feelings. When done properly, this will allow the client to understand her own feelings better.

Dendrow should be aware that Trish and Shelby have never developed a close and trusting relationship. Given her expertise in sexual abuse counseling, Dendrow will have learned that such estrangement can often contribute to the continuation of father-daughter sexual abuse. She will know that a strong mother-daughter bond is a requisite if Shelby is to assume protectiveness and responsibility for her daughter.

Trish's goals should include developing improved self-esteem, assertiveness, and other autonomy-enhancing qualities. These will provide some protection against renewed abuse and a continued life of victimhood. To facilitate such changes, Dendrow will have to allow Trish to exercise independent thinking and judgment.

Dendrow is faced with a dilemma. If she encourages Trish to focus on her discontent with living the life of a Witness, she may be contributing to a further distancing between mother and daughter. The effects of this could be far-reaching. Not only might it prevent strengthening of the mother-daughter bond, but it could also lead to an alienation between Shelby and Dendrow. This alienation could threaten the continuation of therapy as Shelby might stop treatment for herself and Trish. Even if termination did not occur, Trish might feel betrayed by Dendrow, and Dendrow could be perceived as not respecting Shelby's religious values.

If Dendrow discourages lengthy exploration with Trish of religious dissatisfaction, then she could be perceived as lacking adequate empathy, thus promoting a lack of trust. Less than thorough examination of the issue could teach Trish to keep feelings and thoughts to herself, thus subverting the development of assertiveness and autonomy. Inadequate exploration of thoughts/feelings could, perhaps, lead to inadequate resolution of issues and residual resentment; this could ultimately impede the healing process.

As Dendrow works to build rapport with Trish, she needs to listen actively to her own thoughts and feelings. Dendrow should be nonjudgmental and use open-ended questions and reflection of feeling when appropriate. Dendrow must be prepared for a lengthy therapeutic process. After separate group and individual therapy, she should recommend conjoint mother-daughter therapy. There, she will be able to work collectively to target some of the shorter-term issues first. If this therapy is successful, Dendrow may then be able to help mother and daughter reconcile some of their differences. If Trish perceives her lack of participation in teenage activities and lack of involvement with other teens as problematic, then Dendrow could ask Trish to brainstorm and to come up with some activities that her mother might allow her to do. Perhaps Trish will resist at first, saying that her mother would not let her do anything. In such an instance, Dendrow could ask Trish to come up with a list despite the possibility that Shelby might entirely reject it. If Trish is more eager to compile a list, then Dendrow could facilitate the process by providing a way to copy the list.

After several sessions with Trish, Dendrow could approach Trish with the idea of the list. Trish might agree and compile a list that includes such things as miniature golfing with a friend, having a friend visit *her* house, going to certain movies, and going skating during certain hours. If Trish were presently doing none of these things—staying home entirely, ostensibly in protest of her mother's strict policies—she might concede that engaging in even some of the proposed activities was "better than nothing." In concert with being noncoercive and with respecting the rights of minor clients (ACA, 1995, A.3.c), Dendrow should ask Trish if she is willing to discuss these issues in a joint session with her mother. If Trish refuses, Dendrow could help her see that such sharing may promote progress in therapy. Such a disclosure would also be consistent with the helper skill of immediacy, "the helper's ability to discuss with clients what is happening between them in the here and now of any given transaction" (Egan, 1982, p. 201).

If Trish does not express reservations about a session with her mother, then she and Dendrow could discuss when such a meeting might be planned and how to learn whether Shelby would be amenable to it. As Shelby is also Dendrow's client, Dendrow must maintain independence of judgment and act fairly. The suggestion of conjoint therapy must not be coercive. With Trish's permission, Dendrow should tell Shelby that Trish's therapy might benefit if the two had a conjoint session. Dendrow must not, however, attempt to convince Shelby to take part in the session if she expresses outright opposition to it. If, however, this client is undecided about the session, the two could discuss (without breach of confidence) its potential benefits and drawbacks.

In addition to these issues, Dendrow should also address the possible reunification of the family. Ty, sentenced to one year of house arrest and counseling, will be allowed to resume contact with Trish after his therapy is "complete" and after Dendrow gives her approval of such contact. In this context, Dendrow's principal concern must be Trish's welfare. Both Dendrow and Shelby are aware that Jehovah's Witness doctrine allows for divorce in cases of adultery. However, although Trish's sexual abuse fits this definition, Shelby has maintained that, despite what has occurred, she is determined to preserve her marriage. She has stated that the dictates of her faith include showing love and forgiveness. Shelby has made clear her desire to retain her allegiance to her spouse and has declared that she can do this and still keep her child safe from additional abuse.

Dendrow must collaborate closely with Ty's therapist (pursuant to permission from both therapists) to be kept informed of his progress. In concert with the primary counseling mission of protecting client welfare, Dendrow should not consider reunification if Shelby is not able to appreciate the wrongfulness of Ty's actions and to recognize her part in allowing the perpetuation of abuse to continue. Shelby needs to demonstrate that she is able to be assertive, even if it is unpleasant, and to communicate with and protect her child.

Dendrow must be especially aware of Trish's emotional state. Trish must not be coerced into reunification due to feelings of guilt or obligation. This would be to render her once more a thing manipulated. Reunification should not even be considered without family therapy (especially between mother and daughter, and some between father and daughter). Ty must be able to take responsibility for the abuse and assure Trish that she was, in no way, responsible.

If Dendrow believes that contact between the two is likely to jeopardize Trish's welfare, then, in accordance with the principle of nonmaleficence, she should maintain her stance regardless of Shelby's religious convictions. While empathizing with Shelby's plight, sensing her frustration, and recognizing her right to her religious beliefs, Dendrow must stand by her own professional judgment. Providing a congruent model that Shelby can emulate, explaining to Shelby that Trish's welfare is her primary motive, Dendrow should respectfully convey her decision to disallow contact between Trish and her stepfather.

CASE 3: ASSIMILATION, ACCULTURATION, AND THE MINORITY CLIENT

Marta, a 36-year-old Puerto Rican female, began therapy with Meryl Stern, a white, female, middle-class counselor employed in a school-based family counseling program. Stern explained the parameters of therapy to Marta orally as well as in written form. Stern herself spoke some Spanish (although not fluently), and written explanations were supplied in English and in Spanish. Marta stated that she preferred the English instructions. Stern also explained that consultation with other therapists at the center could possibly be necessary, but that only essential information would be provided to them. Marta indicated that she was comfortable with this. Marta's presenting problem was stress, which appeared to be related to a recent marital break-up and difficulty in disciplining her three teenage daughters. As therapy progressed, Marta, born and raised in Puerto Rico, noted that she had difficulty speaking in English and being understood by its native speakers. She further spoke of feeling unable to function in an "Anglo" society although she had resided in the United States for 18 years and had functioned in a job that required her to speak the language. Marta revealed that her husband had physically abused her for many years and had frequently reminded her that he was her intellectual superior. After he severely beat their 17-year-old daughter, Iliana, Marta reported the abuse and her spouse was arrested. The marital break-up followed.

Two of Marta's children—Isabella, age 16, and Iliana—frequently missed school and were beginning to get involved with teens who were experimenting with alcohol and sex. Marta's job required her to work 10-hour days; with so little time at home, she believed that she had little control over her daughters' behavior. Marta's family lived in Puerto Rico, and she was estranged from her former spouse's family, leaving her with complete responsibility for the care of the children. The third daughter, Josefina, age 12, attended a predominantly white, middle-class school and performed well there. Marta feared, however, that she was at high risk of copying her sisters' behavior. Therefore, Marta informed Stern that she was being "careful" with this child by being "strict." However, Marta reported that the more careful she tried to be with Josefina, the more rebellious she became.

Marta also told Stern that she hated her job, but that with her poor command of English, she could probably not hope for more. Marta noted that this was unfortunate, as a different job might allow her more time to spend with her children.

As early as the initial session, Stern told Marta that she had an excellent command of the English language. Although Marta's Spanish accent belied the fact that English was not her first language, her grammar was excellent and her vocabulary was above average.

Because many of Marta's difficulties appeared to be related to Josefina, Stern suggested that Josefina also attend counseling. Sessions were first individual with the eventual goal of mother-daughter sessions. During the initial sessions, Josefina complained that Marta did not allow her to "express her opinions." Marta, on the other hand, contended that Josefina was disrespectful of parental authority and questioned Marta's judgment, something Marta stressed she would never have done with her own mother.

As therapy progressed, Marta frequently asked for reassurance that Stern was able to understand her English. After 10 months of therapy, these questions ceased.

Stern should be aware that merely revealing her assessment of Marta's ability to speak English could not alone change the client's self-assessment. In fact, such verbalizations, might appear to discount the client's feelings or to appear patronizing. Stern needs to know that many immigrants experience anti-immigrant prejudice or are the victims of negative stereotyping or patronizing attitudes that may affect their self-image and self-confidence. She should also recognize that Marta's low self-esteem could have been compounded by her years of being emotionally and physically abused by her husband.

As a beneficent therapist, Stern needs to consider the possible benefits of referring Marta to a Spanish-speaking therapist with whom she shares a common cultural background. With a therapist having these qualities, issues of perceived inequality might be minimized and cultural commonality might serve as a fertile ground for self-disclosure. There is, however, another side to consider. Marta's sense of uneasiness among Anglos could have been a result of having only casual and superficial exposure to them. In addition, suggesting referral to a Latina/Latino therapist might be perceived by the client as further evidence of her inability to communicate or function in mainstream America. It is also possible that Marta would be more reluctant to discuss some of her circumstances with a Hispanic therapist for fear that such a therapist might perceive her as having violated some of the norms of her culture. Viewed in this way, for Stern to remain Marta's therapist could arguably have been in this client's best interest.

Stern should carefully consider whether her experience working with Puerto Rican clients qualifies her to work with this particular client and whether she should consider consultation with another therapist (APA, 1992, 1.08). Even if Stern had some experience counseling Puerto Ricans and could speak some Spanish, she could not (as a non-Hispanic) presume to have complete knowledge of Marta's cultural/ethnic perspectives. She should therefore have asked Marta for permission to consult with other therapists regarding certain cultural perspectives as needed, without divulging any unessential identifying information about Marta. In accordance with the principle of candor, Stern should have explained to Marta that this would be done only if Marta felt comfortable with it, and only in an attempt to enhance the therapist's ability to help the client (ACA, 1995, A.3.a, A.2.b).

At the onset of therapy, Stern may surmise that Marta suffers from low self-esteem stemming from years of abuse and her perceived failure to parent her daughters adequately. Marta's efforts to be "careful" with Josefina may appear to be, at least in part, a result of her sense of failure. In addition, Stern needs to acknowledge the seemingly different levels of acculturation and assimilation of Marta and Josefina, which might have further contributed to the tension between the two.

Acculturation refers to "the acquisition of the cultural patterns of the . . . dominant society" (Atkinson, Morten, & Sue, 1993, p. 10), whereas assimilation refers to the extent to which one becomes integrated into the host culture (Gladding, 1996). Some definitions suggest that true assimilation requires those in both groups to regard each other as equals, freely choosing each other as spouses and friends (Atkinson et al., 1993). Exploration of the dynamics of assimilation and acculturation can allow both therapist and clients to understand better the conflict in the parent-child relationship. Such differences might have, in fact, contributed to further lowering of Marta's self-esteem insofar as she perceived her daughter's persistent questioning of her as culturally inappropriate. Children in Latino families are frequently expected to show appreciation for parental dedication through submitting to family rules (Gladding, 1995).

Josefina attends a primarily white, non-Hispanic, middle-class school. In this cultural context, youngsters are more vocal in their interactions with their parents. Explanations by parents to children about why a certain course of action is taken is fairly routine. In contrast, Marta's socialization occurred in Puerto Rico where such a practice was not commonplace. Josefina, born in the United States, has a stronger identification with being American than does Marta, who still feels uncomfortable in the presence of an all-Anglo social or work setting. Stern needs to see that such differences in perspective may pose some difficulty in the counseling process, but nourishing the mother-daughter bond must remain of paramount importance.

Marta might have experienced guilt not only about her daughters' conduct but also about the dissolution of her marriage and her status as a working mother, roles that conflict with her socialization. Stern should work with Marta to explore her guilt when the client-therapist rapport can support such a discussion. She must remember, however, that her role as a loyal therapist obliges her to avoid imposing any values on her client, even though her own enculturation may be different from Marta's (ACA, 1995, A.4.b).

Similarly, the principle of loyalty requires Stern to clarify the parameters of her counseling relationships with both Marta and Josefina (ACA, 1995, A.8). Consonant with this is an examination of the bounds of confidentiality with regard to Josefina. If she is to become a true partner in the therapeutic process, she will need to know that her confidences will not be abridged unless she reports child abuse or in some way poses a threat to herself or others. As Josefina apparently feels that she has little autonomy, this recognition is essential. However, given Josefina's minor status, Stern should also inform Josefina that she will share with her mother very general statements about the goals and directions of therapy.

As Marta's enculturation dictates an unconditional respect for one's parents, Marta may find the idea of collaboration between therapist and child to the exclusion of the mother disconcerting. Stern must be ready to discuss such feelings and to explore with Marta the rationale behind this process. Stern should be particularly sensitive about this as Marta is already experiencing alienation with regard to Anglo culture. To establish what may appear to be an exclusionary relationship between Stern and Josefina could serve to further Marta's feelings of exclusion and to amplify her sense of low self-esteem. Marta already viewed herself as failing to discipline her daughters and to maintain her marriage, so this perception would likely be countertherapeutic. Stern must, therefore, clarify to Marta that she, too, is aware of the importance and significance that a respectful and close mother-child relationship hold for Marta. She should explain that a major goal of therapy is the reestablishment of this bond. Although some therapists believe that active and directive family therapy serves Hispanic families best (Gladding, 1995), Stern must be careful not to appear overly authoritative. In this way, she will be able to maintain her position of respect without being perceived as intimidating and overbearing.

Through the use of unconditional positive regard and empathetic reflection, Stern can help foster an environment in which Marta will begin to feel accepted, cared for, and valued as a person. As there will be no parameters placed on this acceptance, Marta may begin to feel more secure about expressing her feelings and making self-disclosures. This supportive environment could also benefit Josefina, who has perceived herself as not being respected by her mother and as having had her freedom of expression stifled.

Stern should try not only to facilitate a better mother-daughter relationship but also to help establish conditions under which both mother and daughter feel as if many of their respective individual needs and goals are being met. This will involve not only exploring each client's individual feelings and thoughts but also having conjoint sessions devoted largely to establishing an environment conducive to mutual exchange and expression of feelings and thoughts by both mother and daughter. These conjoint sessions might alternate between individual sessions.

Such an environment of mutual respect and tolerance is likely to be predicated on unconditional positive regard, empathetic understanding, and congruence—among therapist and clients alike. If Stern is able to build this foundation, she can then attempt to initiate conjoint sessions—only, however, with the consent of both Josefina and Marta.

If either client is not amenable to this course of action, then, in concert with respect for client autonomy, Stern should not try to coerce acceptance, but should continue to explore relevant issues with each client. If mother and daughter both agree to participate in joint sessions, then Stern, in accord with the principle of candor, will need to clarify guidelines for these sessions. The guidelines must be respectful of Marta's worldview. Therefore, although both Josefina and Marta will be encouraged to express their feelings and beliefs freely, these expressions should not include swearing, name calling, or overt and blatant disregard by Josefina of Marta's rules. Such a foundation may help Marta feel that her role as a parent will be supported. At the same time, Stern must act diligently to support both clients without seeming to side with either.

Hispanic clients may sometimes prefer somewhat directive and short-term approaches such as behaviorism. To the degree that Stern is comfortable with such an approach, she might consider the viability of taking therapy in this direction. Accordingly, techniques such as contracting might help ensure that compromises agreed on in sessions will be bilaterally fulfilled.

With respect to Marta's perceived departure from the norms of her family and her heritage, Stern should attempt to explore possible feelings of shame and failure. Not only is Marta a working mother, but she has also been divorced. Although divorce is more common among Puerto Ricans than among other Hispanics, there is still a cultural and religious imperative to remain married (Vega, 1990). Marta's feelings of guilt should be explored in the light of her circumstances. Not only was she being beaten by her husband, but her children were severely beaten as well. On the other hand, many Hispanics adhere to the idea of familism, the belief that "the well-being of the family takes precedence over the concerns of individual family members" (Benokraitis, 1996). As a result, Marta may still have been struggling with her decision to get a divorce, especially with the possibility that it might have compromised the family's well-being.

Marta felt estranged from other extended family members as a result of geography or divorce, so she may have been experiencing malaise in this respect as well. It is not unusual for Puerto Rican women to relocate to the mainland to help their adult children raise their children; Marta however, might have felt even more stigmatized as her mother had chosen to remain in Puerto Rico, even given Marta's circumstances. Marta might need to explore her feelings about her own mother. If so, Stern will especially need to convey attitudes of congruence, unconditional positive regard, and empathetic understanding. These attitudes can transcend cultural lines, allowing therapists to enter the phenomenal worlds of their clients.

Guidelines for Multicultural Counseling

The following guidelines for counseling people of differing cultural, ethnic, sexual, or religious backgrounds can be derived from the three case analyses in this chapter. Indicated after each guideline is the basic virtue or principle on which the guideline is based.

GL 1 A therapist is careful to avoid promoting divisiveness between parent and child based on their differing religious or cultural views (nonmaleficence).

GL 2 When the welfare of a minor child is threatened by the religious or cultural practices of a client, the therapist's first priority is protection of the child (nonmaleficence and loyalty).

GL 3 Therapists should carefully consider the levels of acculturation and assimilation of clients with whom they are working (beneficence and loyalty).

GL 4 Therapists help clients make ethical decisions by familiarizing them with the various ethical perspectives that may shape such decisions (beneficence).

GL 5 Therapists should address in therapy discriminatory social or political influences that could affect client perceptions or actions and work with clients to mitigate their impact on the client (fairness).

GL 6 A therapist must be cognizant that the concept of "family" is not uniform. Cultures may adopt various definitions of who is to be included in a "family unit." Therapists must be aware of differences in order to perform therapy more effectively (beneficence).

GL7 Consistent with therapists' responsibilities to provide third-party payers with client information relevant to determination of clients' insurance benefits, therapists refrain from disclosures to third-party payers of irrelevant client information that has serious potential for generating discriminatory treatment of clients in the workplace or other social domain (fairness).

Guidelines 1 and 2 indicate that although therapists have a prima facie obligation to avoid promoting disunity between parent and minor child based on cultural or religious differences, the welfare of a minor child always takes precedence when the safety of the child is at risk.

Guideline 3 underscores the importance of therapists' carefully considering the varying levels of assimilation and acculturation of clients. Therapists must be acutely aware that clients of similar ethnic or religious backgrounds may differ immensely in their behaviors and beliefs, based largely on degrees of cultural entrenchment.

Guideline 4 emphasizes that therapists serve a didactic role in a client's decision-making process by familiarizing the client with various ethical perspectives; these allow the client to make an independent, informed, and educated decision based on clearly identifiable principles.

Guideline 5 discusses the role that therapists have in understanding how long-standing societal prejudices or political directives may influence a client's perspectives and behaviors. Therapists should strive to help alleviate the potentially devastating effects that this could have on the client.

Guideline 6 emphasizes that therapists must be thoroughly acquainted with how any particular culture, group, or unit defines "family." Such knowledge is imperative if a therapist is to provide effective sessions that include people considered "significant" to the functioning of that unit.

Guideline 7 recognizes that therapists have a responsibility to third-party payers to provide information that is relevant to stated, legitimate purposes. In a homophobic dominant culture, disclosing information such as the sexual orientation of a gay client may have serious potential for producing unfair discrimination against the client. When this information is not relevant to determining whether treatment should be covered, making it available would be groundless and contrary to the primary counseling mission.

Summary

This chapter has presented three case studies illustrating the complexities that often accompany multicultural counseling. Ethical analyses and exploration were intended to provide framework and perspective in assisting therapists working with relevantly similar cases.

The first case explored several moral problems involving truthfulness where both telling the truth and omitting it had the potential to cause harm to a third person. As the case dealt with counseling individuals with a homosexual orientation, an essential factor in the analysis was the historical backdrop of prejudice and discrimination that the homosexual population has faced.

The second case involved counseling a Jehovah's Witness mother and daughter in a sexual abuse treatment program. Among the issues discussed were attempting to counsel virtuously while working with a teenager who was rebelling against her parent's religious practices, and adhering to the principle of nonmaleficence when faced with returning a child to a potentially abusive father because the mother's religious beliefs may have supported that return.

The third case explored the dilemmas a therapist may face in deciding whether to counsel or to refer a client whose first language and culture differ from his or her own. Issues of enculturation, assimilation, and bounds of confidentiality were assessed from the perspective of both immigrant mother and American-born child with an eye toward the therapist's establishing and maintaining a stance supportive of the principle of loyalty.

REVIEW QUESTIONS

1. Besides ethnicity and race, what are some of the ways cultural plurality can be manifested?

2. How does the practice of collectivism sometimes create difficulty for individuals attempting to function in mainstream America?

3. In their purest forms, how do the cognitive-behavioral approaches address the qualitative nature of the therapeutic relationship?

4. If a person believes she or he is bound by duty to tell the truth, that person is exemplifying what type of theoretical perspective?

5. Under what conditions may Jehovah's Witnesses sanction divorce?

6. Explain the concepts of assimilation and acculturation.

7. Discuss the Latino idea of familism.

DISCUSSION QUESTIONS

1. Besides ethnicity and race, what are some of the ways that cultural plurality can be manifested?

2. In Case 1, Jeff avoided telling his father that he is homosexual for fear the information would hasten his father's death; but he has come under pressure from his partner, Sam, to disclose this. If Gatsby believes the information has a high probability of contributing to the death of Jeff's father, is she morally obligated to persuade Jeff to withhold the information?

3. Jeff's parents have expressed intolerance toward homosexuality but are unaware that their own son is gay. Is Gatsby promoting dishonesty by supporting Jeff's decision not to inform his parents of his sexual orientation? Discuss how the ethical theories examined in this chapter would be supportive or nonsupportive of this position.

4. Discuss Gatsby's decision not to inform the employee assistance program that part of Jeff's problem is related to his difficulty in disclosing his homosexual orientation to his family (consider the principle of honesty).

5. As a caring therapist, Gatsby is committed to helping to preserve interpersonal relationships and to prevent suffering. Explore additional therapeutic ways in which Gatsby might help to contribute to this goal.

6. Discuss the following regarding Case 2: Because Trish appears to be suffering and is in distress by not being allowed to participate in activities enjoyed by most teenagers, her mother is placing an undue burden on her, and Lisa Dendrow should act as an advocate for allowing Trish such privileges.

7. Respond to the following: Because recidivism rates are generally very high for child molesters, Dendrow should attempt to convince Shelby, regardless of Shelby's religious views, that reunification with Ty is not in the best interest of Trish.

8. In Case 3, Meryl Stern decided, on balance, that Marta's best interests would be served if she continued to treat Marta irrespective of their cultural differences. What overriding circumstances might exist that could justify Stern's referring the client to a Puerto Rican therapist?

9. Stern has advised both Marta and Josefina that, except for information relating to child abuse or harm to self or others, she will share only general information with Marta regarding Josefina's therapy. What would be Stern's moral obligations to Marta if Josefina were to reveal in therapy that she was acting in a

manner that ran counter to her socialization and which Marta disapproved of but in no way posed a threat to herself or others?

10. If Marta asks Stern how she would handle her own daughter's behavior if she were in Marta's place, should Stern give Marta her personal perspective on the matter? What might occur if Stern refuses to respond to this question?

CHAPTER SIX

Avoiding Ethical Impropriety: Problems of Dual-Role Relationships

DUAL-ROLE RELATIONSHIPS INVOLVING
   CONFLICTS OF INTEREST
CASE STUDIES
   Case 1: Sexual Dual-Role Relationships: A Case
      of Mutual Sexual Attraction
   Case 2: Counseling Students: A Case of a
      Nonelective Dual-Role Relationship

ETHICAL STANDARDS FOR ADDRESSING DUAL-
   ROLE RELATIONSHIPS
SUMMARY
REVIEW QUESTIONS
DISCUSSION QUESTIONS

The primary role of a therapist is to provide counseling services, but therapists often assume further professional roles related to their special knowledge and training. They may be consultants, expert witnesses, supervisors, authors, or teachers. As private persons, therapists also assume *nonprofessional* roles. They may be parents, football coaches, consumers, members of the PTA, friends, sexual partners, and countless other things. In their diverse professional and private capacities, therapists can contribute much to the overall happiness of the communities in which they live and work.

When a professional assumes at least one additional professional or personal role with respect to the same client, the relationship thus formed is termed a dual-role or multiple-role relationship. For example, a teacher may also be the supervisor of one of his students/interns, or a counselor may also be a customer of a client/proprietor. Dual-role relationships may occur simultaneously or consecutively (National Association of Social Workers [NASW], 1997, 1.06.c). A therapist has a *consecutive* dual-role relationship when she counsels a former sexual partner or a former student. Although all dual-role relationships are not unethical—that is, they do not have potential to cause significant harm to the client or another—sometimes the blending of the counseling role with certain personal roles or with certain other professional roles can generate serious moral problems.

This chapter considers intricacies of problematic dual-role relationships. Two case studies are presented: one exploring some key issues of sexual relations with clients, and the other exploring some key issues of nonsexual dual-role relationships. From these, four sets of standards regarding ethical management of dual-role relationships are derived.

Dual-Role Relationships Involving Conflicts of Interest

Dual-role relationships are morally problematic when they involve the therapist in a conflict of interest. According to Davis and Stark (in press), "a person has a conflict of interest if he is in a relationship with one or more others requiring the exercise of judgment in the others' behalf but has a special interest tending to interfere with the proper exercise of judgment in that relationship." For example, a therapist's ability to counsel a client may be adversely affected if the counselor is also the client's business partner. If a dual-role relationship impairs the therapist's ability to make judgments that promote client welfare, the therapist has a moral responsibility to avoid such a relationship or to take appropriate steps to safeguard client welfare.

One possible manner of dealing with a dual-role relationship involving a conflict of interest is to inform the client that the conflict exists. In this way, clients are treated as autonomous agents with the power to go elsewhere if and when they so choose. However, although such an approach may accord with candor and consideration for client autonomy, it may not alone resolve the moral problem. The potential for client harm may still persist when the client elects to stay with the relationship. Nonmaleficence—"first do no harm"—should then take priority.

A further approach aiming at mitigating potential for client harm is to make full disclosure to the client *and* seek consultation and supervision in dealing with the conflict (Herlihy & Corey, 1997). According to Herlihy and Corey (1997), although this approach may be more challenging than avoiding dual-role relationships altogether, a willingness to confront ethical challenges is a mark of professionalism.

However, the client's ability to handle the situation must also be taken into account. When the therapist seeks consultation and supervision to deal with a conflict of interest, candor requires that the therapist inform the client of this action. Although different clients may respond differently to disclosure of this information, therapists should consider the implications of this arrangement from the client's perspective. If the therapist cannot trust himself without supervision to act in concert with client welfare, will this adversely affect the client's ability to trust the therapist in this or other situations?

The mere existence of the dual-role relationship may itself present an obstacle for the client. For example, in a relationship in which the client barters for counseling services, the client may feel compelled to treat the therapist in a manner that exceeds ordinary customer expectations. The client's perception may then be more important than the reality. Even if the therapist succeeds in maintaining independence of judgment through consultation and supervision, her behavior may not matter if the client does not perceive the situation this way or if the client is otherwise unable to maintain objectivity.

In some situations, dual-role relationships may be unavoidable. For example, in a rural locality in which there is only one practicing therapist and one bank, the therapist's loan officer may also be the therapist's client. When avoiding the dual role is not possible or feasible, the therapist should take precautions such as informed consent, consultation, supervision, and documentation to guard against impaired judgment and client exploitation (American Counseling Association [ACA], 1995, A.6.a). Viewed in this light, therapists practicing where unavoidable dual-role relationships are likely (for example, in small rural towns) have additional cause for making and maintaining contact with other competent professionals willing to provide consultation or supervision on request.

Morally problematic dual-role relationships may be sexual or nonsexual in nature. Sexual dual-role relationships include those in which therapists engage in sexual relations with current or former clients.

Nonsexual dual-role relationships include those in which the therapist is also the client's supervisor, business partner or associate, friend, employee, relative, or teacher. Even though these relationships are often avoidable, their problematic nature may go unnoticed. For example, in an effort to help a friend in need, a therapist may, with all good intentions, overlook potential for client harm.

Professional and legal standards governing sexual relationships with current clients consistently forbid such relationships. Legal sanctions may include license revocation, civil suits, and criminal prosecution (Anderson, 1996). According to the American Counseling Association *Code of Ethics*, "counselors do not have any type of sexual intimacies with clients and do not counsel persons with whom they have had a sexual relationship" (ACA, 1995, A.7.a). The National Association of Social Workers *Code of Ethics* justifies its own prohibition against providing clinical services to former sexual partners on the grounds that such conduct "has the potential to be harmful to the individual and is likely to make it difficult for the social worker and individual to maintain appropriate professional boundaries" (NASW, 1997, 1.09.d).

The potential harm resulting from sexual activities with clients has been documented. Citing the research of Kenneth S. Pope (1988), Herlihy and Corey (1997) have noted that harm may resemble that suffered by victims of rape, battery, child abuse, and posttraumatic stress. These effects include "ambivalence, guilt, emptiness and isolation, identity/boundary/role confusion, sexual confusion, impaired ability to trust, emotional liability, suppressed rage, cognitive dysfunction, and increased suicidal risk" (p. 24).

The prohibition against sexual activities with current clients has also been extended to students and supervisees. According to the American Psychological Association (APA, 1992) *Ethical Standards*, "psychologists do not engage in sexual relationships with students or supervisees in training over whom the psychologist has evaluative or direct authority, because such relationships are so likely to impair judgment or be exploitative" (1.19.b).

There is, however, less consensus on the question of sex with former clients. Although some states unconditionally regard sex with former clients as sexual misconduct, other state statutes as well as codes of ethics make exceptions. Standard 4.07 of the American Psychological Association (1992) *Ethical Standards* asserts the following:

a. Psychologists do not engage in sexual intimacies with a former therapy patient or client for at least two years after cessation or termination of professional services.

b. Because sexual intimacies with a former therapy patient or client are so frequently harmful to the patient or client, and because such intimacies undermine public confidence in the psychology profession and thereby deter the public's use of needed services, psychologists do not engage in sexual intimacies with former therapy patients and clients even after a two-year interval except in the most unusual circumstances. The psychologist who engages in such activities after the two years following cessation or termination of treatment bears the burden of demonstrating that there has been no exploitation, in light of all relevant factors, including (1) the amount of time that has passed since therapy terminated, (2) the nature and duration of therapy, (3) the circumstances of termination, (4) the patient's or client's personal history, (5) the patient's or client's current mental status, (6) the likelihood of adverse impact on the patient or client and others, and (7) any statements or actions made by the therapist during the course of therapy suggesting or inviting the possibility of a post-termination sexual or romantic relationship with the patient or client.

The American Counseling Association has recently adopted a similar rule stipulating a minimum 2-year waiting period and requiring counselors to "thoroughly examine and document that such relations did not have an exploitative nature" based on criteria similar to those set forth in the above rule (ACA, 1995, A.7.b). The American Association for Marriage and Family Counselors has also adopted a 2-year waiting period (AAMFT, 1991, 1.12). Without stipulating a time period, the recent *Code of Ethics* of the National Association of Social Workers has provided that "social workers should not engage in sexual activities or sexual conduct with former clients because of the potential for harm to the client." The code also states that if social workers act contrary to this prohibition or claim exceptional circumstances, then social workers, not their clients, "assume the full burden of demonstrating that the former client has not been exploited, coerced, or manipulated, intentionally or unintentionally" (NASW, 1997, 1.09.c).

From a rule utilitarian perspective, a rule unconditionally forbidding sex with former clients may be warranted. First, as the above APA rule suggests, the circumstances of excusable sexual relationships with former clients are "most unusual." Second, therapists contemplating sexual relations with former clients may find it difficult to examine and document objectively that such relationships are not exploitive. Their "utilitarian calculations" may be biased. Third, insofar as sexual intimacies with former clients are frequently harmful to clients and tend to undermine public confidence in the profession and its services, permitting such relations risks a high measure of disutility. Accordingly, if therapists avoided sexual relationships with former clients without exception, they would probably maximize overall happiness in the long run.

On the other hand, given discretionary standards such as those of the APA and ACA, it is important that therapists exercise such discretion wisely. The following case study is intended to shed light on confronting conflicts of interest when sexual interests become an issue.

Case Studies

CASE 1: SEXUAL DUAL-ROLE RELATIONSHIPS: A CASE OF MUTUAL SEXUAL ATTRACTION

Bethany Taylor first met Dr. David Walker, a 38-year-old psychologist, when she came to him for marital problems. Bethany, an attractive, 25-year-old woman, had been married to her husband, Charles, for 2 years when she entered therapy. Charles was a wealthy corporate CEO and at the time the couple met, Bethany was a fashion model working between jobs as a waiter in a popular nightclub. When the two were married, Charles insisted that Bethany give up her career goals and stay at home. Bethany cooperated with Charles, resigning from her job and severing all ties with her modeling agency. During the first few weeks of her marriage, after returning from a week-long honeymoon in Europe, she felt reasonably contented. However, as the weeks went on, she began to experience increasing dissatisfaction with her new life, which she subsequently described as "totally empty." Although she was frequently visited by friends, she still felt very much alone. Charles was often away on business and the couple's relationship began to "feel strained" when the two were together. Although they had previously enjoyed an active sex life, the couple gradually became sexually estranged. Bethany thought their relationship might improve if she resumed her modeling career, but when she tried to discuss the matter with Charles, he refused to listen to her, stating "I will not suffer the humiliation of having any wife of mine parading about like a piece of meat." When she suggested that they go to marriage counseling, Charles refused, saying that there was nothing that the two couldn't resolve on their own. However, a close friend convinced Bethany to seek counseling, even though her husband would not agree to come along. The friend recommended Dr. David Walker.

In therapy with Dr. Walker, Bethany often expressed a desire to leave her husband but also expressed fears of "being by herself" and of not "making it on her own" without guidance from her husband. On the one hand, she complained of boredom, loneliness, and desperation; on the other, she expressed reluctance to give up what she now had to return to the precariousness of her former existence. It was a lot "easier and less risky," she said, "just to stay right where I am."

Dr. Walker knew from personal experience how difficult it could be to stand up to the fear of making changes in one's life without any guarantees. Having been through a divorce 3 years earlier after a 13-year marriage, Dr. Walker felt a personal bond with Bethany. He had struggled with similar issues and felt the force of inertia as he mustered up enough inner strength to leave a wife with whom he had lived unhappily for over a decade.

When Bethany began to make romantic overtures toward him—telling him that she found him extremely attractive, that she was falling in love with him, and asking him if he felt the same about her—Dr. Walker found himself in a more perplexing situation. In response to Bethany's query about his feelings toward her, Dr. Walker responded by stating, "I think you are a very attractive woman but as your therapist it would be inappropriate and definitely not in your best interest if I were to become personally involved with you."

Although he considered Bethany's overtures to be a result of transference, he began to question the appropriateness of counseling a woman who awakened so much of his own personal turmoil, and he worried about the possibility of his own countertransference. Dr. Walker was also sexually attracted to Bethany. There had been other occasions in which he was sexually attracted to female clients whom he managed to counsel successfully, but Dr. Walker felt less confident in the present case. At this time, Bethany had been in therapy for 6 months. Although he believed she had made significant progress in this period, he also believed it would be best for her if she were referred to another therapist. He therefore decided to terminate therapy and to refer her.

Dr. Walker explained to Bethany that he had personal problems of his own that made it inappropriate for him to continue as her therapist and that it was in her best interest to accept his referral. Notwithstanding Bethany's repeated pleas to know more, Dr. Walker refused to comment on what exactly those personal problems were except to emphasize that they were his, not her, problems. Bethany declined the referral and, in tears, left his office, neither seeking nor receiving therapy from anyone else again.

Dr. Walker did not himself seek professional counseling for his personal problems. However, as a result of his experience with Bethany, he did subsequently avoid practicing marriage counseling, especially with young, attractive female clients.

About 2 years after ending their professional relationship, Dr. Walker met Bethany while shopping at a supermarket and they began to talk. Bethany explained that she had divorced Charles a year earlier and that she was presently trying to get back into fashion modeling but was finding it difficult to make headway. The two exchanged phone numbers. A week later Dr. Walker called Bethany and asked her out on a date. They subsequently began a sexual relationship.

As we have seen, the primary purpose of a therapist is to promote the welfare of the client. In this case, Dr. Walker's decision to terminate Bethany's counseling was a rational response to the problem of how best to fulfill this primary counseling mission. Dr. Walker was aware that his personal emotions were potentially harmful to Bethany's continued therapeutic advancement. In particular, he was aware that his sexual attraction for this client, coupled with his apparently unresolved feelings about his former marriage and divorce, provided a climate for countertransference. In this regard, Dr. Walker's decision to terminate was consistent with the principle of loyalty insofar as his personal conflict prevented him from maintaining independence of judgment in providing treatment. As provided by APA (1992) Standard 1.13c, a therapist who becomes aware of a personal problem that has potential for interfering with his or her providing professional services should take "appropriate measures," which may include terminating therapy (see Chapter 4).

In referring Bethany to another therapist when he terminated his treatment of her, Dr. Walker further sought to safeguard her welfare. There was, of course, the risk that Bethany might refuse Dr. Walker's referral and never again seek counseling, a possibility that did in fact occur. Dr. Walker then had the problem of deciding which option—referral or continued therapy—ran the greatest chance of minimizing harm and maximizing welfare for this client.

In making this utilitarian determination, however, Dr. Walker could not, mechanically and dispassionately calculate the risks of each available option. On the one hand, he had to try to transcend his own subjective feelings to assess the situation rationally. On the other hand, he had to stay in touch with those very feelings that he sought to transcend in the process of deciding.

Were the emotions he was now experiencing more of an impediment to successful counseling than previous experiences he had had when he chose not to refer a particular client? Was the present case really different from the previous ones? To answer these questions, Dr. Walker could not merely be an impartial and objective observer applying a rational standard, as Kantian ethics would require (see Chapter 1). Nevertheless, while he had to live his feelings to adequately represent them, he also had to attain some measure of rational distance from them.

According to Martin (1997), such "professional distance" can be defined as

> a reasonable response in pursuing professional values by avoiding inappropriate personal involvements while maintaining a sense of personal engagement and responsibility. Under-distancing is the undesirable interference of personal values with professional standards. Over-distancing is the equally undesirable loss of personal involvement, whether in the form of denying one's responsibility for one's actions or in the form of lacking desirable forms of caring about clients and community. (p. 41)

How can a professional determine whether client engagement avoids these extremes and is therefore proper?

Such determination, according to Martin (1997), constitutes an "Aristotelian mean" between these extremes. It must rest with perception and sound judgment enlightened by experience (see Chapter 1). As a general rule, this mean appears to be reached in therapy when the therapist gets as close to the client's situation as possible without losing her ability to assess it rationally, for it is at this point that the therapist's powers of empathetic caring and understanding are at their highest rational level. The point at which a therapist has attained this mean and has therefore stretched her rational capacities to their limits appears to be relative to both situation and individual therapist and may not always be attainable. Thus, while Dr. Walker has successfully treated clients to whom he was sexually attracted, at least some therapists might not be able to work with such clients successfully and had best refer them. On the other hand, Dr. Walker was not sanguine about his ability to work with Bethany without under-distancing himself.

In deciding whether to refer, Dr. Walker needed to remain personally engaged yet detached enough to make a rational judgment about what would be best for his client's welfare. Paradoxically, he had to attain proper distance to decide whether, in counseling Bethany, he would be able to maintain proper distance.

Martin (1997) claims that maintaining such distance within a professional relationship serves at least three important functions. First, it can help professionals to cope efficiently with difficult situations by keeping them from becoming emotionally overwhelmed. Second, proper distance can help in promoting a professional's respect for clients' autonomy. Third, it can help a professional to maintain objectivity. Insofar as loss of professional distance militates against these three functions, serious potential for loss of proper professional distance in counseling Bethany would have afforded Dr. Walker sufficient reason for termination..

Loss of professional distance, in particular under-distancing himself from Bethany, could have destroyed his ability to cope with Bethany's crisis by resulting in countertransference. In such an instance, Dr. Walker's inability to keep personal interests separate from those of client could well have clouded and distorted his professional judgment regarding client welfare and thereby preempted the provision of competent counseling services.

With loss of proper professional distance, Dr. Walker would accordingly have also suffered loss of objectivity, that is "critical detachment, impartiality, the absence of distorting biases and blinders" (Martin, 1997, p. 46). Had Dr. Walker allowed his personal interests and emotions to seep into the professional relationship, his perception would have been biased and as such not objective. For example, in overidentifying with Bethany's plight as an extension of his own negative marital experience, he would no longer have been impartial. He would have had blinders on, interpreting Bethany's circumstances in terms of his own values and interests, seeking resolution not of Bethany's crisis but of his own.

In Dr. Walker's case, loss of proper professional distance could also have affected client autonomy by impairing his powers of empathy. We have seen (Chapter 3) that empathy can be an important autonomy-facilitating virtue. This virtue, however, demands proper professional distance by requiring a therapist to feel as if he were in the client's subjective world without ever losing the "as if" quality. Dr. Walker's failure to keep his own subjectivity separate from that of his client would have precluded the possibility of his accurately sensing the feelings and meanings being experienced by the client, for these experiences would have been filtered through Dr. Walker's own self-interest and personal emotions. As a result, Dr. Walker would not have been able to give his client competent help in accurately clarifying her feelings. However, it is through such increased self-understanding that Bethany could reasonably hope to gain greater control over her own behavior and life circumstances.

Because of the serious possibility that he would not be able to maintain the proper professional distance, Dr. Walker's continued counseling of Bethany might have been colored by his own self-interest and misguided ideas, impeding her progress toward greater autonomy and well-being, thus violating the primary counseling mission. Under these conditions, Bethany's own state of dependency would have made her vulnerable to the exploitation and manipulation that easily arises when a counselor does not clearly separate his or her personal welfare, interests, or needs from those of the client.

Dr. Walker's decision to terminate treatment was in keeping with his moral responsibility not to use his professional power and authority in a manner that might exploit client dependency and vulnerability. The vulnerability of this client was heightened because of the therapist's diminished capacity for objectivity toward her. Therefore, the principle of vulnerability required him to exercise special care to avoid harming her in any way. This additional moral responsibility to take *special care* was discharged by Dr. Walker when, in consideration of his personal conflict, he decided to terminate her treatment.

From a Kantian perspective, the rationale for termination is also apparent. As Bethany's therapist, Dr. Walker had the responsibility of helping her increase her personal autonomy. However, if he had continued her therapy instead of terminating, he would have risked treating her as a means of satisfying his own confused interests and desires rather than treating her as an autonomous agent.

Dr. Walker's motive for terminating Bethany's therapy—namely, to safeguard her welfare—could also consistently be cast as a universal law, as such a law would align with and support the primary counseling mission. Note, however, that not all motives for termination could meet this Kantian standard. For example, had Dr. Walker terminated Bethany's therapy for the express purpose of beginning a sexual relationship with her, this motive would not have universal application for this reason: If therapists consistently and universally sacrificed their clients' welfare whenever it suited their personal interests or needs, clients would not trust their therapists and therefore counseling would not work effectively. Furthermore, to consent to a universal law of such betrayal would be to consent to being treated as an object rather than as an autonomous agent, which no rational person would do. This example illustrates why the ACA now requires therapists who intend to have sexual relationships with former clients to ascertain that they did not terminate therapy as part of a plan to initiate a sexual relationship with the client (ACA, 1995, A.7.b). More generally the ACA also provides that counselors should "avoid actions that seek to meet their personal needs at the expense of clients" (ACA, 1995, A.5.a).

Some have suggested that no violation of client autonomy occurs when a client *consents* to termination of therapy to begin a sexual relationship. After all, is this not respecting the client's will rather than engaging in a form of betrayal? Suppose Bethany were willing to discontinue therapy so she and Dr. Walker could begin a relationship: Would Dr. Walker not have respected her autonomy (self-determination) by obliging her?

If her attraction to Dr. Walker was a case of transference, for him to have a sexual relationship with her would have been to exploit and manipulate her dependency, not to foster her autonomy. As we have seen (Chapter 4), obtaining a client's consent counts as recognition of client autonomy *only* if the consent is freely given and uncoerced. Given Bethany's vulnerable state of mind, how can Dr. Walker be sure that her consent was "free" and "uncoerced"? At the least, with Dr. Walker's own impaired capacity for objectivity and the potential for him to cause serious harm to Bethany, such conduct would have been a blatant violation of Dr. Walker's moral responsibility to safeguard the welfare of a vulnerable client.

In terminating the counseling relationship, should Dr. Walker have told Bethany why he was terminating her therapy? It is arguable that by not fully informing Bethany of the reasons for termination, Dr. Walker had failed to act in a manner befitting a candid and congruent therapist. In support of the principle of candor, the APA provides that "psychologists make reasonable efforts to answer patients' questions and to avoid apparent misunderstandings about therapy"(APA, 1992, 4.01.d). In further support, the ACA provides that "whenever counseling is initiated, and throughout the counseling process as necessary, counselors inform clients of the purposes, goals, techniques, procedures, limitations, potential risks and benefits of services to be performed, and other pertinent information" (ACA, 1995, A.3.a). In still further support, the ACA provides that in terminating counseling, counselors should aim at "securing agreement when possible" (A.11.c).

Unfortunately, Bethany was not given the opportunity to provide informed consent to termination as she was denied information material to termination, information that any client in similar circumstances would reasonably want to know. Thereby, she was not treated as an "end in herself"—that is, as a self-determining agent. Additionally, Dr. Walker left Bethany in a state of frustration and bewilderment. Was she to blame for Dr. Walker's decision to terminate despite his insistence that it was due to "his problem"? Because Dr. Walker had already admitted that he found Bethany attractive, was termination a result of his feelings toward her? Did he really love her? On the other hand, was he just offended by her having told him she was attracted to him? In refusing to disclose his grounds for termination, Dr. Walker failed to achieve adequate closure to therapy, and Bethany was simply left hanging.

Dr. Walker had stated earlier that he found Bethany to be "a very attractive woman"; but this had been at Bethany's prompting, so the statement could have been construed by Bethany as merely an attempt to appease her. Because Dr. Walker did not follow through with an explicit, candid disclosure for ending treatment, therapy ended on an inauthentic note. In failing to acknowledge his own feelings, Dr. Walker missed a final and important opportunity to model congruence and so to encourage Bethany to take similar responsibility for her own future life decisions.

What might Dr. Walker have said to Bethany in response to her request for further information about why he was terminating and referring her?

The truth, as presented along the following lines, would probably have been sufficient: "I have not completely worked through my own divorce, which, coupled with my own sexual attraction for you, has made it difficult for me to remain professionally objective and to provide you with the competent counseling services to which you are entitled. In cases like this, it is my professional responsibility to refer you to someone who will afford you such services." In making disclosure along these lines, Dr. Walker would have responded in a manner befitting a candid and congruent therapist and consistent with the primary counseling mission.

Dr. Walker's experience with Bethany appropriately alerted him to the possibility that his own unresolved feelings surrounding his divorce justified his refusing to accept clients whose profiles were similar to Bethany's. In concert with the principle of loyalty, the APA (1992) cautions psychologists to "refrain from undertaking an activity when they know or should know that their personal problems are likely to lead to harm to patient, client . . . or other person to whom they may owe a professional or scientific obligation" (1.13.a). As his failure to have worked through his own marital issues affected his ability to provide competent counseling services, Dr. Walker also had a professional responsibility to obtain competent counseling for himself. In line with the principle of nonmaleficence, the ACA directs counselors to "refrain from offering or accepting professional services when their physical, mental or emotional problems are likely to harm a client or others. They are alert to the signs of impairment, seek assistance for problems, and, if necessary, limit, suspend, or terminate their professional responsibilities"(ACA, 1995, C.2.g).

In this case, neither Dr. Walker nor Bethany sought therapy for their personal problems after their professional relationship ceased. It was under these circumstances, about 2 years later, that Dr. Walker and Bethany began a sexual relationship.

Quite possibly Bethany's sexual attraction and willingness to begin a sexual relationship with Dr. Walker resulted from the same transference problem that led Dr. Walker to terminate therapy in the first place. Similarly, Dr. Walker's own sexual attraction and willingness to begin a sexual relationship with Bethany might themselves have been an actualization of his previously perceived tendency to countertransfer. If so, the possibility for client manipulation and harm that existed in therapy could be hypothesized to continue to exist in the personal relationship. Furthermore, in his personal relationship with Bethany, Dr. Walker was no longer expected to maintain professional distance or to be objective; therefore, the potential for even greater manipulation of and harm to the client could be hypothesized to exist.

In keeping with the principle of nonmaleficence, Dr. Walker had a professional responsibility to avoid harming others, a class that clearly included former clients. Because his beginning a personal relationship with Bethany placed her at significant risk of harm—and arguably at even greater risk than in their previous professional relationship—Dr. Walker had a professional responsibility to avoid such a relationship with Bethany. In addition, because this potential for harm may be traced to the exercise of power and authority established in the therapeutic context, Dr. Walker could be viewed as having used his *professional* power and authority in a manner inconsistent with Bethany's welfare. The rule of "once a client, always a client" would seem to derive force from the implausibility of supposing that a client's welfare matters only within the professional context and subsequently becomes expendable as soon as therapy is formally ended.

Because professional safeguards were no longer expected in the personal relationship, all knowledge previously acquired in the therapeutic context was no longer insulated from personal use. Thus, by virtue of his personal relation with Bethany, Dr. Walker was no longer expected to remain objective and professionally distanced, yet he still had information previously protected by such professional responsibilities. Considering the emotional dynamics of personal relationships, the potential for misuse of such knowledge will have accordingly increased. For example, in the throes of an emotionally heated disagreement, Dr. Walker might allow his perception to be colored by his intimate knowledge of Bethany's former marriage. This could affect his own verbal, behavioral, and emotional responses to Bethany. If knowledge acquired under a bond of professional confidentiality is subsequently used for personal purposes, the principle of discretion will also be breached. As the APA (1992) states, "Psychologists discuss confidential information obtained in clinical or consulting relationships . . . only for appropriate professional and scientific purposes" (5.03.b); it is clear that use of private client information for personal, self-interested reasons falls outside the purview of such legitimate purposes.

It is possible, of course, that Dr. Walker could manage to keep such private information out of his personal life. Nevertheless, therapists are human beings who have emotions and do not always perform at their best. Therefore, expecting therapists to avoid at all times being influenced by prior clinical knowledge of a person with whom they are in an intimate relationship may be asking too much of the best adjusted therapist. In Dr. Walker's case, however, there were already reasons for supposing that he had unresolved problems that would make such expectations all the more unrealistic.

Furthermore, maintaining such a stature is tantamount to expecting the therapist to fulfill his professional responsibilities within the context of a personal relationship. Role expectations between professional and personal relationships are notoriously inconsistent. Thus, in personal relationships, "there is an expectation that the needs of both parties will be met in a more or less reciprocal manner. It is difficult to consistently put the consumer's needs first if one is also invested in meeting one's own needs. . . . As the incompatibility of expectations increases between roles, so will the potential for misunderstanding and harm" (Kitchener, 1988, p. 219).

Clearly, in starting a sexual relationship with a former client, Dr. Walker acted contrary to the primary counseling mission by taking substantial, unwarranted risks. Even though Dr. Walker waited 2 years before seeing Bethany nonprofessionally, as some standards (for example, APA and ACA) require, there were strong reasons militating against his starting the relationship at all. Had Dr. Walker attempted to show that this relationship did not have an exploitive basis, it is questionable that he would have been in a position to assess the matter objectively. Under the circumstances, it would have been more fitting had he called in a consultant to help him to decide on his course of action (ACA, 1995, C.2.e). An unbiased ethics assessment from an outsider would probably have been more reliable than Dr. Walker's own determination.

It is evident that a 2-year waiting period is not itself a reliable index of warranted sexual relations with former clients. As the APA has suggested, sanction for sexual relations with former clients is most unusual. Had Dr. Walker seen Bethany on a single occasion without having established an ongoing professional relation with her, a subsequent relationship might have been permissible. Here, however, there is still danger of the appearance of conflict of interest—or even worse, of actual exploitation of clients. A profession cannot afford to have its image tarnished. Therapists concerned for the welfare of prospective clients cannot afford to neglect their professional image. A professional known to have had sex with former clients—no matter how well the relation might have been documented—does nothing to promote himself or herself as trustworthy and virtuous in the public eye.

Finally, legal requirements need not always be in harmony with professional standards. Some causes may be morally compelling enough to override obedience to law, but it is unlikely that violation of a state statute in order to engage in a sexual relationship with a former client would qualify. If sexual relations with former clients were legally regarded as sexual misconduct in the state in which Dr. Walker practiced, there would have been further reason, an overriding and compelling reason, for his not engaging in such a relationship with Bethany. In the absence of such a state statute, there would also have been a compelling case against it.

CASE 2: COUNSELING STUDENTS: A CASE OF A NONELECTIVE DUAL-ROLE RELATIONSHIP

Dr. Carver is a professor of counselor education at a local university. He also has a private counseling practice. His students sometimes request counseling for themselves or family members, but he has been careful not to take his students or their family members as clients, referring them instead to other local, qualified therapists. However, he has occasionally agreed to see other university employees; for example, he once counseled his departmental secretary. He has also sometimes taken referrals from his students, such as friends of students, and once counseled a former student.

One such referral, Christi Compton, was a friend of a student in one of Dr. Carver's courses. Christi, a 26-year-old women, sought counseling for depression. She had been institutionalized 3 years earlier for attempting to commit suicide by overdosing on sleeping pills. Prior to Dr. Carver's joining the faculty, Christi had been a graduate student at the university enrolled in the counseling program. When she became seriously depressed, she withdrew from classes. Three weeks later, she attempted suicide.

At the time Christi began therapy with Dr. Carver, she lived alone and was working as a salesperson in a women's clothing store. Christi, a gay woman, had nobody special whom see was seeing. She had previously lived with a partner who abruptly left her for someone else. She sought therapy with Dr. Carver to help overcome her feelings of grief related to the loss of her partner and to find meaning in what she described as a "mean, insensitive, homophobic universe."

As therapy progressed, Christi began to express greater optimism about the prospects for the future. She began to date again and was now seeing someone steadily. Christi reaffirmed her earlier plan to become a therapist. She reentered the counseling program at the university and signed up for her remaining coursework, including Dr. Carver's counseling ethics course, which was a degree requirement.

When Christi informed Dr. Carver (after the fact) that she had signed up for his class, Dr. Carver was taken back. He informed her that doing so would create a conflict of interest for him. Christi proclaimed, however, how it was through Dr. Carver's support that she was ready to return to school in the first place. She pointed out that she needed the course in order to sit for her comprehensive exams, that the course would not be offered again until the following year (which would only postpone her graduation another year), that there was just one section of the course being offered, and that no other university within commuting distance offered the course.

When Dr. Carver suggested referring her to another therapist, Christi became very upset and stated that she did not want to see anyone else. She proclaimed, "Just when things are getting better for me, you want to walk out on me. That's the way things always go for me." And she pleaded with him to continue the therapeutic relationship. Dr. Carver told her he would think about it and let her know at their next weekly session. In the beginning of the next session, he told her that he had decided to retain her as his client. He also informed her that he might find it useful to consult with colleagues on this case from time to time. He also asked her not to disclose to anyone in the class that she was his client. Christi expressed satisfaction with that arrangement.

The semester began and Christi attended Dr. Carver's class. While Christi appeared comfortable with the arrangement, Dr. Carver found the situation increasingly uncomfortable. In discussing dual-role relationships in class, for example, he felt particularly uncomfortable, especially when Christi actively argued in class that there was "nothing wrong with them as long as the therapist and client were in agreement." Dr. Carver did not challenge her argument. Feeling constrained by her presence, he instead glossed quickly over the subject, omitting careful explication of the problematic nature of counseling students and supervisees (in contrast to previous semesters in which he treated this subject in great length).

In grading essay exams, Dr. Carver felt even more uncomfortable. In deciding whether, for example, to give her essay a "C" or a "B" he found it difficult to bracket the question of how hard his client, whom he knew was aiming at getting "A's" and "B's," might take the disappointment of getting a "C." On the one hand, he believed that she needed to learn to cope with disappointment, he also worried about her present ability to do so. Although Dr. Carver was able to "get through" the semester, he felt that his discomfort with the situation had negatively affected both his ability to teach the course and his objectivity in grading.

In therapy, Christi would sometimes talk to Dr. Carver about course material and discussions that had transpired in class. On consideration, however, he believed that the class was now a significant part of her life and that it would be frustrating and counterproductive for Christi to prevent her from speaking freely about matters related to class. Some sessions, however, began to sound more like ethics class than therapy sessions. Dr. Carver did not, however, think it necessary to consult or seek supervision. Moreover, he was reluctant to do so because his colleagues were instructors at the college; he worried about disclosing to them that he was counseling a client as the college had a policy forbidding the counseling of students.

Nevertheless as therapy progressed, Christi began to express renewed vitality for life. She and the person whom she was dating became intimate and decided to live together. Upon completion of the course, she enrolled in classes for the following session. Dr. Carver began phasing down sessions to once every 2 weeks. Thus, when Christi, after having an argument with her partner, attempted suicide again (albeit unsuccessfully), Dr. Carver was shocked and regretful for the manner in which he had handled her case.

This case raises questions surrounding the morality of several types of dual-role relationships: accepting co-workers as clients, accepting current students or their close relatives as clients, accepting referrals from students, and maintaining counseling relationships with clients after they become students.

According to the principle of loyalty, a therapist has a moral responsibility to maintain independence of judgment in acting in matters related to clients' treatment and to take reasonable precautions against loss of such judgment. However, in accepting co-workers as his clients, Dr. Carver voluntarily placed himself in dual-role relationships in which serious potential existed for loss of independence of judgment by both client and therapist. For example, the departmental secretary could feel compelled to do special favors for Dr. Carver, which she would not feel obliged to do for other department members; or she could feel intimidated about making disclosures in therapy for fear of how Dr. Carver might view her professionally. Similarly, Dr. Carver could allow his professional interest in secretarial services to color his counseling services—for example, avoiding confrontation so as not to disrupt the work relationship. While such losses of objectivity and exploitation need not result, given their serious potential, Dr. Carver had a professional and moral responsibility to avoid these dual relationships (ACA, 1995, A.6.a.). Had Dr. Carver agreed to counseling an adjunct on the faculty of another discipline whom he neither knew nor worked with professionally, the case would have been different. The potential for loss of independence of judgment would not have been significant as there would be affiliation without a proximate working relationship.

Professional standards generally also prohibit therapists from recruiting clients for private practice through their place of employment (ACA, 1995, C.3.d). It is not clear that Dr. Carver actively solicited or recruited clients through his workplace, but his willingness to take on co-employees as clients violated the spirit of this proscription, which is to prevent conflicts of interest, real or apparent. Even if Dr. Carver encountered no actual conflict of interest, the appearance of a conflict can also harm a profession by raising public distrust. A virtuous therapist, dedicated to the prosperity of his profession, would avoid apparent conflicts of interest.

Dr. Carver's refusal to take on current students and family members agreed with the principle of loyalty as this policy avoided the serious possibility for the therapist of loss of independence of judgment. The policy of referring rather than counseling students as well as supervisees is standard in professional codes of ethics. For example, according to the ACA *Code of Ethics* (1995), "If students or supervisees request counseling, supervisors or counselor educators provide them with acceptable referrals. Supervisors or counselor educators do not serve as counselor to students or supervisees over whom they hold administrative, teaching, or evaluative roles unless this is a brief role associated with a training program" (F.3.c).

A conflict need not arise in the instruction of former clients. As the student would have been in therapy before becoming a student, the instructional role is not likely to affect past therapy adversely. However, former clients may, and often do, seek additional therapy. It is therefore important that therapists be alert to the possibility that their former clients could request additional therapy while they are students. In such cases, conflict of interest could be avoided by making a suitable referral.

Counseling former students may also have potential for creating future conflicts of interest. If the former student Dr. Carver agreed to counsel was likely to enroll in further courses with Dr. Carver, his acceptance of this individual as a client would have been shortsighted indeed. On the other hand, had the student in question already graduated and received his degree, the potential for future conflict might have been minimal. Due care for avoidance of problematic, future dual-role relationships would therefore support the professional responsibility of therapists to verify the status of former students before accepting them as clients. More generally, such a standard of due care supports a professional responsibility of therapists who teach to decline accepting as a client anyone they know, or have good reason to believe, will become a student in the course of therapy.

In the case of family members of students, the relationship often goes beyond affiliation. Counseling clients often requires involvement by other family members, especially the client's immediate family, so the risk that the student will also become a client can be substantial. Dr. Carver's refusal to counsel family members of students was therefore on firm ground.

The issue of whether to accept referrals *from* students is another matter. Insofar as accepting these referrals cannot be expected to result in dual-role relationships in which the client also becomes a student of the therapist, a policy of accepting unsolicited referrals made by students fits with the principle of loyalty. Admittedly, as a friend of the client, the student may become indirectly involved in the counseling relationship—for instance, as a subject of counseling sessions. Therapists can thereby learn things about their students that may have bearing on the therapist's assessment of the student in her role as teacher. However, the therapist is still afforded some insulation from the student by virtue of not having a counseling relationship with the student. Furthermore, there are many ways in which teachers may learn things about their students outside the teaching context. As teachers and students are members of the same community, they are likely to have mutual acquaintances or shared avenues through which information is disseminated within the community. For example, the professor's next-door neighbor may be his student.

The case of Christi presents a more difficult moral problem. There are several competing interests at stake in this case. First Dr. Carver must regard Christi's physical and mental welfare as well as her interest in advancing her education. Second, Dr. Carver has an interest in providing competent and fair instructional services to all his students.. Third, Dr. Carver's professionalism as an instructor is on the line. His violation of a university policy proscribing counseling of students is a breach of a professional trust he has assumed with the university. Fourth, such a violation might well have untoward effects on his career—for example, disciplinary action by the university and perhaps the loss of his job, especially if he is a relatively new, untenured faculty member. In keeping with the principle of considerateness, Dr. Carver's moral problem is that of addressing the welfare, interests, and needs of the concerned individuals without any unnecessary sacrifices. Because Dr. Carver is a therapist, his primary professional responsibility is to the welfare, interests, and needs of his client. On the other hand, in his capacity as professor, Dr. Carver's primary professional responsibility is to provide fair and competent instruction. Unfortunately, he is torn in incompatible directions in trying to address each of these professional responsibilities at once.

As an instructor, he is expected not to place any of his students at any unfair advantage or disadvantage. Each student should get the grade she deserves. Thus, in its *Statement on Professional Ethics*, the American Association of University Professors (AAUP, 1990, p. 75) asserts that "professors [should] make every reasonable effort to foster honest academic conduct and to ensure that their evaluations of students reflect each student's true merit." As a counselor educator, Dr. Carver has the specific responsibility to train prospective counselors. He therefore has a responsibility to the public not to misrepresent the qualifications of these prospective counselors.

Further, such a public trust requires that any relationships with students tending to thwart teaching effectiveness should be avoided. "As members of an academic institution, professors seek above all to be effective teachers and scholars" (AAUP, 1990, p. 76). Insofar as counseling Christi has compromised his ability to provide fair and effective instructional and evaluation services, Dr. Carver's role as counselor is incompatible with his role as counselor educator.

On the other side, the teacher-student relationship that Dr. Carver has established with Christi is incompatible with the primary counseling mission. As we have seen (Chapter 3), therapy is most likely to be effective when therapists possess and display personal attributes that encourage clients to become more self-directive and independent. Virtuous therapists must possess and display unconditional positive regard for their clients. They accept clients as the persons they are, not the persons the therapists want them to be. The virtuous therapist encourages clients to have their own ideas and feelings, to freely explore them, and to make decisions for themselves.

Teachers as well as therapists have a responsibility to "demonstrate respect for students as individuals and adhere to their proper roles as intellectual guides and counselors" (AAUP, 1990, p. 76); however, it is not part of the role of a therapist formally, objectively, and officially to evaluate and grade their clients. This responsibility falls within the role of the professor, and in particular the role of a counselor educator who is expected as a matter of public trust to evaluate student performance fairly. When Dr. Carver became Christi's teacher, he also assumed a public trust to grade and assess her according to her merit.

This evaluative role is not necessarily inconsistent with a therapist's unconditional positive regard for his client. Nevertheless, it can be confusing to the client who may wonder whether what she says in therapy will affect her grade, or whether it is even appropriate, let alone safe, to get worked up emotionally or to express irrational desires and inner conflicts to a therapist who, as her teacher, is expecting her to be rational. In Christi's case, such client confusion and loss of independence of judgment may have helped to impede therapeutic progress.

The blending of the teacher-student relationship with the therapist-client relationship also probably diverted valuable time from significant, personal issues to course-related matters that would otherwise have been better left for the classroom. Dr. Carver's reasoning that class materials were relevant to Christi's therapy was, if true, itself a negative consequence of a confusion of professional roles. A diligent therapist would have avoided such role blending in the first place if it could reasonably be expected to impair the quality of services rendered.

As an instructor, Dr. Carver had a professional responsibility to be intellectually honest (AAUP, 1990). In the present context, this would include standing behind his moral convictions. Unless Professor Carver were to rationalize away and deny the dangerous consequences of counseling a student, he was remiss in not clearly and carefully emphasizing the dangers of such relationships in a class on professional ethics for prospective counselors. Inasmuch as he failed to do so, he violated a public trust. His failure to present a thorough coverage of dual-role relationships to his class and to correct any misunderstandings about such relationships was dishonest. It was also a breach of the primary responsibility that professors have to their subject "to state the truth as they see it" (AAUP, 1990, p. 75).

Yet, with his client seated before him in his class, Dr. Carver ran a risk of undermining, or appearing to undermine, the very position he had subscribed to in agreeing to counsel that student. To his client, he might have seemed disingenuous, incongruent, and unworthy of trust. In agreeing to counsel his student, Dr. Carver entered a dual-role relationship with inherent conflict of responsibilities and risks to both student and client.

Dr. Carver did not *initiate* the dual-role relationship. He did not intentionally take on a student as his client. Rather, a client elected to become his student. The emerging relationship was a *nonelective* dual-role relationship—that is, one not created by his own actions but rather by those of someone else: his client, in this case. Dr. Carver's decision to counsel Christi was thus more precisely a decision to maintain the dual-role relationship rather than to create one. This, however, did not release Dr. Carver of the moral responsibility to address the problem raised by such a relationship.

Christi had previously been a student at the same university and counseling program in which Dr. Carver taught. Before accepting her as his client, Dr. Carver could have explored with Christi the possibility of her returning to the program. Although Christi may not have had any intention of returning then, Dr. Carver's informing Christi at the outset of his policy of not counseling his students might have set the stage for a more careful approach to the issue by both of them later. It also would have given Christi the opportunity, before establishing a bond with Dr. Carver, to seriously consider pursuing therapy with a different therapist, allowing herself the future option of returning to school. Further, because Dr. Carver at least had reason to suspect that Christi might some day return to school, he had a moral responsibility to provide her with this information as part of her informed consent to therapy.

Once therapy was initiated, Dr. Carver still faced the challenge of deciding whether and how to discontinue the dual-role relationship. In confronting this challenge, Dr. Carver needed to empathize with his client's subjective perspective. Christi perceived the world as "mean, insensitive, and homophobic." As a gay woman, she had apparently encountered antagonism and prejudice from others who lacked moral sensitivity. She had also experienced the loss of a significant other who left her for someone else. With her history of sensitivity to what she perceived as rejection of *her*, coupled with a history of attempted suicide, it is understandable that Dr. Carver did not want to place any unnecessary strain on her emotions. He truly cared for her and wanted to shelter her from harm, even at the expense of violating other important professional responsibilities. Unfortunately, in his zeal to protect her, he also supported her lack of self-assurance and independence, which probably contributed to her second suicide attempt.

Dr. Carver accepted Christi's reasons for maintaining a dual relationship without carefully exploring the implications of doing so. Although he informed her that such an arrangement would create a conflict of interest for him, he failed to inform her of the potential risks of such a dual-role relationship (ACA, 1995, A.3.6) and therefore failed to be candid. These risks, as we have seen, included the potential for loss of independence of judgment for both client and therapist.

Dr. Carver also failed to inform Christi that counseling a student was against university policy and that doing so could cost him his job. Christi wanted to take the course with Dr. Carver out of concern for her own professional advancement. Dr. Carver missed an opportunity to allow Christi to draw out the consistent applications of her own logic.

He also failed to consult on a complex ethical problem about which he apparently had questions. He indicated to Christi that he might seek consultation with colleagues, but he was instead motivated to conceal his predicament from professional colleagues for fear that he would be exposed for his violation. However, according to the ACA *Code of Ethics* (1995), counselors should "take reasonable steps to consult with other counselors or related professionals when they have questions regarding their ethical obligations or professional practice" (C.2.e).

In accepting Christi's reasons for taking the course with him without careful exploration, Dr. Carver missed an opportunity to work with Christi toward a reasonable alternative. For example, the possibility of asking another qualified professor to do a directed independent study was not raised.

In the end, however, if no such alternatives were feasible, the joint exploration of the problem at hand would have made the prospect of a referral appear more reasonable and not merely just another rejection. Such a mutual bond of respect, candor, honesty, congruence, and unconditional regard would have furnished an opportunity to promote greater self-assurance and independence in the client. It would have empowered her to make a free and informed decision about whether to wait another year to take the class and continue in therapy with Dr. Carver or to take the class with Dr. Carver and to accept his referral. Such client empowerment based on mutual respect and understanding would have better supported the primary counseling mission. Instead, Dr. Carver jeopardized client progress toward greater self-assurance, self-directiveness, and independence when he chose to remain in a dual-role relationship that impaired the independence of judgment of both therapist and client and strained therapist-client trust.

Ethical Standards for Addressing Dual-Role Relationships

The following rules of dual-role relationships may be gathered from the case studies and discussions provided in this chapter. They are not intended to be an exhaustive list of all such possible rules, but they are intended to supplement those provided under principles of loyalty and nonmaleficence in Chapter 4.

General Rules Regarding Dual-Role Relationships

GR 1 In considering whether a dual-role relationship is morally problematic and should be avoided or terminated, therapists consider the potential for loss of the client's independence of judgment as well as their own.

GR 2 Therapists consider the adverse effects that pursuing certain types of dual-role relationships, such as sexual relations with former clients, might have on the public image of their profession and avoid apparent conflicts of interest as well as actual ones.

GR 3 Therapists avoid any dual-role relationship in which a serious potential for misappropriation of confidential information exists, as in the use of such information for malicious or self-serving purposes.

GR 4 Therapists who have institutional affiliations—teaching at colleges or universities or working in agencies—avoid providing therapy to other employees with whom they have or are likely to have working relations.

GR 5 Therapists establish and maintain contact with other qualified professionals available to render competent, independent ethics consultation or supervision in case conflicts of interest make the therapists' own judgment questionable.

GR's 1 through 4 are based on the premise that therapists should take reasonable measures to avoid all dual-role relationships that have serious potential for loss of independence of judgment—the client's as well as the therapist's—and conflicts of interest—apparent and actual. These four rules provide key considerations for avoiding such relationships.

When therapists cannot feasibly avoid a conflict of interest, they should fully inform the affected clients about the conflict and, with the clients' consent, seek consultation and/or supervision from other qualified professionals (see GR 5) (ACA, 1995, A.6.a). In satisfying GR 5, therapists who work in agencies should establish and maintain contact with other competent professionals who practice outside their agencies and are therefore more likely to provide independent, nonbiased consultation or supervision. Therapists who practice in isolated rural areas have an especially compelling interest in establishing and maintaining such contacts.

These rules are intended to help guide therapists' decisions regarding dual-role relationships but are not a substitute for careful ethical reflection. For instance, while avoidance of apparent conflicts of interest is important for maintaining professional image, GR 2 must be applied with regard for the welfare, interests, and needs of particular clients. For example, a therapist might justly tolerate public appearance of a conflict of interest in order to prevent serious harm to an identifiable client whereas such involvement purely for personal gain would be unacceptable.

GR 1 stresses that morally problematic dual-role relationships can arise not only when the therapist encounters a conflict of interest but also when the *client's* independence of judgment is impaired. Because either case can result in ineffective or self-defeating therapy, a therapist may have compelling reason for avoiding or terminating a dual-role relationship even when it is only the client's judgment that is adversely affected.

The use of the term *qualified professional* in GR 5 refers to another competent therapist as well as to a competent professional in a related area such as a professional ethicist.

The term *working relations* in GR 4 means direct employee relations arising out of the cooperative performance of specific job-related tasks. Such tasks include secretarial, administrative, custodial, maintenance, committee, and departmental functions. Working relations must involve direct contact, which means exchange of information by face-to-face contact or other channels such as e-mail, phone, or interoffice memo. In general, the more frequent and intimate the job-related contact between therapist and client, the greater the potential for loss of independence of judgment by both parties. Thus, an occasional interoffice memo may not be as risky as ongoing face-to-face contact. The term *working relation* does not apply simply because two individuals have the same employer. In a very large institution such as a state university, it is possible that two employees have no working relation, but this is less likely to be true in smaller institutions such as counseling agencies.

Rules Regarding Sexual Relations with Former Clients

SF 1 Therapists do not engage in sexual relations with current clients and generally avoid sexual relations with former clients. In rare cases in which therapists are considering the propriety of sexual relations with former clients (for instance, in cases where no ongoing therapeutic relationship has been established), they consult with other competent, impartial professionals in documenting the nonexploitive nature of the considered relations.

SF 2 Therapists recognize that their former clients, like current clients, can still be vulnerable to sexual manipulation and therefore avoid taking undue sexual advantage of these individuals. Therapists do not assume that their former clients' agreement to enter into sexual relations with them constitutes freely given consent.

SF 3 If the state in which a therapist practices regards all sexual relations with former clients as sexual misconduct, then therapists do not engage in any such relations even when the relationship might otherwise be proper.

In SF 2, the term *undue sexual advantage* refers to the exploitation of any client weakness related to the prior therapist-client relationship—for example, an unresolved client transference issue, persistent client dependency on the therapist, or the therapist's position of power and authority over the client. Insofar as such client weaknesses may persist after therapy has been terminated, the burden of proof resides with the therapist to show that the client's consent to a sexual relation with the therapist is not a result of weaknesses but a product of the client's autonomous, uncoerced consent (NASW, 1997, 1.09.c). In the rare cases in which this can be shown, SF 1 requires that documentation include the favorable outcome of consultation with at least one other independent, competent professional, as defined above, in addition to the documentation specified in other pertinent standards addressed in this chapter (APA, 1992, 4.07; ACA, 1995, A.7.b).

A virtuous therapist would ordinarily have regard for law, but we have noted that some causes, such as prevention of serious harm to a client, may sometimes militate against compliance with law. Rule SF 3, however, is intended to make clear that satisfaction of the therapist's sexual interests—even when coupled with those of the former client—does not warrant or mitigate the legal transgression.

Rules Regarding Sexual Attraction to Clients

AC 1 Therapists are not disqualified from counseling clients to whom they are sexually attracted so long as they are able to provide these clients with competent, professional services. However, if they have or, in the course of therapy, develop sexual attractions for clients that impair or are likely to impair the therapists' independence of judgment, then they terminate therapy and make appropriate referrals.

AC 2 Therapists do not accept as clients individuals from certain populations (for instance, certain gender and age categories) for whom sexual feelings are likely to impair independence of judgment. In such cases therapists take appropriate steps to overcome their personal problems, such as seeking therapy for themselves, before taking on such individuals as clients.

AC 3 In cases where therapists terminate therapy due to mutual sexual attraction, therapists inform clients of the nature of termination and do not misrepresent or mislead clients as to the cause of termination.

AC 1 assumes that sexual attraction for at least some clients is a frequent occurrence and is not in itself a reason for terminating therapy. AC 1 affords therapists the autonomy to decide whether this attraction is so great as to impair professional judgment. Therapists' sexual attractions for clients may sometimes be related to therapists' own "unfinished business." In such cases, AC 2 recognizes the need for the therapist to address such personal problems therapeutically before counseling groups of clients to whom the sexual attraction may be generalized.

AC 3 is supported by principles of both honesty and candor in requiring therapists with sexual attractions for clients to avoid deception in informing these clients of the grounds for termination.

Rules Regarding Therapy with Students

TS 1 Therapists do not engage in therapy with current students or those with whom current students have intimate relationships. Consistent with client welfare, therapists may engage in therapy with former students.

TS 2 Therapists may not solicit students for referrals, but they may accept unsolicited referrals from students.

TS 3 If, during the course of therapy, therapists' clients also become their students, therapists take reasonable steps to terminate the ensuing dual-role relationships, including terminating therapy and providing appropriate referrals. Therapists inform their clients of all significant risks related to maintaining such dual-role relationships and, consistent with client welfare, decline to remain in both roles. Therapists support and encourage their clients' own informed, autonomous choices in resolving the conflict.

TS 4 Therapists who learn that prospective clients are likely to become their students decline to accept these individuals as clients. As part of their clients' informed consent to therapy, therapists who teach inform potential students (clients whose profiles suggest that they might become students) of a professional responsibility not to engage in therapy with their students.

In TS 1, the term *intimate relationships* includes family members such as parents, stepparents, grandparents, and siblings. The term also includes significant others such as boyfriends or girlfriends, fiancees, and sexual partners. An individual may not have a close relationship with all family members, but the probability that the family bond will implicate the student is substantial enough to justify a strict rule against counseling family members of students. Although TS 2 permits therapists to accept clients through unsolicited referrals from students, note that in concert with TS 1, such permissible, unsolicited referrals do not include individuals with whom students have intimate relationships.

TS 3 provides that therapists should take "reasonable measures" to terminate nonelective dual-role relationships with students. In the context of therapy, this means measures that are consistent with client welfare and that accordingly promote client trust and autonomy. The rule provides that clients be afforded maximal autonomy in deciding how the dual-role relationship will be resolved—for example, whether the student-teacher relationship will be preserved and the therapist-client relationship terminated, or the converse.

TS 4 recognizes the utility of taking preventive measures to increase the likelihood that a nonelective dual-role relationship with students is avoided before it is established by the student. It also conforms with the principle of candor in making clear, from the start, the therapist's professional responsibility not to counsel students. In this way, the therapist's move to discontinue such a relationship, should one later be established, comes as no surprise to the client.

Summary

This chapter has shown how the principle of loyalty discussed in Chapter 4 sets important ethical parameters on virtuous responses to morally problematic dual-role relationships; and it has shown how other professional virtues such as empathy and congruence play supportive roles in addressing these relationships.

Dual-role relationships exist when a professional assumes at least one additional role with respect to a given client. Such relationships are morally problematic when they involve *conflicts of interest*. Conflicts of interest exist when the assumption of dual roles places a strain on the professional's ability to maintain independence of judgment. Dual-role relationships can also be morally problematic when the *client's* independence of judgment is affected by her assumption of dual roles. Even if the therapist encounters no conflict of interest, the client's own inability to cope with the assumption of the dual roles can thwart therapeutic progress.

Two cases were presented and analyzed. The first case, concerning sexual dual-role relationships, raised issues of sexual attraction to clients and sex with former clients. The second case, concerning nonsexual dual-role relationships, raised issues regarding dual-role relationships with co-workers, current students, former students, and the family of students. The second case focused on ethical management of nonelective dual-role relationships with students. These relationships arise when a current client assumes the role of the therapist's student. This contrasts with the converse case in which the therapist elects to take one of her students as a client.

The case analyses presented in this chapter are not intended to illustrate all varieties of sexual and nonsexual dual-role relationships; however, general rules addressing dual-role and multiple-role relationships have been extracted from these cases and can be applied widely. In addition, more specialized rules concerning sexual attraction to clients, sexual relations with former clients, and therapy with students have been extracted. These rules collectively help to define loyal and trustworthy conduct for a therapist in the context of addressing morally problematic dual-role relationships. These standards cannot be mechanically applied, however. At the root of their application is moral sensitivity to the welfare, interests, and needs of clients. Without that, a therapist could not even appreciate the potential for client harm inherent in a problematic dual-role relationship, let alone avoid it.

REVIEW QUESTIONS

1. What is meant by a dual-role or multiple-role relationship?
2. When are dual-role relationships morally problematic?

3. What is meant by a simultaneous dual-role relationship? What is meant by a consecutive dual-role relationship? Provide examples of each.

4. Why do current professional and legal standards forbid any type of sexual intimacy with current clients?

5. Describe at least two different general approaches to dealing with morally problematic dual-role relationships. What are some benefits and disadvantages of each?

6. In deciding whether to engage in a dual-role relationship with a client, why would a therapist's ability to remain objective and unbiased in the relationship not necessarily justify the therapist's engaging in it?

7. What are some examples of so-called unavoidable dual-role relationships? List some possible precautions therapists involved in such situations might take to avoid harm to clients.

8. What is "professional distance" and what functions does it serve in the counseling process?

9. What do professional codes of ethics generally maintain about therapists having sexual intimacy with former clients?

10. What do professional codes of ethics generally maintain about therapists recruiting clients for private practice through their place of employment?

11. What is meant by a nonelective dual-role relationship? In the case of Dr. Carver and Christi (Case 2), why was the dual-role relationship established between these two individuals properly called a nonelective dual-role relationship?

DISCUSSION QUESTIONS

1. Can there be any justified exceptions to professional and legal standards forbidding sexual intimacy with current clients? For example, are sex therapists ever justified in having some form of sexual contact with a client as part of therapy? Defend your view.

2. Do you think that the prohibition against sexual intimacy between therapists and clients applies with equal force to other professions such as law, medicine, and teaching? Is the case for such a prohibition in counseling and psychotherapy any more compelling than in the other professions? Explain.

3. Do you agree with the provisions regarding sexual relationships with former clients as provided by Standard 4.07 of the American Psychological Association *Ethical Standards* (or by similar rules such as A.7.b of the American Counseling Association *Code of Ethics*)? In your estimation, could an absolute (exceptionless) prohibition against sexual relationships with former clients be justified?

4. In the case of Dr. Walker (Case 1), what specific problems and challenges did he confront in trying to maintain professional distance in counseling Bethany? In your estimation, did Dr. Walker succeed in maintaining professional distance in counseling her?

5. In your estimation, did Dr. Walker act appropriately in terminating therapy and making a referral? What reasons, if any, were there for terminating counseling? What risks, if any, were there in referring her?

6. Is it ever ethical for a therapist to terminate therapy for the purpose of beginning a sexual relationship? Would Dr. Walker have been justified in terminating therapy for this purpose if Bethany were consenting and had strong feelings in favor of the idea? Defend your responses.

7. Once Dr. Walker had decided to terminate therapy, did he have a responsibility to tell Bethany why he was terminating therapy? What, in your estimation, should he have told her?

8. If a therapist has a sexual attraction for a client, should the therapist inform the client of this and then let the client decide whether he or she wishes to continue the counseling? Should a therapist adopt a consistent policy of referring clients to whom he or she is sexually attracted? Defend your own position.

9. Was it sufficient for Dr. Walker to have decided not to practice marriage counseling, especially with young, attractive female clients? Did he still have a professional responsibility to seek therapy for himself?

10. Did Dr. Walker act appropriately in beginning a sexual relationship with Bethany 2 years after the termination of therapy? What ethical reasons, if any, were there against Dr. Walker's pursuing a sexual relationship with his former client? What precautions might he have taken before deciding to become involved in a sexual relationship?

11. Suppose that statutes in the state where Dr. Walker practiced did not explicitly forbid sexual relations with former clients. Suppose also that he believed that the nature of the relationship would not be exploitive and that he could satisfactorily document it. Would Dr. Walker have been justified, under these circumstances, in pursuing a sexual relationship with Bethany? Defend your view.

12. Is a therapist ever justified in accepting co-workers as clients? If so, under what conditions? If not, why not?

13. Should therapists ever be permitted to recruit clients for private practice through their place of employment? If so, under what conditions? If not, why not?

14. What ethical problems might arise as a result of counseling former students? In your estimation, do these problems support a general rule forbidding therapists from counseling former students?

15. What ethical problems, if any, might arise in counseling the family of current students? In your estimation, is it ever justified for therapists to counsel family of students?

16. Is there anything wrong with a therapist's accepting unsolicited referrals from students? Defend your view.

17. Discuss some possible steps Dr. Carver (Case 2) might have taken prior to becoming involved in a dual relationship with Christi that might have helped to avoid it in the first place.

18. Why were the primary responsibilities of Dr. Carver as an instructor in a graduate counseling education program in conflict with his responsibilities as Christi's therapist? Discuss some of the potential dangers Dr. Carver risked in blending these two distinct roles.

19. If Dr. Carver did not suffer any loss of independence of judgment in simultaneously counseling and teaching Christi, would this dual-role relationship have been ethically justified? Defend your view.

20. Did Dr. Carver adequately inform Christi about the dangers inherent in such a dual-role relationship? What other alternatives might have been explored? What would you have done if you had been in Dr. Carver's situation?

CHAPTER SEVEN

Suspected Child Abuse: A Therapist's Responsibilities

CHILD ABUSE: SOME GENERAL FACTS
   Sexual Abuse
   Physical Abuse
CASE STUDIES
   Case 1: A Therapist's Responsibility to Report
   Case 2: Child Abuse and a Custody Battle: A
      Therapist's Responsibility to Promote
      Clients' Autonomy

ETHICAL STANDARDS FOR MANAGING
   SUSPECTED CHILD ABUSE
SUMMARY
REVIEW QUESTIONS
DISCUSSION QUESTIONS

Therapists working in the area of child abuse are often confronted with moral dilemmas centered around seemingly irreconcilable choices. The difficulty in making these choices is particularly salient considering the rather precarious position that children often occupy in our society. Even though many contemporary child abuse laws have attempted to focus on protection and prevention, the vulnerability of children and their dependency on adults frequently places them in harm's way. This susceptibility is further heightened by the all too commonplace tendency of many adults to discount as lying a victimized child's allegations of abuse. The issues surrounding the dynamics of child abuse and its aftermath make up an area in the delivery of counseling services that is sometimes wrought with perplexity, frustration, and confusion. It is rare for a working therapist of the 1990s not to be involved in such cases.

This chapter examines two cases of physical and sexual child abuse to illustrate some of the particularly difficult decisions that may confront therapists working with abused children. The case studies also provide ethical standards to assist therapists in grappling with these complex isssues. Some pertinent facts about these two types of abuse are provided below.

Child Abuse: Some General Facts

SEXUAL ABUSE

Sexual abuse of a child by an adult involves the adult's using a child in some way to achieve sexual gratification. Contrary to the misconceptions of some, sexual abuse need not involve touching, although it often does. Acts of sexual abuse may range from watching a child undress or masturbating in the presence of a child to acts of oral sex or vaginal or anal penetration. Although the magnitude of the problem is recognized by many in the therapeutic community, estimates of its prevalence vary. Studies in this area indicate that anywhere from 35% to 40 % of American females have been sexually abused by the age of 18 (Finkelhor, Hotaling, Lewis, & Smith, 1990; Russell, 1986)

It is estimated that 3% to 31% of American male children are sexually molested, but this number may not be truly reflective of the enormity of the problem (Finkelhor et al., 1986). Parents of male children as well as the children themselves are even less likely than female survivors of abuse to report their victimization. Reasons for this underreporting range from homophobia to male gender scripting, which encourages suppressing emotions and presenting a "tough" facade (Briere, Evans, Runtz, & Wall, 1988; Shelden & Shelden, 1989).

Sexual abuse is most often perpetrated by someone known to the child, usually a family member (parents' live-in-lovers included), sometimes a family friend. Only about 10% of all child sexual abuse is perpetrated by a stranger. If allowed to continue, sexual abuse usually escalates. Familial sexual abuse is often intergenerational, and without successful intervention, patterns of abuse often continue to perpetuate themselves.

In instances in which only one parent in the family is committing the abuse, the nonoffending parent is frequently hesitant to support a child's allegations of abuse or even to believe that the child is being truthful. Often this nonoffending parent has witnessed behavior that may be construed as "suspicious" but uses denial and rationalization to avoid dealing with so threatening a problem. When and if a child does disclose the abuse, there is usually great pressure placed on the child to recant these allegations (Summit, 1983). The child may be told that the family will "fall apart," that the child "misinterpreted" what "really" happened, that the child is lying or was dreaming, that the abuse was the child's fault, that the abuse will never happen again, or that the perpetrator will be killed in jail. When the child is unable to withstand this pressure—sometimes exerted by other family members, including other abused siblings—he or she often recants. The uninformed public, reading of allegations dropped and allegations recanted, usually assumes that the child was lying. This perception is a dangerous one as it contributes to the tendency of many adults to disbelieve children and to maintain that they are liars (Summit, 1983).

A child whose allegations are discounted or rationalized by a parent frequently waits for years before attempting to disclose the abuse again. Usually, the abuse continues during this time. Subsequent disclosure is often made to a teacher, a friend, or to the parent of a friend. The child, in an attempt to avoid familial censure, may state that the secret just "slipped out." This demonstrates not only the fear the child experiences in relating the abuse but also the guilt that most children have about their victimization.

In treating survivors of sexual abuse, a therapist must realize that most survivors have ambivalent feelings toward their adult victimizers. This ambivalence is usually quite confusing to the child, who frequently believes that such ambivalence in some way makes him or her abnormal or "crazy." Therapists work with clients to help them reconcile these conflicting feelings (MacFarlane & Waterman, 1986).

Sexually abused children often have low self-esteem, may feel used and different from other children, and may engage in high-risk and self-destructive behavior. Promiscuity and prostitution have been linked to childhood sexual abuse (MacFarlane & Waterman, 1986). The abused person may have difficulty maintaining personal boundaries, which may include trusting inappropriately or being unable to trust at all (Blume, 1990). Many sexually abused females marry abusive men (Mrazek, 1981; Wells, 1981). Studies indicate that about 85% of child molesters were abused as children (Groth, 1982). Child sexual abuse often leads to repetition of the abuse by the victim when he becomes an adult, or even later in childhood (MacFarlane & Waterman, 1986).

PHYSICAL ABUSE

Child physical abuse involves the deliberate inflicting of pain / injury on a child. The criteria for identifying physical abuse differs from state to state. In some states, the presence of a visible mark on a child is evidence that such abuse has occurred. Studies appear to indicate that parents who employ corporal punishment are more likely to abuse their children physically than parents using other types of discipline.

There is increasing controversy in the social and political arena about the utility of corporal punishment and a parent's right to inflict such punishment. Even in states where efforts are made to define physical abuse clearly, there are disagreements about what constitutes "acceptable" corporal punishment and what constitutes abuse.

As with sexual abuse, children who are physically victimized frequently attempt to keep the abuse secret in an attempt to protect the offending parent. This may even include refusing to dress for gym class, even though doing so may result in a failing grade.

Children who are physically abused often have low self-esteem and believe that they are in some way responsible for the abuse. Problems with aggression control and substance abuse may arise as a result of physical victimization. As with sexual abuse, physical abuse is often intergenerational. Victimized females may marry men who are abusive; abused males may themselves be at risk for becoming abusive in interpersonal relationships. (Straus, Gelles, & Steinmetz, 1980; Gelles & Conte, 1990).

Case Studies

CASE 1: A THERAPIST'S RESPONSIBILITY TO REPORT

Mora was a 14-year-old female and the survivor of sexual abuse by her maternal grandfather. Mora's parents were divorced, and Mora was, until recently, frequently left in the care of her grandparents. This occurred despite the fact that Mora's mother, Paula, had been sexually abused as a child by her father. When Mora's allegations of abuse were first reported to the authorities by the mother of Mora's friend, Paula was incredulous. She related that her father had become "a man of God" as evidenced by his frequent involvement in humanitarian church activities. She therefore believed that he had abandoned his previous behaviors, although he had never acknowledged his past nor expressed remorse for it.

Paula slowly, but hesitatingly, began to acknowledge that perhaps some of Mora's allegations could be true. This acknowledgement created a rift between Paula's own mother and herself, as her mother had not ever acknowledged that Paula had been abused as a child. Paula found herself with virtually no emotional support during the ensuing legal process.

The state recommended that both Mora and Paula participate in therapy with a therapist who specialized in this area. Both Mora and Paula were assigned to Jocelyn Sanders, a licensed counselor who specialized in treating survivors of sexual abuse. Mora was to enter group therapy designed for adolescent survivors of incest and Paula was to enter a group for mothers whose children had been sexually abused by family members. Most of these mothers had themselves been sexually abused as children.

Issues to be explored in the adolescent group included feelings of betrayal and guilt, loss of trust, anger, low self-esteem, assertiveness training, and establishing appropriate personal boundaries. The mothers' group worked on issues of betrayal, guilt, parent education, independence, effective communication skills, establishing familial boundaries, and their own childhood molestation.

Mora established a rapport with her therapist and her groupmates. She shared both positive as well as negative feelings in sessions. She focused on many issues, but one of her major problems was coming to terms with her mother 's initial dismissal of her allegations as untrue. Mora was frequently able to express her anger at her mother in this regard. Mora did not know that Paula had also been sexually abused by the same man, as Paula did not want to reveal this. Mora also struggled with issues of self-esteem. She appeared to view herself as "damaged goods" and had difficulty setting self-protective boundaries with her peers. For example, she had been bitten by her boyfriend, but insisted that it was "all in good fun."

Paula struggled in group with issues such as living as a single woman, her relationship with her own mother, and relationships with her daughters, including her difficulty trusting Mora. Paula had become increasingly suspicious that Mora was or would become sexually active. The issue of Paula's own molestation had, to this point, been only superficially explored. Although Paula had not yet shared her own, painful history of sexual abuse with her daughter, she was able to begin doing so with her therapist and the group. Paula also harbored resentment toward her daughter for "having let the abuse go on for so long" and often expressed anger and frustration over raising a teenager. Like her daughter, Paula too, had begun to express trust in the group process. Her revelations became more personal, and she frequently asked questions when the group began to learn effective parenting skills.

About 4 months into therapy, during a group session, Mora revealed that her mother had hit her on her head a few days earlier. Mora claimed that her mother had hit her with her hand and also pulled her by the hair frequently. Mora had no visible physical injuries. The state in which Ms. Sanders practiced had a statute mandating that therapists report all suspected cases of child abuse.

As a competent sexual abuse counselor, Sanders is aware that the dynamics of sexual abuse is largely a function of the victim's loss of a sense of personal autonomy including feelings of powerlessness and loss of self-esteem. Accordingly, Sanders works diligently to create an environment that promotes trust and self-disclosure. In developing such a viable and trusting therapeutic environment, she exhibits various personal qualities that serve to nurture and enhance the client's growth. She cares about her clients regardless of their beliefs or behaviors. Though she herself may have far different beliefs or experiences, she values her clients as individuals and demonstrates concern for them. Her clients do not have to do anything to gain this regard; it is unconditional (Rogers, 1961). In attempting to gain a deeper understanding of her clients' feelings, Sanders believes that she needs to understand them from their own perspectives. In attempting to do this, she tries to empathize with her clients, to enter their subjective world "as if it were your own, but without ever losing the 'as if' quality" (Rogers, 1961, p. 284). This, in part, involves using the technique of reflection as described in Chapter 3. The therapist is also congruent, a "real" person, in her encounters with clients. She does not attempt to wear a facade, and she expresses her feelings related to the counseling process openly. She does not feel threatened by clients' challenges or expressions of disagreement. Through her modeling of unconditional positive regard, empathy, and congruence, Sanders hopes to promote similar attitudes in her clients; and through the bonds of trust that are established, she wants to help these clients make significant strides toward greater autonomy and self-confidence.

As a diligent professional, Sanders does not believe that therapists should have to investigate and screen all the allegations they hear in confidence, as this would divert their attention from the therapy. It would also adversely affect the quality of their services to their clients, especially when time is seriously constrained.

In addition, therapists would then be assuming a dual role. They would be functioning as both counselors and investigators. The investigative role runs counter to the therapeutic posture of the virtuous therapist, which requires unconditional positive regard and trustworthiness. This trust requires that therapists not interrogate, emotionally coerce, or in any other way undermine clients' personal autonomy.

Therapists should, of course, concern themselves with information that they are aware of and which could have impact on clients' welfare. This is different, however, from expecting therapists to know with certainty whether all allegations are true or false and to refrain from reporting any allegations they have determined to be false. Such a role expectation would require therapists to accept clients' disclosures suspiciously and conditionally, thus subverting the very framework of trust on which the virtuous therapist builds a counseling relationship.

In the present case, Sanders is faced with several moral dilemmas. As discussed in Chapter 2, a moral dilemma is a moral problem in which, no matter what is done, someone's welfare will probably suffer. First, Sanders believes that if the allegations of physical abuse are reported, the subsequent investigation would probably yield inconclusive or unfounded findings. Sanders does believe that the abuse has occurred, but her experience with the investigative system leads her to think that the lack of physical evidence coupled with the likelihood that the victim will recant will make a finding of confirmed abuse unlikely. In Sanders's view, there is a significant possibility that Paula would prematurely terminate counseling for both herself and Mora if Sanders reports the incident.

In accordance with the principle of candor, all Sanders's clients are told, prior to the first therapy session, that allegations of child abuse will be reported. Nevertheless, she believes that reporting it in this case would place a strain on the rapport between client and therapist, and could thereby also contribute to premature termination. Sanders is aware that because Paula has not yet been able to acknowledge her own culpability in the sexual abuse of her daughter and is still struggling to maintain a front in public as the ideal mother, the thought of having the truth discovered may be quite threatening. No one outside her own parents and those in the respective groups have any idea that Paula is not in control of life. This image appears to be very important to Paula.

Premature termination would leave Paula with no support system and would leave Mora perhaps more vulnerable to both repeated physical abuse and to possible subsequent sexual abuse. Without further therapy, Paula might again jeopardize her child's safety. As a result of her experience in the field, Sanders knows that many victims of sexual abuse are frequently revictimized, and that the likelihood of revictimization seems to increase in the absence of successful therapy. Furthermore, without the support of the group, Paula might even be more alone and isolated. These conditions are believed to be factors that often contribute to child abuse. Faced with them, she would be more likely to escalate the abuse. Sanders believes that Paula's interest in parenting techniques is a positive sign and thinks that this type of learning could possibly help to prevent further incidents. Sanders, therefore, believes that reporting this abuse could jeopardize Mora's safety.

The second horn of the present dilemma involves the obvious risk that even if therapy continues, Mora could be reassaulted physically by Paula, perhaps seriously. Trust is also an issue here. Mora had trusted enough to risk revealing the abuse to Sanders and the group. Failure to take measures to protect Mora would be a violation of that trust and would reinforce Mora's perception of herself as "damaged goods" and a victim without power over herself.

Sanders, in adhering to the principle of discretion, could not even broach the subject of the allegations to Paula without Mora's permission. Furthermore, if Mora did give her permission for Sanders to do so, would such a disclosure of confidential information prepare Paula to lie when and if such a report were investigated? Would disclosure create even more pressure for Mora to recant her story? Would Mora be physically abused in the 24 hours it might take for the investigation to begin?

Sanders contemplates sharing the accusations with Paula *before* reporting these allegations to the authorities. Paula too is Sanders's client, and disclosure without her knowledge would be less than candid. It would be a violation of the therapist-client trust between Sanders and Paula; and it would be out of line with Sanders's congruent posture and unconditional positive regard for this client.

In consideration of what she might say to Paula, Sanders reasons that she could underscore the positive nature of Mora's own disclosure. This involves the self-protectiveness that Mora has demonstrated, a trait that before this she did not exhibit. Sanders could further discuss with Paula that keeping secrets of this nature contributes to the very atmosphere of secrecy that allowed Mora to be sexually abused. In Sanders's reasoning, she could tell Paula that, although the therapist is obligated by law to report the alleged abuse, she will inform authorities that Paula has been making progress in therapy designed, in part, to address issues of inappropriate mother-child behavior. Above all, Sanders will continue to convey a genuine attitude of care and respect for both clients without implication that disclosure will mark termination of this caring relationship and the availability of therapy.

If Mora rejects the idea of sharing the information with her mother, however, then Sanders confronts another dilemma, for the information about which disclosure is contemplated is confidential. To disclose this information to Paula without Mora's informed and uncoerced consent would be to treat Mora as a "mere means" or object. As we have seen in Chapter 4, the discreet therapist would be disposed against disclosure of confidential information where such disclosure is without clients' consent.

However, even if Mora freely consents to disclosure of the information, Sanders will be mindful of the possible consequences of disclosure. In particular, will Paula perceive Mora as having betrayed her, and will this place Mora's welfare in greater danger than if the alleged abuse is reported without Mora's knowledge beforehand or if it is not reported at all?

Given the primacy of client welfare in the counseling mission, Sanders's decision about whether or not to report the alleged abuse with Paula's foreknowledge or even to report it at all, will be largely dependent on her assessment of what action will best promote her clients' welfare. Regarding Mora's welfare, what action or lack of action would be most likely to leave her both physically safe and to contribute to her continued therapeutic progress? If her mother discontinues treatment, this lack of any check on Paula's behavior could put Mora at risk of further abuse. These considerations must be weighed against the possibility that not reporting the allegations might also allow the abuse to continue or to escalate, causing both physical and emotional harm. Not reporting the allegations could also contribute to Mora's feelings of powerlessness and further reinforce her already low self-esteem and sense of self-worth.

Regarding Paula's welfare, how likely is she to feel betrayed by Sanders if she suspects that Sanders was the one who reported the allegations? Paula has also placed great trust in Sanders and has confided things that were difficult to disclose. Paula has been deserted by her own mother and views the therapeutic setting as a place of safety and security.

The legal issue also has to be considered. State law mandates that cases must be reported if child abuse is suspected. Having had many years of experience working with victims of sexual abuse, Sanders has seen many legitimate cases of abuse investigated and dismissed, leaving no check on either victim or victimizer. On the other hand, not reporting the case could lead to her professional censure and create various civil and criminal problems replete with malpractice allegations. Sanders contemplates the effect that this could have on her present and future clients as well as the effects this course of action could have on her.

Although the client's welfare is of primary concern in making an ethical decision, the virtuous therapist must consider the welfare of all concerned in trying to satisfy as many of the legitimate interests of the persons involved as possible while minimizing the harm. The therapist is also included in those affected by the decision. If therapists were to completely disregard themselves for the sake of their clients, they would then be treating themselves as means, and not as ends. This attitude could result in the potential unhappiness of the therapist; also, it could breed disregard for therapists in general, thus relegating them to the status of mere vehicles. In perpetuating disrespect in this way, the humanness of the therapeutic relationship would be lost.

If Sanders were unable to practice counseling, many people who might benefit from her expertise would not be served. Would she be justified in placing her practice at risk for one client if this means that others in similar or worse situations might never receive her help as a result of this decision? If the number of therapists specializing in the treatment of childhood sexual abuse is quite limited in Sanders's geographical area, this is a realistic concern. The principle of utility might support Sanders in a decision to report this allegation immediately.

Still, Sanders, as a morally courageous professional, is willing to make reasonable personal sacrifices and to take reasonable personal risks for the sake of client welfare. Moreover, as an honest, benevolent professional, Sanders has intrinsic regard for client welfare and is not prone to rationalization, especially when client welfare is at stake.

However, Sanders also has respect for the law. She understands that the useful functions of law would be subverted if people were not in a general habit of obedience to it. In particular, she appreciates the reporting of allegations of child abuse to authorities as being in the best interest of the child, and that without cooperation from mandatory reporters, such as herself, the benefits of having such a law would be undermined. Nevertheless, she is no blind supporter of law and is aware that exceptional cases can and do sometimes occur wherein, based on available evidence, it is highly probable that the reporting of allegations will actually do greater harm to the child than not reporting it. In such cases, it would be self-defeating to comply with the law and contrary to its very spirit.

This situation would be true in certain instances. Suppose an otherwise loving and supportive foster parent slapped a child when state law forbids foster parents to do so. If reported, authorities might place the child back in the custody of an extremely abusive biological parent. Sanders thus must confront the question of whether reporting the allegations in the case of Paula and Mora would be self-defeating in this way.

In this case, such a clear and imminent contravening harm is not evident. Sanders has reason to think that Paula *might* abuse Mora further if the allegations were reported, but she can only speculate that Mora would probably suffer less abuse were Sanders not to report the allegations. Sanders lacks clear, incontrovertible evidence supporting a high probability that the child would suffer an even greater harm if the allegations were reported; therefore, she is disposed to comply with the law, recognizing no overriding reason for noncompliance.

After considering all the morally relevant facts, Sanders reports the allegations to authorities. In concert with the principle of considerateness (Chapter 2), she intends her decision to promote the welfare, interests, and needs of both clients with as little harm to either as possible under these difficult circumstances.

Sanders is aware that Paula may well terminate counseling when she learns of the report. Sanders considers that this situation will be complicated if authorities absolve Paula from any wrongdoing. As discussed previously, this can easily happen even if the charges are true. In this instance, Mora might reason that her disclosure was futile and that disclosures in the future will also be futile. Sanders hopes that the positive counseling experience that Mora has had with her will, in some way, mitigate this perception and allow Mora to trust appropriately again. Sanders hopes that the unconditional positive regard and empathy that were demonstrated in therapy have a lasting impression on both Mora and Paula.

In arriving at her final decision, Sanders decides that there is no clear, incontrovertible evidence that greater client harm will come if she reports the allegations. On the other hand, violating the abuse reporting law could prevent her from practicing counseling. To incur such a personal risk is foolish with so little indication that complying with the law will not cause greater client harm.

Sanders further believes that in this particular case, there is considerable risk that not reporting the abuse would cause Mora to feel discounted and betrayed by Sanders. If Sanders did not believe Mora's allegations of sexual abuse, Mora would have felt unprotected, powerless, and alone. Her relationship with her peers is marked by submissiveness and a lack of assertiveness, as evidenced by her allowing her boyfriend to hurt her in "fun." Sanders believes that Mora's revealing the abuse was not only a cry for help but possibly a way to test Sanders's trustworthiness and concern. To violate such trust may solidify Mora's view that no one can be trusted, and that with nobody to protect her, her only recourse would be to quietly accept her own victimization.

CASE 2: CHILD ABUSE AND A CUSTODY BATTLE: A THERAPIST'S RESPONSIBILITY TO PROMOTE CLIENTS' AUTONOMY

Sally was an 8-year-old female who had disclosed to her school counselor that her father had been sexually abusing her. The school counselor had informed authorities and had also informed Sally's mother of the allegations. Although she was, at the time, separated from a physically and emotionally abusive husband, Sally's mother, Claire, had difficulty believing the allegations. After hearing the allegations from the child herself and talking with Sally's counselor, Claire became convinced that they were true. Until the time these allegations were made, Sally's father, Monte, had not asked for custody of Sally, but had ample visitation with her, including overnight visits. Almost immediately after learning of the investigation of the allegations, Monte hired an attorney to fight for custody. Monte was a prominent businessman, and was able to hire an attorney who was well known in the community and who was Monte's personal friend. Claire had been a housewife for the last 9 years and had few resources of her own. The attorney she subsequently hired was less well known and charged Claire a reduced fee. She often scolded Claire for asking questions about any aspect of the legal issues.

Shortly after the custody fight began, Claire became aware that Monte had begun to circulate stories that Claire was crazy and had coerced Sally into lying about him. Most of the couple's friends sided with Monte, who insisted that Claire had deliberately tarnished his reputation.

The school counselor recommended that Claire begin Sally in therapy to deal with the abuse and other emerging issues. Claire decided to see Dr. Linton, a therapist who was recommended by the counselor. During the course of therapy, Sally disclosed that her father had molested her on several occasions, but had promised her that he would stop if she wanted him to stop.

Sally displayed ambivalent feelings toward Monte but was adamant in her request that she not have to live with him. Sally had also, on innumerable occasions, pretended in session that a seemingly neutral item (e.g., a toy dump truck) was bad and did bad things to the other cars. Sally often stated that she would see whether the truck was still bad, and then played out a scenario wherein the dump truck "hurt" the other cars again.

Based on her experience with play therapy and children and put in the context of Sally's direct disclosures, Linton believed that Sally had been sexually molested by her father. Both before as well as during the 8 months Sally was involved in therapy, a variety of events occurred indicative of the probable direction of the custody judgment. It became apparent to the school counselor, to Dr. Linton, to Claire's attorney, and to Claire's therapist that custody would be awarded to Monte. Although Linton testified about Sally's disclosures and behavior during therapy, the case was decided in Monte's favor. This decision appeared to have been strengthened by the testimony of a close friend of Monte, a woman who alleged that Sally told her she had fabricated the allegations. Sally maintained to all involved that she never said this, but added that this witness promised Sally a new puppy if she would tell the judge that Claire had forced her to lie about Monte. Dr. Linton, the school counselor, Claire's attorney, and Claire believed that the decision to award custody to Monte would put Sally in a most dangerous and compromised position. When Sally became aware she might be sent to live with her father, she implored Dr. Linton "Please don't let them make me live with my dad! Tell them what he did to me!"

As Claire was confronted with the order to relinquish custody to Monte, she was perplexed and distraught. She first experienced denial: She maintained that this decision was a mistake, that a judge could never give custody of a child to a man who had sexually abused that child and that the judge would probably change his mind. Claire's lawyer, however, assured Claire that the order would stand for now, and told her that she could appeal it although it was a difficult case, and she didn't know if she could continue to represent Claire at a reduced fee. Stating that she just wanted to do the right thing for Sally, Claire asked both her own therapist and Dr. Linton if she should flee with Sally.

In the end, however, Claire declared that she had "always obeyed the law" and thus decided to bring Sally to Monte on the mandated day. Her finances having been depleted, she resolved in the interim to secure employment and to vigorously pursue finding another attorney whom she could trust.

In order for Dr. Linton to establish therapeutic rapport and trust with Sally, certain conditions and practices must be in place. Foremost is the issue of training and experience in the treatment of issues associated with possible childhood sexual abuse. According to the principle of competence, a therapist should provide services consistent with her training and experience. Linton's training and experience is appropriate for helping Sally, so Linton will accept this case. Otherwise, she would refer the client to a qualified therapist.

As a virtuous therapist, Dr. Linton is well aware of her priorities. Central to her relationship with Sally is the goal of discovering *Sally's* perspective on any issues she wants to share with Linton. Dr. Linton is aware that this may take time, but she knows that rushing a client may not only involve subtle or overt coercion but may also thwart client autonomy. In this particular case, Linton has learned about the allegations from Claire; however, Linton will not assume them to be true until Sally makes the disclosures to her. This great care to maintain objectivity is part of Linton's effort to maintain the principle of diligence by providing reliable and careful counseling services. She does not question the child about the alleged abuse and greatly minimizes potential allegations of "false" memories. Any such questioning should be in the domain of the appropriate investigators.

To establish an atmosphere of warmth and develop a rapport with Sally, Linton knows that she must demonstrate unconditional positive regard and provide an atmosphere of safety and security. Sally should never be expected to discuss a particular subject; rather, Linton provides an atmosphere wherein Sally is free to pursue in therapy any subject or issue that she chooses. This non-coerciveness is consistent with respect for the autonomy of the client, whether child or adult. As Sally is a child, Dr. Linton will probably use play therapy as part of the treatment regimen. Play therapy may be directed or nondirected. In its directed form, the child is encouraged to play with a particular group of toys and/or to engage in particular play activities (e.g., drawing a picture of one's family). In its nondirected form, the child is free to choose which toys to use and how to use them. Because of her desire to be as objective as possible on the issue of abuse, Linton will probably be inclined to use nondirected play therapy. During these sessions, Sally sometimes speaks about a variety of self-chosen topics during and after her play. Linton must be extremely careful not to pose leading questions, even in response to Sally's more serious disclosures. Instead, Linton makes it a practice to react to such disclosures with responses that allow Sally to amplify in any way she sees fit . Such responses may include "Tell me more about that," "What was that like for you?" "What would you like to happen?"

Throughout the course of therapy, a variety of legal proceedings are occurring. Some do not directly involve Linton, but many do. One of the central legal entailments involves Linton's being subpoenaed by Claire's attorney in the custody suit. If Claire explicitly informs Linton that she wants Linton to testify, Linton believes it will still be ethically necessary to make certain that Sally gives her consent as well. From a legal perspective, Claire's consent may be all that is necessary as Sally is a minor. However, Dr. Linton believes that the trust between Sally and Dr. Linton might be violated if she reveals Sally's intimate disclosures without the child's uncoerced consent. In accordance with the principle of discretion, Linton believes that she should share such disclosures in accordance with Sally's wishes. Because the welfare of her client is of paramount importance, Linton knows that this right should not be abridged. Testifying to help the child remain in a safe environment while compromising her psychological integrity should be avoided to the fullest extent possible.

Linton decides to inform Claire that the rapport and trust she and Sally have developed is based on Linton's respect for Sally's ability for self-determination. Linton realizes that because Sally is a child, this autonomy is limited, but she believes that it should be promoted to the fullest extent possible within the constraints of Sally's age. Linton will tell Claire that she thinks Sally will feel betrayed if disclosures given in confidence are made public unless Sally first gives permission for this to occur. Linton will further explain that one of the issues central to the treatment of survivors of sexual abuse is dealing with loss of trust and a sense of powerlessness. As Linton is having success in reestablishing Sally's sense of trusting appropriately and in instilling a sense of empowerment, Linton does not want to jeopardize this progress.

Dr. Linton knows that her direction will be more easily decided if Sally agrees that Linton should testify. However, Linton is cognizant that this decision must be given freely and without restriction. Linton presents the issue to Sally in an open and unbiased way. Linton will say to Sally, "Sally, your mom and dad both want you to live with them. Because they are having trouble agreeing on this, they both have lawyers to help them talk about this to the judge. The judge will then decide where he thinks it would be best for you to live. Your mom's lawyer has asked me to come to court and to tell the judge the things that you told me about what your dad did to you. I wanted to ask you what you thought of this." If Sally responds that she wants Linton to reveal the content of the sessions, Linton will do so. She now would have obtained permission from both Claire and Sally. Linton's position will then be not only legally sound but ethically sound as well. Linton will also feel comfortable in testifying because she believes that her testimony could help to corroborate allegations of abuse. This is important because such information may keep Sally from living with a parent who has been sexually molesting her.

If Sally refuses to give permission, Linton will find herself in a more difficult position. Legally, she will be secure, as Claire has consented to her testimony, but Linton will be concerned about the possible abridgment of Sally's trust. Linton will then have to balance the probability and degree of harm that might occur as a result of her testifying against the probability and degree of harm that might arise from her not testifying. As a result of her past experience and understanding of the dynamics of sexual abuse, Linton reasons that the likelihood is great that Sally will be reabused by a man who denies the abuse, does not seek treatment, and appears not to regard it as wrong (recall his telling Sally, "I'll stop if you want me to"). She is aware that sexual abuse is not only a violation of a child's body but also of his or her psyche. The sense of loss of control, autonomy, and self-worth often precipitates lifelong crises and problems.

For these reasons, Linton will testify even if Sally dissents. In this case, Linton will try to explain to Sally that her reasons for testifying are to try to protect Sally. Linton will give Sally a chance to respond with whatever feelings she has toward Linton as a result of Linton's decision. Linton will show empathy and unconditional positive regard for Sally and will show that she understands any negative feelings that Sally may have toward her or her intended actions. Linton will explain that although she really would prefer to adhere to Sally's wishes, Linton's primary responsibility, in this instance, is to protect Sally from further harm. Linton will hope that Sally understands that Linton's decision is predicated on her concern and care for Sally's welfare and not on a disregard for the child's wishes.

In further consideration of Sally's welfare, Linton will have to struggle with yet another ethical dilemma. Based on her experience in the field, Linton is quite certain that the court's decision to give custody of Sally to Monte will place Sally in great jeopardy of being reabused. Claire's concern that Sally will be revictimized has created confusion about how she will proceed following this decision. Claire has been considering fleeing with Sally and has asked Linton her opinion on this issue.

Linton is almost certain that Sally will be reabused by her father and is cognizant that Sally is likely not to report this reabuse. Sally will probably learn that such disclosures are not only ineffective in protecting her but place her in a worse situation: living with her father full time. The psychological effects of sexual abuse can be extensive. Should Linton then advise Claire to defy a court order and disappear?

In formulating this decision, Linton must take several factors into account. In her position as therapist, Linton's advice may well be given more weight by Claire than the advice of a nonprofessional. Although the initial subject of fleeing was broached by Claire, Claire is probably vulnerable to any advice by Linton, not only because of Linton's position as therapist but also because of Claire's present crisis situation. As a virtuous therapist, Dr. Linton encourages client autonomy. She believes that a client's decisions should be made freely and without coercion. Suggestions, direct advice, and mandates do not usually contribute to this climate of self-determination. In promoting client autonomy,

Linton attempts to instill in clients a sense of responsibility for their actions and decisions. If Linton were to recommend that Claire leave with Sally, she might be contributing to Claire's avoidance of assuming responsibility for her subsequent actions.

Although Claire is not directly receiving therapeutic services from Linton, she is, in essence, considered a client. Her discussions with Linton about Sally took place in an atmosphere of trust, care, and concern; with only certain noted exceptions, they are also confidential. Linton therefore views the promotion of Claire's autonomy as an essential element in that relationship. This would dictate that Linton not advise Claire to flee with Sally.

Nevertheless, as a candid and honest professional, Linton responds honestly and provides information that Claire would reasonably want to know in formulating her decision. If Claire asks Dr. Linton if it is likely that Sally will be reabused if she lives with Monte, Linton, based on her experience, will respond in the affirmative. If Claire questions whether having been accused of abuse before will scare Monte from taking such risks again, Linton will respond that, in her experience, being accused and then getting away with the abuse, often further contributes to the likelihood that the abuse will not only continue but will also escalate. It is Linton's hope that the provision of such information will empower Claire to make an informed decision, one for which she is prepared to take responsibility.

In considering the welfare of both Sally and Claire, Dr. Linton realizes that advising Claire to flee with Sally would be to influence Claire unduly to make a decision with profound implications for the lives of both clients. If Claire did flee with Sally, she would have become an outlaw; and she would need the determination and ability to escape the law. Under these circumstances, Claire's failure to elude the law could mean even worse repercussions for both Sally and Claire, such as Claire's permanent loss of all visitation rights and imprisonment. As a responsible professional, Dr. Linton is not prepared to make this decision for Claire.

In her effort to promote client welfare, Linton will also discuss with Claire the possibility of other legal options that may help to foster an atmosphere of safety for Sally. As Claire's attorney appears to be hesitant and unenthusiastic about pursuing other legal alternatives, Linton may ask Claire if she has considered consulting with other attorneys, particularly ones with expertise and experience in this area. Linton will be able to share with Claire names of such attorneys, but she will not attempt to coerce Claire into making these contacts.

Linton realizes that Claire is experiencing extreme stress, and she wants to make certain that Claire is availing herself of any outside support that may be available to her. Accordingly, Linton asks whether Claire has been attending therapy sessions with her counselor. If Claire answers yes, Linton may suggest that the two therapists confer with each other on issues related to the welfare of Claire or Sally. Linton will approach Claire in a noncoercive manner, always making it known that the decision rests in Claire's hands. If Claire does give her consent, Linton will exercise discretion in sharing with this therapist only information that Claire has agreed to share. If Linton and Claire agree that some sharing of information involving Sally's sessions may be helpful, then Linton will be certain to ensure that Sally's consent is uncoerced and freely given. If

Sally objects to such disclosures, then Linton will not share the information, even if Claire consents. In this instance, Linton can see no overriding reason not to abide by Sally's wishes as her well-being does not appear to be directly threatened by the nondisclosure of information to her mother's therapist.

Dr. Linton will encourage Claire to continue with her therapy, but she will have a more difficult time saying good-bye to Sally. If Sally cries and becomes agitated at the prospect of living with her father, Linton can listen, show empathy, and express concern. Linton will remind Sally that she was right in disclosing the abuse, although the outcome of things may not be in her best interest. Linton will reinforce with Sally that she does not have to let anyone touch her in any way she finds uncomfortable. Linton will then give Sally a list of numbers she can call if she is ever abused again. Although Linton cannot promise Sally that subsequent disclosures will be acted on in her best interest, she can explain that, in many instances, this does occur.

The conclusion of this case is indeed regrettable. Sally is placed in the custody of a man who has abused and will probably continue to abuse her; and Claire has been required by law to relinquish custody of her daughter, whom she loves, to this man. The progress that Linton has made in the course of therapy with Sally may be substantially undermined in these unfortunate circumstances, and Sally, like her mother, may, as an adult, find an abusive mate who will continue the cycle of abuse for the subsequent generation.

In these unfortunate circumstances, Linton will not rationalize the gravity of the loss. She is a kind and caring person and she has just witnessed a grave injustice perpetrated on an innocent, vulnerable child by a system whose function it is to safeguard the welfare of the innocent and vulnerable. Linton will not have any illusions about this miscarriage of justice.

Nevertheless, Linton will not blame herself for the outcome. As a virtuous therapist, she will have acted responsibly, even though things did not turn out as she would have hoped. She is well aware that acting responsibly does not guarantee a happy ending; and she knows that doing the right thing does not always feel good.

Ethical Standards for Managing Suspected Child Abuse

The following rules for approaching cases involving suspected child abuse are illustrated in the preceding case analyses. The first set of rules consists of Standards for Reporting Suspected Child Abuse (SRs) and is derived from the analysis of Case 1. The second consists of Rules of Respect for Client Autonomy (SAs) and is derived from Case 2. Following each rule, given in parentheses, is the general virtue or principle of virtue on which it is based.

Standards for Reporting Suspected Child Abuse

SR 1 In jurisdictions in which disclosure of suspected child abuse is required, therapists inform clients of this requirement on or before the first therapy session. (Candor)

SR 2 Therapists comply with mandatory reporting laws unless there is clear and incontrovertible evidence establishing a high probability of a greater contravening harm to the child resulting from reporting the allegations. (Nonmaleficence)

SR 3 A therapist avoids dual roles that jeopardize trust between therapist and client, such as therapist and child abuse investigator, when the therapist acts on the state's behalf, screening allegations for veracity as a requisite to reporting them, including interrogation of children allegedly abused. (Loyalty)

SR 4 If the alleged perpetrator of child abuse is the therapist's client, prior to disclosing the allegations to authorities, the therapist first informs the client of her intention to disclose, provided that informing the client prior to disclosing to authorities does not further jeopardize the child's safety, and, if the child is also a client, the child freely consents to it. (Candor, Nonmaleficence, Discretion)

The above standards recognize therapists' moral responsibility to comply with mandatory reporting laws. As SR 2 makes clear, however, this responsibility may be overridden by regard for child welfare in exceptional cases. SR 3 circumscribes this responsibility by proscribing therapists' involvement in state investigations into the veracity of child abuse allegations, as such involvement by therapists would tend to undermine trust, especially between the therapist and the client allegedly abused. Similarly, SR 4 proscribes informing clients suspected of child abuse of the allegations against them when doing so jeopardizes child welfare.

Standards clearly take protection of child welfare as primary in cases involving alleged child abuse. Where state statutes exist that require reporting of suspected child abuse for the purpose of promoting child welfare, the standards are in spirit, if not by strict letter, in concert with these laws.

Rules of Respect for Client Autonomy in Cases of Suspected Child Abuse

SA 1 A therapist patiently remains objective throughout the therapeutic process and avoids all forms of coercion, subtle or overt, including asking leading questions and other forms of closed questions aimed at establishing the truth or falsehood of allegations. (Diligence, Unconditional Positive Regard)

SA 2 A therapist respects the child client's autonomy to the fullest extent possible within the limits of his or her rational capacities, including asking for the child's consent before disclosing his or her confidences in a court proceeding, and appropriately informing the child of any decision to disclose such confidences. (Discretion, Candor)

SA 3 A therapist discloses a child's confidential communications without the child's express consent only if the therapist reasonably believes that such disclosure is necessary to prevent a greater harm, such as preventing the child from suffering further abuse. (Nonmaleficence)

SA 4 A therapist avoids directing, advising, or otherwise encouraging a client to violate judicial decisions regarding child custody or visitation rights but provides the client with all information requisite to an informed decision regarding such matters, including other legal options consistent with the child's welfare. (Candor, Honesty, Unconditional Positive Regard)

Whereas SA 4 safeguards adult clients' autonomy in matters related to child custody and visitation rights, SAs 1 through 3 restrict paternalistic interference with child clients by making clear that children are also individuals whose intrinsic dignity should be respected. According to SAs 2 and 3, the therapist should not discount children's consent just because consent of a parent or legal guardian has been obtained. All children have an intrinsic dignity that should not be violated, but children who have suffered abuse have already been treated as mere objects. To discount input from these children about the handling of personal information and other matters primarily concerning them is once again to treat them as objects, not as persons. As SA 2 provides, disclosure of confidential information without the child's consent can be justified only if a greater harm, such as the reabuse of the child, hangs in the balance. Similarly, SA 1 safeguards the child's autonomy by proscribing any manner of extorting pertinent information from the child.

Summary

In this chapter, two cases involving suspected child abuse have been presented. The first case raised moral problems of whether, when, and how to go about reporting allegations of child abuse when the alleged perpetrator and the alleged victim were both clients and there were potentially damaging effects on client welfare no matter what was done. The second case raised moral problems of how to proceed in the face of probable sexual abuse of a child client, amid court action to grant custody of the child to the alleged perpetrator. Ethical analyses of these cases have been intended to set ethical precedents for addressing similar cases that therapists may confront in their own practices.

In the first case, issues concerning the therapist's responsibility to report allegations of child abuse were important; in the second, issues concerning client autonomy were foremost. Respective ethical analyses of the two cases have yielded Rules of Reporting (SRs) and Rules of Respect for Client Autonomy (SAs). The SRs and SAs present guidelines for making ethical decisions in relevant cases involving child abuse allegations. Although these rules collectively address several of the hard issues common to cases involving child abuse allegations, they do not address all the problems that will arise; nor are they necessarily the only rules that might be extracted from the case analyses. Furthermore, the rules may sometimes need to be weighed and balanced against further, possibly overriding, moral concerns. For example, while SA 1 provides that therapists should avoid all forms of coercion, circumstances might arise in which some form of relatively harmless coercion is unavoidable to prevent a much greater harm to the child. Finally, as the case analyses have shown, a virtuous response to problems of child abuse proceeds from states of character involving emotional, motivational, and attitudinal elements—such as congruence, empathy, and unconditional positive regard—which cannot be captured by rules of conduct alone.

REVIEW QUESTIONS

1. Explain what constitutes sexual abuse of a child.
2. Who are the most common perpetrators of sexual abuse of children?
3. Discuss some of the reasons that children recant their allegations of sexual abuse.
4. How does sexual abuse affect a child's self-esteem?
5. What are some of the reasons for the probable underreporting of incidents of male childhood sexual abuse?
6. Define physical abuse of a child.
7. What are some of the problems that children can develop from having been physically abused?

DISCUSSION QUESTIONS

1. In Case 1, Paula has been progressing in therapy and has been showing an interest in learning parenting skills. Should Sanders continue to work with Paula on these skills and not report Mora's allegations if reporting the alleged abuse increases the risks that Paula will terminate counseling?

2. Respond to the following: "Because Mora is a child, the issue of client confidentiality does not apply to her parents. For this reason, Sanders should have informed Paula of Mora's allegations prior to reporting them.

3. Paula is also a client of Jocelyn Sanders; should this affect Sanders's decision about reporting the alleged abuse of Mora? What difficulties might Sanders face in her relationship with Mora if she does not report the abuse? What difficulties might Sanders encounter in treating Paula if Sanders does not report the abuse?

4. What actions, if any, should Sanders take if Paula prematurely terminates counseling for both herself and for Mora? Consider the principles of honesty, discretion, and nonmaleficence.

5. If Dr. Linton believes that Sally's father has been sexually abusing her and will probably be given custody of her, does she have a moral obligation to advise Claire to disappear or to hide the child? Discuss the moral implications of Dr. Linton's providing Claire with the phone numbers of people who could help her in these endeavors.

6. Discuss the method Dr. Linton used to treat Sally. Might the therapeutic use of open-ended questions and the freedom within the counseling setting have particular significance for Sally? Why or why not?

7. If Sally refuses to give Dr. Linton permission to testify in court, would Linton be morally justified in refusing to testify? What circumstances and possible consequences should be considered in this regard?

8. If Dr. Linton believes that Claire's attorney is not serving Sally's best interests, does she have a moral responsibility to persuade Claire to change attorneys? Consider the concept of autonomy in formulating your ideas.

9. What would be the ethical, legal, and therapeutic implications of Dr. Linton's inviting Monte to participate in the counseling process?

10. If Dr. Linton believes that awarding custody of Sally to Monte poses a threat to Sally's welfare and may be based on perjury and Monte's higher social standing, what avenues of professional recourse might she have? Consider the principles of discretion and candor and nonmaleficence in formulating these options.

CHAPTER EIGHT

Domestic Violence and Abuse: Ethical and Therapeutic Considerations

FACTS ABOUT DOMESTIC ABUSE AND
VIOLENCE
CASE STUDIES
Case 1: Domestic Abuse, Client Autonomy, and
Confidentiality
Case 2: Safeguarding the At-Risk Client:
Therapist Moral Objectivity and
Nonmaleficence

Case 3: Male Victimization: Gender Scripting
and Domestic Violence
GUIDELINES FOR COUNSELING VICTIMS OF
DOMESTIC VIOLENCE
SUMMARY
REVIEW QUESTIONS
DISCUSSION QUESTIONS

The area of domestic abuse can pose some particularly challenging and seemingly unresolvable dilemmas for therapists. Not only might a therapist be struggling to provide effective treatment to a victim who has chosen to remain with her abusive spouse, but the alternative scenario often presents an equally daunting challenge. Because leaving an abusive spouse can often place the victim at an even greater risk, a therapist may sometimes perceive domestic violence cases as almost insurmountable.

Although the literature tends to focus principally on female victims of battering, the frequency of male victimization is probably underreported. The socialization of both genders may contribute to female as well as male domestic violence.

Presented here are case studies illustrating a variety of ethical decisions relevant to the treatment of clients who have suffered domestic abuse. The framework and guidelines provided should help the virtuous therapist in providing effective treatment.

Facts About Domestic Abuse and Violence

The United States Justice Department has defined violence between intimates as murder, rape, robbery, or assault committed by spouses, ex-spouses, boyfriends, or girlfriends. According to a 1994 Department of Justice Report on violence between intimates, 92% of the victims of nonfatal violent crime by a spouse were female, and 89% of victims of nonfatal violent crime were female (U.S. Department of Justice as cited in Lamanna & Reidman, 1997).

In a study by Strauss, Gelles, and Steinmetz regarding violent behavior between couples, the researchers estimated that, at some time, 18% of couples (either husband or wife) reported slapping, 16% throwing something, and almost 25% pushing, shoving, or grabbing during an argument. The rate of using a knife or gun was almost 1 out of 27 couples (Strauss et al., 1992). Here, incidents committed by either husband or wife are included under each category. There is no indication of the genesis of the incidents or whether some of the incidents were self-defensive measures. The researchers acknowledge that these figures may well be a "substantial underestimate." Strauss, Gelles, and Steinmetz report that 49% of situations in their study involved violence by both spouses. However, in statistics gathered in the year prior to their study, they found that in cases where only one spouse was violent the figures were 27% for husbands and 24% for wives (Strauss et al., 1992).

Some view the measures used by Strauss, Gelles, and Steinmetz for reporting incidents of domestic abuse as problematic, especially with respect to "differences in gender response styles, particularly women's tendency to overreport their own aggressive acts and men's tendency to underreport theirs" (Margolin, cited in Walker, 1989, p. 696). In fact, Roy reports that about 50% of females will be battered by their male spouses during the course of their marriages (Roy, 1982).

In addition, many in the area of domestic abuse believe that women's use of violence against men is frequently in response to the men's violence against them (Walker, 1989). According to Walker, "Over half of all women homicide victims are killed by current or former partners" (Walker, 1989, p. 697). Violence against female partners may escalate to even more dangerous levels when the battered partner decides to leave the relationship. In fact, about 75% of the murders of females at the hands of their male partners occurred when the female tried to leave (De Santis, 1990). Steinmetz indicates that abuse by husbands tends to be more damaging than abuse by wives because the men are stronger (Strauss, Gelles, & Steinmetz, 1992).

Domestic violence is most frequently viewed as being cyclical in nature. This cycle is usually understood in terms of violence by a man against a woman, although female on male violence and violence among same-gendered couples may follow this pattern as well. The cycle of domestic abuse can be broken down into three phases. Phase one consists of a period of tension building in which the victim attempts to placate his or her partner to fend off anticipated abuse. During phase two, actual physical battering occurs. At this time, others outside the domestic unit may or may not become involved (Walker, 1984). According to Walker, medical attention is sought in only about 50% of the reported cases of domestic violence perpetrated by a man against his female partner. She postulates that a physiological release of tension after phase two acts as a reinforcer. Frequently, there is a time following phase two (phase 3) during which the abuser becomes attentive to his or her partner and repentant for the abusive behavior (Walker, 1984).

Walker postulates that the cycle of abuse against women is perpetuated by the female's apparent belief that she cannot escape the violence. She uses Seligman's (1975) concept of "learned helplessness" to explain this perceived inability to escape (Walker, 1989). Lawson (1989), using a systems approach to battering, asserts that the continuation of the cycle of wife battering may occur "because it may have served an initial purpose (e.g. tension reduction) and because of the tendency of a system to maintain pattern stability" (p. 364).

Tenets of social learning theory concerned with modeling and observational learning are often used to explain studies showing that men who have witnessed violence between their parents are three times more likely to abuse their wives than those who have not witnessed such violence (Strauss et al., 1992). Lawson (1989) speculates that for the observed battering to be learned and maintained, it must prove to be useful. Thus, it may "restore the authority and control that a male believes are challenged by his wife, particularly if he is not punished for his use of violence" (p. 361). Strict gender scripting dictates that males are to be strong, aggressive, and in control. Males are often viewed as being "sissies" or "wimps" if they express or demonstrate vulnerability, thus reducing the number of options left to a male who feels emasculated. Physical abuse—discipline—of women has historical precedent: English common law held that women were the property of their husbands. "The rule of thumb" allowed a man to beat his wife with anything as long as it was no thicker than his thumb (Wilkerson, 1989).

Some argue that biases in the conceptualization of domestic violence make it difficult for male victims of female aggression to receive attention from mental health professionals, additionally making it more difficult to identify female perpetrators (Macchietto, 1992). Steinmetz holds that male victims of female domestic violence tend to downplay the degree of violence in their relationships, often staying in for financial reasons and out of concern that, in their absence, their children will be victimized. As males are often taught not to hit women, some men may not retaliate against their female abusers (Steinmetz, 1977–1978). The societal expectations for men to be strong and in control may also create an atmosphere in which some abused males refrain from reporting their victimization at the hands of a woman for fear of ridicule (Steinmetz, 1985).

As therapists may encounter cases of domestic violence, they need to be aware of its dynamics and to have an ethical foundation on which to base their clinical decisions. The following cases are representative of many of the issues that therapists may confront.

Case Studies

CASE 1: DOMESTIC ABUSE, CLIENT AUTONOMY, AND CONFIDENTIALITY

Ursula was a 26-year-old married female. She had been married to Tony, age 30, for 6 years and had a daughter, Sharon, age 6. Ursula had married Tony after the birth of their daughter out of love and to give their daughter "legitimacy." At age 19, shortly after Ursula began a relationship with Tony, she began to work, at his behest, as a topless waitress at a local bar. Tony would frequently spend the evenings at Ursula's workplace drinking and watching how customers reacted to Ursula. When Ursula became pregnant, Tony insisted that she continue working in order to "pay the bills." After Sharon's birth, Tony informed Ursula that it was now necessary that she earn more money as they had an extra mouth to feed. Tony informed Ursula that he had spoken to her boss and that he had agreed to give Ursula a job as a topless dancer, a higher paying job. Ursula said she was not sure that this was what she wanted, but Tony insisted, and Ursula gave in without much resistance. Tony continued to watch his wife perform, but he now began to introduce other men to his wife between performances. The purpose of these introductions was to offer Ursula to these men for sex. When Ursula tried to avoid these encounters, Tony demanded that she comply to prove her love for him. Tony's selection of males often seemed devised to repulse and frighten his wife; the men were often dirty or disfigured. Tony would come along on these encounters and sometimes watch. Ursula began to feel totally out of control and degraded. She began to fear contracting AIDS and decided to speak to Tony about this. She informed him of the riskiness of the sex acts and asked that he stop requiring her to do them. Tony gave no response, but Ursula noticed that the frequency of the mandated sex declined somewhat for several months before going back to its prior level.

As time went on, Tony began to insist that Ursula go topless on public beaches. Ursula at first refused to do this as the beaches in question were not topless ones. Tony became agitated and demanded that Ursula comply. Again, she did. Sharon was often present when this was occurring. On one occasion, Tony became enraged that Ursula, already topless, did not have shorts that were "short" enough, so he tore them until Ursula was almost completely exposed. This had been the first violent act that Tony had committed against Ursula. Ursula became worried that this was done in the presence of Sharon and decided to make an appointment for therapy.

Ursula scheduled an appointment with Hannah Mallow, LPC, at a private counseling facility. Ursula revealed that she was at her wits' end, that she did not mind dancing topless, but that she did not want to have sex with other men, nor did she want to appear topless on beaches that prohibited such conduct. She explained that Tony's ripping of her shorts scared her as Sharon was present, and that she was afraid that this could have a harmful effect on the child. Ursula reported that Tony was a good father to Sharon but that he often became angry at Ursula in Sharon's presence. Ursula told Mallow that her family did not know about any of this and that she had told them just that she worked as a waitress in a bar.

Ursula reported coming from the "ideal" family where she and her sisters could "tell Mom anything." "Often, as teens, we'd sit down with Mom over a bottle of wine and just talk and laugh." Ursula stated that her father worked a lot but that she was close to him as well. Ursula reported no family history of substance abuse, child abuse, or spouse abuse. She stated that Tony's father was an alcoholic and that his mother was a devoted wife and mother who met all the demands of her husband and her three sons.

Mallow listened reflectively and nonjudgmentally to Ursula. As the client spoke, Mallow attended to her nonverbal communication. As she discussed her family of origin, Mallow noticed that Ursula's eyes became averted and that she began to vigorously shake her left leg. Mallow suspected that there was something about Ursula's own background that was not being revealed, but based on her counseling experience in general and her work with victims of spousal abuse in particular, she decided not to mention this during the first session.

During this session, Ursula discussed how she felt about Tony, her marriage, Sharon, and the forced sexual encounters. Mallow inquired about the possibility of getting Tony to attend therapy sessions. Ursula responded that not only would Tony "explode" if she asked him this, but that he would "go crazy" if he found out that she was going to counseling. Mallow assured her that confidentiality would be protected.

At the second session, Ursula began to explore the possibility of refusing to dance topless or have sex with other men. She stated that she was considering telling Tony that she would get another job, but that she was unsure that she could make the same amount of money at another job. Ursula was going to explore her options and think further about this.

Ursula never kept her third appointment, and Mallow was unable to reach her at the number provided by Ursula. Mallow was worried and concerned about both Ursula and Sharon. Mallow noted that Ursula had never appeared ready to discuss leaving Tony. For that reason, although the therapist had given Ursula information about shelters, they had never discussed the specific subject of an "escape plan" should the situation worsen. Mallow did not attempt to contact Ursula at home as Tony was not to know about the therapy. Mallow reasoned that not only would an attempt to make such contact possibly violate confidentiality, but it might also lead to an escalation of the abuse should Tony become aware that Ursula had sought counseling.

Five years later, Mallow, inquiring about rates at a local insurance company was surprised when the receptionist in the front office was none other than Ursula. Ursula looked surprised when Mallow entered, but responded, "Hello, m'am, how can I help you?" In respecting Ursula's privacy, Mallow responded that she wanted to speak to an agent about rates.

Mallow noticed that Ursula wore a wedding ring but could not remember whether it was the same ring she wore when married to Tony. She wondered if the two were still married or if Ursula had divorced him and remarried. Had Tony's abuse escalated? Had he ever sought counseling? Mallow wondered whether anything that had transpired in those two counseling sessions could have motivated Ursula to make changes in her life.

Hannah Mallow should be well aware of the importance of active listening in the practice of psychotherapy. As such, she should try to attend to her clients on multiple levels. Mallow must be cognizant of the extremely important role that nonverbal communication plays in the transmission of feelings and messages.

Accordingly, she should focus on both the verbal and the nonverbal content of Ursula's sessions. As Mallow should note, the idyllic childhood that Ursula describes seems incongruent with the body language she exhibits. Mallow should observe that Ursula maintains good eye contact until she begins to speak about her "wonderful" childhood. At this point, she averts her eyes and starts to shake her leg. Mallow would do well to be aware that these behaviors appear to signal some anxiety or discomfort, although Ursula's words do not suggest it. This therapist must make an important decision with regard to the observed behavior. Should she approach her client with this apparent incongruity, or should she remain silent and merely make a note of it? If Mallow were to mention the apparent inconsistency, she might say something like this: "I notice that although you're speaking of such a happy childhood, you appear to be nervous."

Mallow, an experienced therapist, should be aware of the fact that many clients feel uncomfortable disclosing sensitive and personal information before a trusting therapeutic relationship and rapport are established. They often "test the waters" with disclosures that are, in some way, less threatening to them. In fact, premature disclosure often may lead to premature termination of therapy by the client. Although the therapist suspects that Ursula's family history could potentially be helpful in identifying beliefs and patterns of behavior, Mallow will not want to short-circuit treatment. She may reason that even if therapy were not short-circuited, premature disclosure in this instance might interfere with the nurturing of autonomy and empowerment in her client. Ursula has not, to date, been acting autonomously. She has been under the control of Tony and has been acting in accord with his demands. Mallow should not perpetuate this apparent cycle of helplessness and acquiescence by creating an atmosphere where Ursula feels compelled to reveal information that she is not yet ready to share. Ursula seems to have learned to be obedient to authority figures and may feel forced to disclose information to Mallow. As a morally virtuous therapist, Mallow should seek to promote her client's autonomy; thus, during this first session, she should not mention the incongruity between Ursula's verbal and nonverbal language.

Mallow must understand that Ursula is a victim of domestic abuse even though she is not being hit or beaten. She is being coerced into degrading herself and, in the process, putting her very life in danger. As Ursula has disclosed that Tony ripped off most of her shorts in an angry, public fit in the presence of Sharon, the issue of the child's physical and psychological safety becomes paramount. Mallow must be concerned about the child's mental state as well as her safety.

Is subjecting a child to viewing domestic abuse also child abuse? Should Mallow inform the local child welfare agency about the occurrence? Mallow must now confront a *moral problem*. As we've seen in Chapter 2, a moral problem arises when one is confronted with a situation where there is risk to the welfare or interests of a person or persons. Specifically, Mallow must face a moral *dilemma*. A moral dilemma is a moral problem in which no matter what course of action is undertaken, someone's welfare, interests, or needs will be at risk. Should Mallow report the domestic abuse, potentially risking harm to

Ursula or Sharon and jeopardizing the therapeutic relationship, or should she continue, without making any reports, to treat Ursula in the hope that the client will eventually be able to live a healthier and abuse-free lifestyle?

As a discreet therapist, Mallow must try to safeguard clients' confidences. Making such a report will violate her promise to Ursula and possibly compromise the safety of both Ursula and Sharon. Mallow is fairly certain that nothing will be done about the incident if it is reported. She believes that Ursula will probably deny the abuse and that she will terminate therapy. Finally, there is the ever-present possibility that Tony could retaliate, thus creating an even more dangerous situation for the family. As a virtuous therapist, Mallow should recognize her primary function as helping to promote the client's happiness and alleviate her pain. However, as discussed in Chapter 2, therapists must practice in a wider social context, promoting not only client welfare but also the welfare of others who might not necessarily be clients.

Acting in accord with the principle of nonmaleficence, this therapist must attempt to safeguard the welfare of both clients and nonclients. Mallow does not have enough information to know whether such a disclosure, at this point, could threaten the safety of both her client and Sharon. Mallow may reason that she might, if therapy continues, be able to help Ursula change her victim-like pattern of living. She will be aware that there is no information, as yet, that Sharon has been physically or sexually abused by Tony. She should also be aware of current as well as proposed legislative changes governing domestic violence. In some states, legislation has been proposed to increase the sentences of those who have abused their spouses in the presence of children. (See, for example, Bill AB 102, Sentencing: enhancements and aggravations: minors, introduced 01/08/97, Senate Rules Committee, California State Senate.) However, therapists cannot legally breach confidentiality to report spousal abuse unless they have knowledge of something that poses imminent harm to the intended victim. Mallow does not have any evidence that this is the case.

As she listens to Ursula during the initial session, Mallow should see clearly that there are multiple issues needing attention: Ursula's mental state, her physical health (exposure to STDs), Sharon's safety, and Tony's apparent sexual sadism. Mallow should not be too eager to explore too many issues at once. As an experienced clinician, she must be aware that doing so could frighten and overwhelm the client who, at present, does not yet appear ready for broad disclosure. Ursula has made it clear that treatment for Tony is out of the question, so Mallow must work only with Ursula.

As a beneficent therapist, Mallow should be well informed and experienced in the areas in which she practices (ACA, 1995, C.2.b). She should be aware that the abuse, unattended to, will probably continue to escalate. "Violence between intimate partners always gets worse although there may be plateaus and even temporary reversals during periods of legal or extralegal and psychological intervention" (Walker, 1989, p. 697). The therapist has a responsibility to inform Ursula about the dynamics of abusive relationships to help fortify Ursula's decision-making process with factual material. In addition, Mallow as a beneficent counselor should have knowledge of other agencies and programs that may provide assistance to Ursula. As the client's safety could be at risk, Mallow should provide her with information about domestic abuse shelters in the area. She should also tell Ursula about public assistance programs or social service agencies that may provide help with food, electric bills, or other necessities should Ursula decide to leave the marriage. Despite the apparent abuse in the relationship, Mallow must not violate Ursula's autonomy and direct her actions with respect to this decision.

When Ursula terminates therapy prematurely, Mallow must make some difficult decisions. She is no longer in a position to monitor the possible effects that the abuse of Ursula may have on Sharon. She should, therefore, reconsider whether reporting her client's situation is now indicated. Mallow must decide whether Sharon is truly in imminent danger as well as whether reporting the situation has a greater likelihood of creating harm than of preventing it (nonmaleficence). This decision must also be balanced against Mallow's promise to safeguard Ursula's disclosures (discretion).

When Mallow encounters Ursula 5 years after her premature termination, she should be discreet. If Ursula does not greet Mallow in a manner that acknowledges their prior relationship, Mallow must follow her lead. To greet Ursula publicly as someone she knows would violate this former client's rights to confidentiality (discretion). As the welfare of the client is always the therapist's primary responsibility, Mallow must not compromise this to satisfy her curiosity about Ursula's present state.

Therapists often must live with uncertainty about the welfare of their former clients. Although follow-up sessions are sometimes scheduled, they usually occur a few months after therapy has terminated, still leaving the therapist uncertain about long-term results. Cases involving premature termination by the client may be more frustrating and therapists must show restraint and avoid acting coercively in dealing with such situations.

CASE 2: SAFEGUARDING THE AT-RISK CLIENT: THERAPIST MORAL OBJECTIVITY AND NONMALEFICENCE

Karen was a 23-year-old female who had been married to Tim, age 28, for 2 years. She was an executive secretary and her husband was a mid-level corporate executive. The two had dated for 4 months before marrying. During that time, Tim was attentive and romantic, often bringing Karen flowers and gifts. Karen was overwhelmed by Tim's apparent love for her and fell "madly in love" with him. Soon after they married, Karen began to notice changes in Tim's behavior. He began to criticize her mode of dressing, often referring to her as a "whore" or "slut." He told her that her skirts were too short and her blouses too tight. He demanded that she stop wearing makeup as this "was a come-on to other guys" and told her that a woman who has a man shouldn't be "sending out signals" to other men. Karen, shocked by this apparently abrupt change in Tim's behavior, began to question herself. Perhaps she did look like a slut. Perhaps she was, on some level, "sending out signals." She decided to modify her appearance to meet Tim's demands.

One evening, after arriving home from work 30 minutes late, Karen was greeted by an enraged Tim. Tim demanded that Karen confess to having had an after-hours rendezvous with a co-worker. When Karen tried to explain that she had stopped by her friend Sue's house to chat for a few minutes, Tim became more enraged and threw Karen to the ground. Horrified, Karen ran into the bedroom and locked the door, threatening to leave Tim forever. Tim began to cry, begging Karen to forgive him. He explained that it was only because he "loved her so much" that he was afraid of losing her, but that it would never happen again.

The next 2 weeks appeared blissful to Karen. Tim seemed like his "old self." He bought her a diamond bracelet, made her a candlelight dinner, and was extremely attentive. Karen believed that Tim had "learned his lesson."

Karen and Tim subsequently received an invitation from Tim's boss to attend a corporate get-together. Karen was very excited, bought a new dress, and had her nails and hair done. She was very careful to wear only light makeup. Karen thoroughly enjoyed the party. Though a bit apprehensive at first, she felt quite at ease with Tim's co-workers. She noted that Tim appeared to be enjoying himself as well, laughing and conversing with many of the guests.

On the ride home that evening, Tim remained very quiet. Karen's requests about what was bothering Tim went unanswered. When the two arrived home, an angry Tim accused Karen of "coming on" to his boss. "I saw the way you laughed when he talked to you and I saw the way he was looking at you," Tim screamed. "You made a fool of me, and nobody does that." As Karen tried to explain that she was merely trying to socialize, Tim called her a "lying whore" and began to punch her in the face. The beating progressed from punching to kicking and ended with Tim throwing Karen against a wall, leaving Karen bruised and bleeding. Then, still enraged, he got in his car and drove away.

Karen, confused and distraught, tried to make sense of what had just transpired. Tim had been so loving only a few hours before the beating; could she have, without knowing it, done something wrong? Still, she reasoned, there was no excuse to beat her as he did. What should she do? She was too ashamed to tell her family or friends about the incident, especially since they all thought that she and Tim were the "ideal" couple.

When Tim returned, he had calmed down a bit. He told Karen that "men are always looking for an easy conquest, and baby, you made it known that you were available. You can't say more than a few words to these guys or they think you're easy. I've been under a lot of pressure lately, and I shouldn't have reacted like I did, but from now on, be careful. I never want to hurt you again."

Tim's abuse of Karen escalated over the next 2 years. The pattern always seemed the same; Karen would try to please Tim and felt as if she were walking on eggshells. Tim would eventually explode, beating and often severely injuring Karen, later feeling remorse and attempting to romance her again. Karen continued to keep the abuse a secret. This became easier and easier as her circle of friends began to dwindle. Tim disapproved of most of her friends, stating that they were bad influences on her. To avoid conflict, Karen stopped associating with most of them. Tim had also decided that Karen's parents were nosy and intrusive, so Karen limited her time with them to an hour or so every month.

One evening, Karen's boss requested that she attend an impromptu and urgent business meeting with him. The meeting would take an hour and Karen would get home at 6:30 instead of 5:30. Her attendance at the meeting was crucial to her job, so Karen agreed to attend. She attempted to call Tim, but could not reach him, so she left a message on his voice mail. When Karen arrived home, Tim was anxiously waiting. He accused her of having an affair and began to beat her. As Karen struggled to defend herself, the beating intensified. Tim, totally out of control, picked up Karen and threw her out of the living room window. Neighbors called 911 and an unconscious Karen was taken to the hospital.

Tim was subsequently arrested and his father posted bail. Karen suffered a concussion, a dislocated jaw, two broken legs, and severe cuts and abrasions. A domestic abuse counselor from the local shelter visited Karen in the hospital, apprising her of her options and providing her with reading material on spousal abuse. Tim visited daily, bringing gifts and begging Karen to forgive him. Karen was released after 2 weeks and went to her parents' home to recuperate. Tim called daily and Karen decided not to press charges against him; but the state proceeded anyway. Tim was given one year of probation and was mandated to receive counseling and to perform community service. Karen decided also to begin counseling to help her "make some sense" of her life. She was referred to Herbert Hayden, Ph.D., a licensed psychologist and specialist in domestic violence.

After informing Karen of the boundaries of client confidentiality, Dr. Hayden listened attentively as Karen told him her marital history. As an experienced therapist in this area, Hayden was aware that Karen was very confused about her relationship with Tim and on some level was possibly blaming herself for what had happened. When Karen questioned whether a man could be objective about "this sort of thing," Hayden reassured her that he was very capable of objectivity, but he offered to refer her to several excellent female therapists if she so preferred. Hayden stated to Karen that this was purely her decision, and that he would not, in any way, be upset if this is what she chose. Karen said that she would think about it and make her decision the next week. At the next session, she told Hayden that she had thought it over and preferred that he remain her therapist.

During her 5 months in therapy, Karen worked on issues of self-esteem, autonomy, and self-blame for the abuse. She pondered the future of her marriage and struggled about whether she would ever find someone who loved her as much as Tim did. She talked about her belief that he really was changing and that they could have an abuse-free relationship. Karen often alluded to getting back together with Tim and had been conversing with him regularly by phone. Karen reported that Tim's therapy was going wonderfully and that his progress had been extraordinary.

Hayden, an experienced therapist in the area of domestic violence, knew that perpetrators of domestic violence often lie about or exaggerate their progress in therapy. To gain the clearest perspective possible on Tim's progress, Hayden recommended that Karen ask Tony to give permission for his therapist to release information about his sessions to both Karen and to Dr. Hayden. Hayden informed Karen that the process of change for Tim could be quite lengthy and that marital counseling for the couple would probably be advisable if Karen was seriously considering reuniting.

After obtaining releases, Hayden learned that Tim had, under the advisement of his therapist, Dr. Frank Jenkins, terminated his therapy after 3 months. Jenkins informed Hayden that Tim had been going through a "bad" period in his life, had been under great pressure at work, but had moved on to a new job, and was unlikely to abuse Karen again. The therapist suggested that Karen might have some blame in the abuse for not being aware of the stress Tim was under.

Hayden asked Jenkins how much experience he had working with cases of domestic violence. To this Jenkins replied, "Enough to know that it takes two to tango."

Hayden angrily suggested to Jenkins that he become more knowledgeable in this area and hung up the phone. Hayden subsequently told Karen that, although Tim had been terminated from counseling, based on years of experience, he did not believe that adequate progress could be made in such a short time. Hayden also suggested that Jenkins's views on domestic abuse appeared to Hayden to be different from those of most experts in the field.

Karen missed her next appointment and Hayden called to see what had happened. Karen informed Hayden that she and Tim were now in therapy together with Dr. Jenkins. She reported that Jenkins assured the couple that he will have them back together happily in 2 months and that he was "much more hopeful" about the marriage than was Hayden. She thanked Hayden for his help and said "good bye." One year later Hayden read that a pregnant Karen had been killed by Tim while trying to flee to a domestic abuse shelter.

As a competent therapist in the area of domestic abuse, Hayden must be aware of the dynamics of abusive relationships. As such, he should be able, as an integral part of the counseling process, to provide Karen with literature, information, and resources relevant to her current situation. This would allow Karen to explore factual, objective material at her own pace and, additionally, to afford her a broader foundation of knowledge on which to base an autonomous decision regarding the status of her marriage.

In his role as a beneficent therapist, Hayden should act to promote his client's positive psychological growth, in ways that are more likely to ensure relief from frustration and unhappiness. Both competence and beneficence require Hayden to be aware of any facets of the therapeutic relationship that could be potentially damaging to his client. Karen's possible discomfort with a male therapist and her concern about his ability to remain objective when working with a case of male-on-female violence should be an extremely important issue for him. He must understand the importance of remaining neutral as the client makes the decision about whether to continue therapy with him or to seek help from a female counselor.

As an empathetic therapist, Hayden should be able to feel and understand the uncertainty Karen has regarding putting her trust in him. He must care about her unconditionally, regardless of whether she ultimately chooses to continue her therapy with him. Additionally, as a beneficent therapist, Hayden should be willing to and capable of making appropriate referrals to female counselors if this is in the client's best interest (APA, 1992, 1.08; NOSHE, 1994, 5.1).

Hayden, as a discreet therapist, must be cognizant that disclosure of or requests for confidential information should occur only with the client's informed consent unless harm to self or others is imminent. In this situation, Hayden was aware of the necessity for collaboration in domestic abuse cases when reunification of the couple was a distinct possibility. He, therefore, had requested that Karen ask her spouse to complete release forms allowing both her and Hayden access to information regarding the progress of his therapy.

Hayden must strive to function as a competent therapist, so he should also recognize the importance of helping the client gather relevant information as she seeks to make an informed decision about her marriage. He appears to have been aware of the disparity that sometimes exists between a domestic offender's self-reported progress and the clinical assessment of the mental health professional.

Hayden should exercise independence of judgment by making a concerted effort not to allow his beliefs about what Karen should do about her marriage to interfere with her formulation of a self-directed, well-thought-out decision (ACA, 1995, A.4.b). As Karen sought therapy with Hayden after a severe beating, Hayden should be aware of the potential for life-threatening violence should this relationship continue without appropriate therapeutic interventions with both spouses. His discussion of the limits of confidentiality during the initial sessions must include a thorough discussion of his obligation to breach client confidences should Karen's life be in imminent danger. The principle of nonmaleficence requires therapists to safeguard the welfare of clients and others. Hayden must act in a manner that will foster Karen's safety, even if his actions disclose information divulged in confidence.

Hayden's concern over Jenkins possible lack of expertise in the area of domestic abuse appears to be evident as he questioned Jenkins about his experience working with such cases. Hayden also suggested to Karen that Jenkins's views on the issue of domestic violence appeared to be different from those of most therapists in this area. In addition, although Jenkins terminated Tim's counseling after 3 months, declaring him no longer to be in need of individual therapy, Hayden suggested to Karen that in his own experience, such a short course of therapy is generally ineffective.

Although Hayden attempted to act virtuously within the context of his therapeutic relationship with Karen, he appears to have had considerable difficulty in dealing with Dr. Jenkins; in this way, he may also have compromised the integrity of his relationship with his client. Although Hayden acted diligently in informing Karen of his concerns about the brevity of Tim's counseling, he merely alluded to Jenkins's views as "being different from those of most experts in the field." Does this signify that Jenkins uses a family systems approach that focuses on the interpersonal dynamics of wife battering rather than on the intrapersonal dynamics (Lawson, 1989)? Alternatively, does it mean that Jenkins's views and methods are generally unsupported and in conflict with prevailing standards of practice? In compliance with the principles of candor and diligence, Hayden should have given Karen more detailed information explaining what he believed to be the major theoretical and/or practical differences between his and Jenkins's approaches. This would have been difficult for Hayden to do because he never attempted to clarify exactly what Jenkins's theoretical base or modality is.

Hayden, apparently angered by Jenkins's seeming minimization of Tim's culpability, merely questioned Jenkins about his experience in the field. When Jenkins's response appeared to be flippant, Hayden angrily ended the conversation. Had Hayden delved more deeply into Jenkins's qualifications and theories, he might have gotten more information to give Karen and on which to base a moral decision regarding whether to report possible ethical violations. If Hayden suspected that Jenkins was not competent to be treating perpetrators of domestic violence, then he had a *professional* obligation to delve further into the matter (NASW, 1997, 5.01.e). To have been morally objective, Hayden should have attempted to overcome any negative feelings he may have harbored for Dr. Jenkins. We should recall (Chapter 2) that, in being morally objective, one must avoid personal biases, prejudices, or values.

If Hayden had attempted to gather further information from Jenkins and was unsuccessful because of Jenkins's failure to cooperate, or if Jenkins did divulge further information and Hayden believed him to be incompetent, Hayden would have been better prepared to formulate a moral decision. The principle of nonmaleficence holds that the therapist must safeguard the welfare of both clients and nonclients through the noninfliction and prevention of pain and suffering. Under this principle, Hayden would have had a moral responsibility to take actions that would have prevented Jenkins from possibly injuring Karen and other potential spouses of Jenkins's client perpetrators.

If Jenkins did share relevant information with Hayden that led Hayden to believe that Jenkins was incompetent to work in this area, Hayden might have attempted to resolve the problem informally by insisting that Jenkins discontinue therapy with people involved with domestic abuse and get appropriate education and supervision before attempting to work with this population again. This type of arrangement might have been difficult for Hayden to make as he held no supervisory power over Jenkins and would probably be unable to monitor Jenkins's compliance. As a competent therapist, Hayden might have then sought consultation with other professionals (ACA, 1995, H.2.b.) to determine what course of action to take.

After Karen failed to attend her regularly scheduled appointment, Hayden, attempting to be diligent, called her and was informed that she had begun therapy with Dr. Jenkins. Hayden, at this point, should have been aware that Dr. Jenkins had committed a professional ethics violation. "When counselors learn that their clients are in a professional relationship with another mental health professional, they request release from clients to inform the other professionals and strive to establish positive and collaborative professional relationships" (ACA, 1995, C.6.c, A.4).

It appears clear that Jenkins did not demonstrate the trust-establishing quality of honesty in relating to either Hayden or Karen. According to Karen, Jenkins had promised her that she and Tim would be "back together happily" in 2 months. There would not have been any way that Jenkins could have honestly guaranteed this. Making such deceptive claims could, in some states, result in criminal prosecution. For example, according to Florida Statute 491.009(d), disciplinary action may be taken for "false, deceptive, or misleading advertising or obtaining a fee or other thing of value on the representation that beneficial results from any treatment will be guaranteed" (see also Florida Rules, Ch. 59, p-5.001[1]).

Hayden would have had reason to report ethical violations but failed to do so. Perhaps Hayden found himself confronted with a moral dilemma. As discussed in Chapter 2, a moral dilemma exists when regardless of what is done, someone is likely to be hurt. If Hayden had decided to report Jenkins for the possible aforementioned violations, he would have had to obtain Karen's written consent to share details of the case with the various other parties involved. Thus, he would have had to tell Karen that he was about to report Jenkins. Karen might have had serious objections to giving her permission for such personal disclosures. If Karen refused permission, Hayden would not have been able to divulge details of this case (ACA, 1995, H.2.e). He did not, at the time, have any indication that Karen was in imminent danger. Had her safety been in acute jeopardy, Hayden could have broken confidentiality without Karen's permission (APA, 1992, 5.05.a; ACA, 1995, B.1.c).

CASE 3: MALE VICTIMIZATION: GENDER SCRIPTING AND DOMESTIC VIOLENCE

Genelle was a 30-year-old female who had been married for 5 years to Guy, age 35. Genelle was an accountant with a large firm and Guy was a chemist with a mid-size pharmaceutical company. The two had dated for 2 years and had had what Guy described as a tumultuous courtship. They had argued frequently, often breaking up only to reunite several days later.

One evening, shortly after they married, Genelle was feeling particular pressure. It was tax season and she was not sure that she could keep up with her work load. When Guy arrived home, Genelle was working intensely. Guy, concerned that Genelle was becoming exhausted, suggested that the two go out for a quick dinner. Genelle became enraged. "You think that my work is not important just because I'm not a man," she screamed. "If you think that you're going to hold me back by pretending to be concerned about my health, you have another think coming." Guy, confused and somewhat angered himself, began to shout, "Serves me right for caring about you. Next time I just won't give a damn!" Genelle retorted, "As if you give a damn now; you've always been jealous of my success." "What success?" screamed Guy as he angrily ran into his study.

Genelle, now infuriated, sprang up from her chair, following him into the study. When she found the door locked, she began to kick and pound on it. When Guy finally opened the door, Genelle picked up a nearby radio and hit Guy on the head with it. Guy fell to the ground, writhing in pain. Genelle began to cry and to tell Guy how much she loved him. Guy ordered Genelle to stay away from him and slept in the study that night.

The next day, Genelle could not concentrate on her work. She attempted to call Guy at the office every 2 hours, but he refused to speak with her. That evening, Genelle returned home to find Guy packing his clothes. He told her that he was going to a motel to "think things over."

Guy spent one night at the motel before returning home. Genelle had cleaned the house and bought Guy the new set of golf clubs that he had wanted for the past year. She promised that she would never physically assault him again and informed him that she was learning relaxation techniques to help her cope with stress. The next few months went well for the couple.

One Monday morning, 3 months later, Guy and Genelle were both hurrying to get ready for work. As the two shared a bathroom, they often spent time waiting to get a chance to use the facility. On this day, Genelle had an especially early appointment scheduled and she was running late. She requested that Guy get shaved and washed at the office so that she could prepare on time. Guy refused, and Genelle became agitated. She attempted to push him out of the bathroom and when he refused to leave, she reached for her hot curling iron and jammed it on his arm. "If I can't get you to move, maybe this can," she screamed. Guy, shocked and overwhelmed with pain, ran from the bathroom. Genelle hurriedly finished her grooming and left for work. Two hours into the day she called Guy begging his forgiveness. "You know how crazy I get under stress," she said. "Are you all right?" "I'm seeing a lawyer today," replied Guy, "and I'd suggest you see one, too." When Genelle returned home she found Guy's closet cleaned out. She attempted to contact him at work first by phone, and then in person. After three days of this, Guy filed a restraining order against Genelle charging that she was harassing him and interfering with his livelihood. He made no mention of the domestic abuse.

Despite the fact that he was now separated from Genelle and had a restraining order against her, Guy became progressively more depressed. His work began to suffer and he began to question his decision in leaving Genelle. Guy was careful not to tell anyone why he and Genelle had split up. He only said that the two could not get along. Family and friends encouraged Guy to talk about the breakup, but he refused. His friend, Mark, suggested that Guy try counseling and gave him the name of Samantha Sutter, a therapist he had been seeing.

On his first session with Sutter, Guy chronicled his life with Genelle, leaving out the two incidents of abuse. He said that he still loved her, but for reasons that he could not talk about, getting back together was out of the question. Sutter was almost immediately struck by the resemblance between Guy and her 30-year-old brother, Dan. Dan and Sutter had been quite close growing up; however, the relationship had come under considerable strain in recent years since Dan's marriage to Patricia.

During the next four sessions, Guy continued to talk about his family of origin, his work, his life with Genelle, and his struggle to live without his wife. Throughout the sessions, Sutter found herself making mental comparisons between Genelle and Patricia. Here, she thought, is another troublemaker trying to ruin someone's life. When Sutter asked whether Guy was ready to discuss why getting back together was out of the question, Guy stated that Sutter would not understand. "It's just too embarrassing to discuss," he replied, "so I'd rather leave it at that."

On his sixth session, Guy appeared to be very agitated. Genelle was contesting the divorce and Guy was worried about the outcome. "How can I go through with this?" he agonized. "I'm not even sure that this is what I want. Besides, I'll have to let the world know that Genelle abused me." Sutter asked for details, and Guy provided them. During that session, Guy struggled with issues of self-blame and recrimination. "Maybe if I had been a more understanding husband, she wouldn't have lost it," he said.

At the end of the session, Sutter told Guy that she was aware of his embarrassment and confusion about the abuse, but that he was a victim and should not be ashamed. She stated that Genelle would probably never change and that she deserved to be divorced for what she had done. She suggested that Guy tell family and friends the truth.

That week, Guy followed Sutter's advice and resolved to go through with the divorce and inform friends and family about the domestic violence. When he told his male friends about the abuse, several began to laugh and referred to him as a wimp. "I'd have given her a good wallop back," stated one friend. Guy's father told him, "Let's keep this to ourselves, son; people won't understand."

Guy, ashamed and regretful of his decision to disclose the abuse, called Sutter to terminate therapy. "Your advice was lousy," he stated. "I won't be needing your help any more." Sutter attempted to schedule one last appointment with Guy to bring some closure to his issues, but he declined and angrily ended the conversation. Sutter, confused and taken aback, began to question her methods. She decided that she had done nothing wrong and that Guy was being unreasonable.

As Guy appeared reluctant to discuss significant details of his marriage with Sutter, the therapist should have respected his wishes and engaged in active, empathic listening. She must be aware that premature or forced disclosure may lead to client-initiated, premature termination and possible loss of client autonomy. To act beneficently, Sutter needs to recall that Guy has referred to undisclosed material as "embarrassing" and therefore she should approach any related disclosure with special care in an effort to promote his positive, psychological growth and minimization of pain and frustration. This should entail maintaining objectivity, demonstrating empathy, and providing structure and information on which the client can base decisions and actions.

When, during the sixth session, Guy finally revealed what was so embarrassing for him, he indicated fear and apprehension about "telling the world" that Genelle had abused him. According to the principle of candor, it is imperative that Sutter explore with Guy not only his feelings and thoughts regarding the disclosure but that she help to prepare him for the possible negative responses that he will get from others.

To function as a beneficent therapist, Sutter must possess the training, knowledge, and ability to work with abused husbands. This must include an understanding of the gender scripting (the expected behaviors and attributes of males and females in a given society) and strict socialization roles that are operative among a large portion of the population. Because of such gender scripting, males are less likely to report instances of abuse, either physical or sexual (Steinmetz, 1985). Society often presumes that a "real man" would not let himself be abused or would stop the situation immediately.

Guy was reluctant to reveal his abuse to others, perhaps because of these very reasons. Sutter, however, appeared to have left this topic totally unexplored. Instead, she claimed that "Genelle deserved to be divorced" and that Guy should tell others the facts about the abuse.

Sutter, obviously, did not maintain the loyalty imperative to her functioning as a virtuous therapist. As early as the first session, she became aware of a resemblance between Guy and her brother, Dan. Sutter, who had become estranged from Dan, blamed the estrangement on Dan's wife, Patricia, whom she disliked. Sutter was aware that she was comparing the situation of Guy and Genelle with that of Dan and Patricia. According to the principle of loyalty, a therapist must maintain independence of judgment in matters related to issues of the clients' treatment. Sutter did not attempt to come to terms with the countertransference she was experiencing with Guy. She neither sought consultation with a colleague in an attempt to work through this problem nor referred Guy to a therapist who could maintain objectivity with this client. Sutter, having never met nor spoken with Genelle, also indicated that Genelle "would probably never change." In addition to breaching her duty to act loyally, this therapist also seems to have violated prevailing standards of conduct among mental health professionals (APA, 1992, 1.13.a, 1.13.c).

The principle of nonmaleficence emphasizes that therapists safeguard the welfare of clients through the noninfliction and prevention of pain and suffering. "The primary responsibility of counselors is to respect the dignity and to promote the welfare of clients" (ACA, C.2.g). Apparently, Sutter was remiss in this regard as well as she did not give careful and considerate attention to the possible destructive impact that her countertransference could have on Guy. In addition, Sutter also acted coercively in dictating that Guy terminate his marriage and disclose his abuse to others. In this respect, Sutter violated Guy's autonomy and foisted her own attitudes and beliefs on her client. This runs counter to prevailing standards (ACA, 1995, A.5.b) and violates the principle of beneficence as well. Even if Sutter had chosen to consult with a colleague about her difficulty remaining objective, referral might still have been indicated (APA, 1992, 1.13.c).

Sutter thus erred in several respects. She largely ignored Guy's conflicted feelings about divorcing Genelle and curtailed adequate exploration of the issue. She failed to prepare her client for the possible fallout that could occur following his disclosure of abuse, and she instructed him to make the disclosure even though she was aware of his great apprehension in doing so.

Sutter should have been aware of the enormous influence that she might have on her client in her capacity as his therapist. Guy came to counseling, like most clients, in a state of considerable vulnerability. As a result of her seemingly unexplored directiveness, Suttter prevented the growth and development of autonomous behavior by the client. As Guy acted on the advice of Sutter, he could not claim success if the disclosures went well, nor could he hold himself culpable when his disclosures met with ridicule. Thus, not only did Sutter not help to foster in her client a sense of responsibility for self, but she thwarted such development.

When Guy called Sutter to inform her that her "advice" was "lousy," she should have paid careful attention to his words. As Guy implied, Sutter *told* Guy what to do, leaving little room for exploration of relevant issues. Sutter, confused with what had transpired, decided to dismiss Guy's complaints as "unreasonable." She might, as a competent therapist, have chosen to consult with another professional to achieve a better understanding of the situation (ACA, 1995, D.2.a). Sutter, apparently did not submit to more than the most superficial reevaluation of the case, and thus was at high risk for repeating the same behaviors again.

Guidelines for Counseling Victims of Domestic Violence

The following ethical guidelines (GLs) for counseling victims of domestic violence can be derived from the foregoing case analyses. These guidelines are supported by the broader ethical principles, noted parenthetically, following each guideline:

GL 1   Therapists are careful not to coerce clients who are being victimized by their partners into disclosing to those partners that they are attending counseling sessions even for purposes of engaging those partners in therapy (Discretion, Nonmaleficence, and Respect for Client Autonomy).

GL 2   In treating victims of domestic violence, therapists must also consider the safety and potential risk of harm to minor children and may break confidentiality if it appears that a child's physical or psychological welfare is at risk (Nonmaleficence).

GL 3   In working with cases of domestic violence, therapists must be knowledgeable about agencies and programs that could provide information, financial assistance, or shelter for victims should they decide to avail themselves of such services (Beneficence and Competence).

GL 4   In treating a victim or a perpetrator of domestic violence when the couple is considering reunification, therapists for both clients must work together in sharing information relevant to the future safety and security of the victim (Competence and Nonmaleficence).

GL 5 Therapists are aware of the impact that gender scripting and socialization may play in the area of domestic abuse and, in this regard, are sensitive when dealing with victims of both genders (Beneficence and Competence).

GL 6 Therapists are aware of any unresolved personal issues of their own that may interfere with objectivity and seek immediate resolution of those issues, if possible. If immediate resolution does not occur, therapists are obligated to make appropriate referral to another professional (Loyalty).

GL 7 Therapists clarify and explain similarities and differences in theoretical orientation and direction when different agencies or professionals are involved in treating spouses involved in domestic violence (Candor).

GL 8 Therapists avoid making promises or definitive predictions regarding the outcome of therapy (Honesty).

GL 1 stresses that therapists have an obligation to respect the autonomy of their clients by allowing them to make the decision about whether to inform an abusing spouse that the client is presently engaged in therapy. Therapists may attempt to justify coercing such clients into disclosure; however, this action may be problematic for several reasons. In addition to stifling the development of client autonomy, a general goal for most victims of domestic abuse, such action is also a violation of the principle of discretion. In addition, the revelation that a victimized spouse is presently seeking therapy may be seen by the perpetrating partner as evidence of betrayal, thus leading to an escalation in the abusive behavior or to potentially life-threatening actions.

GL 2 emphasizes that harm to minor children witnessing domestic violence is not necessarily limited to actual physical harm incurred by the child. Potential risk of harm, either physical or psychological, must be considered in making a determination regarding the breaking of client-therapist confidentiality.

GL 3 underscores the necessity of therapist familiarity with agencies, networks, shelters, and programs available to victims of domestic abuse for both informational and referral purposes.

GL 4 predicates that, in cases of domestic abuse, both the victim's and the perpetrator's therapist have an ethical obligation to confer with each other regarding the sharing of information and insights relevant to the safety and security of the victim if reunification is a possible goal.

GL 5 emphasizes that therapists must be thoroughly familiar with the effects that gender scripting and socialization may have on both male as well as female victims of domestic abuse in order to understand adequately the client's perspective and motivations. Such familiarity is essential for helping to resolve potential conflicts both interpersonally as well as intrapersonally.

GL 6 indicates that therapists must be aware of any unresolved issues of their own that could compromise the integrity of the therapeutic experience and must seek immediate resolution of them. Referral must be made if this is not possible, as lack of objectivity may lead to client harm.

GL 7 relates to the interface between mental health practitioners, their clients, and other service providers in the context of domestic abuse. As is often the case, mental health practitioners treating clients involved in domestic abuse situations often must interface with multiple agencies or professionals in rendering services. To promote the best service possible for the clients and to ensure some unity and continuity, both professionals and clients must be fully apprised of differences in orientation and techniques among the participating service providers.

GL 8 addresses the issue of irresponsible and misleading promises of therapeutic success. As therapists have no ultimate control over the outcome of services, it is both misleading and dishonest for them to make definitive predictions in this regard.

Summary

In this chapter, three cases were presented. Case 1 involved issues of domestic abuse and client confidentiality and explored some of the moral dilemmas inherent when conflicts between confidentiality and client safety arise. The case was complicated by the fact that a child had witnessed some spousal abuse but, as far as the therapist could tell, had not been directly abused herself.

Case 2 deals with spousal abuse and the therapist's duty to safeguard the welfare of the client and others. In wrestling with this issue, the therapist had to consider the principle of nonmaleficence in multiple contexts including the protection of clients from a seemingly incompetent and unethical clinician.

Case 3 addressed male victimization, domestic violence, and gender scripting. In this context, therapist objectivity, beneficence, and client autonomy were explored. Therapist countertransference and client autonomy were issues that had a dramatic impact on the outcome of the case.

Guidelines for counseling victims of domestic violence were advanced in light of the three aforementioned cases. Collectively, these guidelines emphasize the primacy of avoidance and prevention of client harm and future victimization of the vulnerable. In the process, they also stress the importance of respecting client dignity and autonomy, and therefore, treating victims of domestic violence with honesty and candor. A therapeutic posture that failed to respect the personhood of these clients in these ways would defeat the very point of therapy by perpetuating the state of helplessness and dependence that occasioned the need for therapy in the first place.

REVIEW QUESTIONS

1. According to Walker, what percentage of female homicide victims are killed by their current or former partners?

2. Why might it actually be dangerous for some females to leave their spouses/lovers?

3. Describe the cycle of domestic abuse.

4. Describe what occurs during phase three of the cycle.

5. Witnessing domestic abuse as a child may lead that individual to be an abuser as an adult. What theory attempts to explain this?

6. What was the "rule of thumb" ?

7. What factors might make it difficult to estimate accurately the prevalence of domestic violence against males?

DISCUSSION QUESTIONS

1. Defend or refute the following, making use of factual information as well as the therapeutic trust-establishing virtues: Therapists should actively encourage female victims of spouse abuse to leave their abusing husbands as quickly as possible.

2. Address the following: In Case 1, Hannah Mallow struggles about whether she should report the apparent abuse of Ursula to child welfare authorities as it occurred in the presence of Sharon, a minor child. What position would you take if you were the treating therapist in this case? Support your position.

3. As Ursula terminated therapy prematurely, Mallow no longer had any chance of monitoring the possible harm that her husband's abuse of her might have on Sharon. What course of action, if any, should Mallow have taken at this point?

4. Respond to the following: Due to the brevity of Ursula's period of counseling and her premature termination of therapy, Mallow never discussed possible escape plans with the client. For this reason, Mallow had an ethical obligation to contact Ursula after termination for purposes of possible exploration of this and related issues.

5. Explore the following regarding Case 2: Because Hayden believed that Jenkins was not competent to engage in domestic abuse counseling, he should have immediately reported Jenkins to his respective professional organization and explained the situation to them.

6. What were Hayden's ethical obligations, if any, to Karen after she terminated therapy with him?

7. React to the following and give particulars to support your position: If Hayden had acted more virtuously, Karen's death might have been prevented.

8. In both Case 1 and Case 2, the therapists are presented with situations that could arguably involve disclosure of confidential material to third parties. What are the relevant differences and similarities in each case?

9. Respond to the following: Because Hayden was aware of the severity of Karen's abuse history, he should have actively attempted to dissuade her from ever considering reuniting with Tony.

10. With respect to Case 3, discuss ways in which Sutter demonstrated insensitivity about the impact of gender scripting on Guy.

11. Compare and contrast the ways in which possible gender scripting might have influenced Karen's decisions in Case 2 and Guy's decisions in Case 3.

12. Discuss the impact that consultation with another mental health professional might have had on the way Hayden (Case 1) or Sutter (Case 2) handled their respective cases.

CHAPTER NINE

Confidentiality, Third-Party Harm, and Clients Who Have HIV

SOME GENERAL FACTS ABOUT HIV
THE VIRTUOUS THERAPIST AND THE HIV-
  SEROPOSITIVE CLIENT
CASE STUDIES
  Case 1: Harm to an Identifiable Third Party
  Case 2: Harm to Unidentifiable Third Parties
  Case 3: Harm to a Third-Party Client

STANDARDS FOR DISCLOSURE OF
  CONFIDENTIAL INFORMATION
SUMMARY
REVIEW QUESTIONS
DISCUSSION QUESTIONS

As the AIDS pandemic continues to escalate, therapists are increasingly confronting moral dilemmas involving clients who have HIV (Cohen, 1990). This chapter addresses three representative cases in which clients who have, or are likely to have, HIV are sexually active with unwitting third parties. Focus is on ways therapists should respond to the distinct ethical problems arising in each case. In the light of the analyses, some general ethical standards for confronting these problems are presented.

As discussed in Chapter 2, virtuous responses to ethical problems require adequate understanding of the relevant facts. We begin with some general facts about AIDS, HIV, and HIV transmission. The sections of this chapter on conditions and procedures of disclosure also include further facts pertinent to risk of transmission.

Some General Facts About HIV

Acquired immune deficiency syndrome (AIDS) is a fatal and contagious disease caused by the human immunodeficiency virus (HIV). In the 1990s, it has become a leading cause of death among young adults in the United States. Although in the 1980s most reported deaths from AIDS were among intravenous drug users and homosexual men, the number of reported AIDS cases continues to escalate within the general population (Centers for Disease Control [CDC], 1991). This also increases the likelihood that all psychotherapists will eventually confront ethical problems concerning clients with AIDS or HIV.

HIV invades the T-cells of the human immune system. These are white blood cells that are responsible for stimulating production of antibodies to fight infection. As T-cells are destroyed, the body progressively loses its ability to fight infection. There are presently no vaccines against HIV and no cures for the disease, but some drugs have been developed such as azidothymidine (AZT) and the more recent antiviral drugs, protease inhibitors, that can slow the virus's rate of reproduction and prolong the life of a patient, especially if the drug regimen is begun in the early stages of infection (Mayer, 1990, p. 23; Gostin, 1990, p. 6; Douglas & Pinsky, 1996, p. 6).

There are two major tests for HIV. The most common test is the enzyme immunoassay (EIA) test. This test indirectly tests for HIV by detecting HIV antibodies present in the blood (so-called HIV seropositivity). A person is normally considered to be HIV-seropositive only after the administration of a second EIA as well as a more complex and expensive test, the Western Blot (Brant et al. 1990, p. 127; Douglas & Pinsky, 1996, p. 41).

Not all HIV-seropositive persons are classified as having AIDS. The latter diagnosis is made only if the patient also has specific opportunistic diseases such as Kaposi's sarcoma and pneumocystis carinii (Centers for Disease Control [CDC], 1987).

HIV can be found in blood, blood products, and other body fluids including semen and cervical-vaginal secretions (Leibowitz, 1989, p. 21). The primary mode of transmission is sexual intercourse. The most probable modes of sexual transmission are vaginal and anal intercourse. Latex condoms are effective in preventing the sexual transmission of HIV. Risk of sexual transmission can also be decreased by limiting the number of sexual partners and by selecting partners who do the same (Flaskerud & Nyamathi, 1989, pp. 182–183).

The Virtuous Therapist and the HIV-Seropositive Client

Given the sexually transmittable nature of HIV, what should a therapist do when he learns from a client, through confidential disclosure made in the course of therapy, that the client is, or probably is, HIV-seropositive and is having unprotected sexual intercourse with one or more uninformed individuals? On the one hand, if the therapist discloses client information to protect the welfare of the endangered third party, he may violate client-therapist confidentiality. On the other, if the therapist preserves this confidentiality, he may fail to prevent substantial and preventable third-party harm. In some cases, it may be difficult or impossible for the therapist to maintain confidentiality and still avoid third-party harm. In this chapter, three distinct case studies of this general moral dilemma are presented (Cohen, 1994).

Case Studies

CASE 1: HARM TO AN IDENTIFIABLE THIRD PARTY

Lisa, age 32, was in therapy with Dr. Wayne Talcott to work through a depression. This client's profile included a history of depression and an attempted suicide. After 3 months of therapy, Lisa, who was very resistant to the therapeutic process, reluctantly revealed to Dr. Talcott that she was HIV-seropositive (which she said was probably the result of her former promiscuous lifestyle). She told Dr. Talcott that she had attempted suicide after finding out about her positive HIV status (as determined by two EIA tests and a confirmatory Western Blot). Moreover, Dr. Talcott was aware that Lisa was regularly having vaginal sexual intercourse with her fiancée, Justin, without using any means of protection. When Dr. Talcott asked if Justin knew about her HIV status, Lisa responded that she could not bring herself to tell him because he would then surely leave her.

The principle of candor requires therapists to keep their clients informed about matters related to the counseling process consistent with what clients would reasonably want to know. One provision of such informed consent is that the client must be informed of the nature and limits of confidentiality at an early juncture in therapy, preferably the first session (ACA, 1995, A.3.a). Here, Dr. Talcott should inform Lisa of the confidential nature of the therapist-client relationship. Lisa, like many clients, is resistant to the therapeutic process, so this assurance can facilitate her disclosure of very personal information, which, in turn, may be instrumental to her successfully working through her depression. However, candor as well as honesty requires that Dr. Talcott not misrepresent the limits of confidentiality.

Aware that the primary purpose of counseling is promotion of client welfare and avoidance of third-party harm, Dr. Talcott should recognize the possibility of justified exceptions to confidentiality when they could prevent serious harm to the client or others. He should also be cognizant of legal sanctions for disclosure under such circumstances (see Chapter 4 under Discretion and Confidentiality). Dr. Talcott should therefore inform Lisa of such possible exceptions. This can be done by providing her with some clear illustrations of when breaches would be justified—for instance, to prevent the client from committing suicide or from killing another person.

These illustrations might also include the example of preventing a client from transmitting HIV to a sexual partner although—as will become apparent— the ethical warrant for disclosure in such cases is very provisional. Clearer, less contingent examples might be preferable.

If Dr. Talcott is candid, Lisa will tell him that she is HIV-seropositive and having unprotected sexual intercourse with someone after being informed that confidentiality is not an absolute. As such, if Dr. Talcott were ultimately to decide to disclose any confidential information, the information disclosed would not have been dishonestly exacted from the client.

After Lisa's disclosure, Dr. Talcott should try to get a clear grasp of the moral problem at hand. In light of the primary counseling mission, Dr. Talcott may perceive the problem as how best to promote Lisa's welfare while avoiding harm to Justin. Dr. Talcott will need to gather and inspect the morally relevant facts carefully in confronting this problem.

Because Lisa has had and continues to have unprotected sexual intercourse with Justin, there is a strong probability that Justin will contract HIV in the future or has already done so. If he has not yet contracted the disease, informing him about the potential danger could encourage him to take adequate precautions—for instance, discontinuing sexual intercourse entirely or using protection such as condoms. If Justin has already contracted the disease, telling him will give him the option of early detection, monitoring of the disease through periodic medical examinations, medication to prevent AIDS-related complications, increased longevity, and generally greater control over his life. Dr. Talcott should realize that it is in Justin's best interest to be informed, whether or not he has contracted the disease.

However, Dr. Talcott is also aware that Lisa is presently unwilling to tell Justin herself. Given Lisa's history of depression and attempted suicide, Dr. Talcott has reason to believe that if he tells Justin and Justin subsequently leaves Lisa, she might withdraw into worse depression, lose rapport with the therapist, and again attempt suicide. Dr. Talcott's informing Justin of Lisa's positive HIV status is likely to prevent harm to Justin, but it might adversely affect Lisa.

There is no formula for predicting degrees of danger, but Dr. Talcott, as a competent therapist, can make a reasonable assessment of Lisa's probability of attempting suicide if Justin leaves her. If these prospects appear to be great, involuntary commitment of his client may be indicated. Although this action may save the client's life, it is paternalistic and is likely to run contrary to the interest of the client in not being hospitalized. Moreover, the client is thereby manipulated and treated as a means, even though this is done to save her life. Because Dr. Talcott cares about the autonomy and dignity of his client, he will avoid this option if there are less degrading and restrictive ones available (see Chapter 10).

In line with the primary counseling mission, Dr. Talcott should try first to work within the therapeutic process to convince Lisa to tell Justin herself. This option has the advantage of maintaining confidentiality and therefore the client's trust. It also places the responsibility in the client's own hands, thereby facilitating her self-determination and independence.

If therapy is to stimulate client disclosure, Lisa will need to trust Dr. Talcott and to feel free and safe to explore her own feelings and ideas. Whether this is possible will depend largely on Dr. Talcott's qualities as person and therapist. Lisa has reluctantly disclosed a deep secret. She has been resistant to the counseling process. Progress toward increased client trust and self-reliance is likely to occur only if Dr. Talcott can maintain and convey an attitude of unconditional positive regard for his client notwithstanding her refusal to disclose to Justin. Explaining why he disapproves of such a refusal, he will need to demonstrate empathy for his client. Making no attempt to coerce or intimidate Lisa into changing her mind, Dr. Talcott should abstain from telling Lisa that she is bad, although he should not hide his own ethical stance. Despite Dr. Talcott's disagreement with what Lisa is doing, Dr. Talcott must uphold an attitude of deep, genuine caring so that Lisa is encouraged to explore her own thoughts and feelings freely and to be herself without fear of rejection.

Dr. Talcott should attempt to get inside Lisa's subjective world, understanding what she must be going through in these difficult times and reflecting back this subjectivity with even greater lucidity than Lisa has expressed it. He must approach her, not with doubt and incredulity, but with a deep desire to understand and believe in her; not to detach from and critically assess what she is experiencing, but to "connect with" and partake in it. Thereby, he may help this client to reach greater depths of understanding of what and how she is feeling—her fear of dying, of being out of control, of being abandoned; her anxiety; her anger.

In facilitating such positive growth, Dr. Talcott cannot be a phony. Congruent inside and out, he must deeply care and convey that he cares. He must be there for Lisa and understand her. Even while recognizing that caring is not necessarily a cure, he may realistically hope to facilitate change toward greater client self-directiveness and independence. This will include the increased possibility that Lisa will take up, on her own, the moral responsibility of informing Justin.

Dr. Talcott should recognize that the risks of Justin's contracting the disease increase as time goes on. If he is diligent, he will realize the urgency of the matter and will take action in a timely fashion. Although Dr. Talcott should try at first to facilitate Lisa's self-disclosure, he may reasonably conclude that the only timely disclosure Justin is likely to receive will come from Dr. Talcott's own lips. If so, Dr. Talcott should let Lisa know that he will be informing Justin, for to act without Lisa's knowledge would be to act without candor. This would almost surely destroy the bond of trust formed in therapy. Nor should he tell Lisa of his intent with the implication that it marks the end of his genuine concern for her welfare. To the contrary, a virtuous therapist would continue to convey unconditional positive regard and empathizing.

If Dr. Talcott himself tells Justin of Lisa's HIV status, he should do so discreetly, respecting her privacy as far as ethically feasible under the circumstances. He should not leave the message on an answering machine, or tell Justin through messengers, or discuss the case where others who have no need to know can overhear. Discretion instead requires disclosure *only* to the one at risk.

Dr. Talcott should be morally considerate. He should disclose no more information than necessary to alert Justin of the imminent danger. Only a general statement need be conveyed, such as that there is medical evidence indicating that a current sexual partner is HIV-seropositive. Saying more would be indiscreet, an unwarranted violation of Lisa's privacy.

Nor should Dr. Talcott turn his back on Justin after making the disclosure. Realizing that the information is likely to be traumatic, he should offer Justin his counseling services and, if they are declined, make a suitable referral. Otherwise he will not have exercised due care on Justin's behalf.

CASE 2: HARM TO UNIDENTIFIABLE THIRD PARTIES

Jason, age 25, was in therapy with Dr. Conklin because of problems coping with the knowledge that he was in the early stages of AIDS. Among other problems, Jason was experiencing rejection by close relatives and friends, who dissociated themselves from him when they found that he had AIDS. However, in the course of therapy, Jason revealed to Dr. Conklin that he was engaging in sexual activities with multiple, anonymous sex partners—routinely picking up women at singles bars and having unprotected oral, anal, and genital sex with many of them. When Dr. Conklin advised Jason to cease his promiscuous, high-risk sexual activities and to wear a condom, Jason agreed to do so. However, 2 months later he admitted that his sexual practices had not changed and that he still did not wear a condom.

In this case, Jason knows that he is subjecting others to a deadly disease. Yet, despite this knowledge, he continues to do so. It is easy to understand how one might experience moral outrage at such conduct. However, as a virtuous therapist, Dr. Conklin must try not to allow his personal disapproval of Jason's conduct to taint the quality of his therapy. He will still need to demonstrate deep caring for him, and putting on no facade, empathize with him. Jason is experiencing a deep sense of alienation, abandoned by those he thought really cared about him at a time when he desperately wants their companionship and support. His subjective world is a painful one to be in. Dr. Conklin must be able to put himself in these subjective shoes, feeling what Jason is feeling, and understanding his behavior. Although he will uncover no moral justification for Justin's behavior from this subjectivity, Dr. Conklin can understand it better.

However, Dr. Conklin is human, and his own personal disdain for Jason's conduct may get in the way of such a display, destroying his ability to empathize, clouding his independence of judgment, compromising his loyalty to this client. If that happens, Dr. Conklin should realize it and refer Jason to another therapist, one whose loyalty, he has reason to believe, will not similarly falter.

The case of Jason is significantly different from the case of Lisa. Unlike Lisa's partner, the endangered third parties in Jason's case have all been nameless, and Dr. Conklin does not have a phone number, address, or other means to contact these individuals. In contrast to the first case, of major concern here is the welfare of *future* (prospective) sexual partners who themselves are likely to be nameless, and whose number continues to increase.

Dr. Conklin should work diligently to provide Jason with competent, loyal counseling services. As a virtuous therapist, he will want to help Jason work through his problems because he has intrinsic regard for Jason's own welfare; however, he should also be aware that his success with Jason can be instrumental in helping him stop his dangerous sexual activities. In other words, the most efficacious way Dr. Conklin has for harmonizing intrinsic regard for Jason's welfare and for the welfare of those who may be harmed by him is to provide Jason with his best possible counseling services.

Obviously, there is no guarantee that Jason will change his dangerous sexual activities, even with the help of very competent counseling. He can continue to pay lip service to the idea of giving up these activities without changing his behavior, or he may prematurely discontinue counseling without accepting a referral.

In cases such as these, Dr. Conklin may have done all he can reasonably do. However, one further possibility would be for him to tell the police of the situation. This would involve a breach of confidentiality that would make public information out of very personal, private features of Jason's life, including the fact that he has AIDS. It would probably subject Jason to further, painful discrimination. Moreover, it would be likely to mark the end of any trusting relationship that Jason would have with a therapist and destroy the likelihood of working through his problems in therapy.

Of course, Dr. Conklin could merely threaten to go to the police if Jason does not cease his dangerous sexual activities. Under these conditions, however, the client would cease to be honest with his therapist about his sexual activities, thereby also destroying the therapist's chances of getting the client to alter his sexual conduct.

Reporting Jason to the police assumes that the proper legal machinery is in place to make such an apprisal feasible. First, this option supposes that the state in which Dr. Conklin practices would regard Jason's alleged sexual misconduct as a criminal offense. It also assumes that the police will be motivated to divert scarce resources away from other concerns to pursue such covert operations as observing Jason in bars and other public places. Without reasonable assurance that the police would even respond to the complaint, Dr. Conklin should consider disclosure as pointless.

Second, with no complainants, the police would be required to engage in covert activities to catch the alleged perpetrator in the act of fornication. Consequently, it would be self-defeating for Dr. Conklin to forewarn Jason of his intention to contact the police. For police surveillance to work, Dr. Conklin would need to conspire with the police by deliberately not telling Jason that he was involving the police. However, an honest therapist would be disposed against such deceitful tactics.

Third, an image of therapists as police informants would alienate present as well as prospective clients from trusting their therapists with their secrets. In Kantian terms, a universal law of therapists serving as police informants would undermine the very purpose of therapy—to help clients—by destroying the bond of trust on which it depends.

Fourth, the police would need to have legal grounds for subjecting Jason to an AIDS test or for gaining access to the results of his previous tests.

Fifth, in contrast to the first case, the third parties in this case are engaged in foreseeably high-risk sexual conduct. HIV exists in high proportions within the general population and its primary means of transmission is vaginal and anal sexual intercourse. Individuals should realize that promiscuous or casual sex without adequate safety precautions is high-risk behavior for contracting HIV. The third parties involved already have good reason to avoid such sexual activities and are able to avoid the imminent danger through the exercise of their own rational judgment without the help of a therapist (Cohen, 1995). As suggested in Chapter 2, therapists' moral responsibility to protect third parties from harm may be limited by the third parties' own responsibility for their actions.

Of course, death for sexual indiscretion is too high a price to pay, and therapists who care about other human beings, none of whom are perfect, will feel regret and a sense of tragedy. This should not be rationalized away with the sweeping generalization that "they deserved it, anyway." Dr. Conklin should do whatever he reasonably can about this exigency instead of just allowing it to persist, but what can he reasonably do about it?

Dr. Conklin should do his utmost to discourage sexual promiscuity of clients (those with and without HIV) by educating them about its risks. However, therapists can successfully accomplish this goal only when clients feel free to discuss intimate details of their sex lives with their therapists, and therapists can, in turn, speak candidly with their clients about the risks of sexual promiscuity.

On the other hand, a policy of disclosure under conditions like those described in this case is not likely to discourage sexual promiscuity. On the contrary, by placing great strain on the trust between therapist and client, it may significantly defeat this very purpose. Accordingly, notwithstanding his regrets about not having a better solution to this moral problem, Dr. Conklin should not disclose Jason's HIV status and behavior to the police.

CASE 3: HARM TO A THIRD-PARTY CLIENT

> John and Sue, husband and wife of one year, were seeing Dr. Barns for marital problems that seemed to be getting progressively worse as time went on. In the course of therapy, in an individual session in which Sue was not present, John revealed to Dr. Barns that he was regularly having oral and anal sex with other men—John usually being the recipient in both kinds of sex—without using any means of protection. Unknown to Sue, several evenings each week he would pick up men at gay bars and have sex with them. John also told Dr. Barns that he found these sexual encounters much more gratifying than any heterosexual experience he had ever had. However, Dr. B. was aware that John was also having vaginal sexual intercourse with Sue, and that the two did not use any means of protection. Nevertheless, when Dr. B. advised John to be tested for HIV, John refused, saying that he was better off not knowing. Moreover, he was unwilling to inform Sue of his sexual activities for fear that she would leave him "just as his first wife did when she found out."

One salient difference between this case and the situation with Lisa (Case 1) is that the endangered third party in the present case (Sue) is also one of the therapist's clients. In accordance with the principle of fairness, Dr. Barns should therefore treat Sue in the same equitable fashion as he would treat any other client. Thus Dr. Barns has an equal responsibility of candor toward *both* clients. Not only should Dr. Barns make full disclosure of material facts to John; he should do the same for Sue. Because John is Sue's husband, his sexual activities are materially relevant to the course of Sue's own therapy, and disclosure of them to her would be part of her informed consent.

Still, John has trusted and confided in Dr. Barns, and it is only because of this bond of trust that Dr. Barns has learned about John's promiscuous sexual activities with other men. If Dr. Barns discloses this information to Sue, John would probably view the disclosure as a betrayal of their trust, which would probably mean the end of the counseling relationship and, perhaps, the last time John would ever accept any counseling. As a beneficent, caring therapist, Dr. Barns will not want to lose John as his client.

On the other hand, Dr, Barns also cares about Sue, whom he believes is presently being placed at high risk of contracting HIV. In line with the principle of nonmaleficence, Dr. Barns has a responsibility to protect his client against this risk (National Organization for Human Service Education [NOHSE], 1994, 1.4). If he is to be honest with Sue, he cannot allow her to remain, at least for very long, in a state of ignorance about such an urgent matter.

Out of concern for the welfare of both clients, Dr. Barns should choose the course of action that is most likely to promote the welfare of each as much as possible under the present circumstances. The welfare of each seems best served when Dr. Barns helps to facilitate, through the process of therapy, John's self-disclosure of the pertinent facts to Sue. First, Sue will receive the information she needs to exert significant control over her own life; therapy will proceed, if she decides to pursue it, given a more realistic picture of her marriage and the reasons for saving it.

Second, from the perspective of John's own welfare, it is important that he accept responsibility for the disclosure. John is a homosexual in a primarily heterosexual society in which admitting to be a homosexual typically results in discrimination. It is therefore understandable that John tries to hide behind a heterosexual facade. John's marriage is such a facade; but this is surely not congruence; nor is it personal autonomy—that is, the exercise of control over his own life.

The process of therapy can serve John's welfare by facilitating change toward his increased powers of self-determination. If Dr. Barns exhibits the quality of congruence in relating to John, he will provide an example for John to emulate, thereby helping him to surrender his own phoniness and move toward greater personal autonomy.

If therapy is to facilitate such a positive change, much will depend on Dr. Barns's capacity for unconditional acceptance of John as a person. This unconditional positive regard can provide a model of self-acceptance from which John can, in turn, draw his own positive self-concept. In providing this model, Dr. Barns would send a therapeutic message that would allow John to believe, "My value as a person exists and does not depend on my sexual preference or on what others might say or think of my homosexuality." The success of therapy may, in this instance, depend on whether Dr. Barns, as therapist, conveys this message and John, as client, internalizes it. If John does internalize it, the task of confronting Sue will be much easier for him and more likely to occur.

The success of therapy may also depend on Dr. Barns's ability to empathize, to place himself in the subjective shoes of John but without losing a sense of his own separateness. If Dr. Barns is himself a homosexual, he will need to have worked through any unfinished business of his own that might lead him to overidentify with the feelings of anger, alienation, and frustration that can come from trying to cope with one's homosexuality in a society that treats homosexuals as outcasts. If Dr. Barns is a heterosexual, he will have had to work through any feelings about his own sexuality that might block him from empathizing with his homosexual client. Dr. Barns will have to maintain independence of judgment throughout the therapeutic process, unfaltering in his loyalty to John and Sue alike.

Nevertheless, he may reasonably conclude that therapy is not—and is not likely—to facilitate John's self-disclosure to Sue. As morally autonomous,

Dr. Barns will need to wrestle with the ethical question of whether *he* should make the disclosure or remain silent. On the one hand, there is the possibility that such a disclosure will block any future help that John might reap through therapy—although, unfortunately, the possibility that John will benefit from therapy may have already grown quite dim at this point. On the other hand, Sue's welfare may be jeopardized if she is not informed. Dr. Barns should take account of these respective harms, along with their respective probabilities, and make a decision consistent with what he thinks will bring maximum client welfare under these particular circumstances.

In weighing probabilities, Dr. Barns will need to consider the prospective harm to Sue. It is significant that any evidence is now circumstantial. In contrast to the previous two cases, Dr. Barns does not have conclusive medical evidence on which to base his prediction of harm. Still, he is aware that John is engaging in high-risk sexual activity on a regular basis, and he cannot rationalize away the high probability of harm.

Sue is also Dr. Barns's client. He has a moral responsibility to promote her welfare. To remain silent is to allow a dangerous false impression to persist. It is to masquerade as a helper, inauthentically and incongruently, while knowing information that may eventually kill her.

Had Sue not been a client, the moral problem would have been somewhat different. In general, a bond of trust is presumed to exist between therapists and clients whereas there is no such presumption regarding therapists and non-clients. As a client, Sue therefore has certain reasonable expectations of her therapist that arise from the trust she has been encouraged to repose in her therapist. In particular, she expects that Dr. Barns would not deliberately permit her to remain in ignorance of matters intimately related to her welfare; and certainly her husband's sexual activities do so. The failure to disclose such information to a client is thus a betrayal of this trust.

This does not mean that Dr. Barns should not see a moral problem with nondisclosure were Sue not a client. Nevertheless, in such a case, the lack of conclusive medical evidence (establishing John as HIV-seropositive) would appear to make the case for disclosure less compelling.

Given Sue's status as client, Dr. Barns has a moral responsibility to tell Sue of John's sexual activity, or at least he would be justified in doing so, even though he lacks conclusive medical evidence. Still, he should first make John aware of his intention to give Sue this information, thereby allowing John a final opportunity to do it on his own. Dr. Barns should also convey his willingness to make the disclosure in John's presence—for instance, in a session in which both clients are present. Moreover, Dr. Barns should inform John of exactly what he intends to tell Sue. Therefore, Dr. Barns will remain candid with John throughout the process of disclosure.

Dr. Barns should also exercise discretion in what he discloses. He should restrict the disclosure only to information that is needed to inform Sue of the potential danger. For example, he may say, "John is in a high-risk category for contracting HIV and it would be in your best interest to discuss this matter further with him." He may not say, "John is a homosexual who has had affairs with other men behind your back and now may well have contracted, and infected you with, HIV." While the former statement respects confidentiality as far as is consistent with the purpose of making the disclosure; the latter statement contains unnecessary breaches of confidentiality. Hence, making no wholesale surrender of either principle, Dr. Barns will try his best to harmonize candor and discretion, being "discreetly candid" and "candidly discreet," conceding to each wherever feasible.

Standards for Disclosure of Confidential Information

The American Counseling Association (1995) includes a "Fatal, Contagious Diseases" provision in its *Code of Ethics*. This provision states the following:

> A counselor who receives information confirming that a client has a disease commonly know to be both communicable and fatal is justified in disclosing information to an identifiable third party, who by his or her relationship with the client is at a high risk of contracting the disease. Prior to making a disclosure the counselor should ascertain that the client has not already informed the third party about his or her disease and that the client is not intending to inform the third party in the immediate future. (B.1.d)

This rule, which is a version of a rule previously proposed by Cohen (1990, 1997), provides general guidelines for making disclosure in cases of sexually active HIV-seropositive clients. The following standards—divided into Conditions of Disclosure (CDs) and Procedures of Disclosure (PDs)—amplify on and help to interpret this general rule in the light of the three case analyses presented in this chapter.

Conditions of Disclosure

CD 1 The therapist is aware of medical evidence indicating that the client is HIV-seropositive (for instance, two EIA tests and a confirmatory Western blot).

CD 2 The third party is engaging in a relationship with the client such as unprotected sexual intercourse, which, according to current medical standards, places the third party at high risk of contracting HIV from the client.

CD 3 The client is not likely to disclose his or her HIV status to the third party in the near future; nor is anyone else likely to do so.

CD 4 The third party can be identified and contacted by the therapist without the intervention of law enforcement or other investigative agencies.

CD 5 The third party is not engaging in high-risk sexual activity (such as promiscuous sex without the use of a condom) for which he or she can reasonably be expected to foresee or comprehend the high risk of harm to self.

CDs 1 through 5 collectively provide direction regarding *when* to disclose information that would normally be confidential. When all five conditions are satisfied, a therapist has, other things being equal, a moral responsibility to disclose to the given third party information about this person's risk level. CDs 1 through 3 are conditions under which harm to third parties may be considered imminent enough to warrant disclosure. CD 4 protects clients from unwarranted or unnecessary compromise of welfare, interests, and needs. CD 5 reflects a standard of vulnerability according to which therapists' responsibility to protect third parties from harm is limited by third parties' own responsibility for their actions.

Condition CD 2 refers to a relationship that places a third party at high risk of contracting the disease from an infected individual. Because risks range theoretically on a continuum from 0 to 1, a classification schema is needed for distinguishing high-risk activities from lower-risk activities.

Cohen (1997) has provided such a classification schema. According to his schema, high-risk sexual relationships involve sexual activities that present a probability of infection that, by current medical standards and empirical data, renders them unsafe. These activities involve a high probability of contact with the infected party's blood or semen, which are the body fluids found to have the highest concentrations of HIV virus, with a mucous membrane of the sexual partner—for instance, the linings of the rectum, vagina, mouth, and urethra (Douglas & Pinsky, 1996). These activities include vaginal or rectal intercourse without a condom, fellatio (oral stimulation of the penis) with ejaculation into the partner's mouth, cunnilingus (oral stimulation of the female genitals) during menstruation, and oral-anal contact (Douglas & Pinsky, 1996; Masters, Johnson, & Kolodny, 1992).

Use of latex condoms during vaginal and anal intercourse do not entirely eliminate risk of infection because the condom can break, but such prophylactic measures appear to reduce risk of sexual transmission from high to lower (Centers for Disease Control [CDC], 1988; Cohen, 1997). Although some evidence suggests that consistent withdrawal before ejaculation in vaginal and anal sex affords the receiving partner some protection, there appears to be sufficient grounds for including such an activity within the high-risk range (Cohen, 1997). First, pre-ejaculatory fluid may be a factor in HIV transmission. Second, this method of protection relies exclusively on the responsiveness of the infected partner (De Vincenzi, 1994).

Probabilities within a risk category may vary according to the specific kind of activity and conditions of performance (Cohen, 1997). For example, whereas unprotected vaginal and anal intercourse are both high-risk activities, anal intercourse may present a *higher* risk than vaginal intercourse (Douglas & Pinsky, 1996; Masters et al., 1992). If the HIV-seronegative partner has a genital infection, especially an ulcerative one, the risk of infection from the HIV-seropositive partner appears to increase (De Vincenzi, 1994). Similarly, whereas a sexual activity such as deep mouth kissing is generally regarded as a lower risk activity, this activity may be unsafe and high risk when the HIV-seropositive partner has bleeding gums. Although there is uncertainty about the risk status of nonmenstrual cunnilingus without a protective dam, there is reason to regard this activity as high risk when lesions or other conditions permitting exchange of infected bodily fluids are known or suspected to exist (Cohen, 1997). Finally, the frequency with which any sexual activity is performed may also be a factor because each episode of exposure to infected body fluids heightens the probability of infection (Cohen & Davis, 1994).

Condition CD 3 provides that neither the client nor anyone else is likely to make disclosure to the endangered third party. The reference to "anyone else" may include individuals such as friends or relatives of the client or third party, or it may also include state agencies such as partner notification services. According to Florida Statute 455.2416, practitioners who disclose confidential information to third parties must first inform their clients of the availability of these services. The statute says that practitioners' disclosures are civilly and criminally immune from liability only if clients first refuse to disclose the information themselves and to use partner notification services.

Conditions C1 through C5 are not intended as jointly *necessary and sufficient* conditions of disclosure. First, it is possible for cases to arise in which further conditions are present that make disclosure unwarranted. For example, disclosure may produce a serious harm of equal or greater magnitude to that which is prevented, as when making disclosure to the third party would probably incite this individual to kill or seriously injure the client. Another case may arise if the third party were already dying from a different disease and telling this person of the partner's medical status could reasonably be predicted to affect that person's health or longevity adversely or otherwise serve no redeeming value (Cohen, 1995, 1997).

Second, it is also possible for cases to arise in which therapists have a moral responsibility to disclose certain information or are justified in disclosing it, even though all five conditions have not been satisfied. For example, in case 3, disclosure was warranted even though CD 1 was not satisfied because the evidence on which harm was assessed did not include HIV tests.

In addition to conditions of disclosure, further procedural standards of disclosure (PDs) may be formulated that at least partly define virtuous disclosure style:

Procedures of Disclosure

PD 1 The therapist makes disclosure of otherwise confidential information in a timely fashion so that the very purpose of disclosure is not defeated. (Diligence)

PD 2 The therapist provides the client with the encouragement, understanding, and support conducive to the client's making disclosure on his or her own. (Unconditional positive regard, Empathy, Candor)

PD 3 Prior to disclosure, the therapist informs the client of his or her intention to disclose the pertinent information. (Candor)

PD 4 The therapist avoids coercion and manipulation in effecting client disclosure as by making it a condition of continued therapy or by engaging in any form of lying or deceit. (Unconditional positive regard, Honesty)

PD 5 The therapist makes disclosure directly (for instance, without messengers or answering machines) to only the third party at risk or, in the case of minors, to the legal guardian. (Discretion)

PD 6 The therapist limits disclosure to general information sufficient to inform the third party of the imminent danger. (Discretion)

PD 7 The therapist takes reasonable measures to safeguard the client from physical harm such as self-inflicted harm occasioned by disclosure. (Nonmaleficence)

PD 8 The therapist offers therapy assistance or an appropriate referral to the third party at risk. (Nonmaleficence)

Derived from autonomy-facilitating and trust-establishing counseling virtues, PDs provide fundamental ethical guidelines on how to disclose sensitive information. After each rule, given in parentheses, are the respective virtues or principles undergirding the rule. In making disclosure, when it is warranted, a therapist who neglects one or more of these rules is likely to have needlessly sacrificed client or third-party welfare. On the other hand, respect for these rules provides reasonable assurance that the therapist has acted with due consideration for both client and third party.

Although the concept of a timely disclosure as provided in PD 1 does not lend itself to precise formulation, the timeliness of disclosure is directly proportional to the degree of exposure over a given period. Thus, when intervals between third-party exposure are weeks or months, timely disclosure may be longer than when exposure occurs daily. In the latter case, timely disclosure may mean disclosure within days or hours (Cohen, 1997).

Although a single act of anal or vaginal intercourse can result in HIV transmission, in most cases multiple acts of intercourse have been necessary for infection to occur (Padian, 1987). Estimates of risk of HIV infection from a single sexual episode vary, with some estimates of probability of infection from heterosexual transmission through vaginal intercourse ranging from .2 % to 1% for women and .1% to .5% for men (Langone, 1991; Turner, Miller, & Moses, 1989). The risk of infection from a single episode of anal intercourse with an infected partner may be considerably higher, in the range of 1 in 50 to 100 (Masters et al., 1992). Thus, disclosure in the case of ongoing anal sex may be more urgent than with vaginal sex (Cohen, 1997).

In addition, evidence suggests that the rate of transmission from a single episode of vaginal intercourse may increase according to the stage of advancement of the disease. Thus, De Vincenzi (1994) noted that the transmission rate for 121 couples using condoms inconsistently during an estimated 12,000 sexual contacts was 1 per 1,000. When estimated in relation to the stage of HIV, the rate was significantly higher—5 per 1,000 when the HIV-seropositive partner was in an advanced stage and 0.7 per 1,000 in an asymptomatic stage. Thus urgency of disclosure may also depend on the seropositve person's stage of infection (Cohen, 1997).

Within constraints of timely disclosure, therapists have a moral and professional responsibility to facilitate clients' autonomous self-disclosure. As provided by PD 2, therapists should provide clients with an environment conducive to such disclosure. This requires that therapists understand and demonstrate sensitivity toward the special medical, social, and cultural circumstances of specific client populations (Dworkin & Pincu, 1993). Therapists should themselves be adequately informed about the nature of HIV and its implications for sexual partners and should make reasonable efforts to educate the client about these.

In relating to the client as a person, therapists should convey a genuine, unconditional attitude of acceptance and regard and a willingness to support the person's efforts in confronting the problem of disclosure. Thus, the therapist might offer to be present when the client tells the partner about his or her medical status and to help the client prepare for disclosure such as through role playing (Gray & Harding, 1988; Harding, Gray, & Neal, 1993). If, however, timely disclosure is not likely, therapists should, in accordance with PD 3, inform clients of their intention to disclose the information. Otherwise, therapists fail in their responsibility of candor to their clients.

According to the American Counseling Association's *Code of Ethics* (1995, B.1.f), justified disclosure must be limited to essential information. Given that the primary purpose of disclosure is to warn of the impending danger, essential information is the information that serves this purpose. In accordance with PD 6, such information should include only general medical information—for instance, a broad statement that there is medical evidence indicating that a sexual partner is HIV-seropositive. Particular details such as names of sexual partners or names and addresses of physicians would be superfluous given the stated purpose.

As provided by PD 7, therapists have a responsibility to guard against client harm resulting from disclosure. Although the rate of suicide in HIV-seropositive clients appears to be only slightly higher than in the general population (Rabkin & Rabkin, 1995), HIV-seropositive clients who experience rejection by their sexual partners after the sexual partners have been informed of clients' HIV seropositivity may be at increased risk of depression and suicidality. In such cases, therapists bear a moral responsibility to assess these risks carefully and to respond appropriately to safeguard the welfare of the client (Cohen, 1997). The nature of appropriate paternalistic measures in such cases is discussed in Chapter 10.

Finally, therapists should be aware of the potential psychological effects of disclosure on the HIV-seropositive client's sex partner (Odets, 1995). As provided by PD 8, therapists should be prepared to offer and provide counseling or, when this is not possible, an appropriate referral. The provision of such service or referral respects affected sex partners as ends in themselves and accords with the primary counseling mission by showing due regard for the welfare of third parties.

Summary

In this chapter, three cases were examined in which clients who have, or probably have, HIV are sexually active with third parties. All three cases involve conflict between keeping clients' confidences and preventing third-party harm, but each case also introduces distinct factors. In Case 1, there is one known third party; in Case 2, there are multiple third parties, whose identities are not known. In Case 3, the third party is also a client, and the evidence for HIV in her partner is circumstantial.

Analysis of each case in terms of what a virtuous therapist would do has suggested five general conditions for disclosure of confidential information (CDs). These analyses have also yielded eight procedures (PDs) for making disclosure. Although these guidelines provide general standards of when and how to disclose, they offer no algorithm. Situations may arise that override the need for disclosure even when all CDs are true; in some cases, disclosure may be necessary even though all conditions are not true. Thus, in making determinations about disclosing sensitive information, therapists may need to weigh and balance competing ethical considerations.

In responding appropriately to clients having HIV or full-blown AIDS, therapists will need to be warm, caring, and morally sensitive to the pain, emotional turmoil, and social isolation of people afflicted with this fatal, incurable disease. These personal attributes of virtuous therapists resist complete elaboration in terms of rules.

REVIEW QUESTIONS

1. What is HIV and how is it transmitted?
2. Respond to the following: "HIV is primarily a disease of gays and drug addicts."
3. What factors determine whether a sexual activity is high risk for the transmission of HIV? Provide some examples of high-risk sexual activities.
4. What precautions might be taken to reduce the risk of an otherwise high-risk sexual activity for the transmission of HIV?
5. Can deep mouth kissing ever be considered high risk? Explain.
6. Can the particular stage of HIV infection of an infected individual affect that individual's chance of sexually transmitting the disease? Explain.
7. Can a single episode of sexual intercourse with an HIV-infected sexual partner transmit HIV? Explain.
8. Is there any difference in the risk of heterosexual transmission from women to men as compared to such transmission from men to women? Explain.
9. How is HIV tested?
10. What is meant by HIV-seropositivity?
11. What is the difference between having HIV and having AIDS?

DISCUSSION QUESTIONS

1. In obtaining a client's informed consent to therapy, what exceptions to confidentiality should a therapist present? Should these exceptions include disclosure to prevent a client with HIV from infecting a third party?

2. In the landmark *Tarasoff* case, Prosenjit Poddar, a patient of a psychologist, Dr. Lawrence Moore, at the Cowell Memorial Hospital, University of California at Berkeley, informed the psychologist of his intention to kill a young woman, Tatiana Tarasoff, when she returned home from spending the summer in Brazil. Nobody warned Tatiana or her parents of the potential danger; nor was Poddar detained. The majority opinion of the Supreme Court was that "once a therapist does, in fact, determine, or . . . reasonably should have determined, that a patient poses a serious danger of violence to others, he bears a duty to exercise reasonable care to protect the foreseeable victim of that danger" (*Tarasoff v. Regents of the University of California*, 1976). The defendants, including Moore, were found guilty of a breach of duty to exercise reasonable

care to protect an endangered third party. (For further details of this case see also Chapter 2, Cases for Analysis, Case 2.)

In your estimation, should the logic and conclusion of *Tarasoff* also be applied to Case 1 presented in this chapter? What, if any, relevant similarities and/or differences are there between Poddar and Lisa? Between the circumstances of Dr. Moore and Dr. Talcott? Between those of Tatiana and Justin?

3. The longer Justin goes uninformed, the greater are his chances of contracting the virus. In your estimation, should Dr. Talcott himself immediately inform Justin of the impending danger? Should he work within the therapeutic process to promote Lisa's own disclosure to Justin? Should he be willing to allow Justin to go uninformed if this is the only way of preserving confidentiality? Defend your answers by appealing to morally relevant facts and principles.

4. Respond to the following argument: "Because Justin has been having unprotected sexual intercourse with Lisa for some time now, he probably has the disease anyway. So what could possibly be gained by informing him about the risk of infection?"

5. Is Lisa's history of attempted suicide morally relevant? What steps, if any, do you think Dr. Talcott should take in protecting Lisa from self-inflicted harm, assuming that Dr. Talcott has decided that he will inform Justin of the impending danger?

6. If Dr. Talcott discloses to Justin the danger involved in Justin's sexual activities with Lisa, what information should he disclose? How should he convey this information to him (for example, over the phone, in person, etc.)? How should he decide when to tell? Explain.

7. If Dr. Talcott discloses the information to Justin, should he first inform Lisa of his intention to do so? Explain.

8. If Dr. Talcott discloses the information to Justin, does he then have a moral responsibility to offer him his counseling services? Explain.

9. What differences exist between the circumstances of the endangered third parties of Case 1 and Case 2, as discussed in this chapter? Are these differences morally relevant? Explain.

10. In your estimation, should the logic and conclusion of *Tarasoff* also be applied to Case 2? Explain.

11. How, in your estimation, should Dr. Conklin, in Case 2 respond to Jason's failure to cease his promiscuous, high-risk sexual activities?

12. Discuss some of the psychological and social pressures Jason is likely to be experiencing as a result of having AIDS. How might these pressures relate to Jason's failure to cease his risky sexual behavior? What, if anything, can Dr. Conklin do to help Jason deal more effectively with these pressures?

13. Discuss some of the possible practical as well as moral problems of reporting Jason's sexual activities to the police. On balance, do you think that filing such a report would be a good idea? Explain.

14. In Case 3, the endangered third party, Sue, is also one of Dr. Barns's clients. Discuss the moral significance of this. If Sue were not a client, would the therapist's responsibilities be different? Explain.

15. Why, in Case 3, is Dr. Barns's consistent modeling of congruence and unconditional positive regard toward John of special significance in helping John tell Sue about his sexual activities on his own?

16. In contrast to Cases 1 and 2, there is, in Case 3, no conclusive medical evidence establishing that John is HIV-seropositive. Nevertheless, should Dr. Barns inform Sue that she is at high risk for contracting HIV if it is evident that John will not? Explain.

17. If Dr. Barns did make disclosure to Sue, what information should and should not be disclosed? Explain.

CHAPTER TEN

Paternalistic Intervention, Involuntary Commitment, and Client Autonomy

PATERNALISM IN COUNSELING AND
    PSYCHOTHERAPY
AUTONOMY
MENTAL COMPETENCE
JUSTIFIED PATERNALISM
INVOLUNTARY COMMITMENT
CASE STUDIES
    Case 1: A Pregnant Client with a Bipolar
      Disorder

Case 2: Involuntary Commitment of a Child
Case 3: A Question of Rational Suicide
ETHICAL STANDARDS OF PATERNALISM
SUMMARY
REVIEW QUESTIONS
DISCUSSION QUESTIONS

In Chapter 3, we discussed the autonomy-facilitating virtues and the centrality of client autonomy within the counseling process. Here, we examine the conflicts that sometimes arise between permitting clients to assert their autonomy and acting for the client in what therapists take to be their client's best interests. The general rule is to respect client autonomy, but the line between autonomous decision making and irrational, nonautonomous conduct may be blurred; questions of whether and how to intervene on the client's behalf may present ethical challenges for virtuous therapists.

In this chapter, these challenges are explored. First, concepts central to these issues are examined—in particular, those of paternalism, autonomy, mental competence, and involuntary commitment. Three cases are considered that raise serious moral conflicts for therapists concerning protection of fetal life, child welfare, and suicide intervention.

Paternalism in Counseling and Psychotherapy

Paternalism has been defined as "the interference with a person's liberty of action justified by reasons referring exclusively to the welfare, good, happiness, needs, interests, or values of the person being coerced" (Dworkin, 1971, p.108). In the context of counseling and psychotherapy, paternalistic intervention is objectionable when it impedes clients' autonomous choices or decisions. The value of client autonomy is primary in the promotion of client welfare; therefore, paternalistic interventions that abridge client autonomy may be self-defeating. Further, as the principle of candor requires that therapeutic interventions proceed once clients' informed consent is given, this principle protects clients against paternalistic abridgement of their autonomy. The legitimate place of paternalism within counseling and psychotherapy is thus questionable and controversial.

Given the centrality of autonomy in therapy, an understanding of this concept is necessary. In particular, before one can determine whether particular therapeutic interventions paternalistically abridge clients' autonomy, clarification is needed of what it means for individuals to make autonomous choices. The next section offers this clarification, and the subsequent section applies it to the related concept of mental competence.

Autonomy

According to John Stuart Mill (1947), an autonomous (self-determining) person possesses requisite cognitive and conative capacities to make decisions. In his analysis of what is involved in making a decision for oneself, he states:

> He who chooses his plan for himself employs all his faculties. He must use observation to see, activity to gather materials for decisions, discrimination to decide, and when he has decided, firmness and self-control to hold to his deliberate decision. And these qualities he requires and exercises exactly in proportion as the part of his conduct which he determines according to his own judgment and feelings is a large one. (p. 56)

Mill's "faculties" may be taken as defining fundamental mental operations involved in the process of autonomous decision making. As Mill suggests, a person is more or less autonomous depending on how much or how little he engages these mental operations. People who generally prefer to follow the crowd rather than think for themselves are relatively nonautonomous, whereas those who prefer to work things out for themselves are more autonomous. Thus, autonomy is not an all or nothing concept but exists in degrees.

With Mill's account as a model, autonomous choice or decision making may be understood as engaging four mutually supportive, successive mental operations:

1. Activity to gather materials for decision
2. Observation to see
3. Discrimination to make a deliberate decision
4. Firmness and self-control to hold to one's deliberate decision

Operation 1 relates to the awareness of a problem and the purposive activity of collecting information relevant to its solution. Operation 2 pertains to the use of the various senses—for example, seeing and listening—to obtain this information. Such activity may include direct observation (seeing for oneself) as well as indirect observation (collecting the observations and insights of others). It also may include introspective knowledge (awareness of one's own interests, values, and preferences). Operation 3 involves the deliberative process of coming to a decision based on this information. Operation 4 refers to the willpower and resolve to carry out one's decision without vacillation (Cohen, 1986).

As operation 3 is a rational, deliberative process, it requires additional cognitive activities associated with practical reasoning. Such activities would include foreseeing the probable consequences of pursuing different courses of action based on information gathered in operation 2. These activities would also include evaluating each different course of action and making a selection based on the evaluation. This rational discrimination would also assume a grasp of basic reality such as awareness of who one is, where one is, and what one is doing or intending to do.

Whenever a course of action is rationally judged better or worse, good or bad, right or wrong, a particular standard of value is assumed. Practical reasoning thus always involves commitment to prior values. For example, in choosing to refer a client with whom a conflict of interest has arisen, a virtuous therapist may be guided by values of honesty, beneficence, and loyalty. Without such prior value commitments, the selection of one course of action over another has nothing to commend it.

In choosing for oneself, one engages one's own values. Autonomous choice is accordingly a function of one's own value system. A person who in a manic episode gives away possessions for which he has worked and saved over a lifetime acts "out of character" by contradicting the serious stock he has placed in owning these things. Such uncharacteristic choice is nonautonomous insofar as it is a product of desires and ideas foreign to the person's own characteristic values and ends. Similarly, an honest, law-abiding person who suddenly begins to lie, cheat, and steal to support an escalating drug habit, does not decide autonomously (Cohen, 1986; Macklin, 1982).

An important test of autonomous choice is thus whether one's choice is consistent with one's own value system. A Jehovah's Witness who refuses a life-saving blood transfusion chooses autonomously if this decision is founded on her own religious values. On the other hand, the decision made by the followers of a religious cult to take their own lives is not autonomous if based on manipulation and mind control (Cohen, 1986).

A decision may be said to be autonomous to the extent that Mill's four mental operations are employed in accordance with one's own value system. Individuals can be said to be more or less autonomous depending upon how frequently they make autonomous decisions and the extent to which those decisions are autonomous. A central part of a therapist's job is to help clients become more autonomous as persons.

Mental Competence

When a person lacks the capacity for autonomous decision making, she may be labeled mentally *incompetent*—and *competent* when as she has the capacity for autonomous decision making. A mentally handicapped person may be incompetent to make certain decisions because of her incapacity to appreciate the consequences of her actions (failure of operation 3). A person with schizophrenia who is suffering from auditory or visual hallucinations may be incompetent to make certain decisions because of his incapacity to gather evidence through his senses adequately (failure of operation 2).

Nevertheless, even when individuals are incompetent to make their own decisions, legal guardians who exercise judgment on their behalf can and should act to respect what these individuals might have autonomously chosen for themselves. Thus their values may be respected, regardless of their incompetence. For example, the legal guardian of a comatose person who, when competent, made clear her desire not to be artificially maintained on a respirator has a moral responsibility to request that no such medical intervention be pursued. The exercise of judgment on behalf of a mentally handicapped individual should not depart from the individual's preferences provided that respecting them does not seriously harm the individual or place others in jeopardy. For example, the desire to take walks need not be denied a patient with Alzheimer's disease provided measures are taken to ensure the individual's safety.

An erroneous assumption is often made that mental incompetence is a quality people either have or lack completely. Competence, however, is relative; a person may be mentally competent in one respect but not in another. Thus, a geriatric patient may not be mentally competent to add a column of figures or to tend to his own financial decisions, yet he may be quite competent to decide what time he wishes to eat, whether he wants visitors, and whether he prefers one course of treatment to another (Macklin, 1982).

A person may also be intermittently competent in a given area. Someone with Alzheimer's may be competent to make treatment decisions during periods of lucidity alternating between states of confusion. Sometimes a person is considered mentally competent by having achieved a minimal level of mental competence—for example, he or she understands the nature and consequences of a given course of therapy. There is also a comparative sense in which a person may be more or less competent to make a given decision or type of decision. Thus, a person may be deemed minimally competent to give consent to therapy but, due to psychological pressures, may not be as competent as he or she normally is.

In general, the scope of a person's autonomy is circumscribed by the range of his competencies. The more decisions a person is competent to make, the more autonomous he or she *can* be. Being mentally competent to make decisions for oneself does not, however, make a person autonomous. Some people are competent to make decisions for themselves but seldom do, preferring instead to depend on others. These people may be relatively nonautonomous even though they may be highly competent. Having the mental capacities to make autonomous decisions does not guarantee that a person will exercise those capacities.

Justified Paternalism

Paternalistic intervention by counselors may be justified when it does not seriously thwart the autonomy of the client. For a client who lacks the mental competence to make a certain decision, a therapist who makes that decision for the client may be justified if doing so can avert a serious harm to the client. Such action may accord with the primary mission of counseling by promoting client welfare and need not degrade the client's own autonomy by overriding it. When the client lacks the capacity for autonomous decision making, the client's own autonomy cannot be contravened, for what does not exist cannot be hampered. Further, in cases when the incompetence is temporary—for example, the client is intoxicated—paternalistic intervention to avert a serious harm may elicit the client's future consent, as when sobriety returns. In these cases, the clients' own values are still respected, notwithstanding their temporary incapacity to assert these values for themselves.

In some cases, individuals may be competent—that is, they have the capacity for autonomous choice—but choose to do something contrary to their own welfare or not in accord with their own long-term interests. For example, some people fail to wear their seatbelts when driving to avoid the minor inconvenience of buckling up, despite the knowledge that they would regret not taking the trouble if they were to be seriously injured in an automobile accident. Paternalistic laws requiring people to wear seatbelts have sometimes been justified on the grounds that such a restriction of liberty is consistent with what people would do if they were to act consistently with their own values and long-term interests (Dworkin, 1971).

In the context of counseling, such a rationale for paternalistic intervention must be taken with caution. Therapists' attempts at paternalistically restricting the liberty of competent clients to protect them from themselves can undermine their autonomy and foster dependency. As discussed later in this chapter, prevention of serious harm, such as the client's death, may sometimes warrant restricting the liberty of a competent client. However, whereas a therapist may be justified in helping clients realize the implications of their own values, therapeutic intervention ordinarily must yield to the freely given and informed consent of competent clients.

Involuntary Commitment

Paternalistic interference with individual liberty may take the form of involuntarily detaining or committing a client in an inpatient facility. The rationale typically used to justify involuntary commitment legally and morally has been to provide treatment for mentally ill clients who are likely to harm themselves or others, or who are otherwise incapable of surviving on their own. According to Livermore et al. (1982), where effective treatment is unavailable, as in the case of a patient with Alzheimer's disease, the true rationale for such restriction of liberty may be to provide custodial care.

As corroborated by the oppressive history of involuntary commitment (Szasz, 1978), the concept of "mental illness" is a notoriously vague concept, and its diagnosis, far from being an exact science, may depend on ethical, legal, and social norms as well as the theoretical orientation of the diagnostician (Livermore et al., 1982; Szasz, 1991; Greenberg, 1982). Accordingly, there is need for caution when involuntary commitment is used to abridge a person's liberty. The need for caution has been recognized by legal criteria that regard the mere claim that a person is mentally ill as insufficient grounds for justifying involuntary commitment. Thus, according to the U.S. Supreme Court decision in *O'Connor v. Donaldson* (1975), "a non-dangerous individual who is capable of surviving safely in freedom by himself or with the help of willing or responsible family or friends cannot constitutionally be confined. A finding of 'mental illness' alone cannot justify a state's locking up a person against his will and keeping him indefinitely in simple custodial confinement" (2487). A person with schizophrenia, for example, is not a suitable candidate for involuntary commitment simply because he has been so classified. What is significant is whether this person is dangerous to himself or others. If the person is dangerous, his mental illness might provide an explanation for this dangerousness; but the dangerousness cannot itself be inferred from the illness alone (Livermore et al., 1982).

The prediction of dangerousness can pose a problem for involuntary commitment because there is no precise manner of predicting dangerous acts in all cases (Livermore et al., 1982). In making predictions of dangerousness, a therapist needs to exercise only a "reasonable degree of skill, knowledge and care ordinarily possessed and exercised" by other therapists judging under similar circumstances (*Tarasoff*, 1976, p. 25).

Involuntary commitment of a person presupposes that the person is in some sense incompetent. Incompetence in this context appears to mean that because of a particular mental incapacity—a mental "defect" or "illness"—the person is likely to cause serious bodily harm to self or other (Florida State 394.467[1], 1995). Clients who are incompetent in other ways—for example, have manic episodes or expose themselves in public—may annoy or offend or cause financial harm but may still not pose a threat of bodily harm to themselves or others; they may therefore not be proper candidates for involuntary commitment. Because of the extensive abridgement of freedom involved in involuntary commitment, the harm occasioned by mentally ill persons as a result of their mental illnesses should be serious enough to warrant such an extreme form of paternalism.

Before involuntary commitment is permissible, no other less restrictive means of accomplishing the same purpose should be available. State statutes have recognized the need to tread lightly in the abridgement of personal liberty through involuntary confinement. For example, the Florida Mental Health Act (F.S. 394.467[1]2[b], 1995) requires that "all available less restrictive treatment alternatives which would offer an opportunity for improvement of his or her condition have been judged to be inappropriate." It also requires that no family, friends, or alternative services are available to give the person sufficient help to survive without substantial harm.

Because involuntary commitment can impede clients' autonomy, therapists should avoid such extreme paternalism. This does not mean that there is never a justification for involuntary commitment, but it should be a last resort when no other less restrictive, available alternatives will suffice. The following case illustrates some tensions that might arise between respect for client autonomy and the question of involuntary commitment.

Case Studies

CASE 1: A PREGNANT CLIENT WITH A BIPOLAR DISORDER

Tina Matheson, age 22, is presently employed by the city as a grounds-keeper. She has an apartment with another single woman, Glenda, with whom she splits expenses. The two met when Tina responded to Glenda's classified ad for a roommate to share expenses. Tina has a father residing in the immediate area but they rarely see or speak to one another.

Tina has a bipolar disorder which fluctuates between major depressive and manic episodes. Since the age of 12, she has been in and out of therapy and has been treated with the drug, lithium carbonate. Tina does not have any toxic reactions to lithium, but she has persistently complained of its dulling effects on her personality. This has led her to stop taking her medication intermittently for weeks or sometimes months at a time. During one such period, she experienced psychotic episodes in which she imagined herself a stunt pilot. Boarding a plane at a local air field, she attempted to fly the plane, which subsequently crashed into an adjacent hangar. No one was hurt but the plane was totaled. On another occasion, she imagined herself to be a police detective and she arrested several people, who suffered frustration and minor inconvenience. Each of these occasions led to her hospitalization in a psychiatric facility for brief stays. Several occasions were marked by promiscuous sex. Most other major manic episodes were relatively innocuous in nature with no significant harm incurred by others. Unfortunately, sleep deprivation during major manic episodes coupled with an asthmatic condition sometimes led to physical distress for which she sometimes required hospitalization.

Tina's depressive history was marked by two unsuccessful suicide attempts made when she was 12 and 13, but she has made no other attempt since. Tina prided herself in being able to lift herself from her depressive states without medication through cognitive restructuring techniques that she learned through therapy subsequent to her suicide attempts. These techniques, she has admitted, were ineffectual in her manic phase because of her inability to stay focused.

Two years ago Tina became pregnant from a casual sexual encounter while on one of her manic flights. During her pregnancy, Tina had a serious asthma attack and was hospitalized. While she was in the hospital, however, Tina assumed the role of a nurse and began to make rounds to the other patients. In response to her disordered behavior, she was strapped to the hospital bed where she was constrained for 7 weeks. Because lithium is known to cause birth defects, the medication was not administered.

The hospital sought to have Tina declared legally incompetent and to permit her father as legal guardian to authorize an abortion. It was her father's contention that Tina was not competent to care for a child and that the continued pregnancy was contrary to his daughter's physical and emotional welfare. During this time, Tina lost considerable weight, developed a serious systemic bacterial infection, and eventually miscarried before any legal actions were taken.

While still in the hospital, she was given lithium and released when she scored within the normal range on a psychiatric rating test. At this juncture, Tina, very much distressed over her miscarriage and a sense of having lost control over her own life, sought counseling on a weekly basis with Dr. Harriet Winters. In 2 years of therapy with Dr. Winters, Tina came to trust her therapist. Dr. Winters empathized, was genuine, and she cared. Tina had begun to experience new confidence in her ability to take control of her own life.

As part of the treatment plan, Dr. Winters asked that Tina consistently take her medication, to which Tina consented. Because the issue of taking the medication was one with which Tina had not previously come to terms, the use of the medication became one of several important focal points of therapy. In the 2 years of therapy, she usually did manage to stay on the lithium as agreed. There were a few slip-ups, however. In particular, one month ago, after she stopped taking the medication for a brief period, Tina picked up a man in a bar and had casual sex with him. After finding out that she was once again pregnant, Tina felt as though her present had come full circle with her past.

Tina did not want to lose her child this time. Nor did she want to have a damaged child. While on her medication, she informed Dr. Winters of her intention to discontinue the lithium in order to protect the fetus. The events of her previous pregnancy made her fear that she might be forced to give up her baby. Thus, she made clear to Dr. Winters her wish to carry to term and asked Dr. Winters not to take any action that would put her baby in jeopardy. She made clear that this included involuntary commitment to a mental institution, which she was convinced, based on her previous experience, would make her vulnerable to whatever her father deemed in her "best interest," including an abortion.

Dr. Winters, who had encouraged her client to take charge of her own life, viewed Tina's decision as a positive step in the assertion of her autonomy. At the same time, she realized the risks involved in this decision. Dr. Winters proposed that, after discontinuation of the medication, therapy sessions be conducted on a biweekly schedule. She also told Tina that she would "do her best to safeguard the welfare of her child."

Tina did not show up for the next therapy session. When Dr. Winters called Tina's apartment that morning, Glenda informed Dr. Winters that Tina had not been home all night, that she did not know where she now was, and that the last time she saw her she seemed agitated, was speaking incoherently, and seemed disoriented.

As Tina's therapist, Dr. Winters confronted a difficult moral dilemma. Tina's welfare was intimately bound up with the assertion of her autonomy. Her life had been a struggle to become the pilot of her own fate. Dr. Winters and Tina worked together toward the attainment of such control as a primary goal of therapy. Paradoxically, at precisely the time when she began to harness her rational powers to take control over her own life, she had to relinquish that control in the very act of asserting it. Tina's decision was to have a child and to do whatever she could to ensure that child's welfare. This decision was made in accord with her own values while she was competent.

If Tina was to have a healthy child, she had to willfully stop her medication; but if she stopped her medication, she would lose her ability to decide for herself. This in turn would make her vulnerable to the decisions of others, and these decisions might not accord with her own values. Still, without the intervention of others, there was risk that during major manic or depressive episodes, Tina might jeopardize her own as well as her developing child's welfare.

If Dr. Winters did not respect Tina's autonomous decision to have her child, however, if she pressured her into staying on medication at the expense of the child, then Tina would have surrendered the very point of the therapy. She would have reaffirmed the very nonautonomy that brought her to therapy in the first place.

Dr. Winters's decision to work with Tina in the assertion of her autonomy was thus in concert with the primary counseling mission of promoting client welfare. A crucial problem, however, was not the decision to help her realize her values but how to achieve that end.

As we have seen, an autonomous decision is one in which a person utilizes rational operations to collect, organize, and evaluate data. Dr. Winters could not dictate the outcome of such a process without contravening Tina's autonomy, but her role in helping to facilitate such a rational process was urgent. Tina's decision to stop the medication was indeed an autonomous one. The medication would harm her child. She wanted to have a healthy child; so she needed to stop the medication. No major cognitive failures existed here that would argue against her mental competence.

Tina also reflected on her earlier pregnancy and knew what it was like to be pregnant. She recalled how her father, with the cooperation of the hospital, wanted to terminate her pregnancy without due regard for her own preferences. Thus she did not want once again to come under the control of those who would contravene her autonomy. Her decision to ask Dr. Winters to help her avoid such a pitfall was a competent one. However, to say that it was a competent decision is not to say that it was the best way to accomplish her objectives. As we have seen, decisions may be more or less autonomous. By helping Tina to explore further possible implications of her plan, Dr. Winters could have helped Tina increase her autonomous control over her situation.

For example, would Tina be able to get through the pregnancy without any mishaps to herself or to her child? What was Dr. Winters to do if Tina's major manic or depressive episodes presented a danger to herself, to her child, or to others? Could Dr. Winters, who could not claim to be all-knowing, make a blanket promise to honor Tina's request not to commit her to a hospital? Dr. Winters said she would "do her best to safeguard the welfare of the child," but she did not clearly define what measures she might take. By leaving these questions unexplored, Dr. Winters thus missed an important occasion to allow Tina to have input into managing future problems concerning herself and her child.

When Tina's competence lapsed, when she stopped taking lithium, Dr. Winters faced the intractable situation of speaking for Tina without the benefit of knowing what Tina might have said. To the extent that Dr. Winters failed to help Tina articulate her views before a crisis occurred, her approach was excessively paternalistic.

In accordance with the principle of candor, Dr. Winters had a responsibility to inform Tina of the limits of the therapist's nonintervention. Moreover, in accordance with the principle of nonmaleficence, she had a responsibility to prevent harm to her client. In addition, she had a legal responsibility to take due care for her client's welfare. By not making these moral and legal parameters plain to her client, Dr. Winters thus acted in bad faith.

In response to Tina's request to Dr. Winters to refrain from involuntary commitment, Dr. Winters might have stated more candidly, "I cannot guarantee that once you stop your medication, you will not need to be protected from harm. Your welfare as well as your child's may depend on whether you receive suitable care. If that care can be provided only by commitment to a mental facility, then you should be prepared for this possibility." On hearing this, Tina would have had the opportunity to give informed consent to what Dr. Winters subsequently might do on her behalf. Dr. Winters's failure to inform Tina of these possibilities thus contravened Tina's autonomous choice.

Dr. Winters's proposal to increase therapy sessions to two per week as an alternative to inpatient treatment was naive and raises questions about Dr. Winters's professional competence. The assumption that meaningful therapy could be conducted while the client was on a manic flight made little sense. Indeed, the futility of this may have been gleaned from Tina's own admission of her inability to exert control over her manic episodes.

As a competent therapist, Dr. Winters should have realized that, once the medication was stopped, therapy might need to yield to custodial care. The goal of therapy—to increase client autonomy—would be impossible for a nonautonomous client. Protecting the client from harming herself would, however, be feasible. By failing to distinguish between therapy and custodial care, Dr. Winters thus presented Tina with a false and misleading view of her available options once she discontinued the medication.

Had custodial care, rather than therapy, been stressed, some agreement about how such custody might be arranged could have been broached. For example, was Tina's roommate, Glenda, in a situation to look out for Tina in her pregnancy? Did Tina have any other support system (friends, relatives, etc.) that might have met her custodial needs without the necessity for her commitment to a mental hospital? Were any other facilities such as halfway houses available in the community that could supply the needed custodial care? If any of these existed, involuntary commitment would constitute excessive, unwarranted paternalism.

Unfortunately, Dr. Winters was now faced with having to decide for Tina because Tina was not competent to decide for herself. Still, such decisions as Dr. Winters might make on Tina's behalf could not be made irrespective of Tina's wishes as expressed while she was competent. Tina's situation resembles the case of a medical patient who, while competent, directs that no heroic life prolonging measures be employed should she lapse into an irreversible vegetative state. In such a situation, it would be incorrect to say that since the patient is now incompetent, we can do for her whatever we choose. Rather, a surrogate should make decisions based on the patient's values and wishes (Hastings Center, 1987).

In deference to Tina's competently expressed, prior wishes, Dr. Winters had a moral responsibility to safeguard the welfare of Tina's child, avoiding any unnecessary encroachments on Tina's liberty. If Dr. Winters could manage this by finding adequate custodial care outside of involuntary commitment to a psychiatric facility, this would be the preferred route. However, any route likely to jeopardize Tina's welfare would be self-defeating. Permitting Tina to place herself at serious risk of harm would be inconsistent with Tina's own expressed interest in her developing child's welfare, and it would be inconsistent with the primary counseling aim of promoting client welfare.

One might ask whether Dr. Winters owed her primary allegiance to Tina or to her child. The main purpose of counseling is to promote the welfare, interests, and needs of the client. Because a serious interest of Tina's was safeguarding her child's welfare, promotion of this interest fell within the purview of Dr. Winters's professional responsibility. But what if Tina's continued pregnancy threatened her own life? What if her physical condition deteriorated, as in her previous pregnancy, and the only way to save the life of the mother was to abort the fetus?

Such a decision would ultimately lie with Tina's legal guardian—presumably her father—but Dr. Winters could not remain neutral on the subject. In acting as an advocate for her client, Dr. Winters would need to press her client's autonomously expressed wishes. Tina had said that above all her child's welfare was to be protected, so promotion of that interest would be Dr. Winters's professional responsibility. If Tina's father tried to arrange an abortion, Dr. Winters would need to speak for Tina, vigilantly making her wishes known. To do otherwise would be a betrayal of her client's trust. As a rational, autonomous being, Dr. Winters could not herself wish to be so abandoned.

When a woman chooses to sacrifice her life to save her baby, we ordinarily do not override her wishes. For example, we do not wait until the woman becomes incompetent and then abort her fetus. When a person chooses such a sacrifice, we do not suppose that she has suffered a cognitive breakdown, that she has lost her powers of reason, or that she is not acting in accordance with her own considered values. It may be easier, however, to ascribe such failures to people who suffer from "mental illness" when they make identical, competent requests. Such a response, however, is unjust paternalism. It engenders a double standard and is unfair discrimination. Whatever standard is applied should be consistently applied to all members of society, mentally ill as well as healthy (Livermore et al., 1982). As a trustworthy and fair therapist, Dr. Winters had to be prepared to stand against such inconsistent treatment of her vulnerable client.

CASE 2: INVOLUNTARY COMMITMENT OF A CHILD

Dwayne was a 12-year-old boy who, along with his two brothers, had been subjected to parental neglect as well as sexual and physical abuse from toddlerhood until age 9. On some occasions, Dwayne was forced to remain at the end of his parents' bed while they took turns kicking him.

Dwayne and his two siblings, Frank, age 11 and Mark, age 14, had been, subsequent to the uncovering of the abuse, removed from their homes and placed in a long-term foster home. Although the children's stepfather had been incarcerated on several counts of sexual abuse, the children's biological mother, Nicole, whom the children alleged systematically abused them both sexually and physically, was never brought to trial on any abuse charges. Although the three youngsters had been placed in foster care, Nicole's parental rights had not yet been terminated.

With help from the child welfare agency, the children's foster parent, Debbie, arranged for the three to attend weekly individual and group therapy at a local outpatient sexual abuse treatment facility. When Debbie was unavailable to transport the children to and from their sessions due to work conflicts, the agency provided the transportation. The children were assigned to Vivian Westwood, Licensed Professional Counselor. Ms. Westwood specialized in the treatment of sexually abused children and their families.

Although it could not be proven, Westwood suspected that the children had been sexually abused by other people in addition to their parents. The three had been forced to fend for themselves during the time they lived with their biological mother, often searching through garbage cans for sustenance.

It became evident to Westwood early in therapy that Dwayne suffered from posttraumatic stress disorder. He attempted to avoid any discussions of or references to either his mother or his stepfather and had frequent intense outbursts of anger, usually directed at his siblings. Although he sometimes pushed or hit his siblings, no incidents of severe violence had been reported. An extremely intelligent child with an I.Q. of 140, he maintained an "A" average in school and had no noted difficulties getting along with teachers and other students. He had also bonded with Debbie. He frequently hugged her and smiled in her presence.

Although Dwayne was nonverbal in sessions, Westwood was able to engage him in nondirected play therapy in which he usually drew pictures or played "restaurant." She also worked with Dwayne on issues such as establishing boundaries and respecting privacy. As boundaries had been nonexistent in his family of origin, Dwayne was unfamiliar with locking bathroom doors or knocking before entering someone's room. Therapy proceeded very slowly but appeared to be moving forward.

One Monday morning about one year into therapy, Westwood received a call from Dwayne's foster mother, Debbie, stating that Dwayne had "made a bomb" over the weekend and that she had informed Child Welfare of the occurrence. Debbie stated that although he hadn't detonated the device (built from a household spray can) or made any threats to do so, she was fearful of the possible danger that Dwayne posed to the other two children and that she couldn't supervise him throughout the day as she returned home from work 3 hours after the children arrived home. Child Welfare gave her two choices: allow Dwayne to remain in therapy with Westwood if he could spend one hour after each school day in therapy with her and the rest of the afternoon under supervision at the agency, or put him in an inpatient facility. After consulting with her agency, Westwood informed both Debbie and Child Welfare that the first option was not possible as the agency in question was a busy outpatient facility with only a receptionist to monitor clients in the waiting area. Moreover, she explained that the family had already reached its maximum weekly allowable sessions and agency rules prohibited any additional counseling sessions. The agency was understaffed, and extending the sessions would only cut into times scheduled for other clients. Consequently, at the request of Child Welfare, notwithstanding his claim that he intended no harm, Dwayne was transported to a Medicaid-accepting inpatient hospital for evaluation. He was evaluated and involuntarily committed.

Ned Harris, M.D., was the psychiatrist assigned to the case. He promptly ordered Mellaril and Tofranil and assigned Dwayne to individual and group therapy. When Debbie visited Dwayne several days later, she became concerned. He appeared very lethargic and without vitality. He made little attempt to greet her when she arrived. Debbie subsequently questioned Harris about Dwayne's condition and was then informed about his medication. Debbie was upset that she had not been informed of the decision to medicate Dwayne as he had a hereditary condition that contraindicated certain medications. Mellaril appeared to be one such drug. Harris told Debbie that he did not need her permission to medicate as she was the foster parent. Debbie later found out that Child Welfare also did not know anything about the decision to medicate Dwayne.

Debbie contacted Westwood with her concerns. Westwood, who had obtained releases from Child Welfare to discuss the case with Harris and his associates, subsequently phoned Harris to inquire about Dwayne and to make certain that the medications were not contraindicated. Westwood had done some research after Debbie's call and it appeared that her worries might be justified. Harris assured Westwood that the treatment was appropriate.

Westwood requested privileges to visit Dwayne and they were granted for the following week. At that time Dwayne appeared lethargic and without expression. When Westwood conferred with Harris about Dwayne's progress, Harris remarked, "This is the Mercedes of institutions. I can accomplish in 30 days what takes anybody else 3 years. Dwayne won't talk in sessions. He needs to talk, get it all out. I am medicating him to this extent so that he loses all his defenses and talks." Harris became quite upset when Westwood again questioned the need to medicate so heavily.

Westwood, concerned about Dwayne's treatment, conferred with two of her agency supervisors and the director of the agency. She and they decided that a meeting of all involved was indicated. Harris agreed and a meeting was arranged. Present were Westwood, the agency director, the agency's two supervisors, Harris, the hospital's social worker, the child's guardian ad litem, and a Child Welfare worker. Despite the concern of those outside the hospital, Harris maintained that his treatment was "right on course."

Westwood continued to visit Dwayne on a weekly basis. He had become bloated and more lethargic. He still refused to speak in sessions about anything related to his abuse and his medication dosages were summarily increased. Westwood again called Child Welfare with concerns that Dwayne was not being treated in a proper fashion. However, nothing was done in this regard. Debbie and Westwood both requested that Harris allow an independent psychiatrist to evaluate the case and he refused.

Dwayne was not released after 30 days as Harris had previously indicated. Instead, Harris was able to extend his stay. Sixty days after his admission to the facility, Dwayne was released, still having never uttered a word about his abuse. Debbie immediately took Dwayne to another psychiatrist who weaned him from both medications. Dwayne then resumed therapy with Westwood where he continued for another year. During that time, the usual outbursts of anger at his siblings continued; however, he did not make or use bombs or weapons.

It is arguable that Debbie and Child Welfare overreacted to the danger suggested by Dwayne's act of bomb making. Although he exhibited low tolerance for frustration, Dwayne did not have a history of severe physical aggression, nor did he threaten to harm anyone. It is therefore not evident that he posed a "clear and imminent danger" to himself or others or that his behavior warranted involuntary commitment. On the other hand, as Debbie surmised, there was a clear need for adult supervision.

According to the principle of fairness, therapists should "provide services of equal quality and magnitude consistent with the maximum promotion of the welfare of each client" (see Chapter 4). Involuntarily committing Dwayne for 60 days (double the stay originally indicated) was an extreme abridgement of his liberty. Had Dwayne been an adult with a similar behavioral record, it is unlikely that he would have been subjected to this course of action for the same deed. Because of his status as a minor, Dwayne was vulnerable to the determinations of others. His own assurance that he intended no harm carried no weight. It is thus apparent that Dwayne was a victim of unfair discrimination on the basis of his age (National Association of Social Workers, [NASW], 1997, 4.02).

Presumably, Dwayne was already receiving competent, outpatient treatment from Ms. Westerfield. Confining him involuntarily for the purpose of treatment was therefore questionable. As doing so amounted to complete abnegation of Dwayne's liberty, the urgency for such extreme paternalism needed to be clear and incontrovertible. On the other hand, what Dwayne clearly required was supervision during the 3 hours after school in which Debbie was still at work.

Involuntarily committing Dwayne for treatment indicated confusion about the immediate problem, which was how to avoid leaving the children without adequate supervision.

Dr. Harris's presumption that his own treatment modality was superior to the one already in place and that he could "accomplish in 30 days what takes anybody else 3 years" indicated a mind-set that led him to dismiss blindly the possibility of viable alternative therapies and perspectives. As a result he refused to permit evaluation by an independent psychiatrist, and he refused to consider the possibility that the medication he prescribed was contraindicated in the present case. With this behavior, Dr. Harris failed to act as a beneficent therapist by practicing with reckless disregard for the limits and scope of his own professional knowledge (National Organization for Human Service Education [NOHSE], 1994, 5.1). As we have seen (Chapter 2), a virtuous therapist proceeds with an open mind and does not make and act on decisions without having carefully explored the morally relevant facts—that is, facts relevant to the welfare, interests, and needs of the client. Dr. Harris's inflated sense of power preempted such careful exploration.

Dr. Harris's treatment plan forcibly rendered a child with an I.Q. of 140 lethargic and without ability to express himself. Medication was administered with the aim of forcing Dwayne to "lose all his defenses and talk." Dwayne was thereby treated as an object, not in the least as an autonomous, self-determining individual. No attempt was made at obtaining informed consent from Dwayne for such intrusive therapy. Notwithstanding Dwayne's minor status, a candid therapist would have informed him of the proposed intervention in a manner commensurate with his psychological capacities, sought his assent, and considered his preferences (American Psychological Association [APA], 1992, 4.02c).

Further, a candid therapist would obtain informed consent from the client's legal guardian before administering treatment (APA, 1992, 4.02b). Such consent should be ongoing throughout treatment (American Counseling Association [ACA], 1996, A.3.a). As we have seen (Chapter 4), it should include all information with potential bearing on the welfare, interests, and needs of the client. Inasmuch as Child Welfare was Dwayne's legal guardian, Dr. Harris had a professional responsibility to secure this agency's ongoing, informed consent regarding treatment plans and their potential risks and side effects. As Child Welfare was unaware of the drug regimen and its effects, Dr. Harris was remiss in his responsibility to obtain informed consent from Dwayne's legal guardian.

Although Debbie was not Dwayne's legal guardian, she had been his primary caretaker and had a serious interest in his welfare. This interest would have justified Dr. Harris's seeking consent from Child Welfare to inform Debbie about the treatment plan. In not informing her before undertaking treatment (assuming Child Welfare's prior consent), Dr. Harris acted with disregard for Debbie's autonomy, treating her too as a mere means rather than as an end in herself. Debbie's feelings of having been treated in this way were further disregarded when she was told she had no right to any information because she was not Dwayne's legal guardian. Dr. Harris lacked empathy for the circumstances of one who cared. Also, he showed no moral sensitivity for the welfare, interests, and needs of Dwayne, who needed the support of other adults. Debbie had become a significant and stabilizing force in Dwayne's life. By encouraging her active support rather than alienating her, Dr. Harris might have better promoted his client's needs.

Child Welfare's ultimatum—to extend weekly sessions and use the counseling agency for after-school child supervision or else involuntarily commit Dwayne—might have been drawn too hastily and without careful exploration of alternative possibilities. Because the immediate problem was to find suitable supervision, any well-supervised activity might have provided an alternative. Dwayne had no apparent problems in structured, supervised settings such as the classroom. Well-organized and supervised extracurricular activities—for example, activities involving art, music, athletics, karate, or computers—might have provided suitable, constructive outlets. Furthermore, as Dwayne's legal guardian, Child Welfare had a responsibility to consider his preferences. If Dwayne preferred these alternatives to a hospital stay, there was a presumption in their favor and against involuntary commitment.

Perhaps Child Welfare considered Dwayne a "bad risk." It is easier to incarcerate a client than to take any chances for which legal responsibility can be assigned. On the other hand, moral resolutions to problems need not be easy and risk free. Unfortunately, Child Welfare played it safe at the expense of a vulnerable child for whose welfare it was legally and morally responsible.

Given Child Welfare's refusal to consider any alternatives to involuntary commitment, Ms. Westfield confronted the problem of promoting her client's welfare in the face of the apparent inflexibility of Dr. Harris. Although her attempts at getting Dr. Harris to reconsider his position proved unsuccessful, Ms. Westfield acted appropriately in coming to the defense of her vulnerable client. Visiting her client on a weekly basis and seeing his condition continue to deteriorate with no signs of healthy improvement, it was evident to her that something needed to be done. Unfortunately, her pleas (along with those of others outside the hospital) were ignored by Child Welfare as well as Dr. Harris.

In the end, it was Dwayne, a vulnerable 12-year-old, who paid the price. As a young child, Dwayne was sexually and physically abused by his mother and stepfather and perhaps by others as well. He was reduced to a thing, a mere object to be kicked about with no control over himself. If therapy had a clear mission, it was to help Dwayne gain control over his life, to help him to become more autonomous.

Incarcerating this vulnerable, victimized child "for his own good" and then force-feeding him medication that made him unresponsive, did nothing to build autonomy and everything to keep it down. At a time when positive role models like Debbie and Ms. Westfield entered his life, Dwayne was once again reduced to "thinghood." Cooperative, morally sensitive, mental health workers would have realized the futility of involuntarily committing and medicating into submission a client like Dwayne.

Case 3: A Question of Rational Suicide

Carter James, a 27-year-old former NFL quarterback, had been in an automobile accident 18 months earlier. He had suffered irreversible neurological damage to his spine resulting in complete loss of feeling and movement below his waist with neurological functions remaining intact above his waist. In addition, he suffered third-degree burns over two-thirds of his body. One of his ears needed to be amputated, and his face was severely deformed. Although Carter received skin grafts, they were of little cosmetic value.

Prior to his accident, Carter was at the height of his career and was considered one of the nation's top players. As a handsome, single, young celebrity, he was also pursued by women and had an active sex life. All this, however, changed after the accident. Many of his former "friends" and associates distanced themselves from him. Except for Robert, a friend and former teammate who frequently visited him, he was very much alone.

Despite considerable savings and the ability to get about by use of a wheelchair, Carter chose to live as a recluse in a small, shabby, one-bedroom rented apartment. He had his food delivered by a local grocer and rarely made appearances in public places. His disfigurement made it difficult for him to go out without eliciting ridicule, repulsion, or pity.

Concerned about Carter's psychological well-being, Robert convinced Carter to seek counseling with psychologist Dr. Hershel Dariens. After two sessions, Carter informed Dr. Dariens that he had decided to commit suicide by shooting himself in the head with a gun he owned. Carter stated that his life was "worthless," that he had "absolutely nothing to live for," and that "no life at all is better than the pain of this life." He explained, "I had it all and now I have nothing. I am trapped in this monstrous, broken-down body and the only means of escape is to kill myself. It is my only option."

Dr. Dariens empathized with Carter's plight. He sensed Carter's experiences of loss, emptiness, loneliness, rejection, hopelessness, and desperation, and he understood why Carter was moved to consider suicide. On the other hand, he was not convinced that suicide was his "only option." After all, Carter was not terminally ill, he had money, and might find new meanings in his life despite his physical condition. Yet Dr. Dariens hesitated. Would he be imposing his own values by interfering with Carter's plans? If Carter remained determined to take his own life in these unusual circumstances, would it be justified to try to stop him?

Dr. Dariens asked Carter to sign a contract agreeing not to try to kill himself before their next session so they could explore relevant issues at that time. It was Friday and the next session was scheduled for the coming Monday. Carter refused to sign the contract but said that he would reconsider his decision to commit suicide. He also said that he probably would not kill himself over the weekend but refused to make any promise. Dr. Dariens asked Carter to call him if he was intent on killing himself or if he just wanted to talk. Carter thanked Dr. Dariens for his concern for him and the session came to a close.

Carter did not phone Dr. Dariens that weekend nor did he keep his Monday appointment. Dr. Dariens read in the Sunday newspaper that Carter James had shot himself to death on Saturday evening.

The primary purpose of therapy is to alleviate pain and suffering; in the unfortunate case of Carter James, Dr. Dariens was confronted with the question of whether allowing his client to die was ultimately the best therapy. In cases where the value of living itself is questionable, legal standards and codes of ethics do not provide clear guidance. Relevant codes of ethics typically permit disclosure of confidential information without clients' consent in order to prevent harm to the client or others, but they do not *require* such disclosure. For example, according to the American Psychological Association's *Ethical Standards* (1992), "psychologists disclose confidential information without the consent of the individual only as mandated by law, or where permitted by law for a valid purpose, such as . . . to protect the patient or client or others from harm" (5.05.a). According to the National Association of Social Workers' *Code of Ethics* (1997), "The general expectation that social workers will keep information confidential does not apply when disclosure is necessary to prevent serious, foreseeable, and imminent harm to a client or other identifiable person" (1.07.c). The questions of seriousness of harm, its predictability, and its imminence cannot be codified and must yield to the judgment of the individual therapist. In the case of Carter James, the codes cannot tell us whether preventing suicide should be considered more important than allowing the client to end the unmitigated pain of his life.

While some case law appears to support counselors' responsibility to protect clients from harming themselves if this harm is foreseeable (Anderson, 1996), state statutes do not always make this mandatory. For example, according to Florida Statute 491.0147, confidentiality between a therapist and a client *may* be waived "when there is a clear and immediate probability of physical harm to the patient or client, to other individuals, or to society and the person licensed or certified under this chapter communicates the information only to the potential victim, appropriate family member, or law enforcement or other appropriate authorities."

Some landmark court decisions may also, by extension, support therapists' nonintervention in certain cases similar to the case of Carter James. In *McKay v. Bergstedt* (1990), the Supreme Court of Nevada found in favor of a 31-year-old mentally competent, nonterminal quadriplegic, Kenneth Bergstedt, who sought to affirm his right to die. Bergstedt who was able to read, watch television, orally operate a computer, and occasionally use a wheelchair for ambulation, sought the removal of a respirator that he had lived with for 23 years. Although the majority opinion regarded the removal of the respirator as merely the removal of "an artificial support system" in order to allow a "natural death," Justice Springer, in a dissenting opinion, claimed that it was a case of assisted suicide according to the majority's definition of assisting one in the voluntary and intentional taking of one's own life.

In *Bouvia v. Superior Court* (1986), the California Court of Appeals, Second District, found for Elizabeth Bouvia, a bedridden, nonterminal, competent quadriplegic suffering from cerebral palsy and arthritis, who petitioned the court for the removal of a feeding tube involuntarily administered to preempt her suicide by starvation. The appellate court maintained that patients should be able to enlist the assistance of physicians in ending their lives in comfort and dignity. In a concurring opinion, Associate Justice Compton asserted that the "right to die is an integral part of our right to control our own destinies so long as the rights of others are not affected. That right should, in my opinion, include the ability to enlist the assistance from others, including the medical profession, in making death as painless and quick as possible."

In a further case *In re Claire C. Conroy* (1985) concerning the removal of a nasogastric feeding tube from a nonterminal, incompetent patient, the New Jersey Supreme Court, responding to the appellate decision, maintained that "in cases that do not involve the protection of the actual or potential life of someone other than the decision-maker, the state's indirect and abstract interest in preserving the life of the competent patient generally gives way to the patient's much stronger personal interest in directing the course of his own life" (1223). Although the Court distinguished between the refusal of life-sustaining medical treatment and the commission of suicide, this principle as announced places the decision to end one's life in the hands of the *competent* decision maker. As Carter James was competent to make such a decision, his "personal interest in directing the course of his own life" could be said to have outweighed a state interest in preserving his life.

There may therefore be legal precedent for nonintervention in some cases when competent clients elect to commit suicide because of physical maladies or diseases that cause them unmitigated mental or physical anguish. On the other hand, the courts have frequently distinguished between the withdrawal or refusal of artificial means to preserve life and such other modes of ending life such as guns, poisons, and knives. Some state appellate courts have also relied on this distinction to reverse decisions of trial courts who have rejected the distinction (*Krischer v. McIver,* 1997). Nevertheless, whether this distinction clearly deprives all suicides of legal status is not evident. A competent patient suffering from end-stage bowel cancer who commits suicide by poisoning may be no less defensible than a competent, nonterminal patient such as Kenneth Bergstedt who after 23 years of using a respirator decides to have it disconnected.

In addition, the state of Oregon, by public referendum, has legalized the Oregon Death with Dignity Act (1994), a qualified version of physician-assisted suicide on demand (Snyder & Caplan, 1995). Although the law was subsequently ruled unconstitutional by a federal court, the public's willingness to endorse it was reaffirmed in a second public referendum in November 1997, when Oregonians voted not to repeal the law. This public action indicates a strong social belief that, in at least some cases, interference with a suicide may be unwarranted. Note that the Oregon law includes a provision granting authority in some instances to therapists to determine whether patients were competent to commit suicide. Section 3.03 states that

> if in the opinion of the attending physician or the consulting physician a patient may be suffering from a psychiatric or psychological disorder, or depression causing impaired judgment, either physician shall refer the patient for counseling. No medication to end a patient's life in a humane and dignified manner shall be prescribed until the person performing the counseling detemines that the patient is not suffering from a psychiatric or psychological disorder, or depression causing impaired judgment. (cited in Beauchamp & Veatch, 1996, p. 202)

Therapists can thus expect to play a legislatively defined role in determining whether nonintervention or assistance in clients' commission of suicide is warranted.

Dr. Jack Kevorkian's ability to escape legal sanctions in Michigan for his role in assisting individuals (some of whom were nonterminal) to commit suicide is similarly supportive of a general climate of awareness. Thus, in *People of the State of Michigan v. Jack Kevorkian* (1992), Ciruit Court Judge David F. Breck denied significance to the commonplace distinction between assisted suicide and withdrawal of life support, stating that

> if a person can refuse life-sustaining treatment, then that person should have the right to insist on treatment which will cause death, providing the physician is willing to assist and the patient is lucid and meets rational criteria. While the interests of the State are different when suicide is involved, it appears to this Court that nevertheless the prevailing interest should be the constitutionally protected interests of the individual. The distinction between assisted suicide and the withdrawal of life support is a distinction without merit. But for the doctor's act of disconnecting the life support system, or the act of inserting the I.V. needle, death would not have occurred. There is no morally important difference. (cited in Beauchamp & Veatch, 1996, p. 196)

A similar conclusion was reached by the United States Court of Appeals for the Ninth Circuit in *Compassion in Dying v. Washington* (1996) regarding the right of terminally ill, competent adults to physician-assisted suicide. The court argued that "the line between commission and omission . . . is a distinction without a difference now that patients are permitted not only to decline all medical treatment, but to instruct their doctors to terminate whatever treatment, artificial or otherwise, they are receiving. In disconnecting a respirator, or authorizing its disconnection, a doctor is unquestionably committing an act; he is taking an active role in bringing about the patient's death" (Section V).

The recent passage in Michigan of the Dignified Death Act giving physicians civil and criminal immunity in prescribing dosages of drugs necessary for terminal pain relief has also provided a lawful form of "physician-assisted dying" (American Health Consultants, 1997).

There is currently a rising degree of ambivalence surrounding legal justification for permitting or assisting the suicide of competent individuals whose qualities of life are seriously impaired by their physical conditions. Within this legal uncertainty, therapists will need to exercise moral discretion.

Exercise of such discretion may not be without risk, including legal risks. Therapists should be aware that permitting or assisting suicide may still run counter to the laws of the specific states in which they practice. Nevertheless, moral determinations do not necessarily follow from legal ones. In confronting the moral question, a virtuous therapist still needs to be prepared to reach a moral verdict. Can moral theory help?

From a utilitarian perspective, paternalistic intervention in the unfortunate case of Carter James might have been misguided. Carter's own judgment was that "no life at all is better than the pain of this life." As Carter was not apparently in any serious physical pain, the pain of which he spoke must have been psychological. Nevertheless, as he is the subject of the mental torment, his assessment of its severity cannot be discounted. Requiring Carter to suffer against his will might have preserved his life at the expense of preventing his escape from unbearable pain. A utilitarian approach might have supported Dr. Dariens in not interfering with the client's desire to commit suicide.

On the other hand, although Kantian ethics might appear to condone Carter's suicide as an assertion of client autonomy, this belief system in fact would support the opposite stance. According to Kant, "to use the power of a free will for its own destruction is self-contradictory. If freedom is the condition of life, it cannot be employed to abolish life and so to destroy and abolish itself" (Kant, 1990, pp. 47–48). That is, in taking one's own life, one uses one's freedom or autonomy to destroy the condition of all future freedom. It follows that a therapist who, out of respect for a client's freedom or autonomy, permits a client to take his life, is defeating the purpose of such freedom. Such a therapist respects a client's autonomy only to permit the irreversible and total destruction of that client's autonomy. In pursuing a path of nonintervention out of respect for Carter's freedom or autonomy, Dr. Dariens would, according to this line of thinking, have permitted the destruction of the very autonomy he sought to preserve.

The above argument, however, takes client autonomy as an *absolute* value and assumes that this value must be preserved regardless of the circumstances. When the quality of a client's life has become so severely reduced by the pain of living, such an assumption may be questionable. One might debate whether Carter's life had reached a point that the pain of living justified his ending his life, but the *possibility* of ever reaching such a point cannot so easily be dismissed.

A principle of paternalism related to Kant's has been proposed by Gerald Dworkin. According to Dworkin, paternalistic limitations on individuals' freedom are justified if fully rational individuals would accept them as forms of protection (Dworkin, 1971). Dworkin suggests three related types of decisions on which fully rational individuals would accept at least some paternalistic restrictions. These are (1) decisions that are far-reaching, potentially dangerous, and irreversible; (2) decisions made under extreme psychological pressures when the person is not thinking clearly and calmly; (3) decisions that involve dangers not adequately understood or appreciated by the persons involved. According to Dworkin, in instances of the third class, a person may not know all the pertinent facts; know the facts but not have the requisite willpower to act on them; know the facts but not use them correctly in his or her deliberations.

As Dworkin suggests, decisions to commit suicide often fit into all three of these categories and are therefore decisions for which fully rational individuals would accept some forms of restriction. For example, he suggest the possibility of institutionalizing a cooling off or waiting period before the suicide is permitted.

Was Carter's decision one a fully rational person could embrace?

There is reason to think that Carter's decision to commit suicide was not one a fully rational person could embrace. He was not thinking clearly because he did not appreciate or understand all of the pertinent facts. In concluding that his life was worthless and that he had absolutely nothing to live for, Carter was not considering alternative possibilities and values (Brandt, 1990). For example, he was, in some respects better off than quadriplegics like Kenneth Bergstedt and Elizabeth Bouvia who had little or no control over their upper bodies. Carter was quite mobile with the use of a wheelchair and he apparently had considerable financial means. He also had a friend who cared about him. His appearance made interpersonal transactions uncomfortable for him, but this reaction was largely a function of his own irrational belief that his value as a person depended on the approval of others—indeed, on people he did not even know. Carter had placed a halo about his former life without considering any of its drawbacks (Brandt, 1990). For example, the fact that his former friends and associates no longer wished to maintain contact with him indicated that he had not succeeded in cultivating many meaningful relationships with others in his capacity as a celebrity. Paradoxically, he may have been in a better position to do so after his accident than before it.

The point is not that Carter would have been irrational in ultimately choosing suicide. It is rather that he did not come to his decision in a fully rational manner. If, after careful consideration of his own values, Carter had concluded that death was, on balance, better than continuing to live, this would have been different from discounting all value in continuing to live, which he did.

Because Dr. Dariens had only two counseling sessions with Carter before he announced his suicide plan, the therapist did not have sufficient time to help Carter to work through any of these issues. Thus, Carter's decision was not one a fully rational person could embrace. It was made prematurely before Carter weighed all the relevant issues.

This conclusion does not mean that Carter James was, in some abstract sense, mentally incompetent and lacked the capacity for autonomous decision making. Autonomy is a matter of degrees and one may be competent to make some decisions but not sufficiently competent to make others. Moreover, having the mental capacity to make an autonomous decision does not guarantee that one will exercise that capacity.

To be sure, Carter was not out of contact with reality. He knew who and where he was, his physical handicap was no mere delusion, he appreciated the consequences of shooting himself in the head with a gun, and his decision to kill himself was not clearly out of character and in conflict with his own value system. Carter therefore possessed to some degree the capacity for autonomous decision making. What is less clear is whether, at the time he made his suicide decision, he was competent or competent *enough* to make such a life or death decision. Even if at the time he had the capacity to make this highly autonomous decision, it is still questionable whether he sufficiently exercised this capacity when he chose his own death.

Assessed in terms of Mill's four mental operations, the degree of autonomy Carter exercised in choosing to kill himself appears to have been diminished by his failure to collect adequate information to resolve his problems (failure of operation 1). He may also have lacked clarity in defining these problems. For example, his primary problem was *coping* with his physical condition and its implications for his life. Yet Carter appears to have focused on whether to live with the pain of that condition, as though he had no control whatsoever over this pain.

In addressing whether suicide could ever be rational, Margaret Battin (1995) has proposed five standards. According to Battin, rational suicide decisions, like other rational decisions, must satisfy all or most of the following conditions:

1. *The ability to reason.* The person contemplating suicide does not make any logical errors in moving from premises to conclusions and can see the consequences of the actions or positions he intends to take.
2. *A realistic worldview.* The person does not make reality claims that cannot be justified within a surrounding culture. For example, while the Jehovah's Witness's rejection of blood transfusions can be justified within a certain religious culture, there is no cultural validation for the schizophrenic who thinks he can fly.
3. *Adequacy of information.* The premises from which one reasons must be complete and accurate; for example, one *correctly* believes that one has a terminal illness for which there is no cure.
4. *Avoidance of harm.* The prospective suicide is undertaken to avoid irremediable, relentless mental or physical pain and suffering.
5. *Accordance with fundamental interests.* The suicide is not inconsistent with any serious personal goals founded on the individual's fundamental values; for example, it does not interfere with a political cause or obtaining a better job.

If these standards are applied to the case of Carter James, it is clear that Carter's decision was deficient on at least one count. Carter did not adequately appreciate or understand all the pertinent facts (failure of standard 3 above). On the other hand, it is at least possible that this decision did satisfy all other standards. So is it enough for a suicide to satisfy *most* of these standards in order to be counted as rational?

Even if Carter's decision was consonant with most of the standards, his failures were arguably extensive enough to warrant paternalistic intervention to prevent him from killing himself. Although Carter's decision was rational to a degree, this does not mean that it was rational enough to justify suicide; nor does it mean that it was rational enough to warrant Dr. Dariens's permitting him to commit suicide.

If Carter had unreasonably decided to sell a piece of real estate, there might have been no sufficient reason for interfering. However, as Kantian ethics would stress, Carter's decision was to destroy the very condition of all other autonomous choice, namely his life. In such cases of far-reaching and irreversible decisions, there can be compelling reasons to permit suicide only if all five standards are satisfied.

Expressed in Dworkin's terms, a fully rational therapist would not permit his client to commit suicide if any of Battin's five standards were not satisfied, even if the client was rational and autonomous enough to be considered mentally competent. A client's decision is sufficiently rational to warrant noninterference only if all five standards have been met. This does not mean, however, that satisfaction of all five standards constitutes a sufficient basis for nonintervention.

For example, some arguments for suicide prevention have focused on the prevention of harm to others as when the suicidal client has dependent children (Greenberg, 1982).

To what extent must each of these five standards be satisfied to warrant non-interference with a client's intended suicide? For example, what if a client has some minor error in his thinking? Insofar as any faulty belief or inference stands as a basis for the client's decision to commit suicide, it cannot be considered minor. No error that contributes to a person's death is insignificant.

In applying standards of rationality such as Battin's, therapists need to be cautious not to confuse fundamental value disagreements with fallacious thinking or false premises. For example, Carter may have valued football above all other life activities. Although Dr. Dariens may not have shared his value assessment, this did not make the client wrong. On the other hand, Carter's belief that he had had everything and now had nothing could have been challenged according to Carter's own value system. If queried, Carter might well have conceded that his friendship with Robert was at least worth something.

As a competent therapist, Dr. Dariens should have noticed Carter's inadequate decisional basis. Because Carter was subject to a dangerous and irreversible mistake in judgment due to his lack of clear thinking, Dr. Dariens had a moral responsibility to take reasonable measures to safeguard Carter's welfare. But was there sufficient evidence that he would attempt suicide?

Wubbolding (1996) has suggested six general questions a therapist might ask a client to help facilitate discussion and determine the lethality of a suicide threat:

1. Are you thinking about killing yourself?
2. Have you attempted suicide in the past?
3. Do you have a plan?
4. Do you have the means available to you?
5. Will you make a unilateral no-suicide agreement to stay alive—that is, not to kill yourself accidentally or on purpose—for a specified amount of time?
6. Is there anyone close to you who could prevent you from killing yourself and to whom you could speak when you feel the need to commit suicide?

In Carter's case, the lethality index imbedded in the first five questions provided Dr. Dariens with good reason to take the threat of suicide seriously. It was thus evident that in intervening to prevent Carter's suicide, Dr. Dariens would have acted on adequate predictive evidence. Moreover, given Carter's low self-esteem and general state of psychological vulnerability, it was possible that his suicide threat addressed to Dr. Dariens was an implicit plea for help as in at least some suicide threats (Battin, 1995).

In selecting an intervention strategy, Dr. Dariens should have tried to promote Carter's autonomy as far as was possible. Otherwise, he would have unduly subverted the primary counseling mission, which includes safeguarding client autonomy. Accordingly, the least intrusive form of intervention would have been best.

As suggested by the sixth question above, one possibility might have been to enlist the help of Robert in conducting a suicide watch over the weekend until

Carter's Monday counseling session when Dr. Dariens could reassess the situation. A further, less desirable alternative would have been to detain Carter temporarily in an inpatient facility for observation. This would have been demeaning to Carter. It would have suggested that he was mentally ill and unable to think for himself. It would have divested him of his autonomy. This alternative should have been elected only in the absence of viable outpatient modes of surveillance. Unfortunately, in the present case, it might have been the only alternative available.

If Dr. Dariens had intervened and prevented Carter's suicide, there would have been further opportunity for working through unfinished business with him. In the end, however, after sufficiently working through these issues, if Carter were still committed to ending his own life, Dr. Dariens could not have presumed to know what was best for his client. In such a case, a nonmaleficent therapist would not force a client to live a life of pain and suffering, a life rationally rejected as not worth living according to the client's own values. This sweeping imposition of values dictating how one must live and die would have devoured Carter's personal autonomy rather than preserved it. Such presumption by Dariens would have been unkind and would have lacked empathy for the client's plight. No rational person would choose to be so treated. No therapist with intrinsic regard for client welfare could concede to these terms.

Ethical Standards of Paternalism

The following principles can be gleaned from the three case analyses in this chapter. The first set (the CAs) provides important safeguards against unwarranted, paternalistic abridgements of client autonomy.

Respect for Client Autonomy:

CA 1   In attempting to promote clients' best interests, therapists avoid dictating solutions to life problems and seek instead to encourage and facilitate clients' own rational, autonomous process of exploration and decision making.

CA 2   Therapists do not mislead clients about any legal, professional, or moral limits to therapists' willingness to cooperate with clients' requests. As part of informed consent, therapists inform clients about the nature and circumstances of any paternalistic interventions they might engage in against their clients' will.

CA 3   Therapists avoid paternalistic restriction of clients' freedom and autonomy. In circumstances in which abridgement of clients' freedom or autonomy is unavoidable, therapists choose the least intrusive intervention consistent with client welfare.

CA 4   To the extent feasible, in deciding or acting on behalf of an incompetent client, therapists decide or act in a manner consistent with what they reasonably believe would accord with the preferences and values of the client.

CA 5 Therapists take reasonable steps to advocate clients' autonomously expressed preferences, especially when these clients are not themselves in a position to be their own advocate.

The principles above are especially supported by the "respect for persons" formulation of the Kantian categorical imperative. They guard against treating clients as mere means and promote their treatment as ends in themselves. These principles can also be understood as enjoining modes of conduct whereby therapists demonstrate unconditional positive regard for their clients (see Chapter 3). They set parameters necessary for a noncondemnatory, caring acceptance of clients for who they are rather than what the therapist expects them to be. They help the therapist guard against controlling and manipulating clients and acknowledge the therapeutic value of allowing clients to decide for themselves.

CA 3 proscribes extreme forms of paternalism when less restrictive forms would be effective alternatives. For example, when home care is available, confining a client in a psychiatric hospital involuntarily may be unwarranted.

CA 4 asserts a version of what has sometimes been called the *principle of substituted judgment* (Veatch, 1997, p. 304). This principle acknowledges that even clients deemed incompetent for purposes of making specific decisions may still have preferences or values related to those decisions that should be taken into account. For example, a previously competent client may have been quite clear about her wishes prior to becoming incompetent.

CA 5 recognizes the responsibility of therapists to serve as advocates for vulnerable clients unable to speak effectively for themselves. For example, a presently incompetent client may need the therapist to oppose authorities whose intended actions would undermine the client's previously expressed, competent wishes.

Paternalistic Interventions with Incompetent Clients:

PIC 1 Therapists do not apply standards for restricting the liberty of clients diagnosed as having a mental illness if they would not apply these standards to anyone else in similar circumstances. Therapists expose, denounce, and work toward removal of double standards as they occur in the course of their professional practices.

PIC 2 Therapists are aware of and sensitive to the reality that the minor status of children may make them especially vulnerable to unnecessary, involuntary restriction of their liberty. Therapists seek to protect their minor clients from any unfair, discriminatory actions taken against them.

PIC 3 In determining whether, how, and to what extent paternalistic restriction of a client's freedom is indicated, therapists keep in mind the limits and scope of their own professional knowledge. They proceed with open minds, guided by consideration of the welfare, interests, and needs of the client.

PIC 4 Therapists do not confuse the distinct purposes of custodial care and therapy in addressing the welfare, interests, and needs of clients.

PIC 5 Therapists safeguard and strive to promote the autonomy of clients involuntarily committed to psychiatric facilities. In providing therapy, therapists seek their clients' informed consent to intended interventions to the extent of and in a manner commensurate with the client's ability to understand.

PIC 6 In providing therapy to minor or incompetent clients under state guardianship, therapists take appropriate steps to encourage and to avoid alienating support from foster parents or other caregivers concerned about the clients' welfare.

PIC 7 Therapists countenance involuntary commitment of a client only when no other less restrictive, suitable alternative can be found. Therapists take a firm stand against and do not themselves pursue involuntary commitment of a client for self-interested reasons unrelated to the client's welfare such as avoidance of legal responsibility or personal convenience.

The principles above provide safeguards against unfair or unwarranted abridgements of clients' freedom, especially minor clients and those diagnosed with mental illnesses who are involuntarily confined to psychiatric hospitals.

PIC 1 militates against unfair discrimination against clients diagnosed with mental illnesses. This requires that all similar cases be treated alike. As Livermore et al. (1982) have illustrated, if we are prepared to incarcerate a person with paranoia because he has, statistically, a 40% probability of committing a homicide, then we must be prepared to lock up 60 people out of 100 who will not commit a homicide, whether or not these people have a mental illness. If we are not prepared to do this, by incarcerating the person with paranoia, we have discriminated unfairly against him. In this regard, it is useful to recall (Chapter 2) the importance of avoiding psychiatric labels. Thus the client with paranoia is not simply "a paranoid." Such labels block recognition of clients as distinct human beings and thereby promote overgeneralized, stereotypical attitudes toward them.

PIC 2 similarly reinforces pursuit of nondiscriminatory treatment of minor clients. As provided by PIC 5, such treatment includes recognition of therapists' responsibility to seek the informed consent of minor clients committed to psychiatric facilities to the extent of the clients' capacity to understand. As children are wards of adults, their degree of vulnerability can be considerable, especially in the context of psychiatric confinement. Therapists therefore have considerable responsibility to safeguard this more tender population from unfair or harmful practices. At the same time, the responsibility to protect must include respect for the children's autonomy.

PIC 4 highlights the importance of therapists' candid, honest assessment of the welfare, interests, and needs of clients in judging the suitability of a particular intervention. If a client will not benefit therapeutically from involuntary commitment, it is disingenuous to speak of treatment. If the point is custody, then, as CA 3 provides, the least intrusive intervention consistent with client welfare should be selected. In making such judgments, therapists should be guided by clients' welfare, interests, and needs (PIC 3), not by self-serving reasons (PIC 7).

Suicide Intervention:

SI 1 Therapists diligently seek to promote and preserve clients' freedom to decide for themselves. However, they are aware that some paternalistic restrictions on clients' freedom to decide may sometimes be warranted when these decisions are (1) far-reaching, potentially dangerous, and irreversible; (2) made under extreme psychological duress; or (3) involve dangers not adequately understood or appreciated by the client.

SI 2 Therapists intervene appropriately to prevent the suicide of incompetent clients. Therapists do not infer that a client's competence constitutes sufficient grounds for nonintervention. In cases of far-reaching and irreversible decisions such as suicide, therapists recognize that a competent client may either not be competent enough to make a decision of this magnitude or may fail in efficiently exercising his or her competence.

SI 3 Therapists are prepared to exercise moral discretion in determining whether suicide intervention is warranted. With competent clients whose qualities of life are seriously compromised by their physical conditions, therapists do not assume that ethical verdicts can be reached by appeal to legal rules or precedents alone. Therapists are prepared to exercise moral courage in standing behind what they deem to be a moral determination.

SI 4 Therapists recognize that nonintervention in a client's suicide is extraordinary and requires compelling reasons. Such compelling reasons do not exist unless the client contemplating the suicide (1) exercises the ability to reason without committing logical errors, (2) holds a realistic worldview, (3) applies adequate information, (4) seeks to avoid relentless and irremediable harm, and (5) decides in accordance with his or her own fundamental interests. Therapists do not assume that the existence of these five conditions is always sufficient to justify nonintervention. In making a determination, therapists avoid imposing their own religious or moral view of suicide.

SI 5 In determining the appropriateness of suicide intervention, therapists consider the severity of the pain and suffering of the suicidal client as subjectively experienced, evaluated, and conveyed by the client. In understanding the quality of the client's pain and suffering, therapists rely on their ability to empathize. They avoid imposing their own interpretations and evaluations.

SI 6 Therapists diligently seek to promote and preserve clients' autonomy. However, they also recognize limits to this important objective. When the client's quality of life is severely compromised by pain and suffering, therapists need not assume that it is their overriding responsibility to promote and preserve clients' autonomy by preserving clients' lives.

These principles aim at respect for client autonomy within the scope of nonmaleficence. Balancing both these values, they establish limits to respect for client autonomy when the client contemplates suicide. As SI 1 recognizes, therapists have a primary moral and professional responsibility to foster clients' autonomy. This responsibility, however, is not unconditional. Under circumstances such as the three noted in SI 1, therapists may be justified in paternalistically restricting client freedom. In line with SI 2, under the said conditions, therapists have a further moral responsibility to consider whether clients' decisions are fully autonomous—completely competent and rational, and consistent with the client's own personal goals and fundamental values.

As SI 4 states, warranted nonintervention of a suicide should be regarded as extraordinary. Ordinarily, therapists have a moral, professional, and legal responsibility to intervene to prevent clients' suicide. As SI 2 provides, this responsibility may also extend to competent clients if competence in the minimal sense of understanding the consequences of one's action may fall short of the understanding and rationality sufficient to justify such a far-reaching and irreversible decision.

However, SI 4 allows that, in some cases in which the client suffers from unmitigated distress due to physical disease or malady, the ordinary responsibility to intervene may justly yield to an empathetic respect for the client's decision to die. SI 4 does not require nonintervention when its five conditions are met. Rather, it asserts that when these conditions are satisfied and the client has autonomously decided to end his life, nonintervention would, without compelling reasons to the contrary, be justified. Such compelling reasons might include the effects of the client's death on dependent third parties such as surviving children. However, according to SI 4, such compelling reasons would not include the therapist's view that suicide is sinful or otherwise inherently evil. As SI 6 allows, the attempt by therapists at coercively promoting and preserving clients' autonomy by forcibly rescuing them can be counterproductive.

SI 5 makes clear that the client's autonomous determination that death is preferable to the pain of living must rest with his or her own subjective assessment of pain, not the assessment of the therapist. The therapist can empathize with what the client may be going through, but the painful quality of the suffering is what the client experiences it to be; and it is the client who, in the end, will have to live with this pain.

Finally, SI 3 recognizes the responsibility of therapists to take a moral stand. Such a stand should not be confused with a legal one. In some cases of suicide intervention, there may be ambiguity surrounding what is legal. In this aura of uncertainty, a therapist who takes a morally defensible position may well prevail should she end up in court. The risk that one might not prevail may be an unavoidable cost of exercising moral courage and respect for client autonomy in such unfortunate cases.

Summary

This chapter has undertaken careful inspection of the nature, scope, and limits of client autonomy. Autonomous decision making was shown to be a function of mutually supportive mental activities involving data collection, perception, practical reasoning, exertion of willpower, and decision making according to one's own values. The extent to which a decision is autonomous depends on the degree to which these activities are performed. The concept of mental competence may be defined in terms of the person's capacity to make autonomous decisions; and degrees of competence may be discerned according to one's capacities for engaging in the mental activities described above. A minimal sense of competence may also be distinguished in terms of the person's capacity to foresee the consequences of his or her action.

When clients lack minimal competence for decision making, intervention in their desired courses of action to prevent them from doing serious bodily harm to themselves does not represent an ethical breach of respect for client autonomy. Although therapy requires respect for client autonomy, not all self-regarding client decisions warrant therapists' noninterference. Some client decisions that are far-reaching, potentially dangerous, and irreversible may be insufficiently reasoned, and therapists may have a responsibility to intervene in these cases. Out of respect for client autonomy, the extent of the intervention should be the least intrusive one possible, consistent with client welfare. Involuntary commitment may be indicated but only when less restrictive measures are not realistic options. In making decisions about restricting client liberty, therapists have a responsibility to avoid unnecessary abridgements of client autonomy and self-serving decisions. They should keep open minds and know the limits of their own professional competence or expertise.

In this chapter, three cases were presented that raised conflicts between client autonomy and therapists' concern for client welfare. The first case study addressed the problem of whether and how to respect the autonomy of formerly competent clients who subsequently become incompetent. It also addressed the problem of whether and how to respect autonomous client decisions when doing so would promote third-party welfare (in this case, the welfare of a pregnant client's developing child) at the expense of the client's own life.

The second case study addressed the issue of respect for the autonomy and welfare of minor clients and the need for due care regarding this especially vulnerable population. It also highlighted the importance for therapists of distinguishing between treatment and custodial care.

The third case study addressed the extent of therapists' responsibility in interfering with client suicide. It presented rational criteria for assessing the scope and limits of therapists' interference with client autonomy, especially in cases of suicidal clients whose quality of life is seriously impaired by their physical conditions.

From these three case studies, ethical standards of paternalism were formulated addressing (1) respect for client autonomy; (2) paternalistic liberty restrictions (for instance, involuntary commitment) of incompetent and minor clients; and (3) suicide intervention. These standards complement and support principles and habits of virtuous counseling practice, including principles of trustworthiness, such as candor, and autonomy-facilitating virtues, such as unconditional positive regard. In general, the ethical standards of paternalism collectively support a counseling practice based on promoting and protecting client autonomy within the boundaries of respectful regard for the welfare, interests, and needs of clients.

REVIEW QUESTIONS

1. Describe and illustrate the conditions under which a decision could correctly be called autonomous.

2. Can one decision be more or less autonomous than another? Explain and provide an illustration.

3. What is meant by saying that a person is mentally incompetent?

4. Why can mental competence be said to be relative? Explain the difference between the minimal and comparative senses of mental competence, and give an illustration of each. What is meant by intermittent competence? Provide an illustration.

5. Does being mentally competent automatically make one autonomous? Explain.

6. What is meant by paternalism? Under what general conditions might paternalism be justified? Provide illustrations. Is paternalism in provision of counseling services usually a good idea? Explain.

7. What is the primary rationale usually given for involuntarily committing someone to an inpatient facility?

8. What general legal standards must be satisfied before involuntary commitment could correctly be said to be legally justified?

9. What role has been assigned to counselors in physician-assisted suicide according to the Oregon Death with Dignity Act?

10. Gerald Dworkin mentions three types of decisions for which he thinks "fully rational" individuals would accept paternalistic restrictions. Briefly describe these three types of decisions.

11. Briefly describe and provide illustrations for Margeret Battin's five standards for rational suicide.

DISCUSSION QUESTIONS

1. In Case 1, in what sense did Tina give up control of her life in the very act of taking control of it? Was Tina's decision to stop her medication an autonomous one? Explain.

2. In your estimation, should Dr. Winters have attempted to convince Tina to remain on the medicine despite her pregnancy? Explain.

3. Was Dr. Winters's pledge to "do her best" to protect Tina's pregnancy a suitable response to Tina's plea for help? If you were in Dr. Winters's situation, how would you have responded to this request? Defend your answers.

4. Was Dr. Winters's plan to meet two times per week with Tina after she terminated her medication a good idea? What alternative plans might Dr. Winters

have explored? Could the distinction between custodial care versus therapy have been useful for such purposes? Explain.

5. Under what conditions, if any, would involuntary commitment of Tina have been justified? Explain.

6. What, in your estimation, should Dr. Winters have done if Tina's continuing pregnancy threatened Tina's life? Would defending continuation of Tina's pregnancy, despite risk to her life, have been consistent with the primary counseling mission?

7. In Case 2, in your estimation, was the child welfare agency's ultimatum—that the agency provide counseling and supervision for Dwayne every day after school or that he be placed in an inpatient facility—a reasonable response to the circumstances? Was it fair to Dwayne? Was it fair to the agency? Explain.

8. If you were Westwood, what would you have said or done in response to Child Welfare's demand? Were there any other feasible alternatives besides the two provided by Child Welfare?

9. In your estimation, did Dwayne satisfy the legal conditions necessary to justify involuntarily committing him? Explain.

10. In your estimation, should Dr. Harris have attempted to involve Debbie in the counseling process? If so, in what ways? If not, why not?

11. Do you think Dwayne may have been unfairly discriminated against by Child Welfare because of his minor status? Explain.

12. Dr. Harris did not inform Dwayne that he was to be medicated. Did Harris have a moral responsibility to do so? Defend your position.

13. Discuss some precautions that you think should be taken by the staff at inpatient facilities (therapists, administrators, human service paraprofessionals, psychiatric nurses, etc.) to help ensure that those involuntarily committed will not be mistreated.

14. In your estimation, is the unnecessary involuntary commitment of individuals to inpatient treatment facilities a serious problem today?

15. Does case law on the foreseeable suicide of seriously physically compromised clients like Carter James in Case 3 clearly prescribe a duty of therapists to intervene? Discuss some actual legal cases in support of your answer. What relevant similarities and differences do the cited cases bear to the case of Carter James?

16. Dr. Jack Kevorkian is well known for having assisted the suicides of physically impaired patients, some of whom were not terminally ill. In your estimation, should physician-assisted suicide be available to people as a legal option? If so, what safeguards, if any, would you want to see built into the legal option? Defend your responses.

17. If physician-assisted suicide becomes a legal option, what effect do you foresee this having on the mental health professions?

18. Could a rule permitting therapists' nonintervention in suicide cases like Carter James's be justified by Kantian ethics? Do you agree with Kantian ethics

here? Could such a rule be justified by rule utilitarian ethics? If not, why not? If so, what provisions would this justified rule need to include? What exceptions, if any, would it need to include? Defend your responses.

19. Would a "fully rational individual," in the sense understood by Gerald Dworkin, consent to counselor intervention to prevent suicide in a case like that of Carter James? Explain.

20. Was Carter James's decision to commit suicide competent at least in the minimal sense of the term? In your estimation, was he competent enough to make such a decision? Is anyone ever competent enough to make such a decision? Defend your response.

21. In your estimation, can suicide ever be rational? Was Carter's suicide rational according to Battin's standards? Defend your responses.

22. In your estimation, did Dr. Dariens have sufficient evidence for predicting that Carter would attempt suicide over the weekend? Explain.

23. In your estimation, would Dr. Dariens have acted appropriately had he detained Carter in an inpatient facility for observation over the weekend? (Assume that Robert was unavailable to watch Carter over the weekend.) Defend your response.

REFERENCES

CHAPTER ONE

AMERICAN COUNSELING ASSOCIATION. (1995). *Code of ethics.* Alexandria, VA: Author.

ARISTOTLE. (1941). Nicomachean ethics. In R. McKeon (Ed.), *The basic works of Aristotle* (pp. 935–1112). New York: Random House.

BEABOUT, G. R., & WENNEMANN, D. J. (1994). *Applied professional ethics.* Lanham, MD: University Press of America.

BAYLES, M. D. (1989). *Professional ethics.* (2nd ed.). Belmont, CA: Wadsworth.

ESPIN, OLIVIA M. (1995). Contemporary sexuality and the Hispanic woman. In M. L. Andersen & P. H. Collins (Eds.), *Race, class, and gender* (pp. 423–428). Belmont, CA: Wadsworth.

GILLIGAN, C. (1982). *In a different voice: Psychological theory and women's development.* Cambridge, MA: Harvard University Press.

GILLIGAN, C. (1994a). In a different voice: Women's conception of self and of morality. In S. Stumpf (Ed.), *Philosophy: History and problems* (pp. 725–731). New York: McGraw-Hill.

GILLIGAN, C. (1994b). Moral orientation and moral development. In L. May & S. C. Sharratt (Eds.), *Applied ethics: A multicultural approach* (pp. 261–273). Englewood Cliffs, NJ: Prentice Hall.

GOLDBERGER, N., TARULE, J., CLINCHY, B., & BELENKY, M. (1996). *Knowledge, difference, and power.* New York: HarperCollins.

HINMAN, L. M. (1994). *Ethics: A pluralistic approach to moral theory.* Forth Worth, TX: Harcourt Brace.

KANT, I. (1964). *Groundwork of the metaphysic of morals.* Trans. H. J. Paton. New York: Harper & Row.

KOHLBERG, L. (1987). Indoctrination versus relativity in value education. In G. Sher (Ed.), *Moral philosophy: Selected readings.* New York: Harcourt.

MACINTYRE, A. (1982). *After virtue: A study in moral theory.* Notre Dame, IN: University of Notre Dame Press.

MARTIN, M. W. (1989). *Everyday morality: An introduction to applied ethics.* Belmont, CA: Wadsworth.

MILL, J. S. (1971). Utilitarianism. In S. Gorovitz (Ed.), *Mill: Utilitarianism: Text and critical essays* (pp. 13–57). New York: Bobbs-Merrill.

MORPHIS, M., & RIESBECK, C. K. (1990). Feminist ethics and case-based reasoning: A marriage of purpose. *International Journal of Applied Philosophy, 5*(2), 15–28.

NUSSBAUM, M. C. (1990). *Love's knowledge: Essays on philosophy and literature.* New York: Oxford University Press.

SARTRE, J. P. (1985). *Existentialism and human emotions.* New York: Philosophical Library.

CHAPTER TWO

AMERICAN PSYCHIATRIC ASSOCIATION. (1994). *Diagnostic and statistical manual of mental disorders* (4th ed.). Washington, DC: Author.

ARISTOTLE. (1941). Nicomachean ethics. In R. McKeon (Ed.), *The basic works of Aristotle* (pp. 927–1112). New York: Random House.

COHEN, E. (1988). Pure legal advocates and moral agents: Two concepts of a lawyer in an adversary system. In A. Flores (Ed.), *Professional ideals* (pp. 82–95). Belmont, CA: Wadsworth.

COHEN, E. (1994). *Caution: Faulty thinking can be harmful to your happiness.* Fort Pierce, FL: Trace-WilCo.

COHEN, E. (1995). Ethical standards for counseling sexually active clients with HIV. In W. Odets & M. Shernoff (Eds.), *The second decade of AIDS: A mental health practice handbook.* New York: Hatherleigh Press.

COREY, G. (1996). *Theory and practice of counseling and psychotherapy* (5th ed.). Pacific Grove, CA: Brooks/Cole.

ELLIS, A., & HARPER, R. A. (1975). *A new guide to rational living.* Englewood Cliffs, NJ: Prentice Hall.

FROMM, E. (1955). *The sane society.* New York: Holt, Rinehart & Winston.

GLADDING, S. T. (1996). *Counseling: A comprehensive profession.* Columbus, OH: Merrill.

KITCHENER, K. S. (1986). Teaching applied ethics in counselor education: An integration of psychological processes and philosophical analysis. *Journal of Counseling and Development, 64,* 306–310.

LADD, J. (1982). Philosophical remarks on professional responsibility in organizations. *International Journal of Applied Philosophy, 1*(2), 58–70.

LAZARUS, R. (1969). *Patterns of adjustment and human effectiveness.* New York: McGraw-Hill.

MARTIN, M. W. (1989). *Everyday morality: An introduction to applied ethics.* Belmont, CA: Wadsworth.

NATIONAL ASSOCIATION OF SOCIAL WORKERS. (1997). *Code of ethics.* Washington, DC: Author.

ROGERS, C. R. (1977). *Personal power.* New York: Delacorte Press.

SZASZ, T. (1960). The myth of mental illness. *American Psychologist, 15,* 113–118.

Tarasoff v. Regents of the University of California (1976), California Supreme Court, 17 *California Reporter, 3rd Series,* 425.

VAN HOOSE, W. H., & KOTTLER, J. A. (1985). *Ethical and legal issues in counseling and psychotherapy.* San Francisco: Jossey Bass.

CHAPTER THREE

COREY, G. (1991). *Theory and practice in counseling and psychotherapy* (4th ed.). Belmont, CA: Brooks/Cole.

CLINCHY, B. M. (1996). Connected and separate knowing: Toward a marriage of two minds. In N. Goldberger, J. Tarule, B. Clinchy, & M. Belenky (Eds.), *Knowledge, difference, and power: Essays inspired by women's ways of knowing* (pp. 205–247). New York: HarperCollins.

EVANS, R. I. (1975). *Carl Rogers: The man and his ideas,* New York: E. P. Dutton.

KANT, I. (1964). *Groundwork of the metaphysics of ideals* (H. J. Paton, Trans.). New York: Harper & Row.

MAHONEY, M. J. (1996). Connected knowing in constructive psychotherapy. In N. Goldberger, J. Tarule, B. Clinchy, & M. Belenky (Eds.), *Knowledge, difference, and power: Essays inspired by women's ways of knowing.* (pp. 126–147). New York: HarperCollins.

NUTTIN, J. (1962). *Psychoanalysis and personality: A dynamic theory of normal personality.* New York: Mentor Books.

ROGERS, C. R. (1961). *On becoming a person.* Boston: Houghton Mifflin.

ROGERS, C. R. (1977). *Carl Rogers on personal power: Inner strength and its revolutionary impact.* New York: Delacorte Press.

ROGERS, C. R. (l982). *Interview with Marian.* La Jolla, CA: Center for Studies of the Person.

SARTRE, J. P. (1985). *Existentialism and human emotions.* New York: Philosophical Library.

VAN HOOSE, W. H., & KOTTLER, J. A. (1985). *Ethical and legal issues in counseling and psychotherapy.* San Francisco: Jossey-Bass.

WALEN, S. R., DIGIUSEPPE, R. & DRYDEN, W. (1992). *A practitioner's guide to rational-emotive therapy* (2nd ed.). New York: Oxford University Press.

CHAPTER FOUR

AMERICAN ASSOCIATION OF MARRIAGE AND FAMILY THERAPY. (1991). *Code of ethics.* Washington, DC: Author.

AMERICAN COUNSELING ASSOCIATION. (1995). *Code of ethics.* Alexandria, VA: Author.

AMERICAN PSYCHIATRIC ASSOCIATION ONLINE PRACTICE OF PSYCHIATRY. (Search Date September 6, 1997). The most frequently asked managed care questions 1990–1997 [On-line].

AMERICAN PSYCHOLOGICAL ASSOCIATION. (1992). *Ethical standards.* Washington, DC: Author.

ANDERSON, B. S. (1996). *The counselor and the law* (4th ed.). Alexandria, VA: American Counseling Association.

BAYLES, M. D. (1989). *Professional ethics* (2nd ed.). Belmont, CA: Wadsworth.

BEAUCHAMP, T. L., & CHILDRESS, J. F. (1979). *Principles of biomedical ethics.* New York: Oxford University Press.

Canterbury v. Spence, U.S. Court of Appeals, District of Columbia Circuit, 464 *Federal Reporter, 2nd Series,* 772 (1972).

COHEN, E. D. (1988). Pure legal advocates and moral agents: Two concepts of a lawyer in an adversary system. In A. Flores (Ed.), *Professional ideals.* Belmont, CA: Wadsworth.

COHEN, E. D. (1994). *Caution: Faulty thinking can be harmful to your happiness.* (2nd ed.). Fort Pierce, FL: Trace-WilCo.

COHEN, E. D. (1995). Ethical standards for counseling sexually active clients with HIV. In *The second decade of AIDS: A mental health practice handbook.* New York: Hatherleigh Press.

COMER, D. E. (1995). *Internetworking with TCP/IP: Principles, protocols, and architecture.* (3rd ed., volume 1). Upper Saddle River, NJ: Prentice Hall.

COREY, G., COREY, M. S., & CALLANAN, P. (1988). *Issues and ethics in the helping professions,* (3rd ed.). Belmont, CA: Wadsworth.

CURTIS, C. (1951). The ethics of advocacy. *Stanford Law Review, 4,* 3–23.

DAVIS, J. (1995). Part Two—of a series—becoming managed care-friendly. *The Advocate, 16,* 8, 16.

FRANKENA, W. K. (1973). *Ethics* (2nd ed.). Englewood Cliffs, NJ: Prentice Hall.

GOLDEN, L. (1996). Ethical pitfalls in managed care. In B. Herlihy & G. Corey (Eds.), *ACA ethical standards casebook* (pp. 224–228). Alexandria, VA: American Counseling Association.

HALEY, J. (1976). *Problem-solving therapy: New strategies for effective family therapy.* San Francisco: Jossey-Bass.

HUBER, C. H. (1994). *Ethical, legal and professional issues in the practice of marriage and family therapy* (2nd ed.). Upper Saddle River, NJ: Prentice Hall.

Jaffe v. Redmond, 116 S. Ct. 1923 (1996).

KNAPP, S. J., & VANDECREEK, L. (1985). Psychotherapy and privileged communication in child custody cases. *Professional Psychology: Research and Practice, 16*(3), 398–410.

MABE, A. R., & ROLLINS, S. A. (1986). The role of a code of ethical standards in counseling. *Journal of Counseling and Development, 64*(5), 294–297.

MAPPES, D. C., ROBB, G. P., & ENGELS, D. W. (1985). Conflicts between ethics and law in counseling and psychotherapy. *Journal of Counseling and Development, 64*(4), 246–252.

NATIONAL ASSOCIATION OF SOCIAL WORKERS. (1997). *Code of ethics.* Washington, DC: Author.

NATIONAL ORGANIZATION FOR HUMAN SERVICE EDUCATION. (1994). *Ethical standards for human service workers.* [Code posted on the World Wide Web]. Knoxville, TN: Author. Retrieved May 29, 1998 from the World Wide Web: http://www.nohse.com/ethstand.html

ODETS, W. (1995). Introduction. In W. Odets & M. Shernoff (Eds.), *The second decade of AIDS: A mental health practice handbook* (pp. 1–10). New York: Hatherleigh Press.

PIETROFESA, J. J., PIETROFESA, C. J., & PIETROFESA, J. D. (1990). The mental health counselor and "duty to warn." *Journal of Mental Health Counseling, 12*(2), 129–137.

REMLEY, T. P., JR. (1990). Counseling records: Legal and ethical issues. In B. Herlihy & L. B. Golden (Eds.), *Ethical standards casebook.* Alexandria, VA: American Association for Counseling and Development.

REMLEY, T. P., JR., HERLIHY, B., & HERLIHY, S. B. (1997). The U.S. Supreme Court decision in *Jaffe v. Redmond:* Implications for counselors. *Journal of Counseling and Development, 75*(3), 213–218.

SAMPSON, J. P., JR. (1996). A computer-aided violation of confidentiality. In B. Herlihy & G. Corey (Eds.). *ACA ethical standards casebook* (5th ed.). Alexandria, VA: American Counseling Association.

SHAH, S.A. (1969). Privileged communications, confidentiality, and privacy: Privileged communications. *Professional Psychology, 1*(1), 56–69.

Tarasoff v. Regents of the University of California (1976), California Supreme Court, 17 *California Reporter, 3rd Series,* 425.

VAN HOOSE, W. H., & KOTTLER, J. A. (1985). *Ethical and legal issues in counseling and psychotherapy* (2nd ed.). San Francisco: Jossey-Bass.

CHAPTER FIVE

AMERICAN COUNSELING ASSOCIATION (ACA). (1995). *Code of ethics.* Alexandria, VA: Author.

AMERICAN PSYCHOLOGICAL ASSOCIATION (APA). (1992). *Standards and ethics.* Washington, DC: Author.

ATKINSON, D. R., MORTEN, G., & SUE, D. W. (1993). *Counseling American minorities.* Madison, WI: WCB Brown & Benchmark.

BENOKRAITIS, N. (1996). *Marriages and families.* Upper Saddle River, NJ: Prentice Hall.

DAS, AJIT K. (1995). Rethinking multicultural counseling: Implications for counselor education. *Journal of Counseling and Development, 74*(1), 45.

EGAN, G. (1982). *The skilled helper.* Belmont, CA: Brooks/Cole.

GLADDING, S. T. (1995). *Family therapy.* Englewood Cliffs, NJ: Merrill.

GLADDING, S. T. (1996). *Counseling: A comprehensive profession.* Englewood Cliffs, NJ: Merrill.

NATIONAL ASSOCIATION OF SOCIAL WORKERS (NASW). (1997). *Code of ethics.* Washington, DC: Author.

PEDERSEN, P. (1991). Multiculturalism as a generic approach to counseling. *Journal of Counseling and Development, 70*(1), 6–12.

POORTINGA, Y. H. (1990). Towards a conceptualization of culture for psychology. *Cross-Cultural Psychology Bulletin, 24*(3), 6.

SHANNON, J. W., & WOODS, W. J. (1995). Affirmative psychotherapy for gay men. In D. R. Atkinson & G. Hackett, (Eds.), *Counseling diverse populations.* Madison, WI: WCB Brown & Benchmark.

VEGA, W. A. (1990, November). Hispanic families in the 1980's: A decade of research. *Journal of Marriage and the Family, 52*, 1015–1024.

WATCH TOWER BIBLE AND TRACT SOCIETY OF PENNSYLVANIA. (1997). *Family life that pleases God.* [On-line].

CHAPTER SIX

AMERICAN ASSOCIATION FOR MARRIAGE AND FAMILY THERAPY. (1991). *Code of ethics.* Washington, DC: Author.

AMERICAN ASSOCIATION OF UNIVERSITY PROFESSORS. (1990). Statement on professional ethics. *AAUP Policy Documents and Reports,* 75–76. Washington, DC: Author.

AMERICAN COUNSELING ASSOCIATION. (1995). *Code of ethics.* Alexandria, VA: Author.

AMERICAN PSYCHOLOGICAL ASSOCIATION. (1992). *Standards of ethics.* Washington, DC: Author.

ANDERSON, B. S. (1996). *The counselor and the law* (4th ed.). Alexandria, VA: American Counseling Association.

DAVIS, M., & STARK, A. (in press). *Conflict of interest and the professions.* New York: Oxford University Press.

HERLIHY, B., & COREY, G. (1997). *Boundary issues in counseling: Multiple roles and responsibilities.* Alexandria, VA: American Counseling Association.

KITCHENER, K. S. (1988). Dual role relationships: What makes them so problematic? *Journal of Counseling and Development, 67,* 217–221.

MARTIN, M. W. (1997). Professional distance. *International Journal of Applied Philosophy, 12*(1).

NATIONAL ASSOCIATION OF SOCIAL WORKERS. (1997). *Code of ethics.* Washington, DC: Author.

POPE, K. S. (1988). How clients are harmed by sexual contact with mental health professionals: The syndrome and its prevalence. *Journal of Counseling and Development, 67,* 222–226.

CHAPTER SEVEN

BLUME, E. S. (1990). *Secret survivors: Uncovering incest and its aftereffects in women.* New York: Wiley.

BRIERE, J., EVANS, D., RUNTZ, M., & WALL, T. (1988). Symptomotology in men who were molested as children: A comparison study. *American Journal of Orthopsychiatry, 58*(3), 457–461.

FINKELHOR, D., ARAJI, S., BARON, L., BROWNE, A., PETERS, S. D., & WYATT, G. E. (1986). *Sourcebook on child sexual abuse.* Newbury Park, CA: Sage.

FINKELHOR, D., HOTALING, G., LEWIS, I. A., & SMITH, C. (1990). Sexual abuse in a national survey of men and women: Prevalence, characteristics, and risk factors. *Child Abuse and Neglect, 3*(1), 19–28.

GELLES, R. J. , & CONTE, J. R. (1990). Domestic violence and sexual abuse of children: A review of research in the eighties. *Journal of Marriage and the Family, 52*(4) 1045–1058.

GROTH, A. N. (1982). The incest offender. In S. M. Sgroi (Ed.), *Handbook of clinical intervention in child sexual abuse.* Lexington, MA: Lexington Books.

MACFARLANE, K., & WATERMAN, J., et al. (1986). *Sexual abuse of young children.* New York: Guilford Press.

MRAZEK, P. B. (1981). The nature of incest: A review of contributing factors. In P. B. Mrazek & C. H. Kempe (Eds.), *Sexually abused children and their families.* New York: Pergamon Press.

ROGERS, C. R. (1961). *On becoming a person.* Boston: Houghton Mifflin.

RUSSELL, D. E. H. (1986). *The secret trauma: Incest in the lives of girls and women.* New York: Basic Books.

SHELDEN, V. E., & SHELDEN, R. G. (1989). Sexual abuse of males by females: The problem, treatment modality, and case examples. *Family Therapy, 16,* 249–258.

STRAUS, M. A., GELLES, R. J., & STEINMETZ, S. K. (1980). *Behind closed doors: Violence in the American family.* New York: Doubleday.

SUMMIT, R. (1983). The child sexual abuse accommodation syndrome. *Child Abuse and Neglect, 7,* 177–193.

WELLS, L. (1981). Family pathology and father-daughter incest: Restricted psychopathology. *Journal of Clinical Psychiatry, 42,* 197–202.

CHAPTER EIGHT

AMERICAN COUNSELING ASSOCIATION (ACA). (1995). *Code of ethics.* Alexandria, VA: Author.

AMERICAN PSYCHOLOGICAL ASSOCIATION (APA). (1992). *Standards and ethics.* Washington, DC: Author.

DE SANTIS, MARIE. (1990, June). Hate crimes bill excludes women. *Off Our Backs.*

LAMANNA, M. A., & REIDMAN, A. (1997). *Marriages and families.* Belmont, CA: Wadsworth.

LAWSON, DAVID M. (1989). A family systems perspective on wife battering. *Journal of Mental Health Counseling, 11*(4), 359–374.

MACCHIETTO, JOHN G. (1992). Aspects of male victimization and female aggression: Implications for counseling men. *Journal of Mental Health Counseling, 14*(3), 375–392.

NATIONAL ASSOCIATION OF SOCIAL WORKERS (NASW). (1997). *Code of ethics.* Washington, DC: Author.

NATIONAL ORGANIZATION FOR HUMAN SERVICE EDUCATION. (1994). *Ethical standards for human service workers.* [Code posted on the World Wide Web]. Knoxville, TN: Author. Retrieved May 29, 1998 from the World Wide Web: http://www.nohse.com/ethstand.html

ROY, M. (1982). The nature of abusive behavior. In M. Roy (Ed.), *The abusive partner* (pp. 3–17). New York: Van Nostrand Reinhold.

SELIGMAN, M. E. (1975). *Helplessness: On depression, development, and death.* New York: Wiley.

STEINMETZ, S. K. (1985). Battered husbands: A historical and cross-cultural study. In F. Baumli (Ed.), *Men freeing men: Exploding the myth of the traditional male.* Jersey City, NJ: New Atlantis.

STRAUSS, M. A., GELLES, R. J., & STEINMETZ, S. K. (1992). The marriage license as hitting license. In A. S. Skolnick & J. H. Skolnick (Eds.), *Family in transition* (pp. 203–216). New York: HarperCollins.

STEINMETZ, S. K. (1977–1978). The battered husband syndrome. *Victimology, 2,* 499–509.

WALKER, L. (1984). *The battered woman syndrome.* New York: Springer.

WALKER, L. (1989). Psychology and violence against women. *American Psychologist, 44*(4), 698–702.

WILKERSON, J. K. (1989). Philosopher as social worker. In E. D. Cohen (Ed.), *Philosophers at work.* New York: Holt, Rinehart & Winston.

CHAPTER NINE

AMERICAN COUNSELING ASSOCIATION. (1995). *Code of ethics and standards of practice.* Alexandria, VA: Author.

BRANT, A. M., CLEARY, P. D., & GOSTIN, L. O. (1990). Routine hospital testing for HIV: Health policy considerations. In Lawrence O. Gostin (Ed.), *AIDS and the health care system* (pp. 125–139). New Haven, CT: Yale University Press.

CENTERS FOR DISEASE CONTROL. (1987). Revision of the CDC surveillance case definition for acquired immunodeficiency syndrome. *Morbidity and Mortality Weekly Report, 36.1S,* 1–15.

CENTERS FOR DISEASE CONTROL. (1988). Condoms for prevention of sexually transmitted diseases. *Mortality and Morbidity Weekly Report, 37*, 133–137.

CENTERS FOR DISEASE CONTROL. (1991). The HIV/AIDS epidemic: The first 10 years. *Morbidity and Mortality Weekly Report, 40.22*, 357–369.

COHEN, E. D. (1990). Confidentiality, counseling, and clients who have AIDS: Ethical foundations of a model rule. *Journal of Counseling and Development, 68*, 282–286

COHEN, E. D. (1994). What would a virtuous counselor do? Ethical problems in counseling clients who have HIV. In E. D. Cohen & M. Davis (Eds.), *AIDS: Crisis in professional ethics*. Philadelphia: Temple University Press.

COHEN, E. D. (1995). Ethical standards for counseling sexually active clients with HIV. In W. Odets & M. Shernoff, (Eds.), *The second decade of AIDS: A mental health practice handbook* (pp. 233–254). New York: Hatherleigh Press.

COHEN, E. D. (1997). Confidentiality, HIV, and the ACA code of ethics: The contagious, fatal diseases rule. *Journal of Mental Health Counseling, 19*(4), 349–363.

COHEN, E. D., & DAVIS, L. (1994). *AIDS: Crisis in professional ethics*. Philadelphia: Temple University Press.

DE VINCENZI, I. (1994). A longititudinal study of human immunodeficiency virus transmission by heterosexual partners. *The New England Journal of Medicine, 331*, 341–346.

DOUGLAS, P. H., & PINSKY, L. (1996). *The essential AIDS fact book*. New York: Simon & Schuster.

DWORKIN, S. H., & PINCU, L. (1993). Counseling in the era of AIDS. *Journal of Counseling and Development, 3*, 275–281.

FLASKERUD, J. H. (1989). Overview: AIDS/HIV infection and nurses' needs for information. In J. H. Flaskerud (Ed.), *AIDS/HIV infection: A reference guide for nursing professionals* (pp. 1–18). Orlando FL: Harcourt Brace Jovanovich, Inc.

FLASKERUD, J. H., & NYAMATHI, A. M. (1989). Risk factors and HIV infection. In J. H. Flaskerud (Ed.), *AIDS/HIV infection: A reference guide for nursing professionals* (pp. 169–197). Orlando, FL: Harcourt Brace Jovanovich, Inc.

GOSTIN, L. O. (1990). Hospitals, health care professionals, and persons with AIDS. In L. O. Gostin (Ed.), *AIDS and the health care system* (pp. 3–12). New Haven, CT: Yale University Press.

GRAY, L. A., & HARDING, A. K. (1988). Confidentiality limits with clients who have the AIDS virus. *Journal of Counseling and Development, 66*, 219–223.

HARDING, A. K., GRAY, L. K., & NEAL, M. (1993). Confidentiality limits with clients who have HIV: A review of ethical and legal guidelines and professional policies. *Journal of Counseling and Development, 71*, 297–305.

LANGONE, J. (1991). *AIDS: The facts*. New York: Little, Brown.

LEIBOWITZ, R. E. (1989). Sociodemographic distribution of AIDS. In J. H. Flaskerud (Ed.), *AIDS/HIV infection: A reference guide for nursing professionals* (pp. 19–36). Orlando, FL: Harcourt Brace Jovanovich.

MASTERS, W. H., JOHNSON, V. E., & KOLODNY, R. C. (1992). *Human sexuality* (4th ed.). New York: HarperCollins.

MAYER, K. H. (1990). The natural history of HIV infection and current therapeutic strategies. In L. O. Gostin (Ed.), *AIDS and the health care system* (pp. 21–31). New Haven: Yale University Press.

NATIONAL ORGANIZATION FOR HUMAN SERVICE EDUCATION. (1994). *Ethical standards for human service workers*. [Code posted on the World Wide Web]. Knoxville, TN: Author. Retrieved May 29, 1998 from the World Wide Web: http://www.nohse.com/ethstand.html

ODETS, W. (1995). Survivor guilt in HIV-negative gay men. In W. Odets & M. Shernoff (Eds.), *The second decade of AIDS: A mental health practice handbook* (pp. 201–218). New York: Hatherleigh Press.

PADIAN, N. (1987). Male-to-female transmission of human immunodeficiency virus. *Journal of the American Medical Association, 258*, 788–790.

RABKIN, R., & RABKIN, J. (1995). Management of depression in patients with HIV infection. In W. Odets & M. Shernoff (Eds.), *The second decade of AIDS: A mental health practice handbook* (pp. 11–25). New York: Hatherleigh Press.

TURNER, C. F., MILLER, H. G., & MOSES, L. E. (Eds.). (1989). *AIDS: Sexual behavior and intravenous drug use.* Washington, DC: National Academy Press.

CHAPTER TEN

AMERICAN COUNSELING ASSOCIATION. (1995). *Code of ethics.* Alexandria, VA: Author.

AMERICAN HEALTH CONSULTANTS. (1997, June). Assisted suicide: Michigan law requires doctor/patient discussion of EOL choices. *Medical Ethics Advisor*, pp. 65–66.

AMERICAN PSYCHOLOGICAL ASSOCIATION. (1992). *Ethical standards.* Washington, DC: Author.

ANDERSON, B. S. (1996). *The counselor and the law.* Alexandria, VA: American Counseling Association.

BATTIN, M. P. (1995). *Ethical issues in suicide.* Englewood Cliffs, NJ: Prentice Hall.

BEAUCHAMP, T. L., & VEATCH, R. M. (1996). *Ethical issues in death and dying.* Upper Saddle River, NJ: Prentice Hall.

Bouvia v. Superior Court, 225 Cal. Reporter, 297 (Cal. Ct. App., 2nd D. 1986).

BRANDT, R. (1990). *The morality and rationality of suicide.* In J. Donnelly (Ed.), *Suicide: Right or wrong?* Buffalo, NY: Prometheus Books.

COHEN, E. D. (1986). Paternalism that does not restrict individuality: Criteria and applications. *Social Theory and Practice, 12*(3), 309–335.

Compassion in Dying v. Washington, 79 F. 3d 790, 798 (1996).

DWORKIN, G. (1971). Paternalism. In R. A. Wasserstrom (Ed.), *Morality and the law.* Belmont, CA: Wadsworth.

GREENBERG, D. F. (1982). Involuntary psychiatric commitments to prevent suicide. In R. B. Edwards (Ed.), *Psychiatry and ethics* (pp. 283–298). Buffalo, NY: Prometheus Books.

HASTINGS CENTER. (1987). *Guidelines on the termination of life-sustaining treatment and the care of the dying.* Briarcliff Manor, NY: Author.

In re Claire C. Conroy, 457 A.2d 1232 (1985).

KANT, IMMANUEL. (1990). Duties towards the body in regard to life. In J. Donnelly (Ed.), *Suicide: Right or wrong?* Buffalo, NY: Prometheus Books.

Krischer v. McIver, Florida Supreme Court (1997).

LIVERMORE, J. M., MALMQUIST, C. P., & MEEHL, P. E. (1982). On the justification for civil commitment. In R. B. Edwards (Ed.), *Psychiatry and ethics* (pp. 252–272). Buffalo, NY: Prometheus Books.

MACKLIN, R. (1982). Refusal of psychiatric treatment: Autonomy, competence, and paternalism. In R. B. Edwards (Ed.), *Psychiatry and ethics* (pp. 331–340). Buffalo, NY: Prometheus Books.

McKay v. Bergstedt, 801 P.2d 617 (1990).

MILL, J. S. (1947). *On liberty* (Alburey Castell, Ed.), New York: Appleton-Century-Crofts.

NATIONAL ASSOCIATION OF SOCIAL WORKERS. (1997). *Code of ethics.* Washington, DC: Author.

NATIONAL ORGANIZATION FOR HUMAN SERVICE EDUCATION. (1994). *Ethical standards for human service workers.* [Code posted on the World Wide Web]. Knoxville, TN: Author. Retrieved May 29, 1998 from the World Wide Web: http://www.nohse.com/ethstandard.html

O'Connor v. Donaldson, 422 U.S. 563 (1975). 95 S.Ct. 2486 (1975).

Oregon Death with Dignity Act. (1994).

People v. Kevorkian, No. CR-92-115190-FC (Mich. Cir. Ct., Oakland County, July 21, 1992).

SNYDER, L., & CAPLAN, A. (1995). The dying game: Physician-assisted suicide in Oregon. *The Philadelphia Lawyer, 58*, 34–46.

SZASZ, T. S. (1978). Involuntary mental hospitalization: A crime against humanity. In T. L. Beauchamp & L. Walters (Eds.), *Contemporary issues in bioethics* Belmont, CA: Dickenson Publishing.

SZASZ, T. S. (1991). The myth of mental illness. In T. A. Mapps & J. S. Zembaty (Eds.), *Biomedical ethics* (3rd ed.). New York: McGraw-Hill.

Tarasoff v. Regents of the University of California. (1976). California Supreme Court, 17 *California Reporter, 3rd Series*, 425.

VEATCH, R. M. (1997). *Medical ethics* (2nd ed.). Boston: Jones and Bartlett.

WUBBOLDING, R. E. (1996). Working with suicidal clients. In B. Herlihy & G. Corey (Eds.), *ACA ethical standards casebook* (pp. 267–274). Alexandria, VA: American Counseling Association.

APPENDIX A

ACA *Code of Ethics* and *Standards of Practice,* American Counseling Association (ACA)

PREAMBLE

The American Counseling Association is an educational, scientific, and professional organization whose memebers are dedicated to the enhancement of human development throughout the life-span. Association members recognize diversity in our society and embrace a cross-cultural approach in support of the worth, dignity, potential, and uniqueness of each individual.

The specification of a code of ethics enables the association to clarify to current and future members, and to those served by members, the nature of the ethical responsibilities held in common by its members. As the code of ethics of the association, this document establishes principles that define the ethical behavior of association members. All members of the American Counseling Association are required to adhere to the Code of Ethics and the Standards of Practice. The Code of Ethics will serve as the basis for processing ethical complaints initiated against members of the association.

SECTION A: THE COUNSELING RELATIONSHIP

A.1. Client Welfare

(a) Primary Responsibility. The primary responsibility of counselors is to respect the dignity and to promote the welfare of clients.

(b) Positive Growth and Development. Counselors encourage client growth and development in ways that foster the clients' interest and welfare; counselors avoid fostering dependent counseling relationships.

(c) Counseling Plans. Counselors and their clients work jointly in devising integrated, individual counseling plans that offer reasonable promise of success and are consistent with abilities and circumstances of clients. Counselors and clients regularly review counseling plans to ensure their continued viability and effectiveness, respecting clients' freedom of choice. (See A.3.b.)

(d) Family Involvement. Counselors recognize that families are usually important in clients' lives and strive to enlist family understanding and involvement as a positive resource, when appropriate.

(e) Career and Employment Needs. Counselors work with their clients in considering employment in jobs and circumstances that are consistent with the clients' overall abilities, vocational limitations, physical restrictions, general temperament, interest and aptitude patterns, social skills, education, general qualifications, and other relevant characteristics and needs. Counselors neither place nor participate in placing clients in positions that will result in damaging the interest and the welfare of clients, employers, or the public.

A.2. Respecting Diversity

(a) Nondiscrimination. Counselors do not condone or engage in discrimination based on age, color, culture, disability, ethnic group, gender, race, religion, sexual orientation, marital status, or socioeconomic status. (See C.5.a., C.5.b., and D.1.i.)

(b) Respecting Differences. Counselors will actively attempt to understand the diverse cultural backgrounds of the clients with whom they work. This includes, but is not limited to, learning how the counselor's own cultural/ethnic/racial identity impacts her or his values and beliefs about the counseling process. (See E.8. and F.2.i.)

A.3. Client Rights

(a) Disclosure to Clients. When counseling is initiated, and throughout the counseling process as necessary, counselors inform clients of the purposes, goals, techniques, procedures, limitations, potential risks, and benefits of services to be performed, and other pertinent information. Counselors take steps to ensure that clients understand the implications of diagnosis, the intended use of tests and reports, fees, and billing arrangements. Clients have the right to expect confidentiality and to be provided with an explanation of its limitations, including supervision and/or treatment team professionals; to obtain clear information about their case records; to participate in the ongoing counseling plans; and to refuse any recommended services and be advised of the consequences of such refusal. (See E.5.a. and G.2.)

(b) Freedom of Choice. Counselors offer clients the freedom to choose whether to enter into a counseling relationship and to determine which professional(s) will provide counseling. Restrictions that limit choices of clients are fully explained. (See A.1.c.)

(c) Inability to Give Consent. When counseling minors or persons unable to give voluntary informed consent, counselors act in these clients' best interests. (See B.3.)

A.4. Clients Served by Others

If a client is receiving services from another mental health professional, counselors, with client consent, inform the professional persons already involved and develop clear agreements to avoid confusion and conflict for the client. (See C.6.c.)

A.5. Personal Needs and Values

(a) Personal Needs. In the counseling relationship, counselors are aware of the intimacy and responsibilities inherent in the counseling relationship, maintain respect for clients, and avoid actions that seek to meet their personal needs at the expense of clients.

(b) Personal Values. Counselors are aware of their own values, attitudes, beliefs, and behaviors and how these apply in a diverse society, and avoid imposing their values on clients. (See C.5.a.)

A.6. Dual Relationships

(a) Avoid When Possible. Counselors are aware of their influential positions with respect to clients, and they avoid exploiting the trust and dependency of clients.

Counselors make every effort to avoid dual relationships with clients that could impair professional judgment or increase the risk of harm to clients. (Examples of such relationships include, but are not limited to, familial, social, financial, business, or close personal relationships with clients.) When a dual relationship cannot be avoided, counselors take appropriate professional precautions such as informed consent, consultation, supervision, and documentation to ensure that judgment is not impaired and no exploitation occurs. (See F.1.b.)

(b)   Superior/Subordinate Relationships. Counselors do not accept as clients superiors or subordinates with whom they have administrative, supervisory, or evaluative relationships.

A.7. Sexual Intimacies With Clients

(a)   Current Clients. Counselors do not have any type of sexual intimacies with clients and do not counsel persons with whom they have had a sexual relationship.

(b)   Former Clients. Counselors do not engage in sexual intimacies with former clients within a minimum of 2 years after terminating the counseling relationship. Counselors who engage in such relationship after 2 years following termination have the responsibility to examine and document thoroughly that such relations did not have an exploitative nature, based on factors such as duration of counseling, amount of time since counseling, termination circumstances, client's personal history and mental status, adverse impact on the client, and actions by the counselor suggesting a plan to initiate a sexual relationship with the client after termination.

A.8. Multiple Clients

When counselors agree to provide counseling services to two or more persons who have a relationship (such as husband and wife, or parents and children), counselors clarify at the outset which person or persons are clients and the nature of the relationships they will have with each involved person. If it becomes apparent that counselors may be called upon to perform potentially conflicting roles, they clarify, adjust, or withdraw from roles appropriately. (See B.2. and B.4.d.)

A.9. Group Work

(a)   Screening. Counselors screen prospective group counseling/therapy participants. To the extent possible, counselors select members whose needs and goals are compatible with goals of the group, who will not impede the group process, and whose well-being will not be jeopardized by the group experience.

(b)   Protecting Clients. In a group setting, counselors take reasonable precautions to protect clients from physical or psychological trauma.

A.10. Fees and Bartering (See D.3.a. and D.3.b.)

(a)   Advance Understanding. Counselors clearly explain to clients, prior to entering the counseling relationship, all financial arrangements related to professional services including the use of collection agencies or legal measures for nonpayment. (A.11.c.)

(b)   Establishing Fees. In establishing fees for professional counseling services, counselors consider the financial status of clients and locality. In the event that the established fee structure is inappropriate for a client, assistance is provided in attempting to find comparable services of acceptable cost. (See A.10.d., D.3.a., and D.3.b.)

(c)   Bartering Discouraged. Counselors ordinarily refrain from accepting goods or services from clients in return for counseling services because such arrangements create inherent potential for conflicts, exploitation, and distortion of the professional relationship. Counselors may participate in bartering only if the relationship is not exploitative, if the client requests it, if a clear written contract is established, and if such arrangements are an accepted practice among professionals in the community. (See A.6.a.)

(d)   Pro Bono Service. Counselors contribute to society by devoting a portion of their professional activity to services for which there is little or no financial return (pro bono).

A.11. Termination and Referral

(a)   Abandonment Prohibited. Counselors do not abandon or neglect clients in counseling. Counselors assist in making appropriate arrangements for the continuation of treatment, when necessary, during interruptions such as vacations, and following termination.

(b)   Inability to Assist Clients. If counselors determine an inability to be of professional assistance to clients, they avoid entering or immediately terminate a counseling relationship. Counselors are knowledgeable about referral resources and suggest appropriate alternatives. If clients decline the suggested referral, counselors should discontinue the relationship.

(c)   Appropriate Termination. Counselors terminate a counseling relationship, securing client agreement when possible, when it is reasonably clear that the client is no longer benefiting, when services are no longer required, when counseling no longer serves the client's needs or interests, when clients do not pay fees charged, or when agency or institution limits do not allow provision of further counseling services. (See A.10.b. and C.2.g.)

A.12. Computer Technology

(a)   Use of Computers. When computer applications are used in counseling services, counselors ensure that (1) the client is intellectually, emotionally, and physically capable of using the computer application; (2) the computer application is appropriate for the needs of the client; (3) the client understands the purpose and operation of the computer applications; and (4) a follow-up of client use of a computer application is provided to correct possible misconceptions, discover inappropriate use, and assess subsequent needs.

(b)   Explanation of Limitations. Counselors ensure that clients are provided information as a part of the counseling relationship that adequately explains the limitations of computer technology.

(c)   Access to Computer Applications. Counselors provide for equal access to computer applications in counseling services. (See A.2.a.)

SECTION B: CONFIDENTIALITY

B.1. Right to Privacy

(a)   Respect for Privacy. Counselors respect their clients right to privacy and avoid illegal and unwarranted disclosures of confidential information. (See A.3.a. and B.6.a.)

(b)   Client Waiver. The right to privacy may be waived by the client or his or her legally recognized representative.

(c)   Exceptions. The general requirement that counselors keep information confidential does not apply when disclosure is required to prevent clear and imminent danger to the client or others or when legal requirements demand that confidential information be revealed. Counselors consult with other professionals when in doubt as to the validity of an exception.

(d) Contagious, Fatal Diseases. A counselor who receives information confirming that a client has a disease commonly known to be both communicable and fatal is justified in disclosing information to an identifiable third party, who by his or her relationship with the client is at a high risk of contracting the disease. Prior to making a disclosure the counselor should ascertain that the client has not already informed the third party about his or her disease and that the client is not intending to inform the third party in the immediate future. (See B.1.c and B.1.f.)

(e) Court-Ordered Disclosure. When court ordered to release confidential information without a client's permission, counselors request to the court that the disclosure not be required due to potential harm to the client or counseling relationship. (See B.1.c.)

(f) Minimal Disclosure. When circumstances require the disclosure of confidential information, only essential information is revealed. To the extent possible, clients are informed before confidential information is disclosed.

(g) Explanation of Limitations. When counseling is initiated and throughout the counseling process as necessary, counselors inform clients of the limitations of confidentiality and identify foreseeable situations in which confidentiality must be breached. (See G.2.a.)

(h) Subordinates. Counselors make every effort to ensure that privacy and confidentiality of clients are maintained by subordinates including employees, supervisees, clerical assistants, and volunteers. (See B.1.a.)

(i) Treatment Teams. If client treatment will involve a continued review by a treatment team, the client will be informed of the team's existence and composition.

B.2. Groups and Families

(a) Group Work. In group work, counselors clearly define confidentiality and the parameters for the specific group being entered, explain its importance, and discuss the difficulties related to confidentiality involved in group work. The fact that confidentiality cannot be guaranteed is clearly communicated to group members.

(b) Family Counseling. In family counseling, information about one family member cannot be disclosed to another member without permission. Counselors protect the privacy rights of each family member. (See A.8., B.3., and B.4.d.)

B.3. Minor or Incompetent Clients

When counseling clients who are minors or individuals who are unable to give voluntary, informed consent, parents or guardians may be included in the counseling process as appropriate. Counselors act in the best interests of clients and take measures to safeguard confidentiality. (See A.3.c.)

B.4. Records

(a) Requirement of Records. Counselors maintain records necessary for rendering professional services to their clients and as required by laws, regulations, or agency or institution procedures.

(b) Confidentiality of Records. Counselors are responsible for securing the safety and confidentiality of any counseling records they create, maintain, transfer, or destroy whether the records are written, taped, computerized, or stored in any other medium. (See B.1.a.)

(c) Permission to Record or Observe. Counselors obtain permission from clients prior to electronically recording or observing sessions. (See A.3.a.)

(d) Client Access. Counselors recognize that counseling records are kept for the benefit of clients, and therefore provide access to records and copies of records when requested by competent clients, unless the records contain information that may be misleading and detrimental to the client. In situations involving multiple clients, access to records is limited to those parts of records that do not include confidential information related to another client. (See A.8., B.1.a., and B.2.b.)

(e) Disclosure or Transfer. Counselors obtain written permission from clients to disclose or transfer records to legitimate third parties unless exceptions to confidentiality exist as listed in Section B.1. Steps are taken to ensure that receivers of counseling records are sensitive to their confidential nature.

B.5. Research and Training

(a) Data Disguise Required. Use of data derived from counseling relationships for purposes of training, research, or publication is confined to content that is disguised to ensure the anonymity of the individuals involved. (See B.1.g. and G.3.d.)

(b) Agreement for Identification. Identification of a client in a presentation or publication is permissible only when the client has reviewed the material and has agreed to its presentation or publication. (See G.3.d.)

B.6. Consultation

(a) Respect for Privacy. Information obtained in a consulting relationship is discussed for professional purposes only with persons clearly concerned with the case. Written and oral reports present data germane to the purposes of the consultation, and every effort is made to protect client identity and avoid undue invasion of privacy.

(b) Cooperating Agencies. Before sharing information, counselors make efforts to ensure that there are defined policies in other agencies serving the counselor's clients that effectively protect the confidentiality of information.

SECTION C: PROFESSIONAL RESPONSIBILITY

C.1. Standards Knowledge

Counselors have a responsibility to read, understand, and follow the Code of Ethics and the Standards of Practice.

C.2. Professional Competence

(a) Boundaries of Competence. Counselors practice only within the boundaries of their competence, based on their education, training, supervised experience, state and national professional credentials, and appropriate professional experience. Counselors will demonstrate a commitment to gain knowledge, personal awareness, sensitivity, and skills pertinent to working with a diverse client population.

(b) New Specialty Areas of Practice. Counselors practice in specialty areas new to them only after appropriate education, training, and supervised experience. While developing skills in new specialty areas, counselors take steps to ensure the competence of their work and to protect others from possible harm.

(c) Qualified for Employment. Counselors accept employment only for positions for which they are qualified by education, training, supervised experience, state and national professional credentials, and appropriate professional experience. Counselors hire for professional counseling positions only individuals who are qualified and competent.

(d) Monitor Effectiveness. Counselors continually monitor their effectiveness as professionals and take steps to improve when necessary. Counselors in private practice take reasonable steps to seek out peer supervision to evaluate their efficacy as counselors.

(e) Ethical Issues Consultation. Counselors take reasonable steps to consult with other counselors or related professionals when they have questions regarding their ethical obligations or professional practice. (See H.1.)

(f) Continuing Education. Counselors recognize the need for continuing education to maintain a reasonable level of awareness of current scientific and professional information in their fields of activity. They take steps to maintain competence in the skills they use, are open to new procedures, and keep current with the diverse and/or special populations with whom they work.

(g) Impairment. Counselors refrain from offering or accepting professional services when their physical, mental, or emotional problems are likely to harm a client or others. They are alert to the signs of impairment, seek assistance for problems, and, if necessary, limit, suspend, or terminate their professional responsibilities. (See A.11.c.)

C.3. Advertising and Soliciting Clients

(a) Accurate Advertising. There are no restrictions on advertising by counselors except those that can be specifically justified to protect the public from deceptive practices. Counselors advertise or represent their services to the public by identifying their credentials in an accurate manner that is not false, misleading, deceptive, or fraudulent. Counselors may only advertise the highest degree earned which is in counseling or a closely related field from a college or university that was accredited when the degree was awarded by one of the regional accrediting bodies recognized by the Council on Postsecondary Accreditation.

(b) Testimonials. Counselors who use testimonials do not solicit them from clients or other persons who, because of their particular circumstances, may be vulnerable to undue influence.

(c) Statements by Others. Counselors make reasonable efforts to ensure that statements made by others about them or the profession of counseling are accurate.

(d) Recruiting Through Employment. Counselors do not use their places of employment or institutional affiliation to recruit or gain clients, supervisees, or consultees for their private practices. (See C.5.e.)

(e) Products and Training Advertisements. Counselors who develop products related to their profession or conduct workshops or training events ensure that the advertisements concerning these products or events are accurate and disclose adequate information for consumers to make informed choices.

(f) Promoting to Those Served. Counselors do not use counseling, teaching, training, or supervisory relationships to promote their products or training events in a manner that is deceptive or would exert undue influence on individuals who may be vulnerable. Counselors may adopt textbooks they have authored for instruction purposes.

(g) Professional Association Involvement. Counselors actively participate in local, state, and national associations that foster the development and improvement of counseling.

C.4. Credentials

(a) Credentials Claimed. Counselors claim or imply only professional credentials possessed and are responsible for correcting any known misrepresentations of their credentials by others. Professional credentials include graduate degrees in counseling or closely related mental health fields, accreditation of graduate programs, national voluntary certifications, government-issued certifications or licenses, ACA professional membership, or any other credential that might indicate to the public specialized knowledge or expertise in counseling.

(b)   ACA Professional Membership. ACA professional members may announce to the public their membership status. Regular members may not announce their ACA membership in a manner that might imply they are credentialed counselors.

(c)   Credential Guidelines. Counselors follow the guidelines for use of credentials that have been established by the entities that issue the credentials.

(d)   Misrepresentation of Credentials. Counselors do not attribute more to their credentials than the credentials represent, and do not imply that other counselors are not qualified because they do not possess certain credentials.

(e)   Doctoral Degrees From Other Fields. Counselors who hold a master's degree in counseling or a closely related mental health field, but hold a doctoral degree from other than counseling or a closely related field, do not use the title "Dr." in their practices and do not announce to the public in relation to their practice or status as a counselor that they hold a doctorate.

C.5. Public Responsibility

(a)   Nondiscrimination. Counselors do not discriminate against clients, students, or supervisees in a manner that has a negative impact based on their age, color, culture, disability, ethnic group, gender, race, religion, sexual orientation, or socioeconomic status, or for any other reason. (See A.2.a.)

(b)   Sexual Harassment. Counselors do not engage in sexual harassment. Sexual harassment is defined as sexual solicitation, physical advances, or verbal or nonverbal conduct that is sexual in nature, that occurs in connection with professional activities or roles, and that either (1) is unwelcome, is offensive, or creates a hostile workplace environment, and counselors know or are told this; or (2) is sufficiently severe or intense to be perceived as harassment to a reasonable person in the context. Sexual harassment can consist of a single intense or severe act or multiple persistent or pervasive acts.

(c)   Reports to Third Parties. Counselors are accurate, honest, and unbiased in reporting their professional activities and judgments to appropriate third parties including courts, health insurance companies, those who are the recipients of evaluation reports, and others. (See B.1.g.)

(d)   Media Presentations. When counselors provide advice or comment by means of public lectures, demonstrations, radio or television programs, prerecorded tapes, printed articles, mailed material, or other media, they take reasonable precautions to ensure that (1) the statements are based on appropriate professional counseling literature and practice; (2) the statements are otherwise consistent with the Code of Ethics and the Standards of Practice; and (3) the recipients of the information are not encouraged to infer that a professional counseling relationship has been established. (See C.6.b.)

(e)   Unjustified Gains. Counselors do not use their professional positions to seek or receive unjustified personal gains, sexual favors, unfair advantage, or unearned goods or services. (See C.3.d.)

C.6. Responsibility to Other Professionals

(a)   Different Approaches. Counselors are respectful of approaches to professional counseling that differ from their own. Counselors know and take into account the traditions and practices of other professional groups with which they work.

(b) Personal Public Statements. When making personal statements in a public context, counselors clarify that they are speaking from their personal perspectives and that they are not speaking on behalf of all counselors or the profession. (See C.5.d.)

(c) Clients Served by Others. When counselors learn that their clients are in a professional relationship with another mental health professional, they request release from clients to inform the other professionals and strive to establish positive and collaborative professional relationships. (See A.4.)

SECTION D: RELATIONSHIPS WITH OTHER PROFESSIONALS

D.1. Relationships With Employers and Employees

(a) Role Definition. Counselors define and describe for their employers and employees the parameters and levels of their professional roles.

(b) Agreements. Counselors establish working agreements with supervisors, colleagues, and subordinates regarding counseling or clinical relationships, confidentiality, adherence to professional standards, distinction between public and private material, maintenance and dissemination of recorded information, work load, and accountability. Working agreements in each instance are specified and made known to those concerned.

(c) Negative Conditions. Counselors alert their employers to conditions that may be potentially disruptive or damaging to the counselor's professional responsibilities or that may limit their effectiveness.

(d) Evaluation. Counselors submit regularly to professional review and evaluation by their supervisor or the appropriate representative of the employer.

(e) In-Service. Counselors are responsible for in-service development of self and staff.

(f) Goals. Counselors inform their staff of goals and programs.

(g) Practices. Counselors provide personnel and agency practices that respect and enhance the rights and welfare of each employee and recipient of agency services. Counselors strive to maintain the highest levels of professional services.

(h) Personnel Selection and Assignment. Counselors select competent staff and assign responsibilities compatible with their skills and experiences.

(i) Discrimination. Counselors, as either employers or employees, do not engage in or condone practices that are inhumane, illegal, or unjustifiable (such as considerations based on age, color, culture, disability, ethnic group, gender, race, religion, sexual orientation, or socioeconomic status) in hiring, promotion, or training. (See A.2.a. and C.5.b.)

(j) Professional Conduct. Counselors have a responsibility both to clients and to the agency or institution within which services are performed to maintain high standards of professional conduct.

(k) Exploitative Relationships. Counselors do not engage in exploitative relationships with individuals over whom they have supervisory, evaluative, or instructional control or authority.

(l) Employer Policies. The acceptance of employment in an agency or institution implies that counselors are in agreement with its general policies and principles. Counselors strive to reach agreement with employers as to acceptable standards of conduct that allow for changes in institutional policy conducive to the growth and development of clients.

D.2. Consultation (See B.6.)

(a) Consultation as an Option. Counselors may choose to consult with any other professionally competent persons about their clients. In choosing consultants, counselors avoid placing the consultant in a conflict of interest situation that would preclude the consultant being a proper party to the counselor's efforts to help the client. Should counselors be engaged in a work setting that compromises this consultation standard, they consult with other professionals whenever possible to consider justifiable alternatives.

(b)   Consultant Competency. Counselors are reasonably certain that they have or the organization represented has the necessary competencies and resources for giving the kind of consulting services needed and that appropriate referral resources are available.

(c)   Understanding With Clients. When providing consultation, counselors attempt to develop with their clients a clear understanding of problem definition, goals for change, and predicted consequences of interventions selected.

(d)   Consultant Goals. The consulting relationship is one in which client adaptability and growth toward self-direction are consistently encouraged and cultivated. (See A.1.b.)

D.3. Fees for Referral

(a)   Accepting Fees From Agency Clients. Counselors refuse a private fee or other remuneration for rendering services to persons who are entitled to such services through the counselor's employing agency or institution. The policies of a particular agency may make explicit provisions for agency clients to receive counseling services from members of its staff in private practice. In such instances, the clients must be informed of other options open to them should they seek private counseling services. (See A.10.a., A.11.b., and C.3.d.)

(b)   Referral Fees. Counselors do not accept a referral fee from other professionals.

D.4. Subcontractor Arrangements

When counselors work as subcontractors for counseling services for a third party, they have a duty to inform clients of the limitations of confidentiality that the organization may place on counselors in providing counseling services to clients. The limits of such confidentiality ordinarily are discussed as part of the intake session. (See B.1.e. and B.1.f.)

SECTION E: EVALUATION, ASSESSMENT, AND INTERPRETATION

E.1. General

(a)   Appraisal Techniques. The primary purpose of educational and psychological assessment is to provide measures that are objective and interpretable in either comparative or absolute terms. Counselors recognize the need to interpret the statements in this section as applying to the whole range of appraisal techniques, including test and nontest data.

(b)   Client Welfare. Counselors promote the welfare and best interests of the client in the development, publication, and utilization of educational and psychological assessment techniques. They do not misuse assessment results and interpretations and take reasonable steps to prevent others from misusing the information these techniques provide. They respect the client's right to know the results, the interpretations made, and the bases for their conclusions and recommendations.

E.2. Competence to Use and Interpret Tests

(a)   Limits of Competence. Counselors recognize the limits of their competence and perform only those testing and assessment services for which they have been trained. They are familiar with reliability, validity, related standardization, error of measurement, and proper application of any technique utilized. Counselors using computer-based test interpretations are trained in the construct being measured and the specific instrument being used prior to using this type of computer application. Counselors take reasonable measures to ensure the proper use of psychological assessment techniques by persons under their supervision.

(b) Appropriate Use. Counselors are responsible for the appropriate application, scoring, interpretation, and use of assessment instruments, whether they score and interpret such tests themselves or use computerized or other services.

(c) Decisions Based on Results. Counselors responsible for decisions involving individuals or policies that are based on assessment results have a thorough understanding of educational and psychological measurement, including validation criteria, test research, and guidelines for test development and use.

(d) Accurate Information. Counselors provide accurate information and avoid false claims or misconceptions when making statements about assessment instruments or techniques. Special efforts are made to avoid unwarranted connotations of such terms as IQ and grade equivalent scores. (See C.5.c.)

E.3. Informed Consent

(a) Explanation to Clients. Prior to assessment, counselors explain the nature and purposes of assessment and the specific use of results in language the client (or other legally authorized person on behalf of the client) can understand, unless an explicit exception to this right has been agreed upon in advance. Regardless of whether scoring and interpretation are completed by counselors, by assistants, or by computer or other outside services, counselors take reasonable steps to ensure that appropriate explanations are given to the client.

(b) Recipients of Results. The examinee's welfare, explicit understanding, and prior agreement determine the recipients of test results. Counselors include accurate and appropriate interpretations with any release of individual or group test results. (See B.1.a. and C.5.c.)

E.4. Release of Information to Competent Professionals

(a) Misuse of Results. Counselors do not misuse assessment results, including test results, and interpretations, and take reasonable steps to prevent the misuse of such by others. (See C.5.c.)

(b) Release of Raw Data. Counselors ordinarily release data (e.g., protocols, counseling or interview notes, or questionnaires) in which the client is identified only with the consent of the client or the client's legal representative. Such data are usually released only to persons recognized by counselors as competent to interpret the data. (See B.1.a.)

E.5. Proper Diagnosis of Mental Disorders

(a) Proper Diagnosis. Counselors take special care to provide proper diagnosis of mental disorders. Assessment techniques (including personal interview) used to determine client care (e.g., locus of treatment, type of treatment, or recommended follow-up) are carefully selected and appropriately used. (See A.3.a. and C.5.c.)

(b) Cultural Sensitivity. Counselors recognize that culture affects the manner in which clients' problems are defined. Clients' socioeconomic and cultural experience is considered when diagnosing mental disorders.

E.6. Test Selection

(a) Appropriateness of Instruments. Counselors carefully consider the validity, reliability, psychometric limitations, and appropriateness of instruments when selecting tests for use in a given situation or with a particular client.

(b)   Culturally Diverse Populations. Counselors are cautious when selecting tests for culturally diverse populations to avoid inappropriateness of testing that may be outside of socialized behavioral or cognitive patterns.

E.7. Conditions of Test Administration

(a)   Administration Conditions. Counselors administer tests under the same conditions that were established in their standardization. When tests are not administered under standard conditions or when unusual behavior or irregularities occur during the testing session, those conditions are noted in interpretation, and the results may be designated as invalid or of questionable validity.

(b)   Computer Administration. Counselors are responsible for ensuring that administration programs function properly to provide clients with accurate results when a computer or other electronic methods are used for test administration. (See A.12.b.)

(c)   Unsupervised Test Taking. Counselors do not permit unsupervised or inadequately supervised use of tests or assessments unless the tests or assessments are designed, intended, and validated for self-administration and/or scoring.

(d)   Disclosure of Favorable Conditions. Prior to test administration, conditions that produce most favorable test results are made known to the examinee.

E.8. Diversity in Testing

Counselors are cautious in using assessment techniques, making evaluations, and interpreting the performance of populations not represented in the norm group on which an instrument was standardized. They recognize the effects of age, color, culture, disability, ethnic group, gender, race, religion, sexual orientation, and socioeconomic status on test administration and interpretation and place test results in proper perspective with other relevant factors. (See A.2.a.)

E.9. Test Scoring and Interpretation

(a)   Reporting Reservations. In reporting assessment results, counselors indicate any reservations that exist regarding validity or reliability because of the circumstances of the assessment or the inappropriateness of the norms for the person tested.

(b)   Research Instruments. Counselors exercise caution when interpreting the results of research instruments possessing insufficient technical data to support respondent results. The specific purposes for the use of such instruments are stated explicitly to the examinee.

(c)   Testing Services. Counselors who provide test scoring and test interpretation services to support the assessment process confirm the validity of such interpretations. They accurately describe the purpose, norms, validity, reliability, and applications of the procedures and any special qualifications applicable to their use. The public offering of an automated test interpretations service is considered a professional-to-professional consultation. The formal responsibility of the consultant is to the consultee, but the ultimate and overriding responsibility is to the client.

E.10. Test Security

Counselors maintain the integrity and security of tests and other assessment techniques consistent with legal and contractual obligations. Counselors do not appropriate, reproduce, or modify published tests or parts thereof without acknowledgment and permission from the publisher.

E.11. Obsolete Tests and Outdated Test Results

Counselors do not use data or test results that are obsolete or outdated for the current purpose. Counselors make every effort to prevent the misuse of obsolete measures and test data by others.

E.12. Test Construction

Counselors use established scientific procedures, relevant standards, and current professional knowledge for test design in the development, publication, and utilization of educational and psychological assessment techniques.

SECTION F: TEACHING, TRAINING, AND SUPERVISION

F.1. Counselor Educators and Trainers

(a) Educators as Teachers and Practitioners. Counselors who are responsible for developing, implementing, and supervising educational programs are skilled as teachers and practitioners. They are knowledgeable regarding the ethical, legal, and regulatory aspects of the profession, are skilled in applying that knowledge, and make students and supervisees aware of their responsibilities. Counselors conduct counselor education and training programs in an ethical manner and serve as role models for professional behavior. Counselor educators should make an effort to infuse material related to human diversity into all courses and/or workshops that are designed to promote the development of professional counselors.

(b) Relationship Boundaries With Students and Supervisees. Counselors clearly define and maintain ethical, professional, and social relationship boundaries with their students and supervisees. They are aware of the differential in power that exists and the student's or supervisee's possible incomprehension of that power differential. Counselors explain to students and supervisees the potential for the relationship to become exploitive.

(c) Sexual Relationships. Counselors do not engage in sexual relationships with students or supervisees and do not subject them to sexual harassment. (See A.6. and C.5.b)

(d) Contributions to Research. Counselors give credit to students or supervisees for their contributions to research and scholarly projects. Credit is given through coauthorship, acknowledgment, footnote statement, or other appropriate means, in accordance with such contributions. (See G.4.b. and G.4.c.)

(e) Close Relatives. Counselors do not accept close relatives as students or supervisees.

(f) Supervision Preparation. Counselors who offer clinical supervision services are adequately prepared in supervision methods and techniques. Counselors who are doctoral students serving as practicum or internship supervisors to master's level students are adequately prepared and supervised by the training program.

(g) Responsibility for Services to Clients. Counselors who supervise the counseling services of others take reasonable measures to ensure that counseling services provided to clients are professional.

(h) Endorsement. Counselors do not endorse students or supervisees for certification, licensure, employment, or completion of an academic or training program if they believe students or supervisees are not qualified for the endorsement. Counselors take reasonable steps to assist students or supervisees who are not qualified for endorsement to become qualified.

F.2. Counselor Education and Training Programs

(a) Orientation. Prior to admission, counselors orient prospective students to the counselor education or training program's expectations, including but not limited to the following: (1) the type and level of skill acquisition required for successful completion of the training, (2) subject matter to be covered, (3) basis for evaluation, (4) training components that encourage self-growth or self-disclosure as part of the training process, (5) the type of supervision settings and requirements of the sites for required clinical field experiences, (6) student and supervisee evaluation and dismissal policies and procedures, and (7) up-to-date employment prospects for graduates.

(b)   Integration of Study and Practice. Counselors establish counselor education and training programs that integrate academic study and supervised practice.

(c)   Evaluation. Counselors clearly state to students and supervisees, in advance of training, the levels of competency expected, appraisal methods, and timing of evaluations for both didactic and experiential components. Counselors provide students and supervisees with periodic performance appraisal and evaluation feedback throughout the training program.

(d)   Teaching Ethics. Counselors make students and supervisees aware of the ethical responsibilities and standards of the profession and the students' and supervisees' ethical responsibilities to the profession. (See C.1. and F.3.e.)

(e)   Peer Relationships. When students or supervisees are assigned to lead counseling groups or provide clinical supervision for their peers, counselors take steps to ensure that students and supervisees placed in these roles do not have personal or adverse relationships with peers and that they understand they have the same ethical obligations as counselor educators, trainers, and supervisors. Counselors make every effort to ensure that the rights of peers are not compromised when students or supervisees are assigned to lead counseling groups or provide clinical supervision.

(f)   Varied Theoretical Positions. Counselors present varied theoretical positions so that students and supervisees may make comparisons and have opportunities to develop their own positions. Counselors provide information concerning the scientific bases of professional practice. (See C.6.a.)

(g)   Field Placements. Counselors develop clear policies within their training program regarding field placement and other clinical experiences. Counselors provide clearly stated roles and responsibilities for the student or supervisee, the site supervisor, and the program supervisor. They confirm that site supervisors are qualified to provide supervision and are informed of their professional and ethical responsibilities in this role.

(h)   Dual Relationships as Supervisors. Counselors avoid dual relationships such as performing the role of site supervisor and training program supervisor in the student's or supervisee's training program. Counselors do not accept any form of professional services, fees, commissions, reimbursement, or remuneration from a site for student or supervisee placement.

(i)   Diversity in Programs. Counselors are responsive to their institution's and program's recruitment and retention needs for training program administrators, faculty, and students with diverse backgrounds and special needs. (See A.2.a.)

F.3. Students and Supervisees

(a)   Limitations. Counselors, through ongoing evaluation and appraisal, are aware of the academic and personal limitations of students and supervisees that might impede performance. Counselors assist students and supervisees in securing remedial assistance when needed, and dismiss from the training program supervisees who are unable to provide competent service due to academic or personal limitations. Counselors seek professional consultation and document their decision to dismiss or refer students or supervisees for assistance. Counselors ensure that students and supervisees have recourse to address decisions made to require them to seek assistance or to dismiss them.

(b)   Self-Growth Experiences. Counselors use professional judgment when designing training experiences conducted by the counselors themselves that require student and supervisee self-growth or self-disclosure. Safeguards are provided so that students and supervisees are aware of the ramifications their self-disclosure may have on counselors whose primary role as teacher, trainer, or supervisor requires acting on ethical obligations to the profession. Evaluative components of experiential training experiences explicitly delineate predetermined academic standards that are separate and do not depend on the student's level of self-disclosure. (See A.6.)

(c) Counseling for Students and Supervisees. If students or supervisees request counseling, supervisors or counselor educators provide them with acceptable referrals. Supervisors or counselor educators do not serve as counselor to students or supervisees over whom they hold administrative, teaching, or evaluative roles unless this is a brief role associated with a training experience. (See A.6.b.)

(d) Clients of Students and Supervisees. Counselors make every effort to ensure that the clients at field placements are aware of the services rendered and the qualifications of the students and supervisees rendering those services. Clients receive professional disclosure information and are informed of the limits of confidentiality. Client permission is obtained in order for the students and supervisees to use any information concerning the counseling relationship in the training process. (See B.1.e.)

(e) Standards for Students and Supervisees. Students and supervisees preparing to become counselors adhere to the Code of Ethics and the Standards of Practice. Students and supervisees have the same obligations to clients as those required of counselors. (See H.1.)

SECTION G: RESEARCH AND PUBLICATION

G.1. Research Responsibilities

(a) Use of Human Subjects. Counselors plan, design, conduct, and report research in a manner consistent with pertinent ethical principles, federal and state laws, host institutional regulations, and scientific standards governing research with human subjects. Counselors design and conduct research that reflects cultural sensitivity appropriateness.

(b) Deviation From Standard Practices. Counselors seek consultation and observe stringent safeguards to protect the rights of research participants when a research problem suggests a deviation from standard acceptable practices. (See B.6.)

(c) Precautions to Avoid Injury. Counselors who conduct research with human subjects are responsible for the subjects' welfare throughout the experiment and take reasonable precautions to avoid causing injurious psychological, physical, or social effects to their subjects.

(d) Principal Researcher Responsibility. The ultimate responsibility for ethical research practice lies with the principal researcher. All others involved in the research activities share ethical obligations and full responsibility for their own actions.

(e) Minimal Interference. Counselors take reasonable precautions to avoid causing disruptions in subjects' lives due to participation in research.

(f) Diversity. Counselors are sensitive to diversity and research issues with special populations. They seek consultation when appropriate. (See A.2.a. and B.6.)

G.2. Informed Consent

(a) Topics Disclosed. In obtaining informed consent for research, counselors use language that is understandable to research participants and that (1) accurately explains the purpose and procedures to be followed; (2) identifies any procedures that are experimental or relatively untried; (3) describes the attendant discomforts and risks; (4) describes the benefits or changes in individuals or organizations that might be reasonably expected; (5) discloses appropriate alternative procedures that would be advantageous for subjects; (6) offers to answer any inquiries concerning the procedures; (7) describes any limitations on confidentiality; and (8) instructs that subjects are free to withdraw their consent and to discontinue participation in the project at any time. (See B.1.f.)

(b)   Deception. Counselors do not conduct research involving deception unless alternative procedures are not feasible and the prospective value of the research justifies the deception. When the methodological requirements of a study necessitate concealment or deception, the investigator is required to explain clearly the reasons for this action as soon as possible.

(c)   Voluntary Participation. Participation in research is typically voluntary and without any penalty for refusal to participate. Involuntary participation is appropriate only when it can be demonstrated that participation will have no harmful effects on subjects and is essential to the investigation.

(d)   Confidentiality of Information. Information obtained about research participants during the course of an investigation is confidential. When the possibility exists that others may obtain access to such information, ethical research practice requires that the possibility, together with the plans for protecting confidentiality, be explained to participants as a part of the procedure for obtaining informed consent. (See B.1.e.)

(e)   Persons Incapable of Giving Informed Consent. When a person is incapable of giving informed consent, counselors provide an appropriate explanation, obtain agreement for participation, and obtain appropriate consent from a legally authorized person.

(f)   Commitments to Participants. Counselors take reasonable measures to honor all commitments to research participants.

(g)   Explanations After Data Collection. After data are collected, counselors provide participants with full clarification of the nature of the study to remove any misconceptions. Where scientific or human values justify delaying or withholding information, counselors take reasonable measures to avoid causing harm.

(h)   Agreements to Cooperate. Counselors who agree to cooperate with another individual in research or publication incur an obligation to cooperate as promised in terms of punctuality of performance and with regard to the completeness and accuracy of the information required.

(i)   Informed Consent for Sponsors. In the pursuit of research, counselors give sponsors, institutions, and publication channels the same respect and opportunity for giving informed consent that they accord to individual research participants. Counselors are aware of their obligation to future research workers and ensure that host institutions are given feedback information and proper acknowledgment.

G.3. Reporting Results

(a)   Information Affecting Outcome. When reporting research results, counselors explicitly mention all variables and conditions known to the investigator that may have affected the outcome of a study or the interpretation of data.

(b)   Accurate Results. Counselors plan, conduct, and report research accurately and in a manner that minimizes the possibility that results will be misleading. They provide thorough discussions of the limitations of their data and alternative hypotheses. Counselors do not engage in fraudulent research, distort data, misrepresent data, or deliberately bias their results.

(c)   Obligation to Report Unfavorable Results. Counselors communicate to other counselors the results of any research judged to be of professional value. Results that reflect unfavorably on institutions, programs, services, prevailing opinions, or vested interests are not withheld.

(d) Identity of Subjects. Counselors who supply data, aid in the research of another person, report research results, or make original data available take due care to disguise the identity of respective subjects in the absence of specific authorization from the subjects to do otherwise. (See B.1.g. and B.5.a.)

(e) Replication Studies. Counselors are obligated to make available sufficient original research data to qualified professionals who may wish to replicate the study.

G.4. Publication

(a) Recognition of Others. When conducting and reporting research, counselors are familiar with and give recognition to previous work on the topic, observe copyright laws, and give full credit to those to whom credit is due. (See F.1.d. and G.4.c.)

(b) Contributors. Counselors give credit through joint authorship, acknowledgment, footnote statements, or other appropriate means to those who have contributed significantly to research or concept development in accordance with such contributions. The principal contributor is listed first and minor technical or professional contributions are acknowledged in notes or introductory statements.

(c) Student Research. For an article that is substantially based on a student's dissertation or thesis, the student is listed as the principal author. (See F.1.d. and G.4.a.)

(d) Duplicate Submission. Counselors submit manuscripts for consideration to only one journal at a time. Manuscripts that are published in whole or in substantial part in another journal or published work are not submitted for publication without acknowledgment and permission from the previous publication.

(e) Professional Review. Counselors who review material submitted for publication, research, or other scholarly purposes respect the confidentiality and proprietary rights of those who submitted it.

SECTION H: RESOLVING ETHICAL ISSUES

H.1. Knowledge of Standards

Counselors are familiar with the Code of Ethics and the Standards of Practice and other applicable ethics codes from other professional organizations of which they are member, or from certification and licensure bodies. Lack of knowledge or misunderstanding of an ethical responsibility is not a defense against a charge of unethical conduct. (See F.3.e.)

H.2. Suspected Violations

(a) Ethical Behavior Expected. Counselors expect professional associates to adhere to the Code of Ethics. When counselors possess reasonable cause that raises doubts as to whether a counselor is acting in an ethical manner, they take appropriate action. (See H.2.d. and H.2.e.)

(b) Consultation. When uncertain as to whether a particular situation or course of action may be in violation of the Code of Ethics, counselors consult with other counselors who are knowledgeable about ethics, with colleagues, or with appropriate authorities.

(c) Organization Conflicts. If the demands of an organization with which counselors are affiliated pose a conflict with the Code of Ethics, counselors specify the nature of such conflicts and express to their supervisors or other responsible officials their commitment to the Code of Ethics. When possible, counselors work toward change within the organization to allow full adherence to the Code of Ethics.

(d)   Informal Resolution. When counselors have reasonable cause to believe that another counselor is violating an ethical standard, they attempt to first resolve the issue informally with the other counselor if feasible, providing that such action does not violate confidentiality rights that may be involved.

(e)   Reporting Suspected Violations. When an informal resolution is not appropriate or feasible, counselors, upon reasonable cause, take action such as reporting the suspected ethical violation to state or national ethics committees, unless this action conflicts with confidentiality rights that cannot be resolved.

(f)   Unwarranted Complaints. Counselors do not initiate, participate in, or encourage the filing of ethics complaints that are unwarranted or intend to harm a counselor rather than to protect clients or the public.

H.3. Cooperation With Ethics Committees

Counselors assist in the process of enforcing the Code of Ethics. Counselors cooperate with investigations, proceedings, and requirements of the ACA Ethics Committee or ethics committees of other duly constituted associations or boards having jurisdiction over those charged with a violation. Counselors are familiar with the ACA Policies and Procedures and use it as a reference in assisting the enforcement of the Code of Ethics.

STANDARDS OF PRACTICE

All members of the American Counseling Association (ACA) are required to adhere to the Standards of Practice and the Code of Ethics. The Standards of Practice represent minimal behavioral statements of the Code of Ethics. Members should refer to the applicable section of the Code of Ethics for further interpretation and amplification of the applicable Standards of Practice.

SECTION A: THE COUNSELING RELATIONSHIP

Standard of Practice One (SP-1): Nondiscrimination.

Counselors respect diversity and must not discriminate against clients because of age, color, culture, disability, ethnic group, gender, race, religion, sexual orientation, marital status, or socioeconomic status. (See A.2.a.)

Standard of Practice Two (SP-2): Disclosure to Clients.

Counselors must adequately inform clients, preferably in writing, regarding the counseling process and counseling relationship at or before the time it begins and throughout the relationship. (See A.3.a.)

Standard of Practice Three (SP-3): Dual Relationships.

Counselors must make every effort to avoid dual relationships with clients that could impair their professional judgment or increase the risk of harm to clients. When a dual relationship cannot be avoided, counselors must take appropriate steps to ensure that judgment is not impaired and that no exploitation occurs. (See A.6.a. and A.6.b.)

Standard of Practice Four (SP-4): Sexual Intimacies With Clients.

Counselors must not engage in any type of sexual intimacies with current clients and must not engage in sexual intimacies with former clients within a minimum of 2 years after terminating the counseling relationship. Counselors who engage in such relationship after 2 years following termination have the responsibility to examine and document thoroughly that such relations did not have an exploitative nature.

Standard of Practice Five (SP-5): Protecting Clients During Group Work.

> Counselors must take steps to protect clients from physical or psychological trauma resulting from interactions during group work. (See A.9.b.)

Standard of Practice Six (SP-6): Advance Understanding of Fees.

> Counselors must explain to clients, prior to their entering the counseling relationship, financial arrangements related to professional services. (See A.10. a.-d. and A.11.c.)

Standard of Practice Seven (SP-7): Termination.

> Counselors must assist in making appropriate arrangements for the continuation of treatment of clients, when necessary, following termination of counseling relationships. (See A.11.a.)

Standard of Practice Eight (SP-8): Inability to Assist Clients.

> Counselors must avoid entering or immediately terminate a counseling relationship if it is determined that they are unable to be of professional assistance to a client. The counselor may assist in making an appropriate referral for the client. (See A.11.b.)

SECTION B: CONFIDENTIALITY

Standard of Practice Nine (SP-9): Confidentiality Requirement.

> Counselors must keep information related to counseling services confidential unless disclosure is in the best interest of clients, is required for the welfare of others, or is required by law. When disclosure is required, only information that is essential is revealed and the client is informed of such disclosure. (See B.1. a.+f.)

Standard of Practice Ten (SP-10): Confidentiality Requirements for Subordinates.

> Counselors must take measures to ensure that privacy and confidentiality of clients are maintained by subordinates. (See B.1.h.)

Standard of Practice Eleven (SP-11): Confidentiality in Group Work.

> Counselors must clearly communicate to group members that confidentiality cannot be guaranteed in group work. (See B.2.a.)

Standard of Practice Twelve (SP-12): Confidentiality in Family Counseling.

> Counselors must not disclose information about one family member in counseling to another family member without prior consent. (See B.2.b.)

Standard of Practice Thirteen (SP-13): Confidentiality of Records.

> Counselors must maintain appropriate confidentiality in creating, storing, accessing, transferring, and disposing of counseling records. (See B.4.b.)

Standard of Practice Fourteen (SP-14): Permission to Record or Observe.

> Counselors must obtain prior consent from clients in order to record electronically or observe sessions. (See B.4.c.)

Standard of Practice Fifteen (SP-15): Disclosure or Transfer of Records.

> Counselors must obtain client consent to disclose or transfer records to third parties, unless exceptions listed in SP-9 exist. (See B.4.e.)

Standard of Practice Sixteen (SP-16): Data Disguise Required.

> Counselors must disguise the identity of the client when using data for training, research, or publication. (See B.5.a.)

SECTION C: PROFESSIONAL RESPONSIBILITY

Standard of Practice Seventeen (SP-17): Boundaries of Competence.

> Counselors must practice only within the boundaries of their competence. (See C.2.a.)

Standard of Practice Eighteen (SP-18): Continuing Education.

> Counselors must engage in continuing education to maintain their professional competence. (See C.2.f.)

Standard of Practice Nineteen (SP-19): Impairment of Professionals.

> Counselors must refrain from offering professional services when their personal problems or conflicts may cause harm to a client or others. (See C.2.g.)

Standard of Practice Twenty (SP-20): Accurate Advertising.

> Counselors must accurately represent their credentials and services when advertising. (See C.3.a.)

Standard of Practice Twenty-One (SP-21): Recruiting Through Employment.

> Counselors must not use their place of employment or institutional affiliation to recruit clients for their private practices. (See C.3.d.)

Standard of Practice Twenty-Two (SP-22): Credentials Claimed.

> Counselors must claim or imply only professional credentials possessed and must correct any known misrepresentations of their credentials by others. (See C.4.a.)

Standard of Practice Twenty-Three (SP-23): Sexual Harassment.

> Counselors must not engage in sexual harassment. (See C.5.b.)

Standard of Practice Twenty-Four (SP-24): Unjustified Gains.

> Counselors must not use their professional positions to seek or receive unjustified personal gains, sexual favors, unfair advantage, or unearned goods or services. (See C.5.e.)

Standard of Practice Twenty-Five (SP-25): Clients Served by Others.

> With the consent of the client, counselors must inform other mental health professionals serving the same client that a counseling relationship between the counselor and client exists. (See C.6.c.)

Standard of Practice Twenty-Six (SP-26): Negative Employment Conditions.

> Counselors must alert their employers to institutional policy or conditions that may be potentially disruptive or damaging to the counselor's professional responsibilities, or that may limit their effectiveness or deny clients' rights. (See D.1.c.)

Standard of Practice Twenty-Seven (SP-27): Personnel Selection and Assignment.

> Counselors must select competent staff and must assign responsibilities compatible with staff skills and experiences. (See D.1.h.)

Standard of Practice Twenty-Eight (SP-28): Exploitative Relationships With Subordinates.

Counselors must not engage in exploitative relationships with individuals over whom they have supervisory, evaluative, or instructional control or authority. (See D.1.k.)

SECTION D: RELATIONSHIP WITH OTHER PROFESSIONALS

Standard of Practice Twenty-Nine (SP-29): Accepting Fees From Agency Clients.

Counselors must not accept fees or other remuneration for consultation with persons entitled to such services through the counselor's employing agency or institution. (See D.3.a.)

Standard of Practice Thirty (SP-30): Referral Fees.

Counselors must not accept referral fees. (See D.3.b.)

SECTION E: EVALUATION, ASSESMENT AND INTERPRETATION

Standard of Practice Thirty-One (SP-31): Limits of Competence.

Counselors must perform only testing and assessment services for which they are competent. Counselors must not allow the use of psychological assessment techniques by unqualified persons under their supervision. (See E.2.a.)

Standard of Practice Thirty-Two (SP-32): Appropriate Use of Assessment Instruments.

Counselors must use assessment instruments in the manner for which they were intended. (See E.2.b.)

Standard of Practice Thirty-Three (SP-33): Assessment Explanations to Clients.

Counselors must provide explanations to clients prior to assessment about the nature and purposes of assessment and the specific uses of results. (See E.3.a.)

Standard of Practice Thirty-Four (SP-34): Recipients of Test Results.

Counselors must ensure that accurate and appropriate interpretations accompany any release of testing and assessment information. (See E.3.b.)

Standard of Practice Thirty-Five (SP-35): Obsolete Tests and Outdated Test Results.

Counselors must not base their assessment or intervention decisions or recommendations on data or test results that are obsolete or outdated for the current purpose. (See E.11.)

SECTION F: TEACHING, TRAINING, AND SUPERVISION

Standard of Practice Thirty-Six (SP-36): Sexual Relationships With Students or Supervisees.

Counselors must not engage in sexual relationships with their students and supervisees. (See F.1.c.)

Standard of Practice Thirty-Seven (SP-37): Credit for Contributions to Research.

Counselors must give credit to students or supervisees for their contributions to research and scholarly projects. (See F.1.d.)

Standard of Practice Thirty-Eight (SP-38): Supervision Preparation.

Counselors who offer clinical supervision services must be trained and prepared in supervision methods and techniques. (See F.1.f.)

Standard of Practice Thirty-Nine (SP-39): Evaluation Information.

> Counselors must clearly state to students and supervisees in advance of training the levels of competency expected, appraisal methods, and timing of evaluations. Counselors must provide students and supervisees with periodic performance appraisal and evaluation feedback throughout the training program. (See F.2.c.)

Standard of Practice Forty (SP-40): Peer Relationships in Training.

> Counselors must make every effort to ensure that the rights of peers are not violated when students and supervisees are assigned to lead counseling groups or provide clinical supervision. (See F.2.e.)

Standard of Practice Forty-One (SP-41): Limitations of Students and Supervisees.

> Counselors must assist students and supervisees in securing remedial assistance, when needed, and must dismiss from the training program students and supervisees who are unable to provide competent service due to academic or personal limitations. (See F.3.a.)

Standard of Practice Forty-Two (SP-42): Self-Growth Experiences.

> Counselors who conduct experiences for students or supervisees that include self-growth or self-disclosure must inform participants of counselors' ethical obligations to the profession and must not grade participants based on their nonacademic performance. (See F.3.b.)

Standard of Practice Forty-Three (SP-43): Standards for Students and Supervisees.

> Students and supervisees preparing to become counselors must adhere to the Code of Ethics and the Standards of Practice of counselors. (See F.3.e.)

SECTION G: RESEARCH AND PUBLICATION

Standard of Practice Forty-Four (SP-44): Precautions to Avoid Injury in Research.

> Counselors must avoid causing physical, social, or psychological harm or injury to subjects in research. (See G.1.c.)

Standard of Practice Forty-Five (SP-45): Confidentiality of Research Information.

> Counselors must keep confidential information obtained about research participants. (See G.2.d.)

Standard of Practice Forty-Six (SP-46): Information Affecting Research Outcome.

> Counselors must report all variables and conditions known to the investigator that may have affected research data or outcomes. (See G.3.a.)

Standard of Practice Forty-Seven (SP-47): Accurate Research Results.

> Counselors must not distort or misrepresent research data, nor fabricate or intentionally bias research results. (See G.3.b.)

Standard of Practice Forty-Eight (SP-48): Publication Contributors.

> Counselors must give appropriate credit to those who have contributed to research. (See G.4.a. and G.4.b.)

SECTION H: RESOLVING ETHICAL ISSUES

Standard of Practice Forty-Nine (SP-49): Ethical Behavior Expected.

Counselors must take appropriate action when they possess reasonable cause that raises doubts as to whether counselors or other mental health professionals are acting in an ethical manner. (See H.2.a.)

Standard of Practice Fifty (SP-50): Unwarranted Complaints.

Counselors must not initiate, participate in, or encourage the filing of ethics complaints that are unwarranted or intended to harm a mental health professional rather than to protect clients or the public. (See H.2.f.)

Standard of Practice Fifty-One (SP-51): Cooperation With Ethics Committees.

Counselors must cooperate with investigations, proceedings, and requirements of the ACA Ethics Committee or ethics committees of other duly constituted associations or boards having jurisdiction over those charged with a violation. (See H.3.)

APPENDIX B

Ethical Principles of Psychologists and *Code of Conduct,* American Psychological Association (APA)

INTRODUCTION

The American Psychological Association's (APA's) Ethical Principles of Psychologists and Code of Conduct (hereinafter referred to as the Ethics Code) consists of an Introduction, a Preamble, six General Principles (A–F), and specific Ethical Standards. The Introduction discusses the intent, organization, procedural considerations, and scope of application of the Ethics Code. The Preamble and General Principles are aspirational goals to guide psychologists toward the highest ideals of psychology. Although the Preamble and General Principles are not themselves enforceable rules, they should be considered by psychologists in arriving at an ethical course of action and may be considered by ethics bodies in interpreting the Ethical Standards. The Ethical Standards set forth enforceable rules for conduct as psychologists. Most of the Ethical Standards are written broadly, in order to apply to psychologists in varied roles, although the application of an Ethical Standard may vary depending on the context. The Ethical Standards are not exhaustive. The fact that a given conduct is not specifically addressed by the Ethics Code does not mean that it is necessarily either ethical or unethical.

Membership in the APA commits members to adhere to the APA Ethics Code and to the rules and procedures used to implement it. Psychologists and students, whether or not they are APA members, should be aware that the Ethics Code may be applied to them by state psychology boards, courts, or other public bodies.

This Ethics Code applies only to psychologists' work-related activities, that is, activities that are part of the psychologists' scientific and professional functions or that are psychological in nature. It includes the clinical or counseling practice of psychology, research, teaching, supervision of trainees, development of assessment instruments, conducting assessments, educational counseling, organizational consulting, social intervention, administration, and other activities as well. These work-related activities can be distinguished from the purely private conduct of a psychologist, which ordinarily is not within the purview of the Ethics Code.

The Ethics Code is intended to provide standards of professional conduct that can be applied by the APA and by other bodies that choose to adopt them. Whether or not a psychologist has violated the Ethics Code does not by itself determine whether he or she is legally liable in a court action, whether a contract is enforceable, or whether other legal consequences occur. These results are based on legal rather than ethical rules. However, compliance with or violation of the Ethics Code may be admissible as evidence in some legal proceedings, depending on the circumstances.

In the process of making decisions regarding their professional behavior, psychologists must consider this Ethics Code, in addition to applicable laws and psychology board regulations. If the Ethics Code establishes a higher standard of conduct than is required by law, psychologists must meet the higher ethical standard. If the Ethics Code standard appears to conflict with the requirements of law, then psychologists make known their commitment to the Ethics Code and take steps to resolve the conflict in a responsible manner. If neither law nor the Ethics Code resolves an issue, psychologists should consider other professional materials[1] and the dictates of their own conscience, as well as seek consultation with others within the field when this is practical.

The procedures for filing, investigating, and resolving complaints of unethical conduct are described in the current Rules and Procedures of the APA Ethics Committee. The actions that APA may take for violations of the Ethics Code include actions such as reprimand, censure, termination of APA membership, and referral of the matter to other bodies. Complainants who seek remedies such as monetary damages in alleging ethical violations by a psychologist must resort to private negotiation, administrative bodies, or the courts. Actions that violate the Ethics Code may lead to the imposition of sanctions on a psychologist by bodies other than APA, including state psychological associations, other professional groups, psychology boards, other state or federal agencies, and payors for health services. In addition to actions for violation of the Ethics Code, the APA Bylaws provide that APA may take action against a member after his or her conviction of a felony, expulsion or suspension from an affiliated state psychological association, or suspension or loss of licensure.

PREAMBLE

Psychologists work to develop a valid and reliable body of scientific knowledge based on research. They may apply that knowledge to human behavior in a variety of contexts. In doing so, they perform many roles, such as researcher, educator, diagnostician, therapist, supervisor, consultant, administrator, social interventionist, and expert witness. Their goal is to broaden knowledge of behavior and, where appropriate, to apply it pragmatically to improve the condition of both the individual and society. Psychologists

---

[1]Professional materials that are most helpful in this regard are guidelines and standards that have been adopted or endorsed by professional psychological organizations. Such guidelines and standards, whether adopted by the American Psychological Association (APA) or its Divisions, are not enforceable as such by this Ethics Code, but are of educative value to psychologists, courts, and professional bodies. Such materials include, but are not limited to, the APA's General Guidelines for Providers of Psychological Services (1987), Specialty Guidelines for the Delivery of Services by Clinical Psychologists, Counseling Psychologists, Industrial/Organizational Psychologists, and School Psychologists (1981), Guidelines for Computer Based Tests and Interpretations (1987), Standards for Educational and Psychological Testing (1985), Ethical Principles in the Conduct of Research With Human Participants (1982), Guidelines for Ethical Conduct in the Care and Use of Animals (1986), Guidelines for Providers of Psychological Services to Ethnic, Linguistic, and Culturally Diverse Populations (1990), and Publication Manual of the American Psychological Association (3rd ed., 1983). Materials not adopted by APA as a whole include the APA Division 41 (Forensic Psychology)/American Psychology-Law Society's Specialty Guidelines for Forensic Psychologists (1991).

respect the central importance of freedom of inquiry and expression in research, teaching, and publication. They also strive to help the public in developing informed judgments and choices concerning human behavior. This Ethics Code provides a common set of values upon which psychologists build their professional and scientific work.

This Code is intended to provide both the general principles and the decision rules to cover most situations encountered by psychologists. It has as its primary goal the welfare and protection of the individuals and groups with whom psychologists work. It is the individual responsibility of each psychologist to aspire to the highest possible standards of conduct. Psychologists respect and protect human and civil rights, and do not knowingly participate in or condone unfair discriminatory practices.

The development of a dynamic set of ethical standards for a psychologist's work-related conduct requires a personal commitment to a lifelong effort to act ethically; to encourage ethical behavior by students, supervisees, employees, and colleagues, as appropriate; and to consult with others, as needed, concerning ethical problems. Each psychologist supplements, but does not violate, the Ethics Code's values and rules on the basis of guidance drawn from personal values, culture, and experience.

GENERAL PRINCIPLES
PRINCIPLE A: COMPETENCE
Psychologists strive to maintain high standards of competence in their work. They recognize the boundaries of their particular competencies and the limitations of their expertise. They provide only those services and use only those techniques for which they are qualified by education, training, or experience. Psychologists are cognizant of the fact that the competencies required in serving, teaching, and/or studying groups of people vary with the distinctive characteristics of those groups. In those areas in which recognized professional standards do not yet exist, psychologists exercise careful judgment and take appropriate precautions to protect the welfare of those with whom they work. They maintain knowledge of relevant scientific and professional information related to the services they render, and they recognize the need for ongoing education. Psychologists make appropriate use of scientific, professional, technical, and administrative resources.

PRINCIPLE B: INTEGRITY
Psychologists seek to promote integrity in the science, teaching, and practice of psychology. In these activities psychologists are honest, fair, and respectful of others. In describing or reporting their qualifications, services, products, fees, research, or teaching, they do not make statements that are false, misleading, or deceptive. Psychologists strive to be aware of their own belief systems, values, needs, and limitations and the effect of these on their work. To the extent feasible, they attempt to clarify for relevant parties the roles they are performing and to function appropriately in accordance with those roles. Psychologists avoid improper and potentially harmful dual relationships.

PRINCIPLE C: PROFESSIONAL AND SCIENTIFIC RESPONSIBILITY
Psychologists uphold professional standards of conduct, clarify their professional roles and obligations, accept appropriate responsibility for their behavior, and adapt their methods to the needs of different populations. Psychologists consult with, refer to, or cooperate with other professionals and institutions to the extent needed to serve the best interests of their patients, clients, or other recipients of their services. Psychologists' moral standards and conduct are personal matters to the same degree as is true for any other person, except as psychologists' conduct may compromise their professional responsibilities or reduce the public's trust in psychology and psychologists. Psychologists are concerned

about the ethical compliance of their colleagues' scientific and professional conduct. When appropriate, they consult with colleagues in order to prevent or avoid unethical conduct.

PRINCIPLE D: RESPECT FOR PEOPLE'S RIGHTS AND DIGNITY

Psychologists accord appropriate respect to the fundamental rights, dignity, and worth of all people. They respect the rights of individuals to privacy, confidentiality, self-determination, and autonomy, mindful that legal and other obligations may lead to inconsistency and conflict with the exercise of these rights. Psychologists are aware of cultural, individual, and role differences, including those due to age, gender, race, ethnicity, national origin, religion, sexual orientation, disability, language, and socioeconomic status. Psychologists try to eliminate the effect on their work of biases based on those factors, and they do not knowingly participate in or condone unfair discriminatory practices.

PRINCIPLE E: CONCERN FOR OTHERS' WELFARE

Psychologists seek to contribute to the welfare of those with whom they interact professionally. In their professional actions, psychologists weigh the welfare and rights of their patients or clients, students, supervisees, human research participants, and other affected persons, and the welfare of animal subjects of research. When conflicts occur among psychologists' obligations or concerns, they attempt to resolve these conflicts and to perform their roles in a responsible fashion that avoids or minimizes harm. Psychologists are sensitive to real and ascribed differences in power between themselves and others, and they do not exploit or mislead other people during or after professional relationships.

PRINCIPLE F: SOCIAL RESPONSIBILITY

Psychologists are aware of their professional and scientific responsibilities to the community and the society in which they work and live. They apply and make public their knowledge of psychology in order to contribute to human welfare. Psychologists are concerned about and work to mitigate the causes of human suffering. When undertaking research, they strive to advance human welfare and the science of psychology. Psychologists try to avoid misuse of their work. Psychologists comply with the law and encourage the development of law and social policy that serve the interests of their patients and clients and the public. They are encouraged to contribute a portion of their professional time for little or no personal advantage.

ETHICAL STANDARDS
1. GENERAL STANDARDS

These General Standards are potentially applicable to the professional and scientific activities of all psychologists.

1.01 Applicability of the Ethics Code.

The activity of a psychologist subject to the Ethics Code may be reviewed under these Ethical Standards only if the activity is part of his or her work-related functions or the activity is psychological in nature. Personal activities having no connection to or effect on psychological roles are not subject to the Ethics Code.

1.02 Relationship of Ethics and Law.

If psychologists' ethical responsibilities conflict with law, psychologists make known their commitment to the Ethics Code and take steps to resolve the conflict in a responsible manner.

1.03 Professional and Scientific Relationship.

Psychologists provide diagnostic, therapeutic, teaching, research, supervisory, consultative, or other psychological services only in the context of a defined professional or scientific relationship or role. (See also Standards 2.01, Evaluation, Diagnosis, and Interventions in Professional Context, and 7.02, Forensic Assessments.)

1.04 Boundaries of Competence.

(a)   Psychologists provide services, teach, and conduct research only within the boundaries of their competence, based on their education, training, supervised experience, or appropriate professional experience.

(b)   Psychologists provide services, teach, or conduct research in new areas or involving new techniques only after first undertaking appropriate study, training, supervision, and/or consultation from persons who are competent in those areas or techniques.

(c)   In those emerging areas in which generally recognized standards for preparatory training do not yet exist, psychologists nevertheless take reasonable steps to ensure the competence of their work and to protect patients, clients, students, research participants, and others from harm.

1.05 Maintaining Expertise.

Psychologists who engage in assessment, therapy, teaching, research, organizational consulting, or other professional activities maintain a reasonable level of awareness of current scientific and professional information in their fields of activity, and undertake ongoing efforts to maintain competence in the skills they use.

1.06 Basis for Scientific and Professional Judgments.

Psychologists rely on scientifically and professionally derived knowledge when making scientific or professional judgments or when engaging in scholarly or professional endeavors.

1.07 Describing the Nature and Results of Psychological Services.

(a)   When psychologists provide assessment, evaluation, treatment, counseling, supervision, teaching, consultation, research, or other psychological services to an individual, a group, or an organization, they provide, using language that is reasonably understandable to the recipient of those services, appropriate information beforehand about the nature of such services and appropriate information later about results and conclusions. (See also Standard 2.09, Explaining Assessment Results.)

(b)   If psychologists will be precluded by law or by organizational roles from providing such information to particular individuals or groups, they so inform those individuals or groups at the outset of the service.

1.08 Human Differences.

Where differences of age, gender, race, ethnicity, national origin, religion, sexual orientation, disability, language, or socioeconomic status significantly affect psychologists' work concerning particular individuals or groups, psychologists obtain the training, experience, consultation, or supervision necessary to ensure the competence of their services, or they make appropriate referrals.

1.09 Respecting Others.

In their work-related activities, psychologists respect the rights of others to hold values, attitudes, and opinions that differ from their own.

1.10 Nondiscrimination.

In their work-related activities, psychologists do not engage in unfair discrimination based on age, gender, race, ethnicity, national origin, religion, sexual orientation, disability, socioeconomic status, or any basis proscribed by law.

1.11 Sexual Harassment.

(a)   Psychologists do not engage in sexual harassment. Sexual harassment is sexual solicitation, physical advances, or verbal or nonverbal conduct that is sexual in nature, that occurs in connection with the psychologist's activities or roles as a psychologist, and that either: (1) is unwelcome, is offensive, or creates a hostile workplace environment, and the psychologist knows or is told this; or (2) is sufficiently severe or intense to be abusive to a reasonable person in the context. Sexual harassment can consist of a single intense or severe act or of multiple persistent or pervasive acts.

(b)   Psychologists accord sexual-harassment complainants and respondents dignity and respect. Psychologists do not participate in denying a person academic admittance or advancement, employment, tenure, or promotion, based solely upon their having made, or their being the subject of, sexual harassment charges. This does not preclude taking action based upon the outcome of such proceedings or consideration of other appropriate information.

1.12 Other Harassment.

Psychologists do not knowingly engage in behavior that is harassing or demeaning to persons with whom they interact in their work based on factors such as those persons' age, gender, race, ethnicity, national origin, religion, sexual orientation, disability, language, or socioeconomic status.

1.13 Personal Problems and Conflicts.

(a)   Psychologists recognize that their personal problems and conflicts may interfere with their effectiveness. Accordingly, they refrain from undertaking an activity when they know or should know that their personal problems are likely to lead to harm to a patient, client, colleague, student, research participant, or other person to whom they may owe a professional or scientific obligation.

(b)   In addition, psychologists have an obligation to be alert to signs of, and to obtain assistance for, their personal problems at an early stage, in order to prevent significantly impaired performance.

(c)   When psychologists become aware of personal problems that may interfere with their performing work-related duties adequately, they take appropriate measures, such as obtaining professional consultation or assistance, and determine whether they should limit, suspend, or terminate their work-related duties.

1.14 Avoiding Harm.

Psychologists take reasonable steps to avoid harming their patients or clients, research participants, students, and others with whom they work, and to minimize harm where it is foreseeable and unavoidable.

1.15 Misuse of Psychologists' Influence.

Because psychologists' scientific and professional judgments and actions may affect the lives of others, they are alert to and guard against personal, financial, social, organizational, or political factors that might lead to misuse of their influence.

1.16 Misuse of Psychologists' Work.

(a) Psychologists do not participate in activities in which it appears likely that their skills or data will be misused by others, unless corrective mechanisms are available. (See also Standard 7.04, Truthfulness and Candor.)

(b) If psychologists learn of misuse or misrepresentation of their work, they take reasonable steps to correct or minimize the misuse or misrepresentation.

1.17 Multiple Relationships.

(a) In many communities and situations, it may not be feasible or reasonable for psychologists to avoid social or other nonprofessional contacts with persons such as patients, clients, students, supervisees, or research participants. Psychologists must always be sensitive to the potential harmful effects of other contacts on their work and on those persons with whom they deal. A psychologist refrains from entering into or promising another personal, scientific, professional, financial, or other relationship with such persons if it appears likely that such a relationship reasonably might impair the psychologist's objectivity or otherwise interfere with the psychologist's effectively performing his or her functions as a psychologist, or might harm or exploit the other party.

(b) Likewise, whenever feasible, a psychologist refrains from taking on professional or scientific obligations when pre-existing relationships would create a risk of such harm.

(c) If a psychologist finds that, due to unforeseen factors, a potentially harmful multiple relationship has arisen, the psychologist attempts to resolve it with due regard for the best interests of the affected person and maximal compliance with the Ethics Code.

1.18 Barter (With Patients or Clients).

Psychologists ordinarily refrain from accepting goods, services, or other nonmonetary remuneration from patients or clients in return for psychological services because such arrangements create inherent potential for conflicts, exploitation, and distortion of the professional relationship. A psychologist may participate in bartering only if (1) it is not clinically contraindicated, and (2) the relationship is not exploitative. (See also Standards 1.17, Multiple Relationships, and 1.25, Fees and Financial Arrangements.)

1.19 Exploitative Relationships.

(a) Psychologists do not exploit persons over whom they have supervisory, evaluative, or other authority such as students, supervisees, employees, research participants, and clients or patients. (See also Standards 4.05–4.07 regarding sexual involvement with clients or patients.)

(b) Psychologists do not engage in sexual relationships with students or supervisees in training over whom the psychologist has evaluative or direct authority, because such relationships are so likely to impair judgment or be exploitative.

1.20 Consultations and Referrals.

(a) Psychologists arrange for appropriate consultations and referrals based principally on the best interests of their patients or clients, with appropriate consent, and subject to other relevant considerations, including applicable law and contractual obligations. (See also Standards 5.01, Discussing the Limits of Confidentiality, and 5.06, Consultations.)

(b) When indicated and professionally appropriate, psychologists cooperate with other professionals in order to serve their patients or clients effectively and appropriately.

(c) Psychologists' referral practices are consistent with law.

1.21 Third-Party Requests for Services.

(a) When a psychologist agrees to provide services to a person or entity at the request of a third party, the psychologist clarifies to the extent feasible, at the outset of the service, the nature of the relationship with each party. This clarification includes the role of the psychologist (such as therapist, organizational consultant, diagnostician, or expert witness), the probable uses of the services provided or the information obtained, and the fact that there may be limits to confidentiality.

(b) If there is a foreseeable risk of the psychologist's being called upon to perform conflicting roles because of the involvement of a third party, the psychologist clarifies the nature and direction of his or her responsibilities, keeps all parties appropriately informed as matters develop, and resolves the situation in accordance with this Ethics Code.

1.22 Delegation to and Supervision of Subordinates.

(a) Psychologists delegate to their employees, supervisees, and research assistants only those responsibilities that such persons can reasonably be expected to perform competently, on the basis of their education, training, or experience, either independently or with the level of supervision being provided.

(b) Psychologists provide proper training and supervision to their employees or supervisees and take reasonable steps to see that such persons perform services responsibly, competently, and ethically.

(c) If institutional policies, procedures, or practices prevent fulfillment of this obligation, psychologists attempt to modify their role or to correct the situation to the extent feasible.

1.23 Documentation of Professional and Scientific Work.

(a) Psychologists appropriately document their professional and scientific work in order to facilitate provision of services later by them or by other professionals, to ensure accountability, and to meet other requirements of institutions or the law.

(b) When psychologists have reason to believe that records of their professional services will be used in legal proceedings involving recipients of or participants in their work, they have a responsibility to create and maintain documentation in the kind of detail and quality that would be consistent with reasonable scrutiny in an adjudicative forum. (See also Standard 7.01, Professionalism, under Forensic Activities.)

1.24 Records and Data.

Psychologists create, maintain, disseminate, store, retain, and dispose of records and data relating to their research, practice, and other work in accordance with law and in a manner that permits compliance with the requirements of this Ethics Code. (See also Standard 5.04, Maintenance of Records.)

1.25 Fees and Financial Arrangements.

(a) As early as is feasible in a professional or scientific relationship, the psychologist and the patient, client, or other appropriate recipient of psychological services reach an agreement specifying the compensation and the billing arrangements.

(b) Psychologists do not exploit recipients of services or payors with respect to fees.

(c) Psychologists' fee practices are consistent with law.

(d) Psychologists do not misrepresent their fees.

(e) If limitations to services can be anticipated because of limitations in financing, this is discussed with the patient, client, or other appropriate recipient of services as early as is feasible. (See also Standard 4.08, Interruption of Services.)

(f) If the patient, client, or other recipient of services does not pay for services as agreed, and if the psychologist wishes to use collection agencies or legal measures to collect the fees, the psychologist first informs the person that such measures will be taken and provides that person an opportunity to make prompt payment. (See also Standard 5.11, Withholding Records for Nonpayment.)

1.26 Accuracy in Reports to Payors and Funding Sources.

In their reports to payors for services or sources of research funding, psychologists accurately state the nature of the research or service provided, the fees or charges, and where applicable, the identity of the provider, the findings, and the diagnosis. (See also Standard 5.05, Disclosures.)

1.27 Referrals and Fees.

When a psychologist pays, receives payment from, or divides fees with another professional other than in an employer-employee relationship, the payment to each is based on the services (clinical, consultative, administrative, or other) provided and is not based on the referral itself.

2. EVALUATION, ASSESSMENT, OR INTERVENTION

2.01 Evaluation, Diagnosis, and Interventions in Professional Context.

(a) Psychologists perform evaluations, diagnostic services, or interventions only within the context of a defined professional relationship. (See also Standards 1.03, Professional and Scientific Relationship.)

(b) Psychologists' assessments, recommendations, reports, and psychological diagnostic or evaluative statements are based on information and techniques (including personal interviews of the individual when appropriate) sufficient to provide appropriate substantiation for their findings. (See also Standard 7.02, Forensic Assessments.)

2.02 Competence and Appropriate Use of Assessments and Interventions.

(a) Psychologists who develop, administer, score, interpret, or use psychological assessment techniques, interviews, tests, or instruments do so in a manner and for purposes that are appropriate in light of the research on or evidence of the usefulness and proper application of the techniques.

(b) Psychologists refrain from misuse of assessment techniques, interventions, results, and interpretations and take reasonable steps to prevent others from misusing the information these techniques provide. This includes refraining from releasing raw test results or raw data to persons, other than to patients or clients as appropriate, who are not qualified to use such information. (See also Standards 1.02, Relationship of Ethics and Law, and 1.04, Boundaries of Competence.)

2.03 Test Construction.

Psychologists who develop and conduct research with tests and other assessment techniques use scientific procedures and current professional knowledge for test design, standardization, validation, reduction or elimination of bias, and recommendations for use.

2.04 Use of Assessment in General and With Special Populations.

(a) Psychologists who perform interventions or administer, score, interpret, or use assessment techniques are familiar with the reliability, validation, and related standardization or outcome studies of, and proper applications and uses of, the techniques they use.

(b) Psychologists recognize limits to the certainty with which diagnoses, judgments, or predictions can be made about individuals.

(c) Psychologists attempt to identify situations in which particular interventions or assessment techniques or norms may not be applicable or may require adjustment in administration or interpretation because of factors such as individuals' gender, age, race, ethnicity, national origin, religion, sexual orientation, disability, language, or socioeconomic status.

2.05 Interpreting Assessment Results.

When interpreting assessment results, including automated interpretations, psychologists take into account the various test factors and characteristics of the person being assessed that might affect psychologists' judgments or reduce the accuracy of their interpretations. They indicate any significant reservations they have about the accuracy or limitations of their interpretations.

2.06 Unqualified Persons.

Psychologists do not promote the use of psychological assessment techniques by unqualified persons. (See also Standard 1.22, Delegation to and Supervision of Subordinates.)

2.07 Obsolete Tests and Outdated Test Results.

(a) Psychologists do not base their assessment or intervention decisions or recommendations on data or test results that are outdated for the current purpose.

(b) Similarly, psychologists do not base such decisions or recommendations on tests and measures that are obsolete and not useful for the current purpose.

2.08 Test Scoring and Interpretation Services.

(a) Psychologists who offer assessment or scoring procedures to other professionals accurately describe the purpose, norms, validity, reliability, and applications of the procedures and any special qualifications applicable to their use.

(b) Psychologists select scoring and interpretation services (including automated services) on the basis of evidence of the validity of the program and procedures as well as on other appropriate considerations.

(c) Psychologists retain appropriate responsibility for the appropriate application, interpretation, and use of assessment instruments, whether they score and interpret such tests themselves or use automated or other services.

2.09 Explaining Assessment Results.

Unless the nature of the relationship is clearly explained to the person being assessed in advance and precludes provision of an explanation of results (such as in some organizational consulting, pre-employment or security screenings, and forensic evaluations), psychologists ensure that an explanation of the results is provided using language that is reasonably understandable to the person assessed or to another legally authorized person on behalf of the client. Regardless of whether the scoring and interpretation are done by the psychologist, by assistants, or by automated or other outside services, psychologists take reasonable steps to ensure that appropriate explanations of results are given.

2.10 Maintaining Test Security.

Psychologists make reasonable efforts to maintain the integrity and security of tests and other assessment techniques consistent with law, contractual obligations, and in a manner that permits compliance with the requirements of this Ethics Code. (See also Standard 1.02, Relationship of Ethics and Law.)

3. ADVERTISING AND OTHER PUBLIC STATEMENTS

3.01 Definition of Public Statements.

Psychologists comply with this Ethics Code in public statements relating to their professional services, products, or publications or to the field of psychology. Public statements include but are not limited to paid or unpaid advertising, brochures, printed matter, directory listings, personal resumes or curriculum vitae, interviews or comments for use in media, statements in legal proceedings, lectures and public oral presentations, and published materials.

3.02 Statements by Others.

(a) Psychologists who engage others to create or place public statements that promote their professional practice, products, or activities retain professional responsibility for such statements.

(b) In addition, psychologists make reasonable efforts to prevent others whom they do not control (such as employers, publishers, sponsors, organizational clients, and representatives of the print or broadcast media) from making deceptive statements concerning psychologists' practice or professional or scientific activities.

(c) If psychologists learn of deceptive statements about their work made by others, psychologists make reasonable efforts to correct such statements.

(d) Psychologists do not compensate employees of press, radio, television, or other communication media in return for publicity in a news item.

(e) A paid advertisement relating to the psychologist's activities must be identified as such, unless it is already apparent from the context.

3.03 Avoidance of False or Deceptive Statements.

(a) Psychologists do not make public statements that are false, deceptive, misleading, or fraudulent, either because of what they state, convey, or suggest or because of what they omit, concerning their research, practice, or other work activities or those of persons or organizations with which they are affiliated. As examples (and not in limitation) of this standard, psychologists do not make false or deceptive statements concerning (1) their training, experience, or competence; (2) their academic degrees; (3) their credentials; (4) their institutional or association affiliations; (5) their services; (6) the scientific or clinical basis for, or results or degree of success of, their services; (7) their fees; or (8) their publications or research findings. (See also Standards 6.15, Deception in Research, and 6.18, Providing Participants With Information About the Study.)

(b) Psychologists claim as credentials for their psychological work, only degrees that (1) were earned from a regionally accredited educational institution or (2) were the basis for psychology licensure by the state in which they practice.

3.04 Media Presentations.

When psychologists provide advice or comment by means of public lectures, demonstrations, radio or television programs, prerecorded tapes, printed articles, mailed material, or other media, they take reasonable precautions to ensure that (1) the statements are based on appropriate psychological literature and practice, (2) the statements are otherwise consistent with this Ethics Code, and (3) the recipients of the information are not encouraged to infer that a relationship has been established with them personally.

3.05 Testimonials.

Psychologists do not solicit testimonials from current psychotherapy clients or patients or other persons who because of their particular circumstances are vulnerable to undue influence.

3.06 In-Person Solicitation.

Psychologists do not engage, directly or through agents, in uninvited in-person solicitation of business from actual or potential psychotherapy patients or clients or other persons who because of their particular circumstances are vulnerable to undue influence. However, this does not preclude attempting to implement appropriate collateral contacts with significant others for the purpose of benefiting an already engaged therapy patient.

4. THERAPY

4.01 Structuring the Relationship.

(a) Psychologists discuss with clients or patients as early as is feasible in the therapeutic relationship appropriate issues, such as the nature and anticipated course of therapy, fees, and confidentiality. (See also Standards 1.25, Fees and Financial Arrangements, and 5.01, Discussing the Limits of Confidentiality.)

(b) When the psychologist's work with clients or patients will be supervised, the above discussion includes that fact, and the name of the supervisor, when the supervisor has legal responsibility for the case.

(c) When the therapist is a student intern, the client or patient is informed of that fact.

(d) Psychologists make reasonable efforts to answer patients' questions and to avoid apparent misunderstandings about therapy. Whenever possible, psychologists provide oral and/or written information, using language that is reasonably understandable to the patient or client.

4.02 Informed Consent to Therapy.

(a) Psychologists obtain appropriate informed consent to therapy or related procedures, using language that is reasonably understandable to participants. The content of informed consent will vary depending on many circumstances; however, informed consent generally implies that the person (1) has the capacity to consent, (2) has been informed of significant information concerning the procedure, (3) has freely and without undue influence expressed consent, and (4) consent has been appropriately documented.

(b) When persons are legally incapable of giving informed consent, psychologists obtain informed permission from a legally authorized person, if such substitute consent is permitted by law.

(c) In addition, psychologists (1) inform those persons who are legally incapable of giving informed consent about the proposed interventions in a manner commensurate with the persons' psychological capacities, (2) seek their assent to those interventions, and (3) consider such persons' preferences and best interests.

4.03 Couple and Family Relationships.

(a) When a psychologist agrees to provide services to several persons who have a relationship (such as husband and wife or parents and children), the psychologist attempts to clarify at the outset (1) which of the individuals are patients or clients and (2) the relationship the psychologist will have with each person. This clarification includes the role of the psychologist and the probable uses of the services provided or the information obtained. (See also Standard 5.01, Discussing the Limits of Confidentiality.)

(b) As soon as it becomes apparent that the psychologist may be called on to perform potentially conflicting roles (such as marital counselor to husband and wife, and then witness for one party in a divorce proceeding), the psychologist attempts to clarify and adjust, or withdraw from, roles appropriately. (See also Standard 7.03, Clarification of Role, under Forensic Activities.)

4.04 Providing Mental Health Services to Those Served by Others.

In deciding whether to offer or provide services to those already receiving mental health services elsewhere, psychologists carefully consider the treatment issues and the potential patient's or client's welfare. The psychologist discusses these issues with the patient or client, or another legally authorized person on behalf of the client, in order to minimize the risk of confusion and conflict, consults with the other service providers when appropriate, and proceeds with caution and sensitivity to the therapeutic issues.

4.05 Sexual Intimacies With Current Patients or Clients.

Psychologists do not engage in sexual intimacies with current patients or clients.

4.06 Therapy With Former Sexual Partners.

Psychologists do not accept as therapy patients or clients persons with whom they have engaged in sexual intimacies.

4.07 Sexual Intimacies With Former Therapy Patients.

(a) Psychologists do not engage in sexual intimacies with a former therapy patient or client for at least two years after cessation or termination of professional services.

(b) Because sexual intimacies with a former therapy patient or client are so frequently harmful to the patient or client, and because such intimacies undermine public confidence in the psychology profession and thereby deter the public's use of needed services, psychologists do not engage in sexual intimacies with former therapy patients and clients even after a two-year interval except in the most unusual circumstances. The psychologist who engages in such activity after the two years following cessation or termination of treatment bears the burden of demonstrating that there has been no exploitation, in light of all relevant factors, including (1) the amount of time that has passed since therapy terminated, (2) the nature and duration of the therapy, (3) the circumstances of termination, (4) the patient's or client's personal history, (5) the patient's or client's current mental status, (6) the likelihood of adverse impact on the patient or client and others, and (7) any statements or actions made by the therapist during the course of therapy suggesting or inviting the possibility of a post-termination sexual or romantic relationship with the patient or client. (See also Standard 1.17, Multiple Relationships.)

4.08 Interruption of Services.

(a) Psychologists make reasonable efforts to plan for facilitating care in the event that psychological services are interrupted by factors such as the psychologist's illness, death, unavailability, or relocation or by the client's relocation or financial limitations. (See also Standard 5.09, Preserving Records and Data.)

(b) When entering into employment or contractual relationships, psychologists provide for orderly and appropriate resolution of responsibility for patient or client care in the event that the employment or contractual relationship ends, with paramount consideration given to the welfare of the patient or client.

4.09 Terminating the Professional Relationship.

(a) Psychologists do not abandon patients or clients. (See also Standard 1.25e, under Fees and Financial Arrangements.)

(b) Psychologists terminate a professional relationship when it becomes reasonably clear that the patient or client no longer needs the service, is not benefiting, or is being harmed by continued service.

(c) Prior to termination for whatever reason, except where precluded by the patient's or client's conduct, the psychologist discusses the patient's or client's views and needs, provides appropriate pretermination counseling, suggests alternative service providers as appropriate, and takes other reasonable steps to facilitate transfer of responsibility to another provider if the patient or client needs one immediately.

5. PRIVACY AND CONFIDENTIALITY

These Standards are potentially applicable to the professional and scientific activities of all psychologists.

5.01 Discussing the Limits of Confidentiality.

(a) Psychologists discuss with persons and organizations with whom they establish a scientific or professional relationship (including, to the extent feasible, minors and their legal representatives) (1) the relevant limitations on confidentiality, including limitations where applicable in group, marital, and family therapy or in organizational consulting, and (2) the foreseeable uses of the information generated through their services.

(b) Unless it is not feasible or is contraindicated, the discussion of confidentiality occurs at the outset of the relationship and thereafter as new circumstances may warrant.

(c) Permission for electronic recording of interviews is secured from clients and patients.

5.02 Maintaining Confidentiality.

Psychologists have a primary obligation and take reasonable precautions to respect the confidentiality rights of those with whom they work or consult, recognizing that confidentiality may be established by law, institutional rules, or professional or scientific relationships. (See also Standard 6.26, Professional Reviewers.)

5.03 Minimizing Intrusions on Privacy.

(a) In order to minimize intrusions on privacy, psychologists include in written and oral reports, consultations, and the like, only information germane to the purpose for which the communication is made.

(b) Psychologists discuss confidential information obtained in clinical or consulting relationships, or evaluative data concerning patients, individual or organizational clients, students, research participants, supervisees, and employees, only for appropriate scientific or professional purposes and only with persons clearly concerned with such matters.

5.04 Maintenance of Records.

Psychologists maintain appropriate confidentiality in creating, storing, accessing, transferring, and disposing of records under their control, whether these are written, automated, or in any other medium. Psychologists maintain and dispose of records in accordance with law and in a manner that permits compliance with the requirements of this Ethics Code.

5.05 Disclosures.

(a) Psychologists disclose confidential information without the consent of the individual only as mandated by law, or where permitted by law for a valid purpose, such as (1) to provide needed professional services to the patient or the individual or organizational client, (2) to obtain appropriate professional consultations, (3) to protect the patient or client or others from harm, or (4) to obtain payment for services, in which instance disclosure is limited to the minimum that is necessary to achieve the purpose.

(b) Psychologists also may disclose confidential information with the appropriate consent of the patient or the individual or organizational client (or of another legally authorized person on behalf of the patient or client), unless prohibited by law.

5.06 Consultations.

When consulting with colleagues, (1) psychologists do not share confidential information that reasonably could lead to the identification of a patient, client, research participant, or other person or organization with whom they have a confidential relationship unless they have obtained the prior consent of the person or organization or the disclosure cannot be avoided, and (2) they share information only to the extent necessary to achieve the purposes of the consultation. (See also Standard 5.02, Maintaining Confidentiality.)

5.07 Confidential Information in Databases.

(a) If confidential information concerning recipients of psychological services is to be entered into databases or systems of records available to persons whose access has not been consented to by the recipient, then psychologists use coding or other techniques to avoid the inclusion of personal identifiers.

(b) If a research protocol approved by an institutional review board or similar body requires the inclusion of personal identifiers, such identifiers are deleted before the information is made accessible to persons other than those of whom the subject was advised.

(c) If such deletion is not feasible, then before psychologists transfer such data to others or review such data collected by others, they take reasonable steps to determine that appropriate consent of personally identifiable individuals has been obtained.

5.08 Use of Confidential Information for Didactic or Other Purposes.

(a) Psychologists do not disclose in their writings, lectures, or other public media, confidential, personally identifiable information concerning their patients, individual or organizational clients, students, research participants, or other recipients of their services that they obtained during the course of their work, unless the person or organization has consented in writing or unless there is other ethical or legal authorization for doing so.

(b) Ordinarily, in such scientific and professional presentations, psychologists disguise confidential information concerning such persons or organizations so that they are not individually identifiable to others and so that discussions do not cause harm to subjects who might identify themselves.

5.09 Preserving Records and Data.

A psychologist makes plans in advance so that confidentiality of records and data is protected in the event of the psychologist's death, incapacity, or withdrawal from the position or practice.

5.10 Ownership of Records and Data.

Recognizing that ownership of records and data is governed by legal principles, psychologists take reasonable and lawful steps so that records and data remain available to the extent needed to serve the best interests of patients, individual or organizational clients, research participants, or appropriate others.

5.11 Withholding Records for Nonpayment.

Psychologists may not withhold records under their control that are requested and imminently needed for a patient's or client's treatment solely because payment has not been received, except as otherwise provided by law.

6. TEACHING, TRAINING SUPERVISION, RESEARCH, AND PUBLISHING

6.01 Design of Education and Training Programs.

Psychologists who are responsible for education and training programs seek to ensure that the programs are competently designed, provide the proper experiences, and meet the requirements for licensure, certification, or other goals for which claims are made by the program.

6.02 Descriptions of Education and Training Programs.

(a) Psychologists responsible for education and training programs seek to ensure that there is a current and accurate description of the program content, training goals and objectives, and requirements that must be met for satisfactory completion of the program. This information must be made readily available to all interested parties.

(b) Psychologists seek to ensure that statements concerning their course outlines are accurate and not misleading, particularly regarding the subject matter to be covered, bases for evaluating progress, and the nature of course experiences. (See also Standard 3.03, Avoidance of False or Deceptive Statements.)

(c) To the degree to which they exercise control, psychologists responsible for announcements, catalogs, brochures, or advertisements describing workshops, seminars, or other non-degree-granting educational programs ensure that they accurately describe the audience for which the program is intended, the educational objectives, the presenters, and the fees involved.

6.03 Accuracy and Objectivity in Teaching.

(a) When engaged in teaching or training, psychologists present psychological information accurately and with a reasonable degree of objectivity.

(b)   When engaged in teaching or training, psychologists recognize the power they hold over students or supervisees and therefore make reasonable efforts to avoid engaging in conduct that is personally demeaning to students or supervisees. (See also Standards 1.09, Respecting Others, and 1.12, Other Harassment.)

6.04 Limitation on Teaching.

Psychologists do not teach the use of techniques or procedures that require specialized training, licensure, or expertise, including but not limited to hypnosis, biofeedback, and projective techniques, to individuals who lack the prerequisite training, legal scope of practice, or expertise.

6.05 Assessing Student and Supervisee Performance.

(a)   In academic and supervisory relationships, psychologists establish an appropriate process for providing feedback to students and supervisees.

(b)   Psychologists evaluate students and supervisees on the basis of their actual performance on relevant and established program requirements.

6.06 Planning Research.

(a)   Psychologists design, conduct, and report research in accordance with recognized standards of scientific competence and ethical research.

(b)   Psychologists plan their research so as to minimize the possibility that results will be misleading.

(c)   In planning research, psychologists consider its ethical acceptability under the Ethics Code. If an ethical issue is unclear, psychologists seek to resolve the issue through consultation with institutional review boards, animal care and use committees, peer consultations, or other proper mechanisms.

(d)   Psychologists take reasonable steps to implement appropriate protections for the rights and welfare of human participants, other persons affected by the research, and the welfare of animal subjects.

6.07 Responsibility.

(a)   Psychologists conduct research competently and with due concern for the dignity and welfare of the participants.

(b)   Psychologists are responsible for the ethical conduct of research conducted by them or by others under their supervision or control.

(c)   Researchers and assistants are permitted to perform only those tasks for which they are appropriately trained and prepared.

(d)   As part of the process of development and implementation of research projects, psychologists consult those with expertise concerning any special population under investigation or most likely to be affected.

6.08 Compliance With Law and Standards.

Psychologists plan and conduct research in a manner consistent with federal and state law and regulations, as well as professional standards governing the conduct of research, and particularly those standards governing research with human participants and animal subjects.

6.09 Institutional Approval.

Psychologists obtain from host institutions or organizations appropriate approval prior to conducting research, and they provide accurate information about their research proposals. They conduct the research in accordance with the approved research protocol.

6.10 Research Responsibilities.

Prior to conducting research (except research involving only anonymous surveys, naturalistic observations, or similar research), psychologists enter into an agreement with participants that clarifies the nature of the research and the responsibilities of each party.

6.11 Informed Consent to Research.

(a)   Psychologists use language that is reasonably understandable to research participants in obtaining their appropriate informed consent (except as provided in Standard 6.12, Dispensing with Informed Consent). Such informed consent is appropriately documented.

(b)   Using language that is reasonably understandable to participants, psychologists inform participants of the nature of the research; they inform participants that they are free to participate or to decline to participate or to withdraw from the research; they explain the foreseeable consequences of declining or withdrawing; they inform participants of significant factors that may be expected to influence their willingness to participate (such as risks, discomfort, adverse effects, or limitations on confidentiality, except as provided in Standard 6.15, Deception in Research); and they explain other aspects about which the prospective participants inquire.

(c)   When psychologists conduct research with individuals such as students or subordinates, psychologists take special care to protect the prospective participants from adverse consequences of declining or withdrawing from participation.

(d)   When research participation is a course requirement or opportunity for extra credit, the prospective participant is given the choice of equitable alternative activities.

(e)   For persons who are legally incapable of giving informed consent, psychologists nevertheless (1) provide an appropriate explanation, (2) obtain the participant's assent, and (3) obtain appropriate permission from a legally authorized person, if such substitute consent is permitted by law.

6.12 Dispensing With Informed Consent.

Before determining that planned research (such as research involving only anonymous questionnaires, naturalistic observations, or certain kinds of archival research) does not require the informed consent of research participants, psychologists consider applicable regulations and institutional review board requirements, and they consult with colleagues as appropriate.

6.13 Informed Consent in Research Filming or Recording.

Psychologists obtain informed consent from research participants prior to filming or recording them in any form, unless the research involves simply naturalistic observations in public places and it is not anticipated that the recording will be used in a manner that could cause personal identification or harm.

6.14 Offering Inducements for Research Participants.

(a)   In offering professional services as an inducement to obtain research participants, psychologists make clear the nature of the services, as well as the risks, obligations, and limitations. (See also Standard 1.18, Barter [With Patients or Clients].)

(b)   Psychologists do not offer excessive or inappropriate financial or other inducements to obtain research participants, particularly when it might tend to coerce participation.

6.15 Deception in Research.

(a)   Psychologists do not conduct a study involving deception unless they have determined that the use of deceptive techniques is justified by the study's prospective scientific, educational, or applied value and that equally effective alternative procedures that do not use deception are not feasible.

(b)   Psychologists never deceive research participants about significant aspects that would affect their willingness to participate, such as physical risks, discomfort, or unpleasant emotional experiences.

(c)   Any other deception that is an integral feature of the design and conduct of an experiment must be explained to participants as early as is feasible, preferably at the conclusion of their participation, but no later than at the conclusion of the research. (See also Standard 6.18, Providing Participants With Information About the Study.)

6.16 Sharing and Utilizing Data.

Psychologists inform research participants of their anticipated sharing or further use of personally identifiable research data and of the possibility of unanticipated future uses.

6.17 Minimizing Invasiveness.

In conducting research, psychologists interfere with the participants or milieu from which data are collected only in a manner that is warranted by an appropriate research design and that is consistent with psychologists' roles as scientific investigators.

6.18 Providing Participants With Information About the Study.

(a)   Psychologists provide a prompt opportunity for participants to obtain appropriate information about the nature, results, and conclusions of the research, and psychologists attempt to correct any misconceptions that participants may have.

(b)   If scientific or humane values justify delaying or withholding this information, psychologists take reasonable measures to reduce the risk of harm.

6.19 Honoring Commitments.

Psychologists take reasonable measures to honor all commitments they have made to research participants.

6.20 Care and Use of Animals in Research.

(a)   Psychologists who conduct research involving animals treat them humanely.

(b)   Psychologists acquire, care for, use, and dispose of animals in compliance with current federal, state, and local laws and regulations, and with professional standards.

(c)   Psychologists trained in research methods and experienced in the care of laboratory animals supervise all procedures involving animals and are responsible for ensuring appropriate consideration of their comfort, health, and humane treatment.

(d)   Psychologists ensure that all individuals using animals under their supervision have received instruction in research methods and in the care, maintenance, and handling of the species being used, to the extent appropriate to their role.

(e)   Responsibilities and activities of individuals assisting in a research project are consistent with their respective competencies.

(f) Psychologists make reasonable efforts to minimize the discomfort, infection, illness, and pain of animal subjects.

(g) A procedure subjecting animals to pain, stress, or privation is used only when an alternative procedure is unavailable and the goal is justified by its prospective scientific, educational, or applied value.

(h) Surgical procedures are performed under appropriate anesthesia; techniques to avoid infection and minimize pain are followed during and after surgery.

(i) When it is appropriate that the animal's life be terminated, it is done rapidly, with an effort to minimize pain, and in accordance with accepted procedures.

6.21 Reporting of Results.

(a) Psychologists do not fabricate data or falsify results in their publications.

(b) If psychologists discover significant errors in their published data, they take reasonable steps to correct such errors in a correction, retraction, erratum, or other appropriate publication means.

6.22 Plagiarism.

Psychologists do not present substantial portions or elements of another's work or data as their own, even if the other work or data source is cited occasionally.

6.23 Publication Credit.

(a) Psychologists take responsibility and credit, including authorship credit, only for work they have actually performed or to which they have contributed.

(b) Principal authorship and other publication credits accurately reflect the relative scientific or professional contributions of the individuals involved, regardless of their relative status. Mere possession of an institutional position, such as Department Chair, does not justify authorship credit. Minor contributions to the research or to the writing for publications are appropriately acknowledged, such as in footnotes or in an introductory statement.

(c) A student is usually listed as principal author on any multiple-authored article that is substantially based on the student's dissertation or thesis.

6.24 Duplicate Publication of Data.

Psychologists do not publish, as original data, data that have been previously published. This does not preclude republishing data when they are accompanied by proper acknowledgment.

6.25 Sharing Data.

After research results are published, psychologists do not withhold the data on which their conclusions are based from other competent professionals who seek to verify the substantive claims through reanalysis and who intend to use such data only for that purpose, provided that the confidentiality of the participants can be protected and unless legal rights concerning proprietary data preclude their release.

6.26 Professional Reviewers.

Psychologists who review material submitted for publication, grant, or other research proposal review respect the confidentiality of and the proprietary rights in such information of those who submitted it.

7. FORENSIC ACTIVITIES

7.01 Professionalism.

Psychologists who perform forensic functions, such as assessments, interviews, consultations, reports, or expert testimony, must comply with all other provisions of this Ethics Code to the extent that they apply to such activities. In addition, psychologists base their forensic work on appropriate knowledge of and competence in the areas underlying such work, including specialized knowledge concerning special populations. (See also Standards 1.06, Basis for Scientific and Professional Judgments; 1.08, Human Differences; 1.15, Misuse of Psychologists' Influence; and 1.23, Documentation of Professional and Scientific Work.)

7.02 Forensic Assessments.

(a) Psychologists' forensic assessments, recommendations, and reports are based on information and techniques (including personal interviews of the individual, when appropriate) sufficient to provide appropriate substantiation for their findings. (See also Standards 1.03, Professional and Scientific Relationship; 1.23, Documentation of Professional and Scientific Work; 2.01, Evaluation, Diagnosis, and Interventions in Professional Context; and 2.05, Interpreting Assessment Results.)

(b) Except as noted in (c), below, psychologists provide written or oral forensic reports or testimony of the psychological characteristics of an individual only after they have conducted an examination of the individual adequate to support their statements or conclusions.

(c) When, despite reasonable efforts, such an examination is not feasible, psychologists clarify the impact of their limited information on the reliability and validity of their reports and testimony, and they appropriately limit the nature and extent of their conclusions or recommendations.

7.03 Clarification of Role.

In most circumstances, psychologists avoid performing multiple and potentially conflicting roles in forensic matters. When psychologists may be called on to serve in more than one role in a legal proceeding—for example, as consultant or expert for one party or for the court and as a fact witness—they clarify role expectations and the extent of confidentiality in advance to the extent feasible, and thereafter as changes occur, in order to avoid compromising their professional judgment and objectivity and in order to avoid misleading others regarding their role.

7.04 Truthfulness and Candor.

(a) In forensic testimony and reports, psychologists testify truthfully, honestly, and candidly and, consistent with applicable legal procedures, describe fairly the bases for their testimony and conclusions.

(b) Whenever necessary to avoid misleading, psychologists acknowledge the limits of their data or conclusions.

7.05 Prior Relationships.

A prior professional relationship with a party does not preclude psychologists from testifying as fact witnesses or from testifying to their services to the extent permitted by applicable law. Psychologists appropriately take into account ways in which the prior relationship might affect their professional objectivity or opinions and disclose the potential conflict to the relevant parties.

7.06 Compliance With Law and Rules.

In performing forensic roles, psychologists are reasonably familiar with the rules governing their roles. Psychologists are aware of the occasionally competing demands placed upon them by these principles and the requirements of the court system, and attempt to resolve these conflicts by making known their commitment to this Ethics Code and taking steps to resolve the conflict in a responsible manner. (See also Standard 1.02, Relationship of Ethics and Law.)

8. RESOLVING ETHICAL ISSUES
8.01 Familiarity With Ethics Code.

Psychologists have an obligation to be familiar with this Ethics Code, other applicable ethics codes, and their application to psychologists' work. Lack of awareness or misunderstanding of an ethical standard is not itself a defense to a charge of unethical conduct.

8.02 Confronting Ethical Issues.

When a psychologist is uncertain whether a particular situation or course of action would violate this Ethics Code, the psychologist ordinarily consults with other psychologists knowledgeable about ethical issues, with state or national psychology ethics committees, or with other appropriate authorities in order to choose a proper response.

8.03 Conflicts Between Ethics and Organizational Demands.

If the demands of an organization with which psychologists are affiliated conflict with this Ethics Code, psychologists clarify the nature of the conflict, make known their commitment to the Ethics Code, and to the extent feasible, seek to resolve the conflict in a way that permits the fullest adherence to the Ethics Code.

8.04 Informal Resolution of Ethical Violations.

When psychologists believe that there may have been an ethical violation by another psychologist, they attempt to resolve the issue by bringing it to the attention of that individual if an informal resolution appears appropriate and the intervention does not violate any confidentiality rights that may be involved.

8.05 Reporting Ethical Violations.

If an apparent ethical violation is not appropriate for informal resolution under Standard 8.04 or is not resolved properly in that fashion, psychologists take further action appropriate to the situation, unless such action conflicts with confidentiality rights in ways that cannot be resolved. Such action might include referral to state or national committees on professional ethics or to state licensing boards.

8.06 Cooperating With Ethics Committees.

Psychologists cooperate in ethics investigations, proceedings, and resulting requirements of the APA or any affiliated state psychological association to which they belong. In doing so, they make reasonable efforts to resolve any issues as to confidentiality. Failure to cooperate is itself an ethics violation.

8.07 Improper Complaints.

Psychologists do not file or encourage the filing of ethics complaints that are frivolous and are intended to harm the respondent rather than to protect the public.

NASW Code of Ethics

PREAMBLE

The primary mission of the social work profession is to enhance human well-being and help meet the basic human needs of all people, with particular attention to the needs and empowerment of people who are vulnerable, oppressed, and living in poverty. A historic and defining feature of social work is the profession's focus on individual well-being in a social context and the well-being of society. Fundamental to social work is attention to the environmental forces that create, contribute to, and address problems in living.

Social workers promote social justice and social change with and on behalf of clients. "Clients" is used inclusively to refer to individuals, families, groups, organizations, and communities. Social workers are sensitive to cultural and ethnic diversity and strive to end discrimination, oppression, poverty, and other forms of social injustice. These activities may be in the form of direct practice, community organizing, supervision, consultation, administration, advocacy, social and political action, policy development and implementation, education, and research and evaluation. Social workers seek to enhance the capacity of people to address their own needs. Social workers also seek to promote the responsiveness of organizations, communities, and other social institutions to individuals' needs and social problems.

The mission of the social work profession is rooted in a set of core values. These core values, embraced by social workers throughout the profession's history, are the foundation of social work's unique purpose and perspective:

service
social justice
dignity and worth of the person
importance of human relationships
integrity
competence.

This constellation of core values reflects what is unique to the social work profession. Core values, and the principles that flow from them, must be balanced within the context and complexity of the human experience.

PURPOSE OF THE NASW CODE OF ETHICS

Professional ethics are at the core of social work. The profession has an obligation to articulate its basic values, ethical principles, and ethical standards. The NASW Code of Ethics sets forth these values, principles, and standards to guide social workers' conduct. The Code is relevant to all social workers and social work students, regardless of their professional functions, the settings in which they work, or the populations they serve.

The NASW Code of Ethics serves six purposes:

1. The Code identifies core values on which social work's mission is based.
2. The Code summarizes broad ethical principles that reflect the profession's core values and establishes a set of specific ethical standards that should be used to guide social work practice
3. The Code is designed to help social workers identify relevant considerations when professional obligations conflict or ethical uncertainties arise.
4. The Code provides ethical standards to which the general public can hold the social work profession accountable.
5. The Code socializes practitioners new to the field to social work's mission, values, ethical principles, and ethical standards.
6. The Code articulates standards that the social work profession itself can use to assess whether social workers have engaged in unethical conduct. NASW has formal procedures to adjudicate ethics complaints filed against its members. In subscribing to this Code, social workers are required to cooperate in its implementation, participate in NASW adjudication proceedings, and abide by any NASW disciplinary rulings or sanctions based on it.

The Code offers a set of values, principles, and standards to guide decision making and conduct when ethical issues arise. It does not provide a set of rules that prescribe how social workers should act in all situations. Specific applications of the Code must take into account the context in which it is being considered and the possibility of conflicts among the Code's values, principles, and standards. Ethical responsibilities flow from all human relationships, from the personal and familial to the social and professional.

Further, the NASW Code of Ethics does not specify which values, principles, and standards are most important and ought to outweigh others in instances when they conflict. Reasonable differences of opinion can and do exist among social workers with respect to the ways in which values, ethical principles, and ethical standards should be rank ordered when they conflict. Ethical decision making in a given situation must apply the informed judgment of the individual social worker and should also consider how the issues would be judged in a peer review process where the ethical standards of the profession would be applied.

Ethical decision making is a process. There are many instances in social work where simple answers are not available to resolve complex ethical issues. Social workers should take into consideration all the values, principles, and standards in this Code that are relevant to any situation in which ethical judgment is warranted. Social workers' decisions and actions should be consistent with the spirit as well as the letter of this Code.

In addition to this Code, there are many other sources of information about ethical thinking that may be useful. Social workers should consider ethical theory and principles generally, social work theory and research, laws, regulations, agency policies, and other relevant codes of ethics, recognizing that among codes of ethics social workers should consider the NASW Code of Ethics as their primary source. Social workers also should be aware of the impact on ethical decision making of their clients' and their own personal values and cultural and religious beliefs and practices. They should be aware of any conflicts between personal and professional values and deal with them responsibly. For additional guidance social workers should consult the relevant literature on professional ethics and ethical decision making and seek appropriate consultation when faced with ethical dilemmas. This may involve consultation with an agency-based or social work organization's ethics committee, a regulatory body, knowledgeable colleagues, supervisors, or legal counsel.

Instances may arise when social workers' ethical obligations conflict with agency policies or relevant laws or regulations. When such conflicts occur, social workers must make a responsible effort to resolve the conflict in a manner that is consistent with the values, principles, and standards expressed in this Code. If a reasonable resolution of the conflict does not appear possible, social workers should seek proper consultation before making a decision.

The NASW Code of Ethics is to be used by NASW and by individuals, agencies, organizations, and bodies (such as licensing and regulatory boards, professional liability insurance providers, courts of law, agency boards of directors, government agencies, and other professional groups) that choose to adopt it or use it as a frame of reference. Violation of standards in this Code does not automatically imply legal liability or violation of the law. Such determination can only be made in the context of legal and judicial proceedings. Alleged violations of the Code would be subject to a peer review process. Such processes are generally separate from legal or administrative procedures and insulated from legal review or proceedings to allow the profession to counsel and discipline its own members.

A code of ethics cannot guarantee ethical behavior. Moreover, a code of ethics cannot resolve all ethical issues or disputes or capture the richness and complexity involved in striving to make responsible choices within a moral community. Rather, a code of ethics sets forth values, ethical principles, and ethical standards to which professionals aspire and by which their actions can be judged. Social workers' ethical behavior should result from their personal commitment to engage in ethical practice. The NASW Code of Ethics reflects the commitment of all social workers to uphold the profession's values and to act ethically. Principles and standards must be applied by individuals of good character who discern moral questions and, in good faith, seek to make reliable ethical judgments.

ETHICAL PRINCIPLES

The following broad ethical principles are based on social work's core values of service, social justice, dignity and worth of the person, importance of human relationships, integrity, and competence. These principles set forth ideals to which all social workers should aspire.

VALUE: Service

> **Ethical Principle:** *Social workers' primary goal is to help people in need and to address social problems.*

Social workers elevate service to others above self-interest. Social workers draw on their knowledge, values, and skills to help people in need and to address social problems. Social workers are encouraged to volunteer some portion of their professional skills with no expectation of significant financial return (pro bono service).

VALUE: Social Justice

> **Ethical Principle:** *Social workers challenge social injustice.*

Social workers pursue social change, particularly with and on behalf of vulnerable and oppressed individuals and groups of people. Social workers' social change efforts are focused primarily on issues of poverty, unemployment, discrimination, and other forms of social injustice. These activities seek to promote sensitivity to and knowledge about oppression and cultural and ethnic diversity. Social workers strive to ensure access to needed information, services, and resources; equality of opportunity; and meaningful participation in decision making for all people.

VALUE: Dignity and Worth of the Person

> **Ethical Principle:** *Social workers respect the inherent dignity and worth of the person.*

Social workers treat each person in a caring and respectful fashion, mindful of individual differences and cultural and ethnic diversity. Social workers promote clients' socially responsible self-determination. Social workers seek to enhance clients' capacity and opportunity to change and to address their own needs. Social workers are cognizant of their dual responsibility to clients and to the broader society. They seek to resolve conflicts between clients' interests and the broader society's interests in a socially responsible manner consistent with the values, ethical principles, and ethical standards of the profession.

VALUE: Importance of Human Relationships

> **Ethical Principle:** *Social workers recognize the central importance of human relationships.*

Social workers understand that relationships between and among people are an important vehicle for change. Social workers engage people as partners in the helping process. Social workers seek to strengthen relationships among people in a purposeful effort to promote, restore, maintain, and enhance the well-being of individuals, families, social groups, organizations, and communities.

VALUE: Integrity

> **Ethical Principle:** *Social workers behave in a trustworthy manner.*

Social workers are continually aware of the profession's mission, values, ethical principles, and ethical standards and practice in a manner consistent with them. Social workers act honestly and responsibly and promote ethical practices on the part of the organizations with which they are affiliated.

VALUE: Competence

> **Ethical Principle:** *Social workers practice within their areas of competence and develop and enhance their professional expertise.*

Social workers continually strive to increase their professional knowledge and skills and to apply them in practice. Social workers should aspire to contribute to the knowledge base of the profession.

ETHICAL STANDARDS
1. SOCIAL WORKERS' ETHICAL RESPONSIBILITIES TO CLIENTS
1.01 Commitment to Clients

> Social workers' primary responsibility is to promote the well-being of clients. In general, clients' interests are primary. However, social workers' responsibility to the larger society or specific legal obligations may on limited occasions supersede the loyalty owed clients, and clients should be so advised. (Examples include

when a social worker is required by law to report that a client has abused a child or has threatened to harm self or others.)

1.02 Self-Determination

Social workers respect and promote the right of clients to self-determination and assist clients in their efforts to identify and clarify their goals. Social workers may limit clients' right to self-determination when, in the social workers' professional judgment, clients' actions or potential actions pose a serious, foreseeable, and imminent risk to themselves or others.

1.03 Informed Consent

(a) Social workers should provide services to clients only in the context of a professional relationship based, when appropriate, on valid informed consent. Social workers should use clear and understandable language to inform clients of the purpose of the services, risks related to the services, limits to services because of the requirements of a third-party payer, relevant costs, reasonable alternatives, clients' right to refuse or withdraw consent, and the time frame covered by the consent. Social workers should provide clients with an opportunity to ask questions.

(b) In instances when clients are not literate or have difficulty understanding the primary language used in the practice setting, social workers should take steps to ensure clients' comprehension. This may include providing clients with a detailed verbal explanation or arranging for a qualified interpreter or translator whenever possible.

(c) In instances when clients lack the capacity to provide informed consent, social workers should protect clients' interests by seeking permission from an appropriate third party, informing clients consistent with the clients' level of understanding. In such instances social workers should seek to ensure that the third party acts in a manner consistent with clients' wishes and interests. Social workers should take reasonable steps to enhance such clients' ability to give informed consent.

(d) In instances when clients are receiving services involuntarily, social workers should provide information about the nature and extent of services and about the extent of clients' right to refuse service.

(e) Social workers who provide services via electronic media (such as computer, telephone, radio, and television) should inform recipients of the limitations and risks associated with such services.

(f) Social workers should obtain clients' informed consent before audiotaping or videotaping clients or permitting observation of services to clients by a third party.

1.04 Competence

(a) Social workers should provide services and represent themselves as competent only within the boundaries of their education, training, license, certification, consultation received, supervised experience, or other relevant professional experience.

(b) Social workers should provide services in substantive areas or use intervention techniques or approaches that are new to them only after engaging in appropriate study, training, consultation, and supervision from people who are competent in those interventions or techniques.

(c) When generally recognized standards do not exist with respect to an emerging area of practice, social workers should exercise careful judgment and take responsible steps (including appropriate education, research, training, consultation, and supervision) to ensure the competence of their work and to protect clients from harm.

1.05 Cultural Competence and Social Diversity

(a)   Social workers should understand culture and its function in human behavior and society, recognizing the strengths that exist in all cultures.

(b)   Social workers should have a knowledge base of their clients' cultures and be able to demonstrate competence in the provision of services that are sensitive to clients' cultures and to differences among people and cultural groups.

(c)   Social workers should obtain education about and seek to understand the nature of social diversity and oppression with respect to race, ethnicity, national origin, color, sex, sexual orientation, age, marital status, political belief, religion, and mental or physical disability.

1.06 Conflicts of Interest

(a)   Social workers should be alert to and avoid conflicts of interest that interfere with the exercise of professional discretion and impartial judgment. Social workers should inform clients when a real or potential conflict of interest arises and take reasonable steps to resolve the issue in a manner that makes the clients' interests primary and protects clients' interests to the greatest extent possible. In some cases, protecting clients' interests may require termination of the professional relationship with proper referral of the client.

(b)   Social workers should not take unfair advantage of any professional relationship or exploit others to further their personal, religious, political, or business interests.

(c)   Social workers should not engage in dual or multiple relationships with clients or former clients in which there is a risk of exploitation or potential harm to the client. In instances when dual or multiple relationships are unavoidable, social workers should take steps to protect clients and are responsible for setting clear, appropriate, and culturally sensitive boundaries. (Dual or multiple relationships occur when social workers relate to clients in more than one relationship, whether professional, social, or business. Dual or multiple relationships can occur simultaneously or consecutively.)

(d)   When social workers provide services to two or more people who have a relationship with each other (for example, couples, family members), social workers should clarify with all parties which individuals will be considered clients and the nature of social workers' professional obligations to the various individuals who are receiving services. Social workers who anticipate a conflict of interest among the individuals receiving services or who anticipate having to perform in potentially conflicting roles (for example, when a social worker is asked to testify in a child custody dispute or divorce proceedings involving clients) should clarify their role with the parties involved and take appropriate action to minimize any conflict of interest.

1.07 Privacy and Confidentiality

(a)   Social workers should respect clients' right to privacy. Social workers should not solicit private information from clients unless it is essential to providing services or conducting social work evaluation or research. Once private information is shared, standards of confidentiality apply.

(b)   Social workers may disclose confidential information when appropriate with valid consent from a client or a person legally authorized to consent on behalf of a client.

(c)   Social workers should protect the confidentiality of all information obtained in the course of professional service, except for compelling professional reasons. The general expectation that social workers will keep information confidential does not apply when disclosure is necessary to prevent serious, foreseeable, and imminent harm to a client or other identifiable person or when laws or regulations require disclosure without a client's consent. In all instances, social workers should disclose the least amount of confidential information necessary to achieve the desired purpose; only information that is directly relevant to the purpose for which the disclosure is made should be revealed.

(d) Social workers should inform clients, to the extent possible, about the disclosure of confidential information and the potential consequences, when feasible before the disclosure is made. This applies whether social workers disclose confidential information on the basis of a legal requirement or client consent.

(e) Social workers should discuss with clients and other interested parties the nature of confidentiality and limitations of clients' right to confidentiality. Social workers should review with clients circumstances where confidential information may be requested and where disclosure of confidential information may be legally required. This discussion should occur as soon as possible in the social worker–client relationship and as needed throughout the course of the relationship.

(f) When social workers provide counseling services to families, couples, or groups, social workers should seek agreement among the parties involved concerning each individual's right to confidentiality and obligation to preserve the confidentiality of information shared by others. Social workers should inform participants in family, couples, or group counseling that social workers cannot guarantee that all participants will honor such agreements.

(g) Social workers should inform clients involved in family, couples, marital, or group counseling of the social worker's, employer's, and agency's policy concerning the social worker's disclosure of confidential information among the parties involved in the counseling.

(h) Social workers should not disclose confidential information to third-party payers unless clients have authorized such.

(i) Social workers should not discuss confidential information in any setting unless privacy can be ensured. Social workers should not discuss confidential information in public or semipublic areas such as hallways, waiting rooms, elevators, and restaurants.

(j) Social workers should protect the confidentiality of clients during legal proceedings to the extent permitted by law. When a court of law or other legally authorized body orders social workers to disclose confidential or privileged information without a client's consent and such disclosure could cause harm to the client, social workers should request that the court withdraw the order or limit the order as narrowly as possible or maintain the records under seal, unavailable for public inspection.

(k) Social workers should protect the confidentiality of clients when responding to requests from members of the media.

(l) Social workers should protect the confidentiality of clients' written and electronic records and other sensitive information. Social workers should take reasonable steps to ensure that clients' records are stored in a secure location and that clients' records are not available to others who are not authorized to have access.

(m) Social workers should take precautions to ensure and maintain the confidentiality of information transmitted to other parties through the use of computers, electronic mail, facsimile machines, telephones and telephone answering machines, and other electronic or computer technology. Disclosure of identifying information should be avoided whenever possible.

(n)   Social workers should transfer or dispose of clients' records in a manner that protects clients' confidentiality and is consistent with state statutes governing records and social work licensure.

(o)   Social workers should take reasonable precautions to protect client confidentiality in the event of the social worker's termination of practice, incapacitation, or death.

(p)   Social workers should not disclose identifying information when discussing clients for teaching or training purposes unless the client has consented to disclosure of confidential information.

(q)   Social workers should not disclose identifying information when discussing clients with consultants unless the client has consented to disclosure of confidential information or there is a compelling need for such disclosure.

(r)   Social workers should protect the confidentiality of deceased clients consistent with the preceding standards.

1.08 Access to Records

(a)   Social workers should provide clients with reasonable access to records concerning the clients. Social workers who are concerned that clients' access to their records could cause serious misunderstanding or harm to the client should provide assistance in interpreting the records and consultation with the client regarding the records. Social workers should limit clients' access to their records, or portions of their records, only in exceptional circumstances when there is compelling evidence that such access would cause serious harm to the client. Both clients' requests and the rationale for withholding some or all of the record should be documented in clients' files.

(b)   When providing clients with access to their records, social workers should take steps to protect the confidentiality of other individuals identified or discussed in such records.

1.09 Sexual Relationships

(a)   Social workers should under no circumstances engage in sexual activities or sexual contact with current clients, whether such contact is consensual or forced.

(b)   Social workers should not engage in sexual activities or sexual contact with clients' relatives or other individuals with whom clients maintain a close personal relationship when there is a risk of exploitation or potential harm to the client Sexual activity or sexual contact with clients' relatives or other individuals with whom clients maintain a personal relationship has the potential to be harmful to the client and may make it difficult for the social worker and client to maintain appropriate professional boundaries. Social workers—not their clients, their clients' relatives, or other individuals with whom the client maintains a personal relationship—assume the full burden for setting clear, appropriate, and culturally sensitive boundaries.

(c)   Social workers should not engage in sexual activities or sexual contact with former clients because of the potential for harm to the client. If social workers engage in conduct contrary to this prohibition or claim that an exception to this prohibition is warranted because of extraordinary circumstances, it is social workers—not their clients—who assume the full burden of demonstrating that the former client has not been exploited, coerced, or manipulated, intentionally or unintentionally.

(d)   Social workers should not provide clinical services to individuals with whom they have had a prior sexual relationship. Providing clinical services to a former sexual partner has the potential to be harmful to the individual and is likely to make it difficult for the social worker and individual to maintain appropriate professional boundaries.

1.10 Physical Contact

Social workers should not engage in physical contact with clients when there is a possibility of psychological harm to the client as a result of the contact (such as cradling or caressing clients). Social workers who engage in appropriate physical contact with clients are responsible for setting clear, appropriate, and culturally sensitive boundaries that govern such physical contact.

1.11 Sexual Harassment

Social workers should not sexually harass clients. Sexual harassment includes sexual advances, sexual solicitation, requests for sexual favors, and other verbal or physical conduct of a sexual nature.

1.12 Derogatory Language

Social workers should not use derogatory language in their written or verbal communications to or about clients. Social workers should use accurate and respectful language in all communications to and about clients.

1.13 Payment for Services

(a) When setting fees, social workers should ensure that the fees are fair, reasonable, and commensurate with the services performed. Consideration should be given to clients' ability to pay.

(b) Social workers should avoid accepting goods or services from clients as payment for professional services. Bartering arrangements, particularly involving services, create the potential for conflicts of interest, exploitation, and inappropriate boundaries in social workers' relationships with clients. Social workers should explore and may participate in bartering only in very limited circumstances when it can be demonstrated that such arrangements are an accepted practice among professionals in the local community, considered to be essential for the provision of services, negotiated without coercion, and entered into at the client's initiative and with the client's informed consent. Social workers who accept goods or services from clients as payment for professional services assume the full burden of demonstrating that this arrangement will not be detrimental to the client or the professional relationship.

(c) Social workers should not solicit a private fee or other remuneration for providing services to clients who are entitled to such available services through the social workers' employer or agency.

1.14 Clients Who Lack Decision-Making Capacity

When social workers act on behalf of clients who lack the capacity to make informed decisions, social workers should take reasonable steps to safeguard the interests and rights of those clients.

1.15 Interruption of Services

Social workers should make reasonable efforts to ensure continuity of services in the event that services are interrupted by factors such as unavailability, relocation, illness, disability, or death.

1.16 Termination of Services

(a) Social workers should terminate services to clients and professional relationships with them when such services and relationships are no longer required or no longer serve the clients' needs or interests.

(b) Social workers should take reasonable steps to avoid abandoning clients who are still in need of services. Social workers should withdraw services precipitously only under unusual circumstances, giving careful consideration to all factors in the situation and taking care to minimize possible adverse effects. Social workers should assist in making appropriate arrangements for continuation of services when necessary.

(c) Social workers in fee-for-service settings may terminate services to clients who are not paying an overdue balance if the financial contractual arrangements have been made clear to the client, if the client does not pose an imminent danger to self or others, and if the clinical and other consequences of the current nonpayment have been addressed and discussed with the client.

(d) Social workers should not terminate services to pursue a social, financial, or sexual relationship with a client.

(e) Social workers who anticipate the termination or interruption of services to clients should notify clients promptly and seek the transfer, referral, or continuation of services in relation to the clients' needs and preferences.

(f) Social workers who are leaving an employment setting should inform clients of appropriate options for the continuation of services and of the benefits and risks of the options.

2. SOCIAL WORKERS' ETHICAL RESPONSIBILITIES TO COLLEAGUES

2.01 Respect

(a) Social workers should treat colleagues with respect and should represent accurately and fairly the qualifications, views, and obligations of colleagues.

(b) Social workers should avoid unwarranted negative criticism of colleagues in communications with clients or with other professionals. Unwarranted negative criticism may include demeaning comments that refer to colleagues' level of competence or to individuals' attributes such as race, ethnicity, national origin, color, sex, sexual orientation, age, marital status, political belief, religion, and mental or physical disability.

(c) Social workers should cooperate with social work colleagues and with colleagues of other professions when such cooperation serves the well-being of clients.

2.02 Confidentiality

Social workers should respect confidential information shared by colleagues in the course of their professional relationships and transactions. Social workers should ensure that such colleagues understand social workers' obligation to respect confidentiality and any exceptions related to it.

2.03 Interdisciplinary Collaboration

(a) Social workers who are members of an interdisciplinary team should participate in and contribute to decisions that affect the well-being of clients by drawing on the perspectives, values, and experiences of the social work profession. Professional and ethical obligations of the interdisciplinary team as a whole and of its individual members should be clearly established.

(b) Social workers for whom a team decision raises ethical concerns should attempt to resolve the disagreement through appropriate channels. If the disagreement cannot be resolved, social workers should pursue other avenues to address their concerns consistent with client well-being.

2.04 Disputes Involving Colleagues

(a) Social workers should not take advantage of a dispute between a colleague and an employer to obtain a position or otherwise advance the social workers' own interests.

(b) Social workers should not exploit clients in disputes with colleagues or engage clients in any inappropriate discussion of conflicts between social workers and their colleagues.

2.05 Consultation

(a) Social workers should seek the advice and counsel of colleagues whenever such consultation is in the best interests of clients.

(b) Social workers should keep themselves informed about colleagues' areas of expertise and competencies. Social workers should seek consultation only from colleagues who have demonstrated knowledge, expertise, and competence related to the subject of the consultation.

(c) When consulting with colleagues about clients, social workers should disclose the least amount of information necessary to achieve the purposes of the consultation.

2.06 Referral for Services

(a) Social workers should refer clients to other professionals when the other professionals' specialized knowledge or expertise is needed to serve clients fully or when social workers believe that they are not being effective or making reasonable progress with clients and that additional service is required.

(b) Social workers who refer clients to other professionals should take appropriate steps to facilitate an orderly transfer of responsibility. Social workers who refer clients to other professionals should disclose, with clients' consent, all pertinent information to the new service providers.

(c) Social workers are prohibited from giving or receiving payment for a referral when no professional service is provided by the referring social worker.

2.07 Sexual Relationships

(a) Social workers who function as supervisors or educators should not engage in sexual activities or contact with supervisees, students, trainees, or other colleagues over whom they exercise professional authority.

(b) Social workers should avoid engaging in sexual relationships with colleagues when there is potential for a conflict of interest. Social workers who become involved in, or anticipate becoming involved in, a sexual relationship with a colleague have a duty to transfer professional responsibilities, when necessary, to avoid a conflict of interest.

2.08 Sexual Harassment

Social workers should not sexually harass supervisees, students, trainees, or colleagues. Sexual harassment includes sexual advances, sexual solicitation, requests for sexual favors, and other verbal or physical conduct of a sexual nature.

2.09 Impairment of Colleagues

(a) Social workers who have direct knowledge of a social work colleague's impairment that is due to personal problems, psychosocial distress, substance abuse, or mental health difficulties and that interferes with practice effectiveness should consult with that colleague when feasible and assist the colleague in taking remedial action.

(b)   Social workers who believe that a social work colleague's impairment interferes with practice effectiveness and that the colleague has not taken adequate steps to address the impairment should take action through appropriate channels established by employers, agencies, NASW, licensing and regulatory bodies, and other professional organizations.

2.10 Incompetence of Colleagues

(a)   Social workers who have direct knowledge of a social work colleague's incompetence should consult with that colleague when feasible and assist the colleague in taking remedial action.

(b)   Social workers who believe that a social work colleague is incompetent and has not taken adequate steps to address the incompetence should take action through appropriate channels established by employers, agencies, NASW, licensing and regulatory bodies, and other professional organizations.

2.11 Unethical Conduct of Colleagues

(a)   Social workers should take adequate measures to discourage, prevent, expose, and correct the unethical conduct of colleagues.

(b)   Social workers should be knowledgeable about established policies and procedures for handling concerns about colleagues' unethical behavior. Social workers should be familiar with national, state, and local procedures for handling ethics complaints. These include policies and procedures created by NASW, licensing and regulatory bodies, employers, agencies, and other professional organizations.

(c)   Social workers who believe that a colleague has acted unethically should seek resolution by discussing their concerns with the colleague when feasible and when such discussion is likely to be productive.

(d)   When necessary, social workers who believe that a colleague has acted unethically should take action through appropriate formal channels (such as contacting a state licensing board or regulatory body, an NASW committee on inquiry, or other professional ethics committees).

(e)   Social workers should defend and assist colleagues who are unjustly charged with unethical conduct.

3. SOCIAL WORKERS' ETHICAL RESPONSIBILITIES IN PRACTICE SETTINGS

3.01 Supervision and Consultation

(a)   Social workers who provide supervision or consultation should have the necessary knowledge and skill to supervise or consult appropriately and should do so only within their areas of knowledge and competence.

(b)   Social workers who provide supervision or consultation are responsible for setting clear, appropriate, and culturally sensitive boundaries.

(c)   Social workers should not engage in any dual or multiple relationships with supervisees in which there is a risk of exploitation of or potential harm to the supervisee.

(d)   Social workers who provide supervision should evaluate supervisees' performance in a manner that is fair and respectful.

3.02 Education and Training

(a)   Social workers who function as educators, field instructors for students, or trainers should provide instruction only within their areas of knowledge and competence and should provide instruction based on the most current information and knowledge available in the profession.

(b) Social workers who function as educators or field instructors for students should evaluate students' performance in a manner that is fair and respectful.

(c) Social workers who function as educators or field instructors for students should take reasonable steps to ensure that clients are routinely informed when services are being provided by students.

(d) Social workers who function as educators or field instructors for students should not engage in any dual or multiple relationships with students in which there is a risk of exploitation or potential harm to the student. Social work educators and field instructors are responsible for setting clear, appropriate, and culturally sensitive boundaries.

3.03 Performance Evaluation

Social workers who have responsibility for evaluating the performance of others should fulfill such responsibility in a fair and considerate manner and on the basis of clearly stated criteria.

3.04 Client Records

(a) Social workers should take reasonable steps to ensure that documentation in records is accurate and reflects the services provided.

(b) Social workers should include sufficient and timely documentation in records to facilitate the delivery of services and to ensure continuity of services provided to clients in the future.

(c) Social workers' documentation should protect clients' privacy to the extent that is possible and appropriate and should include only information that is directly relevant to the delivery of services.

(d) Social workers should store records following the termination of services to ensure reasonable future access. Records should be maintained for the number of years required by state statutes or relevant contracts.

3.05 Billing

Social workers should establish and maintain billing practices that accurately reflect the nature and extent of services provided and that identify who provided the service in the practice setting.

3.06 Client Transfer

(a) When an individual who is receiving services from another agency or colleague contacts a social worker for services, the social worker should carefully consider the client's needs before agreeing to provide services. To minimize possible confusion and conflict, social workers should discuss with potential clients the nature of the clients' current relationship with other service providers and the implications, including possible benefits or risks, of entering into a relationship with a new service provider.

(b) If a new client has been served by another agency or colleague, social workers should discuss with the client whether consultation with the previous service provider is in the client's best interest.

3.07 Administration

(a) Social work administrators should advocate within and outside their agencies for adequate resources to meet clients' needs.

(b)   Social workers should advocate for resource allocation procedures that are open and fair. When not all clients' needs can be met, an allocation procedure should be developed that is nondiscriminatory and based on appropriate and consistently applied principles.

(c)   Social workers who are administrators should take reasonable steps to ensure that adequate agency or organizational resources are available to provide appropriate staff supervision.

(d)   Social work administrators should take reasonable steps to ensure that the working environment for which they are responsible is consistent with and encourages compliance with the NASW Code of Ethics. Social work administrators should take reasonable steps to eliminate any conditions in their organizations that violate, interfere with, or discourage compliance with the Code.

3.08 Continuing Education and Staff Development

Social work administrators and supervisors should take reasonable steps to provide or arrange for continuing education and staff development for all staff for whom they are responsible. Continuing education and staff development should address current knowledge and emerging developments related to social work practice and ethics.

3.09 Commitments to Employers

(a)   Social workers generally should adhere to commitments made to employers and employing organizations.

(b)   Social workers should work to improve employing agencies' policies and procedures and the efficiency and effectiveness of their services.

(c)   Social workers should take reasonable steps to ensure that employers are aware of social workers' ethical obligations as set forth in the NASW Code of Ethics and of the implications of those obligations for social work practice.

(d)   Social workers should not allow an employing organization's policies, procedures, regulations, or administrative orders to interfere with their ethical practice of social work. Social workers should take reasonable steps to ensure that their employing organizations' practices are consistent with the NASW Code of Ethics.

(e)   Social workers should act to prevent and eliminate discrimination in the employing organization's work assignments and in its employment policies and practices.

(f)   Social workers should accept employment or arrange student field placements only in organizations that exercise fair personnel practices.

(g)   Social workers should be diligent stewards of the resources of their employing organizations, wisely conserving funds where appropriate and never misappropriating funds or using them for unintended purposes.

3.10 Labor-Management Disputes

(a)   Social workers may engage in organized action, including the formation of and participation in labor unions, to improve services to clients and working conditions.

(b)   The actions of social workers who are involved in labor-management disputes, job actions, or labor strikes should be guided by the profession's values, ethical principles, and ethical standards. Reasonable differences of opinion exist among social workers concerning their primary obligation as professionals during an actual or threatened labor strike or job action. Social workers should carefully examine relevant issues and their possible impact on clients before deciding on a course of action.

4. SOCIAL WORKERS' ETHICAL RESPONSIBILITIES AS PROFESSIONALS

4.01 Competence

(a) Social workers should accept responsibility or employment only on the basis of existing competence or the intention to acquire the necessary competence.

(b) Social workers should strive to become and remain proficient in professional practice and the performance of professional functions. Social workers should critically examine and keep current with emerging knowledge relevant to social work. Social workers should routinely review the professional literature and participate in continuing education relevant to social work practice and social work ethics.

(c) Social workers should base practice on recognized knowledge, including empirically based.

4.02 Discrimination

Social workers should not practice, condone, facilitate, or collaborate with any form of discrimination on the basis of race, ethnicity, national origin, color, sex, sexual orientation, age, marital status, political belief, religion, or mental or physical disability.

4.03 Private Conduct

Social workers should not permit their private conduct to interfere with their ability to fulfill their professional responsibilities.

4.04 Dishonesty, Fraud, and Deception

Social workers should not participate in, condone, or be associated with dishonesty, fraud, or deception.

4.05 Impairment

(a) Social workers should not allow their own personal problems, psychosocial distress, legal problems, substance abuse, or mental health difficulties to interfere with their professional judgment and performance or to jeopardize the best interests of people for whom they have a professional responsibility.

(b) Social workers whose personal problems, psychosocial distress, legal problems, substance abuse, or mental health difficulties interfere with their professional judgment and performance should immediately seek consultation and take appropriate remedial action by seeking professional help, making adjustments in workload, terminating practice, or taking any other steps necessary to protect clients and others.

4.06 Misrepresentation

(a) Social workers should make clear distinctions between statements made and actions engaged in as a private individual and as a representative of the social work profession, a professional social work organization, or the social worker's employing agency.

(b) Social workers who speak on behalf of professional social work organizations should accurately represent the official and authorized positions of the organizations.

(c) Social workers should ensure that their representations to clients, agencies, and the public of professional qualifications, credentials, education, competence, affiliations, services provided, or results to be achieved are accurate. Social workers should claim only those relevant professional credentials they actually possess and take steps to correct any inaccuracies or misrepresentations of their credentials by others.

4.07 Solicitations

(a) Social workers should not engage in uninvited solicitation of potential clients who, because of their circumstances, are vulnerable to undue influence, manipulation, or coercion.

(b) Social workers should not engage in solicitation of testimonial endorsements (including solicitation of consent to use a client's prior statement as a testimonial endorsement) from current clients or from other people who, because of their particular circumstances, are vulnerable to undue influence.

4.08 Acknowledging Credit

(a) Social workers should take responsibility and credit, including authorship credit, only for work they have actually performed and to which they have contributed.

(b) Social workers should honestly acknowledge the work of and the contributions made by others.

5. SOCIAL WORKERS' ETHICAL RESPONSIBILITIES TO THE SOCIAL WORK PROFESSION

5.01 Integrity of the Profession

(a) Social workers should work toward the maintenance and promotion of high standards of practice.

(b) Social workers should uphold and advance the values, ethics, knowledge, and mission of the profession. Social workers should protect, enhance, and improve the integrity of the profession through appropriate study and research, active discussion, and responsible criticism of the profession.

(c) Social workers should contribute time and professional expertise to activities that promote respect for the value, integrity, and competence of the social work profession. These activities may include teaching, research, consultation, service, legislative testimony, presentations in the community, and participation in their professional organizations.

(d) Social workers should contribute to the knowledge base of social work and share with colleagues their knowledge related to practice, research, and ethics. Social workers should seek to contribute to the profession's literature and to share their knowledge at professional meetings and conferences.

(e) Social workers should act to prevent the unauthorized and unqualified practice of social work.

5.02 Evaluation and Research

(a) Social workers should monitor and evaluate policies, the implementation of programs, and practice interventions.

(b) Social workers should promote and facilitate evaluation and research to contribute to the development of knowledge.

(c) Social workers should critically examine and keep current with emerging knowledge relevant to social work and fully use evaluation and research evidence in their professional practice.

(d) Social workers engaged in evaluation or research should carefully consider possible consequences and should follow guidelines developed for the protection of evaluation and research participants. Appropriate institutional review boards should be consulted.

(e) Social workers engaged in evaluation or research should obtain voluntary and written informed consent from participants, when appropriate, without any implied or actual deprivation or penalty for refusal to participate; without undue inducement to participate; and with due regard for participants' well-being, privacy, and dignity. Informed consent should include information about the nature, extent, and duration of the participation requested and disclosure of the risks and benefits of participation in the research.

(f) When evaluation or research participants are incapable of giving informed consent, social workers should provide an appropriate explanation to the participants, obtain the participants' assent to the extent they are able, and obtain written consent from an appropriate proxy.

(g) Social workers should never design or conduct evaluation or research that does not use consent procedures, such as certain forms of naturalistic observation and archival research, unless rigorous and responsible review of the research has found it to be justified because of its prospective scientific, educational, or applied value and unless equally effective alternative procedures that do not involve waiver of consent are not feasible

(h) Social workers should inform participants of their right to withdraw from evaluation and research at any time without penalty.

(i) Social workers should take appropriate steps to ensure that participants in evaluation and research have access to appropriate supportive services.

(j) Social workers engaged in evaluation or research should protect participants from unwarranted physical or mental distress, harm, danger, or deprivation.

(k) Social workers engaged in the evaluation of services should discuss collected information only for professional purposes and only with people professionally concerned with this information.

(l) Social workers engaged in evaluation or research should ensure the anonymity or confidentiality of participants and of the data obtained from them. Social workers should inform participants of any limits of confidentiality, the measures that will be taken to ensure confidentiality, and when any records containing research data will be destroyed.

(m) Social workers who report evaluation and research results should protect participants' confidentiality by omitting identifying information unless proper consent has been obtained authorizing disclosure.

(n) Social workers should report evaluation and research findings accurately. They should not fabricate or falsify results and should take steps to correct any errors later found in published data using standard publication methods.

(o) Social workers engaged in evaluation or research should be alert to and avoid conflicts of interest and dual relationships with participants, should inform participants when a real or potential conflict of interest arises, and should take steps to resolve the issue in a manner that makes participants' interests primary.

(p) Social workers should educate themselves, their students, and their colleagues about responsible research practices.

6. SOCIAL WORKERS' ETHICAL RESPONSIBILITIES TO THE BROADER SOCIETY

6.01 Social Welfare

Social workers should promote the general welfare of society, from local to global levels, and the development of people, their communities, and their environments. Social workers should advocate for living conditions conducive to the fulfillment of basic human needs and should promote social, economic, political, and cultural values and institutions that are compatible with the realization of social justice.

6.02 Public Participation

Social workers should facilitate informed participation by the public in shaping social policies and institutions.

6.03 Public Emergencies

> Social workers should provide appropriate professional services in public emergencies to the greatest extent possible.

6.04 Social and Political Action

(a)   Social workers should engage in social and political action that seeks to ensure that all people have equal access to the resources, employment, services, and opportunities they require to meet their basic human needs and to develop fully. Social workers should be aware of the impact of the political arena on practice and should advocate for changes in policy and legislation to improve social conditions in order to meet basic human needs and promote social justice.

(b)   Social workers should act to expand choice and opportunity for all people, with special regard for vulnerable, disadvantaged, oppressed, and exploited people and groups.

(c)   Social workers should promote conditions that encourage respect for cultural and social diversity within the United States and globally. Social workers should promote policies and practices that demonstrate respect for difference, support the expansion of cultural knowledge and resources, advocate for programs and institutions that demonstrate cultural competence, and promote policies that safeguard the rights of and confirm equity and social justice for all people.

(d)   Social workers should act to prevent and eliminate domination of, exploitation of, and discrimination against any person, group, or class on the basis of race, ethnicity, national origin, color, sex, sexual orientation, age, marital status, political belief, religion, or mental or physical disability.

APPENDIX D

Ethical Standards of Human Service Professionals, National Organization for Human Service Education (NOHSE)

PREAMBLE

Human services is a profession developing in response to and in anticipation of the direction of human needs and human problems in the late twentieth century. Characterized particularly by an appreciation of human beings in all of their diversity, human services offers assistance to its clients within the context of their community and environment. Human service professionals, regardless of whether they are students, faculty or practitioners, promote and encourage the unique values and characteristics of human services. In so doing human service professionals uphold the integrity and ethics of the profession, partake in constructive criticism of the profession, promote client and community well-being, and enhance their own professional growth.

The ethical guidelines presented are a set of standards of conduct which the human service professional considers in ethical and professional decision making. It is hoped that these guidelines will be of assistance when the human service professional is challenged by difficult ethical dilemmas. Although ethical codes are not legal documents, they may be used to assist in the adjudication of issues related to ethical human service behavior.

Human service professionals function in many ways and carry out many roles. They enter into professional-client relationships with individuals, families, groups and communities who are all referred to as "clients" in these standards. Among their roles are caregiver, case manager, broker, teacher/educator, behavior changer, consultant, outreach professional, mobilizer, advocate, community planner, community change organizer, evaluator and administrator. The following standards are written with these multifaceted roles in mind.

THE HUMAN SERVICE PROFESSIONAL'S RESPONSIBILITY TO CLIENTS

STATEMENT 1 Human service professionals negotiate with clients the purpose, goals, and nature of the helping relationship prior to its onset as well as inform clients of the limitations of the proposed relationship.

STATEMENT 2 Human service professionals respect the integrity and welfare of the client at all times. Each client is treated with respect, acceptance and dignity.

STATEMENT 3 Human service professionals protect the client's right to privacy and confidentiality except when such confidentiality would cause harm to the client or others, when agency guidelines state otherwise, or under other stated conditions (e.g., local, state, or federal laws). Professionals inform clients of the limits of confidentiality prior to the onset of the helping relationship.

STATEMENT 4 If it is suspected that danger or harm may occur to the client or to others as a result of a client's behavior, the human service professional acts in an appropriate and professional manner to protect the safety of those individuals. This may involve seeking consultation, supervision, and/or breaking the confidentiality of the relationship.

STATEMENT 5 Human service professionals protect the integrity, safety, and security of client records. All written client information that is shared with other professionals, except in the course of professional supervision, must have the client's prior written consent.

STATEMENT 6 Human service professionals are aware that in their relationships with clients power and status are unequal. Therefore they recognize that dual or multiple relationships may increase the risk of harm to, or exploitation of, clients, and may impair their professional judgment. However, in some communities and situations it may not be feasible to avoid social or other nonprofessional contact with clients. Human service professionals support the trust implicit in the helping relationship by avoiding dual relationships that may impair professional judgment, increase the risk of harm to clients or lead to exploitation.

STATEMENT 7 Sexual relationships with current clients are not considered to be in the best interest of the client and are prohibited. Sexual relationships with previous clients are considered dual relationships and are addressed in Statement 6 (above).

STATEMENT 8 The client's right to self-determination is protected by human service professionals. They recognize the client's right to receive or refuse services.

STATEMENT 9 Human service professionals recognize and build on client strengths.

THE HUMAN SERVICE PROFESSIONAL'S RESPONSIBILITY TO THE COMMUNITY AND SOCIETY

STATEMENT 10 Human service professionals are aware of local, state, and federal laws. They advocate for change in regulations and statutes when such legislation conflicts with ethical guidelines and/or client rights. Where laws are harmful to individuals, groups or communities, human service professionals consider the conflict between the values of obeying the law and the values of serving people and may decide to initiate social action.

STATEMENT 11 Human service professionals keep informed about current social issues as they affect the client and the community. They share that information with clients, groups and community as part of their work.

STATEMENT 12 Human service professionals understand the complex interaction between individuals, their families, the communities in which they live, and society.

STATEMENT 13 Human service professionals act as advocates in addressing unmet client and community needs. Human service professionals provide a mechanism for identifying unmet client needs, calling attention to these needs, and assisting in planning and mobilizing to advocate for those needs at the local community level.

STATEMENT 14 Human service professionals represent their qualifications to the public accurately.

STATEMENT 15 Human service professionals describe the effectiveness of programs, treatments, and/or techniques accurately.

STATEMENT 16 Human service professionals advocate for the rights of all members of society, particularly those who are members of minorities and groups at which discriminatory practices have historically been directed.

STATEMENT 17 Human service professionals provide services without discrimination or preference based on age, ethnicity, culture, race, disability, gender, religion, sexual orientation or socioeconomic status.

STATEMENT 18 Human service professionals are knowledgeable about the cultures and communities within which they practice. They are aware of multiculturalism in society and its impact on the community as well as individuals within the community. They respect individuals and groups, their cultures and beliefs.

STATEMENT 19 Human service professionals are aware of their own cultural backgrounds, beliefs, and values, recognizing the potential for impact on their relationships with others.

STATEMENT 20 Human service professionals are aware of sociopolitical issues that differentially affect clients from diverse backgrounds.

STATEMENT 21 Human service professionals seek the training, experience, education and supervision necessary to ensure their effectiveness in working with culturally diverse client populations.

THE HUMAN SERVICE PROFESSIONAL'S RESPONSIBILITY TO COLLEAGUES

STATEMENT 22 Human service professionals avoid duplicating another professional's helping relationship with a client. They consult with other professionals who are assisting the client in a different type of relationship when it is in the best interest of the client to do so.

STATEMENT 23 When a human service professional has a conflict with a colleague, he or she first seeks out the colleague in an attempt to manage the problem. If necessary, the professional then seeks the assistance of supervisors, consultants or other professionals in efforts to manage the problem.

STATEMENT 24 Human service professionals respond appropriately to unethical behavior of colleagues. Usually this means initially talking directly with the colleague and, if no resolution is forthcoming, reporting the colleague's behavior to supervisory or administrative staff and/or to the Professional organization(s) to which the colleague belongs.

STATEMENT 25 All consultations between human service professionals are kept confidential unless to do so would result in harm to clients or communities.

THE HUMAN SERVICE PROFESSIONAL'S RESPONSIBILITY TO THE PROFESSION

STATEMENT 26 Human service professionals know the limit and scope of their professional knowledge and offer services only within their knowledge and skill base.

STATEMENT 27 Human service professionals seek appropriate consultation and supervision to assist in decision-making when there are legal, ethical or other dilemmas.

STATEMENT 28 Human service professionals act with integrity, honesty, genuineness, and objectivity.

STATEMENT 29 Human service professionals promote cooperation among related disciplines (e.g., psychology, counseling, social work, nursing, family and consumer sciences, medicine, education) to foster professional growth and interests within the various fields.

STATEMENT 30 Human service professionals promote the continuing development of their profession. They encourage membership in professional associations, support research endeavors, foster educational advancement, advocate for appropriate legislative actions, and participate in other related professional activities.

STATEMENT 31 Human service professionals continually seek out new and effective approaches to enhance their professional abilities.

THE HUMAN SERVICE PROFESSIONAL'S RESPONSIBILITY TO EMPLOYERS

STATEMENT 32 Human service professionals adhere to commitments made to their employers.

STATEMENT 33 Human service professionals participate in efforts to establish and maintain employment conditions which are conducive to high quality client services. They assist in evaluating the effectiveness of the agency through reliable and valid assessment measures.

STATEMENT 34 When a conflict arises between fulfilling the responsibility to the employer and the responsibility to the client, human service professionals advise both of the conflict and work conjointly with all involved to manage the conflict.

THE HUMAN SERVICE PROFESSIONAL'S RESPONSIBILITY TO SELF

STATEMENT 35 Human service professionals strive to personify those characteristics typically associated with the profession (eg., accountability, respect for others, genuineness, empathy, pragmatism).

STATEMENT 36 Human service professionals foster self-awareness and personal growth in themselves. They recognize that when professionals are aware of their own values, attitudes, cultural background, and personal needs, the process of helping others is less likely to be negatively impacted by those factors.

STATEMENT 37 Human service professionals recognize a commitment to lifelong learning and continually upgrade knowledge and skills to serve the populations better.

STATEMENT 38 Human service professionals recognize a commitment to lifelong learning and continually upgrade knowledge and skills to serve the populations better.

AAMFT Code of Ethics, American Association for Marriage and Family Therapy

The Board of Directors of the American Association for Marriage and Family Therapy (AAMFT) hereby promulgates, pursuant to Article 2, Section 2.013 of the Association's Bylaws, the Revised AAMFT Code of Ethics effective August 1, 1991.

The AAMFT Code of Ethics is binding on Members of AAMFT in all membership categories, AAMFT Approved Supervisors, and applicants for membership and the Approved Supervisor designation (hereafter, AAMFT Member).

If an AAMFT Member resigns in anticipation of, or during the course of an ethics investigation, the Ethics Committee will complete its investigation. Any publication of action taken by the Association will include the fact that the Member attempted to resign during the investigation.

Marriage and family therapists are strongly encouraged to report alleged unethical behavior of colleagues to appropriate professional associations and state regulatory bodies.

1. RESPONSIBILITY TO CLIENTS

Marriage and family therapists advance the welfare of families and individuals. They respect the rights of those persons seeking their assistance, and make reasonable efforts to ensure that their services are used appropriately.

1.1   Marriage and family therapists do not discriminate against or refuse professional service to anyone on the basis of race, gender, religion, national origin, or sexual orientation.

1.2   Marriage and family therapists are aware of their influential position with respect to clients, and they avoid exploiting the trust and dependency of such persons. Therapists, therefore, make every effort to avoid dual relationships with clients that could impair professional judgment or increase the risk of exploitation. When a dual relationship cannot be avoided, therapists take appropriate professional precautions to ensure judgment is not impaired and no exploitation occurs. Examples of such dual relationships include, but are not limited to, business or close personal relationships with clients. Sexual intimacy with clients is prohibited. Sexual intimacy with former clients for two years following the termination of therapy is prohibited.

1.3 Marriage and family therapists do not use their professional relationships with clients to further their own interests.

1.4 Marriage and family therapists respect the right of clients to make decisions and help them to understand the consequences of these decisions. Therapists clearly advise a client that a decision on marital status is the responsibility of the client.

1.5 Marriage and family therapists continue therapeutic relationships only so long as it is reasonably clear that clients are benefiting from the relationship.

1.6 Marriage and family therapists assist persons in obtaining other therapeutic services if the therapist is unable or unwilling, for appropriate reasons, to provide professional help.

1.7 Marriage and family therapists do not abandon or neglect clients in treatment without making reasonable arrangements for the continuation of such treatment.

1.8 Marriage and family therapists obtain written informed consent from clients before videotaping, audiorecording, or permitting third party observation.

2. CONFIDENTIALITY

Marriage and family therapists have unique confidentiality concerns because the client in a therapeutic relationship may be more than one person. Therapists respect and guard confidences of each individual client.

2.1 Marriage and family therapists may not disclose client confidences except: (a) as mandated by law; (b) to prevent a clear and immediate danger to a person or persons; (c) where the therapist is a defendant in a civil, criminal, or disciplinary action arising from the therapy (in which case client confidences may be disclosed only in the course of that action); or (d) if there is a waiver previously obtained in writing, and then such information may be revealed only in accordance with the terms of the waiver. In circumstances where more than one person in a family receives therapy, each such family member who is legally competent to execute a waiver must agree to the waiver required by subparagraph (d).

   Without such a waiver from each family member legally competent to execute a waiver, a therapist cannot disclose information received from any family member.

2.2 Marriage and family therapists use client and/or clinical materials in teaching, writing, and public presentations only if a written waiver has been obtained in accordance with Subprinciple 2.1(d), or when appropriate steps have been taken to protect client identity and confidentiality.

2.3 Marriage and family therapists store or dispose of client records in ways that maintain confidentiality.

3. PROFESSIONAL COMPETENCE AND INTEGRITY

Marriage and family therapists maintain high standards of professional competence and integrity.

3.1 Marriage and family therapists are in violation of this Code and subject to termination of membership or other appropriate action if they: (a) are convicted of any felony; (b) are convicted of a misdemeanor related to their qualifications or functions; (c) engage in conduct which could lead to conviction of a felony, or a misdemeanor related to their qualifications or functions; (d) are expelled from or disciplined by other professional organizations; (e) have their licenses or certificates suspended or revoked or are otherwise disciplined by regulatory bodies; (f) are no longer competent to practice marriage and family therapy because they are impaired due to physical or mental causes or the abuse of alcohol or other substances; or (g) fail to cooperate with the Association at any point from the inception of an ethical complaint through the completion of all proceedings regarding that complaint.

3.2 Marriage and family therapists seek appropriate professional assistance for their personal problems or conflicts that may impair work performance or judgment.

3.3 Marriage and family therapists, as teachers, supervisors, and researchers, are dedicated to high standards of scholarship and present accurate information.

3.4 Marriage and family therapists remain abreast of new developments in family therapy knowledge and practice through educational activities.

3.5 Marriage and family therapists do not engage in sexual or other harassment or exploitation of clients, students, trainees, supervisees, employees, colleagues, research subjects, or actual or potential witnesses or complainants in investigations and ethical proceedings.

3.6 Marriage and family therapists do not diagnose, treat, or advise on problems outside the recognized boundaries of their competence.

3.7 Marriage and family therapists make efforts to prevent the distortion or misuse of their clinical and research findings.

3.8 Marriage and family therapists, because of their ability to influence and alter the lives of others, exercise special care when making public their professional recommendations and opinions through testimony or other public statements.

4. RESPONSIBILITY TO STUDENTS, EMPLOYEES, AND SUPERVISEES

Marriage and family therapists do not exploit the trust and dependency of students, employees, and supervisees.

4.1 Marriage and family therapists are aware of their influential position with respect to students, employees, and supervisees, and they avoid exploiting the trust and dependency of such persons. Therapists, therefore, make every effort to avoid dual relationships that could impair professional judgment or increase the risk of exploitation. When a dual relationship cannot be avoided, therapists take appropriate professional precautions to ensure judgment is not impaired and no exploitation occurs. Examples of such dual relationships include, but are not limited to, business or close personal relationships with students, employees, or supervisees. Provision of therapy to students, employees, or supervisees is prohibited. Sexual intimacy with students or supervisees is prohibited.

4.2 Marriage and family therapists do not permit students, employees, or supervisees to perform or to hold themselves out as competent to perform professional services beyond their training, level of experience, and competence.

4.3 Marriage and family therapists do not disclose supervisee confidences except: (a) as mandated by law; (b) to prevent a clear and immediate danger to a person or persons; (c) where the therapist is a defendant in a civil, criminal, or disciplinary action arising from the supervision (in which case supervisee confidences may be disclosed only in the course of that action); (d) in educational or training settings where there are multiple supervisors, and then only to other professional colleagues who share responsibility for the training of the supervisee; or (e) if there is a waiver previously obtained in writing, and then such information may be revealed only in accordance with the terms of the waiver.

5. RESPONSIBILITY TO RESEARCH PARTICIPANTS

Investigators respect the dignity and protect the welfare of participants in research and are aware of federal and state laws and regulations and professional standards governing the conduct of research.

5.1 Investigators are responsible for making careful examinations of ethical acceptability in planning studies. To the extent that services to research participants may be compromised by participation in research, investigators seek the ethical advice of qualified professionals not directly involved in the investigation and observe safeguards to protect the rights of research participants.

5.2 Investigators requesting participants' involvement in research inform them of all aspects of the research that might reasonably be expected to influence willingness to participate. Investigators are especially sensitive to the possibility of diminished consent when participants are also receiving clinical services, have impairments which limit understanding and/or communication, or when participants are children.

5.3 Investigators respect participants' freedom to decline participation in or to withdraw from a research study at any time. This obligation requires special thought and consideration when investigators or other members of the research team are in positions of authority or influence over participants. Marriage and family therapists, therefore, make every effort to avoid dual relationships with research participants that could impair professional judgment or increase the risk of exploitation.

5.4 Information obtained about a research participant during the course of an investigation is confidential unless there is a waiver previously obtained in writing. When the possibility exists that others, including family members, may obtain access to such information, this possibility, together with the plan for protecting confidentiality, is explained as part of the procedure for obtaining informed consent.

6. RESPONSIBILITY TO THE PROFESSION

Marriage and family therapists respect the rights and responsibilities of professional colleagues and participate in activities which advance the goals of the profession.

6.1 Marriage and family therapists remain accountable to the standards of the profession when acting as members or employees of organizations.

6.2 Marriage and family therapists assign publication credit to those who have contributed to a publication in proportion to their contributions and in accordance with customary professional publication practices.

6.3 Marriage and family therapists who are the authors of books or other materials that are published or distributed cite persons to whom credit for original ideas is due.

6.4 Marriage and family therapists who are the authors of books or other materials published or distributed by an organization take reasonable precautions to ensure that the organization promotes and advertises the materials accurately and factually.

6.5 Marriage and family therapists participate in activities that contribute to a better community and society, including devoting a portion of their professional activity to services for which there is little or no financial return.

6.6 Marriage and family therapists are concerned with developing laws and regulations pertaining to marriage and family therapy that serve the public interest, and with altering such laws and regulations that are not in the public interest.

6.7 Marriage and family therapists encourage public participation in the design and delivery of professional services and in the regulation of practitioners.

7. FINANCIAL ARRANGEMENTS

Marriage and family therapists make financial arrangements with clients, third party payors, and supervisees that are reasonably understandable and conform to accepted professional practices.

7.1 Marriage and family therapists do not offer or accept payment for referrals.

7.2 Marriage and family therapists do not charge excessive fees for services.

7.3 Marriage and family therapists disclose their fees to clients and supervisees at the beginning of services.

7.4 Marriage and family therapists represent facts truthfully to clients, third party payors, and supervisees regarding services rendered.

8. ADVERTISING

Marriage and family therapists engage in appropriate informational activities, including those that enable laypersons to choose professional services on an informed basis.

GENERAL ADVERTISING

8.1 Marriage and family therapists accurately represent their competence, education, training, and experience relevant to their practice of marriage and family therapy.

8.2 Marriage and family therapists assure that advertisements and publications in any media (such as directories, announcements, business cards, newspapers, radio, television, and facsimiles) convey information that is necessary for the public to make an appropriate selection of professional services. Information could include: (a) office information, such as name, address, telephone number, credit card acceptability, fees, languages spoken, and office hours; (b) appropriate degrees, state licensure and/or certification, and AAMFT Clinical Member status; and (c) description of practice. (For requirements for advertising under the AAMFT name, logo, and/or the abbreviated initials AAMFT, see Subprinciple 8.15, below).

8.3 Marriage and family therapists do not use a name which could mislead the public concerning the identity, responsibility, source, and status of those practicing under that name and do not hold themselves out as being partners or associates of a firm if they are not.

8.4 Marriage and family therapists do not use any professional identification (such as a business card, office sign, letterhead, or telephone or association directory listing) if it includes a statement or claim that is false, fraudulent, misleading, or deceptive. A statement is false, fraudulent, misleading, or deceptive if it (a) contains a material misrepresentation of fact; (b) fails to state any material fact necessary to make the statement, in light of all circumstances, not misleading; or (c) is intended to or is likely to create an unjustified expectation.

8.5 Marriage and family therapists correct, wherever possible, false, misleading, or inaccurate information and representations made by others concerning the therapist's qualifications, services, or products.

8.6 Marriage and family therapists make certain that the qualifications of persons in their employ are represented in a manner that is not false, misleading, or deceptive.

8.7 Marriage and family therapists may represent themselves as specializing within a limited area of marriage and family therapy, but only if they have the education and supervised experience in settings which meet recognized professional standards to practice in that specialty area.

ADVERTISING USING AAMFT DESIGNATIONS

8.8 The AAMFT designations of Clinical Member, Approved Supervisor, and Fellow may be used in public information or advertising materials only by persons holding such designations. Persons holding such designations may, for example, advertise in the following manner:

- Jane Doe, Ph.D., a Clinical Member of the American Association for Marriage and Family Therapy.

Alternately, the advertisement could read,

- Jane Doe, Ph.D., AAMFT Clinical Member.
- John Doe, Ph.D., an Approved Supervisor of the American Association for Marriage and Family Therapy.

Alternately, the advertisement could read,

- John Doe, Ph.D., AAMFT Approved Supervisor.
- Jane Doe, Ph.D., a Fellow of the American Association for Marriage and Family Therapy.

Alternately, the advertisement could read,

- Jane Doe, Ph.D., AAMFT Fellow.

More than one designation may be used if held by the AAMFT Member.

8.9 Marriage and family therapists who hold the AAMFT Approved Supervisor or the Fellow designation may not represent the designation as an advanced clinical status.

8.10 Student, Associate, and Affiliate Members may not use their AAMFT membership status in public information or advertising materials. Such listings on professional resumes are not considered advertisements.

8.11 Persons applying for AAMFT membership may not list their application status on any resume or advertisement.

8.12 In conjunction with their AAMFT membership, marriage and family therapists claim as evidence of educational qualifications only those degrees (a) from regionally accredited institutions or (b) from institutions recognized by states which license or certify marriage and family therapists, but only if such state regulation is recognized by AAMFT.

8.13 Marriage and family therapists may not use the initials AAMFT following their name in the manner of an academic degree.

8.14 Marriage and family therapists may not use the AAMFT name, logo, and/or the abbreviated initials AAMFT or make any other such representation which would imply that they speak for or represent the Association. The Association is the sole owner of its name, logo, and the abbreviated initials AAMFT. Its committees and divisions, operating as such, may use the name, logo, and/or the abbreviated initials, AAMFT, in accordance with AAMFT policies.

8.15 Authorized advertisements of Clinical Members under the AAMFT name, logo, and/or the abbreviated initials AAMFT may include the following: the Clinical Member's name, degree, license or certificate held when required by state law, name of business, address, and telephone number. If a business is listed, it must follow, not precede the Clinical Member's name. Such listings may not include AAMFT offices held by the Clinical Member, nor any specializations, since such a listing under the AAMFT name, logo, and/or the abbreviated initials AAMFT would imply that this specialization has been credentialed by AAMFT.

8 .16 Marriage and family therapists use their membership in AAMFT only in connection with their clinical and professional activities.

8.17 Only AAMFT divisions and programs accredited by the AAMFT Commission on Accreditation for Marriage and Family Therapy Education, not businesses nor organizations, may use any AAMFT-related designation or affiliation in public information or advertising materials, and then only in accordance with AAMFT policies.

8.18 Programs accredited by the AAMFT Commission on Accreditation for Marriage and Family Therapy Education may not use the AAMFT name, logo, and/or the abbreviated initials, AAMFT. Instead, they may have printed on their stationery and other appropriate materials a statement such as:

The (name of program) of the (name of institution) is accredited by the AAMFT Commission on Accreditation for Marriage and Family Therapy Education.

8.19 Programs not accredited by the AAMFT Commission on Accreditation for Marriage and Family Therapy Education may not use the AAMFT name, logo, and/or the abbreviated initials, AAMFT. They may not state in printed program materials, program advertisements, and student advisement that their courses and training opportunities are accepted by AAMFT to meet AAMFT membership requirements.

INDEX

Abortion, 232, 235
Abuse, of children, 165–167
    domestic, 185–187, 202
    physical, 167
    reporting of, 170–173, 179–180
    sexual, 165–167
Acculturation, 130, 133
Acquired immune deficiency syndrome
    (AIDS), 207–208,
    see also Human immunodeficiency
        virus (HIV)
Advertising, false and deceptive, 198
Ambiguity, in ethical decision making,
    42–43
American Assocation for Marriage and
    Family Therapy (AAMFT), 88, 261,
    263
    Code of ethics, unabridged, 337–344
American Association of University
    Professors (AAUP),
    Statement on professional ethics, 153,
        154, 263
American Counseling Association (ACA),
    73, 259, 261, 262, 264, 266
    Code of ethics and standards of practice,
        unabridged, 269–292
    selected rules with abridgements,
        74–75, 77, 78, 82, 83, 88, 89, 92–93,
        94, 95, 98, 99, 102, 217
American Psychological Association
    (APA), 73, 261, 262, 263, 264, 266
    *Ethical principles of psychologists and code
        of conduct*, unabridged, 293–314
    selected rules with abridgements, 74,
        75, 77, 89, 94, 98, 139–140
Applied professional ethics, 24–25
Aristotle, ancient Greek philosopher, 19
    and virtue ethics, 19–22, 64–65, 143, 260
Assimilation, 130, 133

Autonomy-facilitating attitudes:
    as moral virtues, 64–65
    and client trust, 65
Autonomy-facilitating virtues, functions
    in counseling ethics, 48
Autonomy:
    in decision making, 226–227, 233
    moral, 43–44
    respect for in clients, 249–250

Bartering for services, 99, 101, 138
Battin, M., 247, 248, 266
Bayles, M., 25, 72, 76, 78, 80, 83, 89, 95, 99,
    102, 259, 261
Beneficence, principle of, 88
    and codes of ethics, 88–89
    distinguished from benevolence, 90
    see also Competence, professional
Benevolence, virtue of, 90
Bentham, J., 7, 25
Bipolar disorder, case of client with,
    231–235
Bouvia v. Superior Court, 242, 266

Candor, principle of, 76
    and codes of ethics, 77–78
    and disclosure of fees for services, 77,
        79
    and full disclosure, 78
    and informed consent, 78–82
    and termination of therapy, 146
    and third-party reimbursement, 79
Canterbury v. Spence, 78, 261
Care ethics, 14–19, 105–106, 120
Categorical imperative, *see* Kant, I., ethics
    of
Children, *see* Minor clients
Clinchy, B., 17, 62–63, 260
Cognitive-behavioral approaches, 116

Cohen, E. D., 33, 42, 76, 84, 90, 207, 208, 213, 217, 218, 219, 220, 221, 227, 260, 261, 265, 266
Collectivism, 116
Compassion in Dying v. the State of Washington, 244, 266
Competence, mental, *see* Mental competence of client
Competence, professional, 88–92, 234, 250
Computers, use of, 102
  see also Records, computer storage of
Confidentiality of client information, 77, 78–79, 82–88, 94, 96–97, 133, 134, 171, 180, 181, 194, 198, 242
Conflicts of interest, 93–94, 98, 150, 160
  apparent, 149, 151, 156, 157
  defined, 99, 160
  with third-party payers, 100–101
Congruence, 56, 57, 146, 169
Consent of client to therapy:
  freely given, 80–81, 145
  informed, 84, 159, 176, 178–179, 181
  validity of, 80–81
  see also Candor
Consultation with other professionals, 89, 92–93, 98, 99, 138–139, 148, 150, 151, 155, 156, 157, 158, 197, 201, 202, 238
Corey, G., 33, 56, 57, 76, 138, 139, 260, 261
Counseling:
  and client autonomy and trust, 47–48, 49
  primary purpose of, 32–33, 35, 49
Countertransference, 100, 103, 142, 144, 147, 201
Courage, moral, 44, 49, 252, 253
Credentials, therapist, 74, 79
Culture, definition of, 115–116
Curtis, C., 76, 261

Deception of client, 72–73, 75–76
Decision by indecision, 42–43, 49
Decisions, ethical, 3–5, 25–26
  five stages of, 35–47, 49
Demographic variables, 115
Descriptive ethics, 5–6
Diagnosis of mental disorders, 101
  see also Diligence
Dignified Death Act (Michigan), 244
Diligence, principle of, 94
  and codes of ethics, 94–95
  and diagnosing mental disorders, 97
  and keeping of counseling records, 94, 95, 96–97
  and political action, 97
  and scheduling of appointments, 94, 97
Disclosure by client, premature, 200

Discretion, principle of, 82
  and codes of ethics, 82–83
  and confidentiality, 83–88
Discrimination, 102, 133, 134, 235, 238, 250
Dishonesty, 75
Domestic violence and abuse, 185–187
  cycle of, 186–187
  defined, 185
  differences in gender response styles, 186
  of men, 186, 187
  and rule of thumb, 187
  of women, 186–187
Dual-role relationships, 93–94, 98–99, 100, 137–164, 169, 180
  conflict of interest in, 138
  with co-workers, 151, 156, 157
  defined, 137
  ethical standards of, 156–160
  with family of students, 152
  nonelective, 149, 154–155, 159, 160
  sexual and nonsexual, 139
  simultaneous distinguished from consecutive, 137
  unavoidable, 138–139
Due care, 93, 95, 152, 234, 254
Dworkin, G., 225, 229, 245–246, 247, 266

Elison v. Brady, 94
Empathy, 56, 61–64
Employee Assistance Program (EAP), 118, 122
Employment, accepting, 88, 90–91
Ethical principles, summarized, 40–41
Ethical theory, 6–7
Ethics:
  definition of, 5
  types of, 5–25
Ethnocentric variables, 115
Expressive traits, 116

Facts, identifying morally relevant, 38–39, 239
Fairness, principle of, 102, 238
  and codes of ethics, 102
  and managed care, 102–104
False memories, 175
Familism, 132
Family therapy, confidentiality in, 83, 88
Feeling good, distinguished from doing what is right, 37–38
Fees for services:
  determining, 102
  and quality of services, 104
  and sliding scales, 103, 104
Feminist theories of knowledge, 116
  and connected knowing, 17, 62–63

Fiduciary model of professional ethics, 72, 76
Finkelhor, D., 166, 263
Freudian psychoanalysis, 116

Gelles, R., 167, 185, 186, 263, 264
Gender scripting, 187, 201
Genovese, Kitty, case of, 45–46
Gifts, accepting from client, 101–102
Gilligan, C., 14, 16–18, 259
Gladding, S., 130, 260, 262
Group therapy:
    confidentiality in, 83, 87–88
    and prevention of client harm, 93
Guardianship, legal, 81, 228, 232, 239, 240, 251

Haley, J., 63–64, 75, 261
Harm to others, *see* Third-party harm; Nonmaleficence; and Human immunodeficiency virus
Hedonistic ethics, 7, 22–23, 32
Helplessness, learned, 186
Herlihy, B., 138, 139, 263
Hinman L., 15, 18, 259
Honesty, principle of, 74
    and professional codes of ethics, 74–75
    and deception, 75–76
    toward nonclients, 76
    and truthfulness, 75
Human immunodeficiency virus (HIV), 91, 207–211, 213–214, 216–222
    and conditions of disclosure, 217–219
    and condoms, 208, 217, 218
    and confidentiality, 82, 84, 208, 209, 210, 211, 212, 214, 216–221
    facts about, 207–208
    HIV seropositivity, 208, 217
    and partner notification services, 219
    and procedures of disclosure, 219–221
    and risk assessment of sexual behaviors, 213, 216, 218, 220
    and suicidal clients, 210, 221
    and third-party harm, 208–217
    see also Acquired immune deficiency syndrome
Human welfare, defined, 32

Illogical thinking, forms of, 41–42
Immediacy, 127
Incompetence, professional, 89, 197
Independence of judgment, *see* Loyalty and conflicts of interest
In re Claire C. Conroy, 243, 266
Instrumental traits, 116
Insurance companies, defrauding, 101

Interests:
    client, 34, 80
    common human, 35, 78–80
Involuntary commitment, 229–231, 236–240, 254
    and mental incompetence, 130
    and prediction of dangerousness, 230

Jaffee v. Redmond, 86, 261
Jehovah's Wittnesses, 123–124
    and divorce, 127

Kant, I.:
    18th-century German philosopher, 10
    ethics of, 10–14, 25–26, 60, 119, 143, 145, 250, 259, 266
Kevorkian, J., 244
Kitchener, K., 36, 148, 263
Krischer v. McIver, 243, 266

Ladd, J., 44, 260
Law:
    distinguished from codes of ethics, 4–5
    distinguished from morality, 3–4, 43
Legal incompetence, 232
Loyalty, principle of, 98
    and codes of ethics, 98–99
    and conflicts of interest, 99–102

MacIntyre, A., 21, 22, 24, 259
Macklin, R., 227, 228, 266
Mahoney, M. J., 62, 260
Managed care, 102–104
Marriage, same sex, 121
Martin, M., 25, 143, 144, 259, 260
McKay v. Bergstedt, 242, 266
Mental competence of client, 227–229, 232, 249, 250–251, 252, 253–254
    as condition of valid consent to therapy, 81
    intermittent, 228
    minimal and comparative senses of, 228, 246
Mill, J. S., 7–8, 22–23, 25, 226, 246–247, 259, 266
Minor clients:
    and confidentiality, 82, 131, 171, 176, 180
    and conflicts of interest, 100
    and conflicts of values, 126–127, 130, 133, 134
    and discrimination against, 238, 250, 251
    and informed consent, 81, 125, 131, 171, 176–177, 180
    and involuntary commitment of, 236–240
Moral considerateness, principle of, 39–40, 41, 45, 73

Morality, distinguished from expedience, 42
Moral problems, 35–38, 48, 104–105
and moral dilemmas, 37–38, 119, 190
and morally relevant facts, 38–39
and moral objectivity, 37
and moral sensitivity, 36–37, 49
Morphis, M., and Riesbeck, C., 16–18, 259
Multicultural:
counseling guidelines, 133–134
definition of, 115–116
training, 89
Multiple-role relationships, *see* Dual-role relationships
Multiple therapists in treatment of one client, 197–198
National Association of Social Workers (NASW), 73, 260, 262, 263, 264, 266
Code of ethics, unabridged, 315–332
selected rules with abridgements, 77–78, 83, 89, 92, 95, 98, 99, 102
National Organization for Human Service Education (NOHSE), 73, 262, 264, 265, 266
Ethical standards of human service professionals, unabridged, 333–336
selected rules with abridgements, 73, 74, 82, 89, 92, 95, 102
Needs, client, 34–35
Nonmaleficence, principle of, 92
and codes of ethics, 92–93
distinguished from nonmalevolence, 93
Nonmalevolence, virtue of, 93

O'Connor v. Donaldson, 230, 266
Oregon Death with Dignity Act, 243, 266

Paradoxical directions, 75–76
Paternalism, in counseling and psychotherapy, 225–226, 234
defined, 225
ethical standards of, 249–253
justification of, 228–229, 245–246
see also Involuntary commitment
People of the State of Michigan v. Jack Kevorkian, 244, 267
Personal problems of therapists, and counseling effectiveness, 98
Person-centered approach to counseling, 55
Philosophical analysis:
conducting a, 39–42
reaching a decision in light of, 42–43
Philosophical ethics, 6
Play therapy, 175
Pope, K. S., 139, 263

Practice:
concept of, defined, 22
and counseling, 32
and internal virtues, 22–23
Privacy, protection of client, *see* Confidentiality; Discretion
Privileged communication, 85–87
Probability, in ethical decision making, 40, 43
Problems, intellectual distinguished from practical, 35–36
Pro bono professional services, 102, 103, 104
Professional, being a, 34
Professional distance, 143–144
and empathy, 144
and objectivity, 144, 147–148, 151
Publication and respect for client confidentiality, 85

Recording of client sessions, 79–80
Records, counseling:
client access to, 77–78, 80
confidentiality of, 82, 94
computer storage of, 96–97
main purpose of, 95
Recruitment of clients, 99, 151
Referrals, client, 100, 101, 103, 104, 142, 143, 144, 156, 158, 159, 196, 201, 203
Reflection, 169
Research and experimentation, 74–75, 78
Responsibility, moral, 44–47, 49
defined, 44
and job-related responsibility, 46–47, 49
and legal responsibility, 46–47, 49, 240
of therapists to third parties, 33
Rights, concept of, 13–14
Rogers, C., 47, 55–57, 58–59, 61–62, 169, 260, 261, 263
Rule ethics, 7–14
Rule of thumb, *see* Domestic violence

Sartre, J. P., 21, 56, 57
Scheduling of client appointments, *see* Diligence
Sensitivity, moral, 91, 155, 160, 239
see also Moral problems
Sexual attraction, between therapists and clients, 141–149, 158–159
Sexual harassment, 92, 94
Sexual relationships:
with current clients, 92, 93–94, 99, 139
with former clients, 92, 93–94, 139–140, 142, 147–149, 156, 157–158
Staff, respect for client confidentiality among, 82, 84

Steinmetz, S., 167, 185, 186, 201
Strauss, M., 167, 185, 186, 187, 264
Students:
   accepting referrals from, 152–153, 159
   counseling of, 99, 152, 159–160
   sexual relationships with, 139
Subpoena, complying with, 87
Substituted judgment, principle of, 250
Suicide, of client, 149, 155, 231–235,
     240–249, 252–253, 254
   and Kantian ethics, 245, 247
   physician-assisted, 243–244
   and prediction of lethality of threat,
     248–249
   standards of rationality, 245, 247
   and utilitarianism, 244–245
Summit, R., 166, 264
Supervision, 88–89, 91, 92–93, 94, 99,
     138–139, 151, 152, 156, 157
   and sexual relationships, 139
Szasz, T., 32, 229

Tarasoff v. Board of Regents of the University
   of California, 52–53, 87, 230
Termination of therapy, 92–93, 99, 100, 142,
     145–146, 158, 159
   and Kantian ethics, 145
   premature, 170, 192
Third-party harm, as exception to
   confidentiality, 82, 87
   see also Nonmaleficence
Third-party payers, 97, 133, 134
Training, of counselor, *see* Competence,
   professional
   of employees, 94

Transference, 142, 145, 147, 158
Trust-establishing virtues, functions in
   counseling ethics, 48
Trustworthiness:
   distinguished from being trusted, 72–73
   principles of, 41, 73–74
   and professional codes of ethics, 73

Unconditional positive regard, 56, 58–61,
     154, 250
Utilitarianism, 7–10, 119–120, 143
   act distinguised from rule, 7–8, 26
   and care ethics, 15
   and rights, 14
   and sexual relationships with former
     clients, 140
   and virtue ethics, 19, 22–24, 26

Value conflicts with clients, 98, 101
Virtue ethics, 19–24, 120
Virtues, moral, 64
   criterion of selection, 23–24, 33, 72
   relation between professional and
     moral, 34, 49
   see also Virtue ethics
Vulnerability, client, 33, 44, 45, 72, 84, 145,
     146, 233, 235, 240, 250, 251
   principle of, 41

Walker, L., 185, 186, 187, 191, 264
Wubbolding, R. E., 248

TO THE OWNER OF THIS BOOK:

We hope that you have found *The Virtuous Therapist: Ethical Practice of Counseling and Psychotherapy* useful. So that this book can be improved in a future edition, would you take the time to complete this sheet and return it? Thank you.

School and address: ————————————————————————————

Department: ———————————————————————————————

Instructor's name: ————————————————————————————

1. What I like most about this book is: ————————————————

——————————————————————————————————————

——————————————————————————————————————

2. What I like least about this book is: ————————————————

——————————————————————————————————————

——————————————————————————————————————

3. My general reaction to this book is: ————————————————

——————————————————————————————————————

4. The name of the course in which I used this book is: ——————

——————————————————————————————————————

5. Were all of the chapters of the book assigned for you to read? ——————

   If not, which ones weren't? ————————————————————

6. In the space below, or on a separate sheet of paper, please write specific suggestions for improving this book and anything else you'd care to share about your experience in using the book.

——————————————————————————————————————

——————————————————————————————————————

——————————————————————————————————————

——————————————————————————————————————

——————————————————————————————————————

Optional:

Your name: _____ Date: _____

May Brooks/Cole quote you, either in promotion for *The Virtuous Therapist: Ethical Practice of Counseling and Psychotherapy* or in future publishing ventures?

Yes: _____ No: _____

Sincerely,

Elliot D. Cohen
Gale Spieler Cohen

FOLD HERE

FOLD HERE

IN-BOOK SURVEY

At Brooks/Cole, we are excited about creating new types of learning materials that are interactive, three-dimensional, and fun to use. To guide us in our publishing/development process, we hope that you'll take just a few moments to fill out the survey below. Your answers can help us make decisions that will allow us to produce a wide variety of videos, CD-ROMs, and Internet-based learning systems to complement standard textbooks. If you're interested in working with us as a student Beta-tester, be sure to fill in your name, telephone number, and address. We look forward to hearing from you!

In addition to books, which of the following learning tools do you currently use in your counseling/human services/social work courses?

_____ **Video** _____ in class _____ school library _____ own VCR

_____ **CD-ROM** _____ in class _____ in lab _____ own computer

_____ **Macintosh disks** _____ in class _____ in lab _____ own computer

_____ **Windows disks** _____ in class _____ in lab _____ own computer

_____ **Internet** _____ in class _____ in lab _____ own computer

How often do you access the Internet? _____

My own home computer is:

_____ Macintosh _____ DOS _____ Windows _____ Windows 95

The computer I use in class for counseling/human services/social work courses is:

_____ Macintosh _____ DOS _____ Windows _____ Windows 95

If you are NOT currently using multimedia materials in your counseling/human services/social work courses, but can see ways that video, CD-ROM, Internet, or other technologies could enhance your learning, please comment below:

_____

_____

_____

Other comments (optional): _____

_____

Name _____Telephone _____

Address _____

School _____

Professor/Course_____

You can fax this form to us at (408) 375-6414; e:mail to: info@brookscole.com; or detach, fold, secure, and mail.